To the memory of Eduardo White

Contents

List of Figures and Tables

ix

Preface

Small and medium-sized enterprises (SMEs) established in developed countries have carried out foreign direct investment in developing countries, and participated in technology agreements with local counterparts based in these nations, for at least thirty years. Due to the fact that individually most of those initiatives do not involve significant sums of productive resources, particularly when compared with a typical operation implemented by, or with, the participation of large transnational corporations, few efforts have been made by academics to study the main features of this phenomenon.

In order to contribute to the knowledge on this subject, the International Development Research Centre (IDRC) of Canada decided to support an international project that was coordinated by the Centro de Estudios de Dessarrollo y Relaciones Economicas Internacionales (CEDREI) from Buenos Aires. The endeavour consisted in putting together a team of thirteen research groups based in seven developed countries – Canada, France, Germany, Italy, Japan, the United Kingdom and the United States – and six developing countries – Argentina, Brazil, India, Korea, Mexico and Singapore. This team was responsible for (1) discussing the focus to be given to the study, (2) identifying the firms in supplier as well as recipient countries to be studied, as well as (3) performing the interviews and preparing the country reports.

The project focused on the technology transfer process to developing countries by SMEs. It was considered appropriate in this respect to analyse first the main factors behind SMEs internationalisation. Here the basic thrust of the research was to verify to what extent the received theories developed to explain the foreign expansion of large undertakings were useful in understanding SMEs' overseas involvement. The studies performed in each of the developed countries mentioned above shed light on this issue and, as will also be evident for the reader of this book, came out with interesting findings as to the extent that some common patterns were more significant than country specific variables in explaining the behaviour of SMEs internationally. In the same vein, the researchers gathered information on the basic features that characterised those SMEs that participated in foreign production initiatives. Were these firms leaders in their field? Had they a salient record as regards R&D efforts? What was their international experience before committing resources in a foreign venture in a developing country? Had they a clearly defined strategy as to their overseas involvement? These were some of the questions posed to the firms studied.

The second main topic of study was to understand the nature and main features of the technology transfer process to developing countries. Here the different researchers went on to investigate the typical contents of the transfer and the modes adopted by SMEs when they did business abroad. Was the process well 'packaged' to suit a given demand in a recipient country or were the SMEs heavily dependent on the capabilities that existed in these environments? Had SMEs a clear preference for some organisational forms, including equity arrangements and contractual forms? How did SMEs surpass their *a priori* expected limitations to transfer resources internationally?

The third main interest of the research had to do with the impact on recipient firms and countries of the international operations of SMEs. This was a crucial aspect of the study since the project was particularly interested in verifying the extent to which developing countries could profit from SMEs as alternative or complementary sources of productive resources (compared to, say, indigenous firms and large transnational companies). The research was designed to illuminate issues such as the capacity of SMEs in transferring up-to-date technologies, of easing the balance of payments bottlenecks in host countries, or upgrading local workforces, of maintaining a permanent commitment to the recipient economy, and so on.

Besides defining the focus of the research, the other important challenge of the project was to put together a sample of firms that included a variety of countries of origin, industrial sectors, organisational forms and recipient countries. This phase of the study was particularly cumbersome. The list of SMEs that had invested or transferred technology through contractual agreements was constructed following a given sequence: first, from developing country records non-large transnational corporations with operations in developing countries were identified; secondly, the size of these firms was checked by developed country researchers in order to see if they could be considered SMEs in terms of the project's criteria;[1] thirdly, once this phase was over, each team in North as well as South countries, prepared its own list of firms to be interviewed with the aim of including a diversified sample and transmitted it to CEDREI; and finally, as far as possible, CEDREI tried to ensure that both the supplier as well as the recipient firm participating in the same technology transfer experience were interviewed. As a result of this intensive exchange of information, 234 SMEs and recipient firms (including SMEs' subsidiaries, majority or minority partners, as well as domestic firms that had concluded a technology agreement) were interviewed. In a third of cases both the technology supplier and recipient were interviewed.

The information collected by each research group was sent to the CEDREI team in order for it to prepare the global overview of the study.[2] Each group also produced a country report. This book assembles most of these documents and as such represents the first work to be published on the international experience of SMEs from various countries of origin, as well as their activities in a selected group of developing countries.

It is proper to emphasise before concluding these remarks that the research project on which this book is based was designed and implemented by the late Eduardo White. He provided, from the start of the project, a clear orientation as to what should be its main objectives, selected the team of research collaborators, organised the three meetings of the research team and participated in the first drafts of the global overview, as well as of some country papers. White was convinced that SMEs were a source of productive resources for developing countries that deserved serious attention and devoted many years to conducting studies on the matter. For those of us who had the pleasure of sharing his enthusiasm on this research project it is a great satisfaction to have helped him in finishing this job.

Buenos Aires   JAIME CAMPOS
Leeds   PETER BUCKLEY
Bradford   HAFIZ MIRZA

Notes

1. The project adopted a criterion of size based on the number of employees, that is, a firm to be considered an SME had to employ up to 1000 employees. Also to be included in the sample it had to be an independent undertaking.
2. Jaime Campos, Alejandra Herrera, Javier Cardozo and Eduardo White, with the collaboration of Marcelo Sierra, *Technology Transfer to Developing Countries by Small and Medium-Sized Enterprises* (CEDREI, 1991).

Notes on the Contributors

Peter J. Buckley is Professor of International Business at the University of Leeds and was formerly Professor of Managerial Economics at the University of Bradford Management Centre and Visiting Professor at the Universities of Reading and Paris I: Panthéon, Sorbonne. He has published and edited numerous books and articles on international business. He is a former Vice-President of the Academy of International Business and former Chair of its UK region. In 1985 he was elected a Fellow of the Academy for 'outstanding achievements' in that field.

Jaime Campos has a MA in Economics, Yale University, and a Licenciate in Sociology, Argentine Catholic University. He is consultant to various international organisations and Director of CEDREI (Centre of Studies on Development and International Economic Relations). Currently, he is Executive Director of Argentina's Investment Foundation. He is the co-author of *Technology Transfer to Developing Countries by Small and Medium-Sized Enterprises* (1993).

Javier Cardozo is Senior Executive at Metrovías, the Buenos Aires Subway System. He has an MA in Technology from the University of Sussex.

Michel Delapierre is Chargé de Recherches at CNRS (Centre National de la Recherche Scientifique) and Director of CEREM (Centre de Recherches sur l'Entreprise Multinationale). He is co-author of *Grappes technologiques, les nouvelles strategies d'entreprise* (1986) and *Les Firmes multinationales. Des firmes au coeur d'industries mondialisées* (1995).

Ashok V. Desai is Consultant Editor of *Business Standard*, an Indian financial daily. In 1991–3, as Chief Consultant to the Ministry of Finance, he helped in the reforms carried out by the Indian Government. In the 1970s he was Head of the Economics Department at the University of the South Pacific and in the 1980s he coordinated the Energy Research Group for the International Development Research Centre, Ottawa. Since the 1960s he has been associated with the National Council of Applied Economic Research in Delhi, where he carried out a number of studies on industry and trade.

Anna Falzoni is a researcher based at CERPEM, University of Bari.

Afonso Fleury is Head of the Production Engineering Department at the University of Sao Paulo, Brazil. He is a consultant in industrial organisation for public and private institutions. He has published books on work organisation (1983), technology management (1987) and organisational learning and innovation (1995).

Pan Eng Fong is currently on leave from the National University of Singapore and is Ambassador for Singapore in Belgium. In 1991–2 he was Visiting Professor at the Graduate School of Business, Columbia University, and in 1993–4 he was Visiting School Associate Fellow at the Institute of Southeast Asian Studies. He is co-author of *Foreign Investment and Industrialisation in Malaysia, Singapore, Taiwan and Thailand* (1991) and author of *Regionalisation and Labour Flows in Pacific Asia* (1993).

Masataka Fujita is currently Transnational Corporations Affairs Officer for the United Nations Conference on Trade and Development. He has masters' degrees from Pennsylvania State University and from Waseda University, Tokyo, where he also completed his doctoral thesis in 1985. He is author of *Small and Medium-sized Transnational Corporations: Role Impact and Policy Implications* (1993).

Benjamin Gomes-Casseres is Associate Professor of International Business, Graduate School of International Economics and Finance, Brandeis University, Waltham, Mass. From 1985 to 1995 he was Associate Professor at the Graduate School of business Administration, Harvard University, Boston, Mass. He is author of *The Alliance Revolution: The New Shape of Business Rivalry* (1997) and *International Trade and Competition: Cases and Notes in Strategy and Management* (with David B. Yoffie) (2nd edn, 1994).

Alejandro Herrera is Advisor to the President of Brazil on Telecommunications. He was formerly a Director of the Argentina Technology Fund. He is author of *La revolución technológica y la telefonía argentina* (1989).

Tomás Kohn is Professor of Management and International Business, Boston University School of Management, Boston, Mass.

He is author of *Strategic Management in Developing Countries: Case Studies* (with James E. Austin, 1990) and *Instructor Manual for Strategic Management on Developing Countries: Case Studies* (also with James E. Austin) 1990.

B. Nino Kumar is Professor and Chair of Business Economics and International Management, Universitat Erlangen-Nurberg. From 1988 to 1992 he was Professor and Chair of General Business Economics at the Universitat der Bundeswehr, Hamburg. He is co-editor of *Handbuch der internationalen Internehmenstätigkeit* (1992), and author of *Deutsche Unternehmen in den USA* (1989) and *Fuhrungsprobleme internationaler Gemeinschaftsunternehmen* (1975).

Won-Young Lee is currently Director of the Policy Research Division of the Science and Technology Institute in Seoul, Korea. He is also a member of the Presidential Commission on the Twenty-first Century. He was Research Fellow of the Korea Development Institute from 1983 to 1993, and a Visiting Professor of the University of California, San Diego, in 1991. He is author of *An Industry and Trade Model of South Korea* (1993), *Challenging the Future: Changes in Industry Structure and Policy Response* (1988) and *Research and Development Investment and Tax Incentives* (1984).

Miguel H. Marquez is a consultant, and was formerly Assistant Director and researcher, Energy Research Program at the University of Chile. He has written *The Privatisation of the Chilean Electrical Industry and Sustainable Development* (1996) and *Renewable Energy Sources: An Option for Sustainable Development* (1996).

Hafiz Mirza is Professor of International Business at the University of Bradford Management Centre. His principle research interests include the political economy of Japanese internationalisation, transnational corporations and the transfer of business culture, SME transnationals and the international transfer of technology and regionalisation and zones of growth. He has published widely, including many articles in journals such as the *Journal of International Business Studies*, *Management International Review* and *International Business Review*. His book on multinationals and the Singapore economy was an early examination of technology transfer and development in NIEs and he has several books forthcoming. He is currently involved in a number of projects with UNCTAD, the UN Economic Commission for Africa and ASEAN on foreign direct investment and the international transfer of technology and business culture.

Jorge Niosi is Director of CIRST (Centre interuniversitaire de recherche sur la science et la technologie) and a Fellow of the Royal Society of Canada. He is Professor at the University of Quebec, Montreal, and in 1995–6 was Visiting Scholar at the Center for Economic Policy Research, Stanford University. He is the author of *Technology and National Competitiveness* (1991), *Technological Alliances in Canadian Industry* (1995), and *New Technology Policy and Social Innovations in the Firm* (1994).

Terutomo Ozawa is Professor of Economics, Colorado State University, Fort Collins, Colorado, USA. He serves on the Editorial Advisory Board for *Transnational Corporations*, an UNCTAD journal, on the Editorial Board for the *International Business Review*, and on the Review Board for *International Trade Journal*. He is author of *Recycling Japan's Surpluses for Developing Countries* (1989), *Multinationalism, Japanese Style: Political Economy of Outward Dependency* (1979 and 1982) and co-author of *Japan's General Trading Companies: Merchants of Economic Development* (1989).

Annukka Paloheimo is a researcher at the School of Management, National University of Singapore.

Marcelo Sierra is an economist at the Funación Invertir, Argentina.

H. Steinmann has been Professor and Chair of Business Economics and General Management at Universität Erlangen-Nurnberg since 1970. He is author of *Das GroBunternehmen im Interessenkonflikt* (1969), *Grundlagen der Unternehmensethik*, 2 Aufl. (1994) and *Management. Grundlagen der Unternehmensfuhrung*, 3 Aufl. (1993).

Gianfranco Viesti is Lecturer in International Economics, University of Bari, and Director of CERPEM, a centre of social and economic studies. In the past, he has taught in other Italian universities, including Bocconi University of Milan. His books include The *Italian Multinationals* (1986), *Il difficile sviluppo dell'industria nel Mezzogiorno* (F. Angeli, 1984), *I distretti industriali: crisi o evoluzione?* (1992).

Eduardo White was a lawyer from the Buenos Aires University and Licenciate in Sociology from the University of Rome. He was formerly consultant to various international organisations and Advisor to the Centre on Transnational Corporations of the United Nations. He was a former Director of CEDREI (Centre of Studies on Development and International Economic Relations) and was the author of *Las Empresas Multinacionales Latinoamericanas* (1973).

1 Introduction

Peter J. Buckley and Hafiz Mirza

1.1 TECHNOLOGY TRANSFER AND THE INNOVATION PROCESS

It has long been conventional to distinguish between invention (the idea creating a new product or process) and innovation (the application of the idea in a commercial setting). The process of commercialising technology is now seen as a much more complicated process, involving technical feasibility testing, commercial development and design as well as other issues. Technological development is a continuous, dynamic process and constant reinvestment in updating technology is essential.

The strategic behaviour of the firm must strike a balance between capitalising its technological advantages and slowing diffusion of that technology. It is of course not in the interests of the firm that its technology should diffuse to others. This reduces the firm's appropriation of returns from technological advance. The appropriability problem is central to the choice between licensing (the market sale of knowledge in some form) and foreign direct investment, in which control is retained by internalising the technology (Buckley and Casson, 1976). Firms must balance the costs and benefits of obtaining a return from technological advance by utilising it themselves or by transferring it to outsiders.

This project concentrates on the means used to transfer technology by small and medium-sized enterprises (SMEs). Section 2 examines technology transfer by multinational enterprises (MNEs) and section 3 analyses the role of SMEs in technology transfer. Section 4 presents the types of technology transfer mode open to companies and section 5 links this to the current project.

1.2 MULTINATIONAL ENTERPRISES AND TECHNOLOGY TRANSFER

The exploitation of a technological lead is a major competitive weapon and a major reason for foreign direct investment (Buckley and Casson,

1976, 1985; Casson, 1979). The multinational enterprise can be re-garded as an institution designed to prevent technological diffusion (Johnson, 1970). The actual situation is somewhat more complex than this. The multinational firm plays a threefold role in the technology process: (1) as a creator of new technology, (2) as an adopter of new technology into commercial products and processes (in the process of which it undertakes risk) and (3) as a vehicle for transferring tech-nology internationally, both by internal and external means.

From the host country's point of view, a major concern is to obtain the *use* of the technology. It is not necessary to produce technology in order to use it. In fact there are a number of strategies open to the host country in order to gain technology-intensive goods: (1) import the goods which embody the technology, (2) import the producer goods embodying the technology in order to manufacture the final goods, (3) import the technology itself and carry out production and (4) pro-duce the technology itself. Most countries employ a mix of strategies (1)–(3) because the resource cost of technology creation is so high, except possibly in a very narrow area of specialisation. It is a fallacy to believe that route (4), technology creation, is always optimal.

The vast majority of external transfer of technology to independent foreign firms is done by firms which either *are* MNEs (companies which have a number of controlled foreign subsidiaries) or *could be* MNEs (companies which have considered the possibility of having controlled subsidiaries overseas). Thus in the great majority of cases where technology is transferred overseas outside the originating firm, the alternative route of foreign direct investment (FDI) will have been considered. This is not to rule out the possibility that the transfer does not have some (even total) control over the recipient of the technology when the market route is chosen. This non-ownership (non-equity) control can be very important.

Intermediate routes of transferring technology, such as the joint venture, involve some sharing of control, reward and risk. A complex analysis of modes of technology transfer by MNEs can be undertaken, involving issues such as the extent of resource transfer, time and space limita-tions on the use of resources, the mode of transfer (internal or exter-nal) and whether this transfer occurs via equity or non-equity ventures.

It should be remembered that the process of transferring technology is difficult and time-consuming. As Hall and Johnson (1970) say

Technology can be transferred in two basic forms. One form embraces physical items such as drawings, tools, machinery, process information, specifications and patents. The other form is personal contact. Put simply, knowledge is always embodied in something or somebody, the form being important for determining the transfer process and cost.

Technology transfer is thus a relationship, not an act.

The minimisation of transaction costs is the key to the choice of form of technology transfer. In many cases, the most efficient institution for transferring technology internationally is the multinational firm. Several studies of the technology transfer process point to the costs of transmitting and absorbing all the relevant unembodied knowledge (Teece, 1977. p. 247). A study of Australian licensors pointed to the large costs of communication and back-up services for licencees (Carstairs and Welch, 1981). It is safe to assume that these costs are reduced when the transfer is internal to the firm. Furthermore, the time lag in licensing is greater than that on internal transfers (Mansfield, Romeo and Wagner, 1979). Licensing involves continuing expense on the part of the licensor to ensure the successful transfer and policing of his rights. The role of (expensive) skilled personnel is crucial.

Nevertheless, licensing is still the preferred route for the transfer of technology by MNEs in certain circumstances. These might be in smaller markets, with more dated technology and where licensing reduces head-to-head competition (perhaps by cross-licensing deals). Some host countries restrict foreign ownership, and licensing may be a second best choice in these circumstances. It is also the case that restrictions on the ability of firms to finance and manage foreign subsidiaries may lead to licensing. A special case of this may be internationally-orientated SMEs.

1.3 SMALL AND MEDIUM-SIZED ENTERPRISES AND TECHNOLOGY TRANSFER

Small and medium-sized enterprises often play a specialised role in creating, transferring and adapting technology. They are often uniquely suited to the creation and development of niche technologies. Indeed their survival is often linked to innovation in 'small-firm industries' (industries with low economies of scale and significant entry barriers for larger operations) (Buckley, 1989). With respect to international technology transfer, it is often smaller firms who seek out foreign sources of technology and then adopt the technology to their own national conditions – as the empirical chapters of this book show.

Perhaps what is less appreciated is that SMEs play a major role in the export of technology from advanced countries. Again it is arguable that they have certain unique attributes which enable them to be successful in the international transfer of technology. Their specialised products and technology, 'hands-on' style of management and attitudes to risk enable rapid and effective transfer. Often the types of technology in which they are specialised are especially suited to less developed countries.

On both the supplier and recipient sides of technology transfer, therefore, SMEs have an important role to play.

1.4 TYPES OF TECHNOLOGY TRANSFER

It is possible to characterise the forms of technology transfer by reference to a number of dimensions. This is done in Table 1.1 (following Buckley, 1983). The dimensions cover ownership (equity or non-equity), possible time and space limitations on the use of the technology transferred, the scope of the transfer of resources and rights and the mode of transfer (internalised or market).

Using these dimensions, it is possible to classify the modes of international cooperation into (at least) eleven distinctive types ranging from wholly-owned subsidiaries to much looser forms of cooperation such as licensing deals of various kinds, joint ventures and alliances. The factors which govern the firm's selection of mode of transfer are fascinating and are illuminated throughout this volume.

1.5 INTRODUCTION TO THIS VOLUME

This book is result of a truly multinational effort. Teams from seven technology-supplying countries and six recipient countries coordinated their efforts in examining technology transfer by SMEs. This effort was coordinated by the late Eduardo White (to whom this book is dedicated) assisted by Jaime Campos, and the logistical problems of this alone were monumental. Frequent meetings of the teams took place and the result is truly and properly a cooperative effort. In addition, Chapter 2 reports on a parallel UN study which helps to place the remaining chapter of this book in a broader context.

Part I of the book examines the role of SMEs in foreign direct investment and the policy implications of SMEs' role in technology transfer. In Part II, technology suppliers are examined on a country-by-country basis, and the same procedure is followed for recipients in Part III. Clearly, each national 'team' conducted the basic research but, as far as possible, the approaches were standardised and focused on the central themes on the project.

Table 1.1 A typology of international cooperation modes

Form of cooperation	Equity or non-equity	Time limited or unlimited	Space limited	Transfer of resources and rights	Mode of transfer
1 Wholly-owned foreign subsidiaries	Equity	Unlimited	At discretion of MNE	Whole range	Internal
2 Joint ventures	Equity	Unlimited	Agreed	Whole range?	Internal
3 Foreign minority holdings	Equity	Unlimited	Limited	Whole range?	Internal
4 'Fade out' agreements	Equity	Limited	Nature of agreement	Whole range? for limited period	Internal changing to market
5 Licensing	Non-equity	Limited by contract	May include limitation in contract	Limited range	Market
6 (Franchising)	Non-equity	Limited by contract	Yes	Limited + support	Market
7 Management contracts	Non-equity	Limited by contract	May be specified	Limited	Market
8 'Turnkey ventures'	Non-equity	Limited	Not usually	Limited in Time	Market
9 'Contractual joint ventures'	Non-equity	Limited	May be agreed	Specified by contract	Mixed
10 International sub-contracting	Non-equity	Limited	Yes	Small	Market
11 Alliances	Usually non-equity	Limited	Yes	Variable	Non-market

Part I

Overview: The Role of Small and Medium-sized Enterprises in Foreign Direct Investment

2 Small and Medium-sized Enterprises in Foreign Direct Investment

Masataka Fujita

2.1 INTRODUCTION

The increased participation of small and medium-sized enterprises (SMEs) in international production is a phenomenon worthy of research and analysis. For the purposes of this chapter, SMEs are defined as firms which employ 'less than' 500 people in manufacturing, 'less than' 100 in wholesale trade and 'less than' 50 in retail trade and other services[1] (this definition differs from that used in the study reported by the bulk of this book – see the Preface). Although several studies have taken note of the general phenomenon of SMEs,[2] there is a need to assess whether small and medium-sized transnational corporations (TNCs) differ from large TNCs in their behaviour and in their effects on home and host-country economies. Such differences, if they can be substantiated, should be incorporated into national economic policies on foreign direct investment (FDI).

Academic neglect of SMEs has been due partly to lack of information data and partly to the inadequacy of the traditional theory of transnationalisation, which focuses on firm size as a key determinant of FDI. In view of the changing world economy, with diverse forms of corporate actors, economic theories of FDI and TNC behaviour are evolving.

The intent of this chapter is to examine available evidence on the role of SMEs in both national economies and the world economy and the assess the importance of SMEs in FDI world-wide. Section 2.2 will examine the importance and role of SMEs in their own national economies. Our sample is a group of 18 developed countries[3] and the comparative analysis is based on the determinants of numbers of SMEs, levels of employment created, value of sales and value added generated and labour productivity. The role of SMEs in their national economies will be assessed in terms of employment-creation, innovation and export value.

Section 2.3 will assess the process of transnationalisation of SMEs, focusing on factors that motivate SMEs to go abroad and whether they differ from those affecting large TNCs. Section 2.4 will analyse SME FDI trends, drawing on a data base being developed at the United Nations Centre on Transnational Corporations. After an overview, sub-sections will detail differing FDI patterns of United States, European and Japanese SMEs. Section 2.5 will discuss the implications of the analysis for developing countries.

2.2 THE IMPORTANCE AND ROLE OF SMEs IN NATIONAL ECONOMIES

The Importance of SMEs in the Economy

The post-1974 oil crisis marks the beginning of governmental and academic interest in SMEs and their contribution to national economies. Many large firms failed to adjust to abrupt changes in demand and relative costs. National governments faced inflation, unemployment and declining or stagnant investment. Theorists and policy-makers believed that SMEs could alleviate some of these problems by being more responsive to changed market conditions than large firms. The hypothesis was that being individually owned or operated by a small team of managers, SMEs were able to move quickly in response to change, that being price-takers in most markets they did not aggravate inflationary pressures and, due to their relatively higher share of net firm formation, would contribute to innovation of products, processes and organisation.

Although criteria differ among nations, there are some useful generalisations that can be made from a comparison of the importance of SMEs in their economies. This chapter uses four measures to evaluate their importance: the relative number of SMEs in the economy, their share of employment, their share of sales and their share of value added across industries – manufacturing, wholesale trade, retail trade, and other services. Based on the above measures, even after bringing into account country differences, SMEs have a relatively high degree of importance in national economies as compared to large firms (Table 2.1).[4] SMEs also seem to be more important in wholesale and retail trade and other services than in manufacturing. An overall trend to an increased share of SMEs as defined by the above-mentioned measures is further confirmed in Table 2.2. There are of course exceptions to the trend, such as in retail trade in Norway and Sweden, and wholesale

Table 2.1 SMEs: no. of enterprises/establishments, employment, value of sales and value added, latest available year[a]

Country	Number of enterprises/establishments (Thousands)	Employment (Thousands)	Value of sales[a] (Million dollars)	Value added[b] (Million dollars)	SMEs as % of all enterprises/establishments (%)			
					Number of enterprises/establishments	Number of employment	Value of sales	Value added
			Manufacturing[c]					
Australia (1985)[d]	22.6	543.4	32 149.8	12 805.5	98.7	51.9	46.2	44.7
Austria (1985)[e]	7.6	326.9	21 101.1	6 947.6	89.5	56.1	52.8	54.1
Belgium (1970)[d]	56.2	695.8	...	...	99.4	57.1	...	...
Canada (1984)[d]	36.1	1 266.8	132 121.7	47 451.5	98.9	67.9	60.3	63.6
Denmark (1986)	7.3	320.5	...	...	98.7	77.1	...	...
Finland (1984)[d]	18.1	227.3	11 474.6	...	99.4	43.8	32.6	...
France (1986)[i,f]	21.1	1 580.4	117 821.0	45 127.1	92.5	47.0	37.4	40.7
Germany, Fed. Rep. of, (1986)[d,a]	41.8	3 362.2	229 724.1	69 957.2	93.8	46.6	33.5	34.5
Ireland (1983)	5.0	164.6	7 923.3	3 049.0	97.8	81.1	83.6	84.0
Italy (1982)[d,h]	24.7	1 662.5	102 167.0	...	96.9	53.4	49.0	...
Japan (1986)[i]	434.2	8 577.1	934.986.1	345 609.9	99.6	78.7	61.9	65.3
Netherlands (1985)[j]	8.5	454.5	37 553.5	...	97.5	57.5	47.6	...
New Zealand (1979)	9.4	222.7	7 978.7	2 428.8	99.3	78.2	78.8	75.6
Norway (1982)[k]	12.7	220.1	16 706.0	4 376.7	97.9	62.4	58.2	56.4
Sweden (1986)	8.7	470.1	...	...	97.4	61.2	...	...
Switzerland (1985)	41.0	613.9	...	...	99.6	77.0	...	...
United Kingdom (1983)	100.8	2 699.3	...	47 462.4	98.4	53.2	...	47.6
United States (1982)	343.2	11 074.8	1 054 145.9	441 184.1	98.5	62.2	53.8	53.5

continued on page 12

Table 2.1 continued

Country	Number of enterprises/establishments	Employment	Value of sales[a]	Value added[b]	SMEs as % of all enterprises/establishments (%)			
	(Thousands)		(Million dollars)		Number of enterprises/establishments	Number of employment	Value of sales	Value added
Wholesale trade[l]								
Austria (1983)[m]	56.9	263.9	37 980.0	4472.5	98.3	63.0	51.7	56.7
Belgium (1970)[d]	34.8	160.0	...	...	99.4	75.3	...	...
Finland (1984)[d,n]	32.7	117.3	13 299.3	...	98.5	44.5	35.7	...
Germany, Fed. Rep. of (1985)[d,c]	39.7	561.4	162 137.6	...	96.5	58.1	56.4	...
Japan (1985)	410.3	3 427.2	1 056 951.0	...	99.3	85.7	58.9	...
New Zealand (1983)[d]	4.3	72.2	12 957.9	...	98.9	88.3	83.3	...
Norway (1986)[p]	16.6	65.8	25 778.2	...	96.3	58.5	57.6	...
Switzerland (1985)	16.6	117.9	...	...	99.9	79.3	...	...
United States (1982)	318.4	3 159.7	870 987.2	...	99.0	84.2	77.3	...
Retail trade[q]								
Australia (1980)	100.3	488.3	36 100.7	7 631.4	98.6	72.7	72.2	73.2
Belgium (1970)[d]	132.4	235.2	...	...	99.8	70.7	...	...
Germany, Fed. Rep. of (1985)[d,r]	139.3	1 008.9	68 548.5	...	98.0	52.2	46.5	...
Japan (1985)	1 621.9	5 569.6	338 518.0	...	99.6	88.0	79.4	...
New Zealand (1983)[d]	24.8	129.9	8 176.7	...	99.6	85.5	86.5	...
Norway (1986)[p]	37.8	117.6	19 181.6	...	99.2	88.8	86.6	...

Sweden (1985)[s]	64.8	...	12 112.3	...	98.8	...	70.3	...
Switzerland (1985)	53.0	201.3	...	...	99.1	77.5	...	...
United Kingdom (1984)[d]	229.0	1 010.0	38 294.3	...	99.2	43.4	34.8	...
United States (1982)	1 195.0	9 189.8	658 158.1	...	96.4	67.5	66.5	...
Services excluding wholesale and retail trade[q]								
Australia (1980)[f]	22.3	188.1	5 562.8	2 643.1	97.3	75.8	75.5	71.0
Belgium (1970)[d,u]	181.9	476.6	...	...	99.1	60.6	...	...
Germany, Fed. Rep. of (1985)[d,v]	124.7	866.8	21 465.7	...	96.5	54.0	43.7	...
Japan (1982)[w]	536.0	1 896.0	33 422.9	...	99.8	96.5	95.8	...
New Zealand (1983)[d,x]	15.4	78.5	1 691.4	...	99.5	84.0	87.6	...
Switzerland (1985)	188.1	967.1	...	...	97.8	62.6	...	...
United States (1982)[y]	1 146.5	5 997.1	259 744.0	...	97.3	57.3	64.0	...

Notes:

[a] Figures based on establishment basis are overestimated as small and medium-sized establishments owned by large enterprises are included.

[b] Converted to United States dollars by using the period average exchange rates for the year.

[c] Defined as enterprises/establishments with employment less than 500.

[d] On enterprise basis.

[e] Includes Zentralbueros USW.

[f] Excludes enterprises with employment less than 19. Data for all industries (enterprises au bénéfice réel normal) are 530 436 (99.6 per cent) for number of enterprises, 6 212 039 (56.5 per cent) for number of employment and $527.6 billion (59.0 per cent) for sales in 1985.

[g] Includes Handwork for enterprise with more than 20 employment, includes mining.

h Excludes enterprises with employment less than 19.

i Excludes establishments with employment less than 3.

j Includes only activity units with employment more than 10.

k Defined as establishments with employment less than 199.

l Defined as enterprises/establishments with employment less than 100.

m Includes retail trade. Employment less than 49.

n Includes retail trade, restaurants and hotels. Employment less than 49.

o Only enterprises with more than DM 1 million in annual sales.

p Defined as establishments with employment less than 29.

q Defined as enterprises/establishments with employment less than 50.

r Only enterprises with more than DM 0.25 million in annual sales.

s Defined as establishments with sales size of 0–24.9 million kroner.

t Includes only recreation, personal and other services (motion picture theatres, cafes and restaurants, hotels, accommodation, licensed bowling clubs, licensed golf clubs, licensed clubs n.e.c., laundries and dry cleaners, man's hairdressers and woman's hairdressers and beauty salons).

u Includes only construction, restaurants, reparations, transport and communications, credit, assurance and business services institutions and other services.

v Includes only construction, hotels and restaurants. For construction, only enterprises with 20 or more employees, and for hotels and restaurants, only enterprises with more than DM 50 000 in annual sales. All enterprises in hotels and restaurants (number of enterprises 114 167) are counted as small and medium enterprises as they are not classified in employment sizes of more than 10.

w Only restaurants.

x Includes only restaurants and hotels and personal and household services.

y Hotels, personal and business services, repair services, amusement and recreation services, health services (excluding hospitals), legal services, selected educational services, social services, non-commercial museums, art galleries and botanical and zoological gardens, selected membership organizations and miscellaneous services.

Source: UNCTC, based on official national sources.

Table 2.2 Changes in the share of SMEs in trade, various periods, percentage points

Country/Items	Manufacturing[a]		Wholesale trade[b]	Retail trade[c]	
Australia					
Establishments	+0.2	(1975–80)	...	...	
	+0.2	(1980–5)			
Employment	+7.0	(1975–80)	...	...	
	+16.5	(1980–5)			
Sales	+1.2	(1975–80)	...	...	
	+3.0	(1980–5)			
Value added	+1.0	(1975–80)	...	...	
	+3.2	(1980–5)			
Austria					
Establishments	+4.4	(1980–5)	...	−0.4	(1971–6)[d]
				+0.2	(1976–83)[d]
Employment	+3.5	(1980–5)	...	−2.4	(1976–6)[d]
				−2.6	(1976–83)[d]
Gross product	+2.6	(1980–5)	...	+0.8	(1971–6)[d]
				−3.8	(1976–83)[d]
Net product	+1.0	(1980–5)	...	+0.9	(1971–6)[d]
				−2.1	(1976–83)[d]
Canada					
Establishments	+0.2	(1980–4)	...	...	
Employment	+2.5	(1980–4)	...	...	
Sales	+0.3	(1980–4)	...	...	
Value added	+2.0	(1980–4)	...	...	

continued on page 16

16

Table 2.2 continued

Country/ Items	Manufacturing[a]	Wholesale trade[b]	Retail trade[c]
Denmark			
Establishments	− (1981–6)	..	..
Employment	+2.4 (1981–6)	..	..
Finland			
Enterprises	+0.2 (1976–80)	..	+0.3 (1976–80)[e]
	+0.2 (1980–4)	..	+0.4 (1980–4)[e]
Employment	+2.3 (1976–80)	..	+4.6 (1976–80)[e]
	+1.4 (1980–4)	..	−0.9 (1980–4)[e]
Sales	+0.5 (1976–80)	..	+2.2 (1976–80)[e]
	−2.1 (1980–4)	..	+1.1 (1980–4)[e]
France			
Enterprises		− (1981–5)[f]	..
Employment		−3.2 (1981–5)[f]	..
Sales		1.9 (1981–5)[f]	..
Germany, Fed. Rep. of			
Enterprises	−0.2 (1980–6)[g]	..	..
Employment	−0.6 (1980–6)[g]	..	..
Gross product	+0.4 (1980–6)[g]	..	..
Value added	−0.2 (1980–6)[g]	..	..
Ireland			
Enterprises	+0.4 (1980–3)	..	..

Employment	+3.3 (1980–3)	…		…		
Gross product	+3.5 (1980–3)	…		…		
Net product	+6.1 (1980–3)	…		…		
Italy						
Enterprises	– (1975–9)[h]	– (1979–82)[h]	…			
Employment	–1.5 (1975–9)[h]	+1.2 (1979–82)[h]	…			
Turnover	–0.4 (1975–9)[h]	–0.8 (1979–82)[h]	…			
Japan						
Establishments	+0.2 (1973–81)	– (1981–6)	+0.3 (1974–9)	– (1979–85)	– (1974–9)	–0.1 (1979–85)
Employment	+4.5 (1973–81)	+0.5 (1981–6)	+4.5 (1974–9)	+0.4 (1979–85)	–0.9 (1979–85)	
Sales	+0.6 (1973–81)	+1.2 (1981–6)	+5.8 (1974–9)	–2.6 (1979–85)	+0.4 (1974–9)	+0.2 (1979–85)
Value added	+3.4 (1973–81)	+0.8 (1981–6)	…			
Netherlands						
Establishments	+0.3 (1976–80)	– (1980–5)	…			
Employment	+1.2 (1976–80)	+0.3 (1980–5)	…			
Sales	–0.4 (1976–80)	–2.2 (1980–5)	…			

17

continued on page 18

Table 2.2 continued

Country/Items	Manufacturing[a]	Wholesale trade[b]	Retail trade[c]
New Zealand			
Establishments	+0.1 (1975–9)	+1.2 (1978–83)[i]	– (1978–83)
Employment	−1.1 (1975–9)	+5.7 (1978–83)[i]	−1.8 (1978–83)
Sales	−3.0 (1975–9)	+5.5 (1978–83)[i]	−0.2 (1978–83)
Value added	−4.1 (1975–9)	…	…
Norway			
Establishments	…	+0.2 (1974–80)[y]; +1.1 (1980–6)[y]	– (1974–80)[y]; +0.1 (1980–6)[y]
Employment	…	−1.9 (1974–80)[y]; +3.0 (1980–6)[y]	+1.3 (1974–80)[y]; −0.6 (1980–6)[y]
Sales	…	+1.8 (1974–80)[y]; +6.6 (1980–6)[y]	−0.4 (1974–80)[y]; −2.6 (1980–6)[y]
Sweden			
Establishments	– (1980–6)	…	−0.4 (1975–80)[k]; −0.4 (1980–5)[k]
Employment	+1.4 (1980–6)	…	…
Sales	…	…	−6.4 (1975–80)[k]; −7.1 (1980–5)[k]
Switzerland			
Establishments	−0.1 (1975–85)	+0.9 (1975–85)	+0.1 (1975–85)
Employment	−1.3 (1975–85)	−1.5 (1975–85)	+4.0 (1975–85)

United States			
Establishments	−2.4 (1976–80)	−1.4 (1976–80)	−2.2 (1976–80)[l]
	+0.5 (1980–6)	−1.6 (1980–6)	−5.9 (1980–6)[l]
Employment	−0.7 (1976–80)	−2.2 (1976–80)	−5.0 (1976–80)[l]
	+1.5 (1980–6)	−1.7 (1980–6)	−5.7 (1980–6)[l]

Notes:

[a] Defined as enterprises/establishments with lower than 500 employment, unless otherwise stated.

[b] Defined as enterprises/establishments with less than 100 employment, unless otherwise stated.

[c] Defined as enterprises/establishments with less than 50 employment, unless otherwise stated.

[d] Wholesale and retail trades. Employment less than 49.

[e] Wholesale trade, retail trade and restaurants and hotels.

[f] All industries.

[g] Includes mining, excludes enterprises with less than 19 employment.

[h] Excludes enterprises with less than 19 employment.

[i] Employment less than 49.

[j] Employment less than 19.

[k] Establishments with less than 24.9 million kroner in sales.

[l] Employment less than 99.

Source: UNCTC, based on official national sources.

Table 2.3   Labour intensity in Japan,[a] FY 1980–6

Industry	SMEs[b]	Large enterprises	All enterprises
	1980		
Primary[c]	1.955	0.143	0.591
Manufacturing	0.718	0.162	0.318
Services[d]	1.152	0.343	0.517
All industries[d]	0.913	0.254	0.418
	1983		
Primary[c]	0.851	0.076	0.314
Manufacturing	0.634	0.119	0.244
Services[d]	1.149	0.291	0.446
All industries[d]	0.839	0.202	0.339
	1986		
Primary[c]	0.977	0.041	0.241
Manufacturing	0.499	0.093	0.194
Services[d]	1.076	0.226	0.338
All industries[d]	0.697	0.161	0.264

[a] Labour–capital ratio. Unit for capital is million yen and unit for labour is number of employment.
[b] Defined as enterprises whose capital is less than 100 million yen in primary and manufacturing, and 10 million yen in services.
[c] Agriculture, fishing and forest, and mining.
[d] Excludes banks and other financial companies.

Sources: Ministry of Finance, *Zaisei Kinyu Tokei Geppo (Monthly Report of Fiscal and Financial Statistics)*, no. 355 (November 1981), no. 390 (October 1984), and no. 425 (September 1987).

and retail trade in the United States, where the share of SMEs is declining due to reconstruction and consolidation in response to global competition.

The Role of SMEs

SMEs as Job Generators

Although the labour–capital ratio varies from country to country and from industry to industry, SMEs tend to be more labour-intensive than large firms. For example, in Japan the labour–capital ratio in all industries is approximately four times higher in SMEs than in large firms, although this ratio has been decreasing for both SMEs and large firms (Table 2.3).[5] The labour–capital ratio is particularly high in services, indicating that services are able to absorb more employment than any other sector. The exceptions to these general observations are manufacturing in Finland and the then Federal Republic of Germany where large firms provided more than half of total employment and to wholesale trade in Finland, the Federal Republic of Germany, Norway and retail trade in the United Kingdom where large firms account for 40–50 per cent of employment. A decline in manufacturing employment was experienced in various countries and this decline was largely due to the loss of jobs in large firms. Austria, Canada, Finland and the United States are typical examples (Table 2.4). In Italy and Japan the loss of manufacturing employment in large firms was compensated for by an increase in employment by SMEs. The decline of traditional manufacturing sectors such as steel, shipbuilding and textiles and the result of rationalisation are largely responsible for increased unemployment in large firms. However, overall employment may remain constant due to the growth of services in all economies. Among the four countries for which data is complete (Italy, Japan, Switzerland and the United States), three countries (all but Italy) show increased employment in services in both SMEs and large firms. In Italy, employment in large services firms declined but was more than offset by jobs created in services SMEs. The growth of services SMEs in Japan is substantial, accounting for three-quarters of all increases in total employment in all industries between 1975 and 1986.

Although there is agreement on the tendency of SMEs to create more jobs per unit of capital than large firms, analysts are divided over the exact proportions, and also over the source of employment growth in SMEs. According to the United States Small Business Administration, employment changes due to net births (births minus deaths) and net internal growth (expansion minus contraction) accounted for 45 per cent and 55 per cent of total change in employment respectively for SMEs (less than 499 employees) and 96 per cent and 4 per cent respectively for large firms (more than 500 employees) between 1980 and 1986.[6] Growth in United States SMEs is equally the result of formation and expansion, while for large firms growth has been mainly due to net births.[7] Since some proportion of the births of large firms is the result of expansion by SMEs, the role of SMEs in growth and employment is even larger.

If SMEs hire more labour, how productive is that labour compared to large firms? In general, labour productivity is lower in SMEs due to a high labour-intensity of production (Table 2.5). In Japan and the

Table 2.4 Employment growth,[a] various periods

Country/ industry	Changes in employment (000)			Contributing share (%)		
	SMEs	LEs	All	SMEs	LEs	All
Australia (1975–85)						
Manufacturing	−79.0	−106.4	−185.4	−42.6	−57.4	−100.0
Austria (1980–5)						
Manufacturing	−5.2	−39.3	−44.6	−11.7	−88.3	−100.0
Services[b]	2.9	17.5	20.4	14.1	85.9	100.0
Canada (1980–4)						
Manufacturing	−43.3	−85.8	−129.1	−33.5	−66.5	−100.0
Denmark (1981–6)						
Manufacturing	43.8	4.1	47.9	91.3	8.7	100.0
Finland (1976–84)						
Manufacturing	−1.6	−50.8	−52.4	−3.2	−96.8	−100.0
Services[c]	9.0	−11.3	−2.3	393.0	−493.0	−100.0
France (1981–5)						
All industries[d]	−396.3	316.6	−79.7	−497.4	397.4	−100.0
Germany, Fed. Rep. of (1975–86)						
Primary[e]	−11.2	−33.3	−44.6	−25.2	−74.8	−100.0
Manufacturing	−373.3	−172.5	−545.8	−68.4	−31.6	−100.0
Ireland (1980–3)						
Manufacturing	−11.9	−11.6	−23.5	−50.7	−49.3	−100.0
Italy (1971–81)						
Primary	20.8	6.0	26.8	77.6	22.4	100.0
Manufacturing	607.0	−134.9	472.1	128.6	−28.6	100.0
Services	1 624.3	−199.5	1 424.8	114.0	−14.0	100.0
All industries	2 252.1	−328.4	1 923.7	117.1	−17.1	100.0
Japan (1975–86)						
Primary	–	−26.4	−26.4	0.1	−100.1	−100.0
Manufacturing	991.3	−313.4	677.9	146.2	−46.2	100.0
Services	7 007.9	1 711.9	8 719.8	80.4	19.6	100.0
All industries	7 999.2	1 372.1	9 371.3	85.4	14.6	100.0
Netherlands (1976–85)						
Manufacturing	−67.9	−75.0	−142.9	−47.5	−52.5	−100.0
New Zealand (1975–84)						
Manufacturing[f]	7.2	17.4	−4.6	−9.4	70.6	100.0

Country/ industry	Changes in employment (000)			Contributing share (%)		
	SMEs	LEs	All	SMEs	LEs	All
Services[g]	32.1	4.8	36.9	87.0	13.0	100.0
Norway (1980–6)						
Primary[e,h]	0.7	6.5	7.2	9.6	90.4	100.0
Manufacturing[h]	−14.8	−21.1	−35.9	−41.3	−58.7	−100.0
Services[i]	13.3	6.1	19.4	68.4	31.6	100.0
Sweden (1980–6)						
Primary[e]	–	−3.1	−3.1	1.2	−101.2	−100.0
Manufacturing	−40.3	−45.7	−86.0	−46.9	−53.1	−100.0
Switzerland (1975–85)						
Primary	16.2	1.0	17.2	94.3	5.7	100.0
Manufacturing	−132.6	−24.2	−156.9	−84.5	−15.5	−100.0
Services	258.0	117.5	375.4	68.7	31.3	100.0
All industries	141.6	94.2	235.8	60.0	40.0	100.0
United States (1980–6)						
Primary	118	−50	68	173.5	−73.5	100.0
Manufacturing	567	−1 746	−1 178	48.2	−148.2	−100.0
Services	5 963	5 618	11 581	51.5	48.5	100.0
All industries	6 648	3 822	10 470	63.5	36.5	100.0

Notes: SMEs – small and medium-sized firms.

LEs – large firms.

[a] SMEs are defined as enterprises/establishments whose employment is less than 499 in primary and manufacturing, less than 99 in wholesale trade and less than 49 in retail trade and other services. For Finland, the Federal Republic of Germany, France, Ireland and Italy, figures are on enterprise basis. For other countries, figures are on establishment basis, in which small and medium establishments owned by large enterprises are included.

[b] For 1976–83. Only wholesale and retail trades in which employment is less than 49 for SMEs.

[c] Only wholesale and retail trades, restaurants and hotels in which employment is less than 49 for SMEs.

[d] For SMEs, employment is less than 499.

[e] Only mining.

[f] For SMEs employment is less than 99 regardless of industries.

[g] For 1978–83. Only wholesale trade, retail trade, restaurants and hotels, and personal and household services in which employment is less than 49 for SMEs.

[h] For SMEs, employment is less than 199.

[i] Only commerce (wholesale and retail trades) in which employment is less than 19 for SMEs.

Source: UNCTC, based on official national sources.

Table 2.5 Labour productivity: sales and value added per employment, SMEs and large firms (LEs)[a], latest available year, 000 dollars

Country	Sales per employment				Value added per employment			
	Manufacturing[b]	Wholesale trade[c]	Retail trade[d]	Services excluding wholesale and retail trades[d]	Manufacturing[b]	Wholesale trade[c]	Retail trade[d]	Services excluding wholesale and retail trades[d]
Australia								
SMEs	59.2 (1985)	73.9 (1980)	29.6 (1980)[e]	...	23.6 (1985)	...	15.6 (1980)	14.1 (1980)[e]
LEs	77.5 (1985)	75.3 (1980)	30.0 (1980)[e]	...	31.5 (1985)	...	15.2 (1980)	18.0 (1980)[e]
All	66.5 (1985)	74.3 (1980)	29.7 (1980)[e]	...	27.4 (1985)	...	15.5 (1980)	15.0 (1980)[e]
Austria								
SMEs	64.5 (1985)	143.9	... (1983)[y]	...	21.3 (1985)	16.9	... (1983)[y]	...
LEs	75.1 (1985)	104.1	... (1983)[y]	...	22.7 (1985)	22.2	... (1983)[y]	...
All	68.5 (1985)	129.2	... (1983)[y]	...	22.0 (1985)	18.9	... (1983)[y]	...
Canada								
SMEs	104.3 (1984)	...	...	...	37.5 (1984)	...	...	...
LEs	158.0 (1984)	...	...	...	55.3 (1984)	...	...	...
All	118.5 (1984)	...	...	...	42.2 (1984)	...	...	...
Finland								
SMEs	50.5 (1984)	113.4	... (1984)[g]	...	...	...	...	...
LEs	81.5 (1984)	163.9	... (1984)[g]	...	...	...	...	...
All	67.9 (1984)	141.4	... (1984)[g]	...	...	...	...	...
France								
SMEs	74.6 (1986)[h]	...	...	...	28.6 (1986)[h]	...	...	...
LEs	108.0 (1986)[h]	...	...	...	36.8 (1986)[h]	...	...	...
All	93.7 (1986)[h]	...	...	...	33.0 (1986)[h]	...	...	...

	(1986)^i	(1985)y	(1985)^k	(1985)^j	(1986)^j		
Germany, Fed. Rep. of							
SMEs	68.3	288.8 67.9	85.4 24.8	20.8	...	...	...
LEs	120.5	310.2 85.4	37.4	35.1	...	...	...
All	96.0	297.7 76.3	30.6	28.4	...	...	...
Ireland	(1983)		(1983)	(1983)			
SMEs	48.1	...	...	18.5	...	...	...
LEs	40.2	...	...	15.1	...	...	...
All	46.7	...	...	17.9	...	...	...
Italy	(1982)^m						
SMEs	61.5	...	...	...	...		
LEs	73.3	...	...	...	...		
All	67.0	...	...	...	...		
Japan	(1986)^n	(1985)	(1985)	(1982)^o	(1986)^n		
SMEs	109.0	308.4 60.8	17.6	40.3	...	...	...
LEs	248.9 1	292.9 115.8	21.0	79.4	...	...	...
All	138.7	449.0 67.4	17.7	48.6	...	...	...
Netherlands	(1985)^p						
SMEs	82.6	...	...	...	...	...	...
LEs	123.2	...	...	...	...	...	...
All	99.8	...	...	...	...	...	...
New Zealand	(1979)	(1983)	(1983)	(1983)^q	(1979)		
SMEs	35.8	179.5 62.9	21.5	10.9	...	...	...
LEs	34.7	269.6 57.7	16.0	12.7	...	...	...
All	35.6	190.1 62.2	20.7	11.3	...	...	...

continued on page 26

Table 2.5 continued

Country	Sales per employment				Value added per employment			
	Manufacturing[b]	Wholesale trade[c]	Retail trade[d]	Services excluding wholesale and retail trades[d]	Manufacturing[b]	Wholesale trade[c]	Retail trade[d]	Services excluding wholesale and retail trades[d]
Norway								
SMEs	75.9 (1982)[r]	391.8 (1986)[s]	163.1 (1986)[s]	...	19.9 (1982)[r]	...	...	...
LEs	90.3 (1982)	406.4 (1986)	201.1 (1986)	...	25.6 (1982)	...	...	...
All	81.3 (1982)	397.8 (1986)	167.4 (1986)	...	22.0 (1982)	...	...	...
United Kingdom								
SMEs	...	...	37.9 (1984)	...	17.6 (1983)	...	...	...
LEs	...	...	54.5 (1984)	...	22.0 (1983)	...	...	...
All	...	...	47.3 (1984)	...	19.6 (1983)	...	...	...
United States								
SMEs	95.2 (1982)	275.7 (1982)	71.6 (1982)	43.3 (1982)	39.8 (1982)	...	...	...
LEs	134.4 (1982)	429.9 (1982)	74.9 (1982)	32.7 (1982)	56.8 (1982)	...	...	...
All	110.0 (1982)	300.1 (1982)	72.7 (1982)	38.8 (1982)	46.3 (1982)	...	...	...

Notes:

a For Australia (only manufacturing), Canada, Finland, the Federal Republic of Germany, France, Italy, New Zealand and the United Kingdom (only retail sales) figures are on enterprise basis. For other countries, figures are on establishment basis, in which small and medium establishments owned by large enterprises are included. Converted to US dollars by using the period average exchange rate for the year.

b Defined as enterprises/establishments with employment less than 500.

c Defined as enterprises/establishments with employment less than 100.

d Defined as enterprises/establishments with employment less than 50.

e Includes only recreation, personal and other services (motion picture theatres, cafes and restaurants, hotels, accommodation, licensed bowling clubs, licensed golf clubs, licensed clubs n.e.c., laundries and dry cleaners, men's hairdressers and women's hairdressers and beauty salons).

f Wholesale and retail trades.

g Wholesale trade, retail trade, restaurants and hotels. Defined as enterprises with employment less than 49.

h Excludes enterprises with employment less than 19. Data for all industries (enterprises au bénéfice réel normal) are $84.9 thousand for SMEs, $76.9 thousand for large enterprises and $85.1 thousand for all enterprises in sales per employment in 1985.

i Includes Handwerk for enterprises with more than 20 employment.

j Only enterprises with more than DM 1 million in annual sales.

k Only enterprises with more than DM 0.25 million in annual sales.

l Includes only construction, hotels and restaurants. For construction, only enterprises with 20 or more employees, and for hotels and restaurants, only enterprises with more than DM 50 000 in annual sales. All enterprises in hotels and restaurants (number of enterprises 114 167) are counted as small and medium enterprises as they are not classified in employment sizes of more than 10.

m Excludes enterprises with employment less than 19.

n Excludes establishments with employment less than 3.

o Only restaurants.

p Includes only activity units with employment more than 10.

q Includes only restaurants and hotels and personal and household services.

r Defined as establishments with employment less than 199.

s Defined as establishments with employment less than 29.

Source: UNCTC, based on official national sources.

Federal Republic of Germany, labour productivity in manufacturing
SMEs is about half that of large firms. In Japanese wholesale and
retail trade, labour productivity of SMEs is only one-fourth and one-
half of large firms respectively. However, in countries such as Australia,
Austria, Italy, New Zealand and Norway, differences in labour
productivity between firms are small and in specific sectors in Australia
(retail trade), Austria (wholesale and retail trade), Ireland (manufacturing), New Zealand (manufacturing, retail trade, other services), and
United States (other services), SMEs' labour productivity is higher
than that of large firms either in terms of sales per employee or value
added per employee.

SMEs as Innovators

The role of SMEs as innovators is not as clearly demonstrated by
data as is their job-creation role. First, there is a problem of definition.
Many surveys and statistics do not clearly differentiate innovation (the
application of technological advances and products and processes) from
invention (the discovery of a new product or process). Secondly,
innovation of products and processes is more easily defined, and thus
measured, than organisational innovations. Finally, there is the problem
of separation of data on innovation within large firms where births
and deaths of products and processes occur within product lines and
divisions and do not show up in data on net firm formation.

The measure traditionally used has been research and development
(R&D) expenditure per employee related to the number of patents for
new products or production processes per employee. However, this
measure does not capture a unique feature of SMEs, which is that
owners and managers are often themselves innovators. For example,
in Japan more than half the SMEs' innovations reported in 1986 (52
per cent) were created by SME employers, as opposed to large firms
where 72 per cent of innovations were created by research technicians.[8]
Also large firms are more likely to separate R&D expenditures and
R&D departments. During 1975–84, only 9–17 per cent of Japanese
SMEs reported explicit R&D activities, as opposed to 62–75 per cent
of large firms.[9]

Taking available data for 1982 for the United States, SMEs registered
2089 innovations and large firms 2830. (Table 2.6). The number of
innovations per million employees was 36.2 for SMEs and 31 for large
firms.[10] Data for that year suggests that the share of SMEs in the
number of innovations exceeds their share in R&D expenditures. In

Table 2.6   Distribution of innovations by industry, United States, 1982

Industry	SMEs[a]	Large firms	Total
Primary	2	106	108
Agriculture	–	4	4
Mining	2	102	104
Manufacturing	1954	2455	4409
Services	133	269	402
Construction	3	24	27
Wholesale trade	75	77	152
Retail trade	–	9	9
Transportation, communications and utilities	9	21	30
Finance, insurance and real estate	14	68	82
Other services	32	70	102
All industries	2089	2830	4919

Note:
[a] Firms with fewer than 500 employment.

Source: US Small Business Administration, *The State of Small Business: A Report of the President, 1985* (Washington, DC, US Government Printing Office, May 1985), Table 2.11, p. 130.

the United Kingdom, the innovation share of SMEs increased from 23 per cent in 1965–9, 29 per cent in 1975–9 and to 38 per cent in 1980–3 in total number of innovations.[11] In the Federal Republic of Germany, SMEs seem to exhibit a better ability for the practical application of inventions than large firms.[12]

The data on innovation indicates that the total number of innovations is positively related to R&D expenditures, skilled labour and the degree to which large firms comprise the industry, at the same time as it is negatively related to concentration and unionisation.[13] Thus the data is somewhat inconclusive. A tentative conclusion from cross-country and cross-industry data could be that innovative activity is unrelated to firm size. In certain types of industries such as the new technologies – microelectronics, new materials, biotechnology, etc. – SMEs, particularly technologically advanced SMEs that grow at a faster rate than ordinary SMEs, seem to be the vanguard of innovation. However, the same conclusion cannot be applied across the board.

SMEs as Exporters

In four countries (France, Italy, the Netherlands and Norway), for which
data on exports by firm size is available, the share of exports by SMEs
is more than a third of the total (Table 2.7). In France (all industries)
and Italy (manufacturing), SMEs export almost as much as large firms.
In the Netherlands, 70 out of 177 manufacturing firms which exported
more than 100 million guilders ($30.1 million) in 1985 were SMEs.
In France, the Netherlands and Norway, the export ratio (export/sales)
is positively related to firm size. In Italy, the export ratio is not affected
by firm size. In three countries (France, the Netherlands, Norway),
exports by SMEs grew at a faster rate than those by large firms during the periods examined.[14] Elsewhere, except for France, the share of
SMEs in exports is less than their share in total sales, implying a
greater involvement of SMEs in domestic markets. In the Netherlands,
45 per cent of SMEs produced solely for the domestic market in 1985,
while only 11 per cent of large firms confined themselves to the domestic
consumer.

   For other countries, complete data is not available and is somewhat
inconclusive. For the United States, the Small Business Administration
estimates for 1985 that half of the value added of goods exported by
manufacturers was accounted for by firms with fewer than 500
employees.[15] Another source indicates that 86 500 of 100 000 United
States exporters exported less than 50 shipments annually, most of
them being SMEs, and that they accounted for 12 per cent of total
export value.[16]

   In Japan, the export value of SME products was 4324 billion yen
($29.9 billion) in 1988, accounting for 12.7 per cent of total merchandise
exports, down from 14.7 per cent in 1983 and 13.3 per cent in 1985.
Barriers to exports include management's technical skills, marketing
abilities, financing, tariff and non-tariff trade barriers.[17] One study indicates that major barriers for non-exporters or marginal exporters are
strategic limitations (lack of capacity or capital) and procedural and
technical complexity (shipping complexity, uncertainty of shipping cost,
complexity of trade documentation), and that these can be overcome
by internal actions or through education. External barriers, such as
government policy, contextual differences and local competition affected
all firms equally.[18] Computations as to the potential export gains from
increased exports by SMEs are difficult to make. However, it can be
said that the gains, both to the firms and to their national economies,
are enormous.

In addition to their positive contributions to employment, innovation and exports, SMEs expand consumer choice by catering to consumer needs for diversification, sophistication and specialisation. While larger firms provide relatively standardised products in larger volumes to national markets, SMEs tend to supply niche or specialised products in small volumes to specific markets. An example of this is the traditional handicrafts industries of Europe that preserve the distinctiveness of national products.[19]

General conclusions are difficult, given the scarcity of data. However a tentative relationship does emerge from the data available. The ranking of countries available for the share of SMEs value added in manufacturing (Table 2.1) seems to be related positively to the ranking of countries by the growth rate of *per capita* value added in manufacturing.[20]

2.3 THE INTERNATIONALISATION PROCESS FOR SMEs

The internationalisation process refers to the undertaking by a firm of production outside its home country. The various forms of internationalisation include FDI, licensing, corporate alliances, management contracts, sub-contracting, technology transfers, joint ventures, etc. SMEs use all the above-mentioned forms of internationalisation. However, the degree of internationalisation (defined as the share of SMEs engaged in internationationalisation) is lower in every category than that of large firms (for example, see Table 2.20, p. 60–1).

There are several explanations for this low degree of internationalisation. SMEs have been relatively reluctant to internationalise as they are unfamiliar with foreign markets. However, recent technological developments in communications, transportation and financial sectors provide improved opportunities to exploit international markets. Risk and cost concerns impact SMEs more than large firms, since even one business failure may mean the demise of the firm. The recent expansion of international communications, travel and financial services have reduced the costs and time frame of obtaining more accurate, larger volumes of information on foreign markets, of travelling to the location to reach a final decision, of raising funds in international capital markets and using increasingly liberalised banking services.

The reasons that the SMEs overseas are for the most part similar to large TNCs. SMEs expand into international markets when they seek access to less expensive labour and raw materials, when they face

Table 2.7 Manufacturing exports, by country, employment and sales,[a] billion dollars and %

Employment size	France[b] 1981 Exports	France[b] 1981 Exports to sales ratio	France[b] 1985 Exports	France[b] 1985 Exports to sales ratio	Italy[c] 1979 Exports	Italy[c] 1979 Exports to sales ratio	Italy[c] 1982 Exports	Italy[c] 1982 Exports to sales ratio	Netherlands[d] 1976 Exports	Netherlands[d] 1976 Exports to sales ratio	Netherlands[d] 1985 Exports	Netherlands[d] 1985 Exports to sales ratio	Norway 1980 Exports	Norway 1980 Exports to sales ratio	Norway 1982 Exports	Norway 1982 Exports to sales ratio
0–4	8.4	8.7	6.9	10.0	...	...	...	...	...	...	...	...	–	1.8	–	1.6
5–9	4.7	6.9	5.1	8.4	...	...	...	...	...	...	...	...	–	3.1	–	2.8
10–19	6.5	10.1	5.5	9.7	...	...	...	...	0.2	10.4	0.5	14.6	0.1	6.0	0.1	6.4
20–49	17.0	12.5	15.3	13.2	4.2	17.6	4.0	17.1	1.0	20.6	1.7	24.4	0.4	9.1	0.4	9.4
50–99	9.8	12.7	8.9	13.2	5.0	21.7	4.7	21.8	2.2	34.1	2.7	38.6	0.6	14.1	0.5	13.7
100–199	10.8	14.7	9.3	14.5	8.7	23.7	5.9	22.3	2.3	32.5	3.9	42.3	1.0	18.7	0.9	17.8
200–499	13.6	14.0	17.6	18.8	8.2	24.5	7.5	24.0	3.4	38.5	5.6	49.2				
500–999	12.1	16.8	12.0	18.5	5.2	22.5	5.5	20.6								
1000–1999	9.4	14.8	9.7	17.6	4.0	19.4	3.6	22.4								
2000–4999	15.8	11.7	12.1	15.3	3.8	20.8	5.4	22.7	16.0[e]	55.0[e]	23.6[e]	57.2[e]	5.4[f]	38.8[f]	4.4[f]	36.5[f]
5000–9999	10.9	14.7	10.4	16.7	3.2	28.7	2.9	34.3								
10 000–19 999	5.2	25.1	6.0	23.7	2.6	24.4	5.5	29.9								
More than 20 000	22.6	23.3	20.5	25.2	8.1	33.4	3.7	27.9								
Total	146.7	13.7	139.3	15.6	50.5	23.5	48.5	23.3	25.1	43.0	38.0	48.1	7.6	23.5	6.3	21.9
1–499	70.8	11.5	68.6	13.0	23.7	22.1	22.0	21.5	9.1	31.1	14.3	38.1	2.2[g]	11.9[g]	1.9[g]	11.4[g]
More than 500	75.9	16.5	70.7	19.2	26.8	24.9	26.5	25.0	16.0	55.0	23.6	37.2	5.4[f]	38.8[f]	4.4[f]	36.5[f]

Notes:

[a] Converted to US dollars by using the period average exchange rates for the year.

[b] All industries (enterprises au bénéfice réel normal). The exports to sales ratio for only manufacturing in 1986 as follows:

Employment size	Exports to sales ratio
20–49	9.7
50–99	13.5
100–199	18.7
200–499	21.3
More than 500	33.9
Total	27.5

No amounts of exports are given.

[c] Excludes firms with employment less than 19.

[d] Excludes firms with less than 9 employment.

[e] Figures are for firms with more than 500 employment.

[f] Figures are for firms with more than 200 employment.

[g] Figures are for firms with less than 199 employment.

Source: UNCTC, based on official national sources.

stagnating demand or a saturated market in home countries, and when they have a fear of losing their foreign market share due to various tariff or non-tariff barriers. A special case are SMEs that are specialised suppliers of parts and components and follow their larger customers in their foreign operations – the 'drag effect'. These 'drag-effect' SMEs are becoming increasingly important due to their special relationship as subcontractors. The rise of small and medium-sized TNCs is also affected by the growth of services, since services industries contain more SMEs than does manufacturing.

The process by which specific firms internationalise differs, depending on what specific factors motivate the move abroad. From available data on the United Kingdom, for example, it seems that about two-thirds of SMEs engaged first in exporting their products, and then established foreign sales agents or sales subsidiaries before plunging into foreign production.[21] Interestingly, there seems to be a positive correlation between the eventual success of a foreign production subsidiary and the number of steps taken to get to that point.

The exception to the above principle seems to be the technologically advanced SMEs who internationalise in the early stages of their firms' life, often collaborating with foreign firms on advancing technologies. These SMEs derive ownership advantages from their innovations in microelectronics, biotechnology and new materials, for example, optical fibres.

The process also depends on the type of product. For standardised products where scale economies are important, SMEs either license or move production abroad to take advantage of lower average production costs. However, SMEs that produce standardised products for which scale economies are crucial do not remain SMEs for long, as they either expand internally into large TNCs or become the targets of takeovers by large TNCs. In products where scale economies are less important, such as furniture making and tool making, SMEs are more likely to internationalise as independent producers.

SMEs that produce niche products and are large in terms of market share behave in a manner similar to large TNCs regarding foreign direct investment. They are able to find interstices in world markets because of their specialised products. Size must thus, be defined in relation to the market, not just in terms of internal resources, to explain the internationalisation behaviour of firms.

2.4 FOREIGN DIRECT INVESTMENT BY SMALL AND MEDIUM-SIZED TNCs

A Global Overview

The United Nations Centre on Transnational Corporations (UNCTC) is in the process of putting together a database on the overall development and global trends and patterns of small and medium-sized TNCs. The definitive cut-off for small and medium-sized TNCs in this study is firms with less than 500 employees in all sectors, including retail trade and other services.[22] As of May 1989 the UNCTC database covered 18 developed countries, identifying 735 TNCs. The analysis in this section is based on this database, and is thus an interim report on global trends.

The bulk of FDI, if defined in value terms, is still accounted for by large TNCs. Even in Japan, where the ratio of SME FDI to all FDI is probably greater than other countries, the share of FDI by SMEs is still only one-fifth, as of the early to mid-1980s.[23] In the United States, only 3 per cent of SMEs (less than 1000 employees) were transnational, while 87 per cent of large firms (more than 10 000 employees) were transnational in 1987. This phenomenon holds across countries since SMEs, even when they engage in FDI, make relatively small foreign investments. However, in terms of the number of foreign investments or number of firms involved in FDI, the share of SMEs increases substantially. Again in the case of Japan, about 40 per cent of the number of investments was attributed to SMEs between 1980 and 1986. An even sharper contrast exists with regard to the United Kingdom where SMEs (firms with net assets under £2 million) accounted for 7 per cent of book value of FDI and 66 per cent of total numbers of FDI transactions in 1981.

Turning now to the general characteristics of SMEs that have invested overseas, it can be observed that in 1986–7, these SMEs had on average 3.2 foreign affiliates (Table 2.8). TNCs based in Western European countries had more foreign affiliates than the average of this sample. Smaller European countries in particular, such as Denmark, Ireland, Sweden, Finland and Switzerland, had higher numbers of SMEs engaged in FDI. This is the result of small domestic markets that lead to an earlier saturation point; firms that are still SMEs by international standards can be large by domestic standards. In contrast, countries with a large domestic market, such as the United States, have a lower proportion of SMEs that are internationalised.

Table 2.8   No. of foreign affiliates of small and medium-sized TNCs based in 18 developed countries, by country of origin,[a] 1986–7

Region/ country	Total no. of TNCs surveyed	Total no. of foreign affiliates	No. of foreign affiliates per company
North America			
Canada	43	127	2.95
United States	171	426	2.49
Total	214	553	2.58
Japan	120	438	3.65
Europe			
Austria	7	20	2.86
Belgium	34	84	2.47
Denmark	17	104	6.12
Finland	11	44	4.00
France	23	63	2.74
Germany, Fed. Rep.	59	237	4.02
Ireland	9	38	4.22
Italy	24	69	2.88
Netherlands	23	60	2.61
Norway	28	103	3.68
Sweden	28	113	4.04
Switzerland	24	95	3.96
United Kingdom	78	278	3.56
Total	365	1308	3.58
Oceania			
Australia	16	35	2.19
New Zealand	20	35	1.75
Total	36	70	1.94
Total	735	2369	3.22

Note:

[a] Includes all identified foreign entities regardless of forms of organisation (i.e. subsidiaries, branches, representative offices, etc.). Small and medium-sized TNCs here are those whose employment is less than 500 in all sectors. Thus it includes services TNCs which are beyond the employment criteria used for the discussion of SMEs in earlier sections. Banks, insurance and other financial companies are excluded.

Source: UNCTC, database on small and medium-sized TNCs.

Another characteristic of FDI by SMEs is that it is concentrated in developed market economies. More than 80 per cent of foreign affiliates of 735 SMEs from the 18 developed countries sampled were in other developed market economies in 1986–7 (Table 2.9). Three-quarters of Western European SMEs' foreign affiliates were within Western Europe. Finland, Ireland and the United Kingdom have substantial investment by SMEs in the United States – a quarter of all SME investment. 60 per cent of Canadian SME foreign afiliates were in the United States while only 16 per cent of United States affiliates were in Canada. United States SMEs prefer Western European, especially the United Kingdom: one-fifth of total United States SME foreign affiliates and 36 per cent of United States SME foreign affiliates in Europe are in the United Kingdom. In Oceania, two-thirds of New Zealand's SMEs' foreign affiliates are in Australia, but only 22 per cent of Australian SMEs foreign affiliates are in New Zealand.

Among developed countries, the exceptions are Japan and to a lesser degree Australia, which tend to direct their FDI from SMEs to developing countries. About half of the foreign affiliates owned by 120 Japanese SMEs were in developing market economies in 1986–7. For both Japan and Australia, the United States is the largest host country, although the South and East Asia region (excluding China) hosts more of their SME affiliates. Latin America is the major developing country host region for United States SMEs, while Western European SME investment is spread across Africa, South and East Asia, the Middle East and Latin America.[24]

Only eight out of 735 SMEs surveyed have foreign affiliates in centrally planned economies (CPEs). China and Czechoslovakia are the only host countries in this group. Five Japanese and two United States companies have one affiliate each in China. In Czechoslovakia, one Norwegian SME has an affiliate.[25]

A comparison of the above pattern with the distribution of foreign affiliates by 593 of the largest TNCs shows that 73 per cent of about 38 000 foreign affiliates of those large TNCs are located in developed countries, with Europe as the largest host region at 63 per cent of developed country affiliates. Latin America at 14 per cent and South and East Asia at 8 per cent were the largest developing country host regions.[26] In comparison, SMEs' FDI is 80 per cent concentrated in developed countries, with 17 per cent in the United States alone (11 per cent for large TNCs). Among developing countries for SMEs, South and East Asia are relatively more important as hosts than Latin America, largely due to the relative position of FDI of United States SMEs in

Table 2.9 Geographical distribution of foreign affiliates of small and medium-sized TNCs based in 18 developed countries, by country of origin,[a] 1986–7, %

Region/country	World	Developed market economies					Developing market economies						Centrally planned economies[d]
	Total	North America	Of which: United States	Japan	Western Europe	Other countries[b]	Total	Africa	South and East Asia	Latin America	Middle East	Other countries[c]	
North America													
Canada	100.0	92.1	62.2	62.2	0.0	26.0	2.4	7.9	–	1.6	6.3	–	–	–
United States	100.0	82.6	16.2	–	6.1	54.0	6.3	16.9	0.7	5.2	11.0	–	–	0.5
Total	100.0	84.0	26.0	14.3	4.9	47.7	5.4	14.0	0.5	4.3	9.9	–	–	0.4
Japan	100.0	46.6	20.0	27.4	–	15.5	2.3	52.3	6.0	30.6	6.2	0.7	–	1.1
Europe													
Austria	100.0	100.0	15.0	10.0	–	85.0	–	–	–	–	–	–	–	–
Belgium	100.0	89.3	7.1	7.1	–	81.0	1.2	10.7	7.1	2.4	1.2	–	–	–
Denmark	100.0	94.2	8.7	8.7	1.0	82.7	1.9	5.8	–	1.9	2.9	1.0	–	–
Finland	100.0	93.2	27.3	22.7	2.3	63.6	–	6.8	–	4.5	2.3	–	–	–
France	100.0	92.1	19.0	15.9	1.6	65.1	6.3	7.9	6.3	1.6	–	–	–	–
Germany, Fed. Rep.	100.0	91.1	13.1	10.1	2.1	72.2	3.0	8.9	0.0	3.0	4.2	0.0	–	–
Ireland	100.0	92.1	26.3	26.3	–	65.0	–	7.9	2.6	2.6	2.6	–	–	–
Italy	100.0	91.3	11.6	11.6	1.4	70.3	–	8.7	–	1.4	7.2	–	–	–
Netherlands	100.0	86.7	11.7	11.7	–	75.0	–	13.3	1.7	6.7	1.7	1.7	1.7	–
Norway	100.0	94.2	14.6	9.7	–	79.6	–	4.9	1.9	2.9	–	–	–	1.0

Sweden	100.0	99.1	10.6	9.7	–	00.5	–	0.9	–	0.9	–	–	–	–
Switzerland	100.0	91.6	15.0	12.6	3.2	69.5	3.2	0.4	–	6.3	2.1	–	–	–
United Kingdom	100.0	90.3	33.1	23.4	0.7	43.2	13.3	9.7	0.7	5.4	2.9	0.4	0.4	–
Total	100.0	92.1	17.7	14.1	1.1	69.0	4.3	7.0	1.4	3.4	2.4	0.4	0.2	0.1
Oceania														
Australia	100.0	57.1	20.6	22.9	2.9	11.4	14.3	42.9	–	42.9	–	–	–	–
New Zealand	100.0	85.7	11.4	3.6	–	5.7	69.6	14.3	–	11.4	2.9	–	–	–
Total	100.0	71.4	20.0	15.7	1.4	0.6	41.4	20.6	–	27.1	1.4	–	–	–
Total	100.0	81.4	22.0	16.6	1.0	52.4	5.3	18.3	2.2	10.0	4.9	0.3	0.1	0.3

Notes:

[a] Includes all identified foreign entities regardless of forms of organization (i.e. subsidiaries, branches, representative offices, etc.). Small and medium-sized TNCs here are those whose employment is less than 500 in all sectors. Thus includes services TNCs which are beyond the employment criteria used for the discussion of SMEs in earlier sections. Banks, insurance and other financial companies are excluded.

[b] Australia, Israel, New Zealand and South Africa.

[c] Cyprus, Malta, Turkey and Yugoslavia.

[d] Includes China.

Source: UNCTC, database on small and medium-sized TNCs.

Latin America (11 per cent of their total as opposed to 22 per cent of large United States TNCs' FDI).

The concentration of FDI in developed countries can be explained by the gradual approach taken by SMEs in their internationalisation strategy. Firms start with investment in markets whose characteristics are similar to those in their home countries in terms of culture and life styles. Since foreign investment is a relatively new trend for SMEs, there is greater concentration by SMEs in similar markets.

In terms of sectoral distribution, the UNCTC data base indicates that 70 per cent of small and medium-sized TNCs were in manufacturing in 1986–7 (Table 2.10). The rest were mostly in services, including trade.[27] The average number of foreign affiliates per SME was four in services and three in manufacturing. Service SMEs, particularly transport and storage companies, need a greater spread of location worldwide to conduct their international business. Focusing on total numbers of TNCs, SMEs are concentrated in the distribution trade (wholesale and retail) and capital goods production (mostly mechanical equipment).

As measured by the distribution of foreign affiliates, SME FDI in developed countries is largely concentrated in manufacturing while SME FDI in developing countries is almost equally concentrated between manufacturing and services, although developed market economies continue to be hosts to more services small and medium-sized TNCs than developing countries (Table 2.11). In particular, the transport and storage sector has half of its foreign affiliates in developing countries with a high concentration in Africa due to Liberia's 'flags of convenience' policy. About one-quarter of foreign affiliates of SMEs in distribution trade, non-metallic mineral products and electrical equipment are located in developing countries, of which two-thirds are in South East Asia. In the non-metallic mineral products and electrical equipment areas developing countries, in particular South and East Asia, have comparative advantages in production. In comparison with a sectoral breakdown of total FDI, SMEs show a higher propensity to invest in developed countries in manufacturing than large TNCs, while in services SME investment in developed countries is on a par with that of all TNCs.[28]

To summarize, SMEs are globally less internationalised than large TNCs. Of the SMEs that are internationalised, there is a greater concentration in other developed economies for SMEs than for large TNCs. In a sectoral breakdown, SMEs are more prominent in the internationalisation of services as opposed to manufacturing and in

Table 2.10   No. of foreign affiliates of small and medium-sized TNCs based in 18 developed countries, by sector of parent,[a] 1986–7

Industry	Total no. of TNCs surveyed	Total no. of foreign affiliates	No. of foreign affiliates per company
Primary	25	86	3.44
Manufacturing			
Food and beverage	35	113	3.23
Textiles and clothing	45	101	2.24
Paper and allied	33	83	2.52
Chemicals and allied	56	202	3.61
Non-metallic mineral products	11	32	2.91
Metals	57	186	3.26
Mechanical equipment	105	328	3.12
Electrical equipment	64	172	2.69
Transport equipment	12	22	1.83
Other manufacturing	96	278	2.90
Total	514	1517	2.95
Services			
Construction	24	93	3.88
Distributive trade	87	307	3.53
Transport and storage	25	129	5.16
Real estate	7	29	4.14
Other services	52	207	3.98
Total	195	765	3.92
All industries	734	2368	3.23

Note:
[a] Sectors are classified according to the primary business of the company. Those companies whose lines of business are unknown are excluded.

Source: UNCTC, data base on small and medium-sized TNCs.

terms of location, Western Europe is the largest home and host region of SMEs.

The Japanese Dimension

The relatively high importance of SMEs in the Japanese economy is mirrored by the importance of FDI by Japanese SMEs in the general upsurge of total Japanese FDI since the mid-1980s. This rise in Japanese

Table 2.11 Geographical distribution of foreign affiliates of small and medium-sized TNCs based in 18 developed countries, by sector of parent,[a] 1986–7, %

Industry	World Total	Developed market economies						Developing market economies						Centrally planned economies[d]
		Total	North America	Of which: United States	Japan	Western Europe	Other countries[b]	Total	Africa	South and East Asia	Latin America	Middle East	Other countries[c]	
Primary	100.0	86.0	50.0	33.7	–	33.7	2.3	14.0	3.5	–	10.5	–	–	–
Manufacturing														
Food and beverage	100.0	91.2	23.0	17.7	0.9	65.5	1.8	8.8	8.9	5.3	2.7	–	–	–
Textiles and clothing	100.0	81.2	13.9	9.9	–	53.5	13.9	16.8	2.0	13.9	1.0	–	–	2.0
Paper and allied	100.0	91.6	21.7	21.7	–	67.5	2.4	8.4	–	4.8	3.6	–	–	–
Chemicals and allied	100.0	82.2	19.3	13.9	2.0	56.4	4.5	17.8	0.5	9.4	7.9	–	–	–
Non-metallic mineral products	100.0	75.0	12.5	9.4	–	56.3	6.3	25.0	–	18.8	6.3	–	–	–
Metals	100.0	87.1	21.5	15.6	2.7	58.6	4.3	12.9	–	10.2	2.2	0.5	–	–
Mechanical equipment	100.0	88.4	18.9	15.2	3.0	63.7	2.7	11.0	1.2	4.6	0.9	–	0.6	–
Electrical equipment	100.0	78.5	15.1	8.1	1.2	57.0	5.2	21.5	0.0	17.4	4.1	–	–	–
Transport equipment	100.0	86.4	27.3	22.7	4.5	40.9	13.6	13.6	4.5	9.1	–	–	–	0.7
Other manufacturing	100.0	84.2	23.0	18.0	1.8	53.6	5.8	15.1	–	10.4	4.7	–	–	0.7
Total	100.0	85.1	19.7	15.0	1.8	58.7	4.9	14.5	0.6	9.5	4.2	0.3	–	0.4
Services														
Construction	100.0	81.7	22.6	20.4	–	51.6	7.5	17.2	3.2	7.5	5.4	1.1	–	1.1
Distributive trade	100.0	75.2	22.1	16.6	2.6	43.3	7.2	24.4	1.6	19.2	2.6	1.0	–	0.3
Transport and storage	100.0	54.3	14.0	10.9	0.8	32.6	7.0	45.7	21.7	10.1	14.0	–	–	–

Real estate	100.0	82.8	34.5	24.1	–	44.8	3.4	17.2	–	3.4	10.3	–	3.4	–
Other services	100.0	77.8	29.5	22.7	2.4	41.1	4.8	22.2	1.4	15.9	4.3	–	0.5	–
Total	100.0	73.5	23.3	18.0	1.8	42.0	6.4	26.3	5.1	14.8	5.6	0.5	0.3	0.3
All industries	100.0	81.4	22.0	16.6	1.8	52.4	5.3	18.3	2.2	10.9	4.9	0.3	0.1	0.3

Notes:

[a] Sectors are classified according to the primary business of the company. Those companies whose lines of business are unknown are excluded.

[b] Australia, Israel, New Zealand and South Africa.

[c] Cyprus, Malta, Turkey and Yugoslavia.

[d] Includes China.

Source: UNCTC, data base on small and medium-sized TNCs.

Table 2.12   Japan: flows of FDI[a] by SMEs,[b] 1974–86

Year[c]	FDI by SMEs		FDI by all firms		Share of investments by SMEs	
	No. of investments	Value ($ million)	No. of investments	Value ($ million)	No. of investments (%)	Value (%)
1974	615	129	1912	2 396	32.2	5.4
1976	542	99	1652	3 462	32.8	2.9
1978	1219	381	2395	4 599	50.9	8.3
1980	1100	806	2442	4 693	45.0	17.2
1982	927	1033	2604	7 808	35.6	13.2
1983	943	839	2546	7 074	37.0	11.9
1984	1028	1645	2656	10 276	38.7	16.0
1985	967	1707	2513	11 190	38.5	15.3
1986	1239	2899	3053	19 840	40.6	14.6

Notes:
[a] On approval/notification basis. As notification criteria of investment value have changed from more than 3 million yen to 10 million yen since April 1984, the data is not consistent before and after 1983.
[b] The definition of Japanese SMEs is as follows: in manufacturing, capital is less than 100 million yen and employment is less than 300; in wholesale trade, capital is less than 30 million yen and employment is less than 100; and in retail trade and other services capital is less than 10 million yen and employment is less than 50. This definition applies to tables 2.13–2.15.
[c] Fiscal year before 1980 and calendar year after 1982.

Source: Ministry of International Trade and Industry.

FDI by SMEs is due mainly to trade frictions and protectionism, the 'drag effect' and the loss of export competitiveness. Trade frictions and the 'drag effect' changed the direction of FDI flows towards developed countries, in particular the United States. The appreciation of the yen since 1985 has once again raised the importance of Asia as a host region. Loss of their international markets to companies from developing countries, particularly the Newly Industrialising Countries (NICs), coupled with the appreciation of the yen, has spurred Japanese SMEs to became involved in international production. In contrast, the 1970s boom of FDI by Japanese SMEs was caused mainly by labour shortages in Japan.

There is no data on FDI stock value by size of company from Japan. However, if we examine past flow data, FDI stock value by SMEs can be estimated at between 10–13 per cent of total FDI, amounting to $19–24 billion in 1988. Total FDI also accelerated in the 1980s, with average outflows by SMEs increasing by 2.3 times between the periods 1980–3 and 1984–6. For large TNCs, FDI increased 2.1 times in the same periods (Table 2.12). The share of FDI outflow by SMEs increased from 16 per cent during 1980–3 to 18 per cent during 1984–6. These shares represent a substantial increase over the 3–8 per cent shares of the 1970s. In addition, the value per investment increased from \$0.2–0.3 million in the 1970s to about \$2 million in the mid-1980s. The trend for increased numbers and increased value of SME FDI holds true even if adjusted for currency valuation and inflation.

Sectoral and geographical breakdown of FDI is available only by the number of investment cases. According to this measure, manufacturing FDI cases accounted for about one-third of total new equity investment, 2724 cases out of a total of 7095 during the period 1974–88. Since 1985 this share has climbed to 40 per cent. During 1986–8, 53 per cent of the new FDI was in services, but this was a decline from previous periods (Table 2.13). In manufacturing FDI, the share of Asia, which had decreased to one-half, has again grown since 1985. The appreciation of the yen in 1985 forced Japanese SMEs to use less expensive Asian labour in production for export to Japan or to international markets to retain their competitiveness. In Asia, about 20 per cent of finished goods and 16 per cent of parts and components produced by Japanese affiliates were exported to Japan at end 1987, a share that was expected to be 31 and 32 per cent respectively by the early 1990s.[29]

In comparison to the geographical distribution of FDI by large firms, FDI by SMEs is slightly more concentrated in developed countries, particularly North America (Table 2.14). However, for both small and medium-sized TNCs and large TNCs, Asia is the second largest host region after North America. FDI by SMEs is also more concentrated in these two regions than that by large TNCs (sample standard deviation of the share in seven regions is 20.1 for small and medium-sized TNCs and 13.9 for large TNCs). Since FDI by SMEs is relatively recent, concentration in more similar regions is no surprise. With regard to sectoral distribution, the importance of Asia in manufacturing FDI and North America in services FDI is more prominent for Japanese SMEs (Table 2.14). In manufacturing, the share of SMEs' FDI was higher in light industries (food, textiles, woods, pulp and paper) and lower in heavy industries (chemicals, iron and non-ferrous metals, and machinery) than that of large firms during 1977–86. The post-1985 period has seen the rise of FDI by SMEs in services other than commerce, largely due to the impetus of real estate firms and restaurants.

SMEs are still not internationalised to the same extent as large TNCs according to a survey by the Japanese Ministry of Trade and Industry (MITI). The stock of foreign equity and loan investment by SMEs

Table 2.13 Japan: regional and sectoral distribution of FDI by SMEs,[a] 1974–88, %

Region/country territory/sector	1974–9[b]	1980–5	1986–8	1986	1987	1988
Total no. of investments	1963	1845	3287	599	1063	1625
Regional distribution						
Developed countries	53.2	61.1	54.8	54.0	53.6	55.8
North America	44.7	50.6	44.2	44.2	42.8	45.0
Europe	6.7	7.9	6.3	6.5	4.9	7.2
Oceania	1.8	2.6	4.3	3.3	5.9	3.6
Developing countries	46.8	39.0	45.2	46.0	46.4	44.1
Asia	38.8	35.3	43.4	43.1	44.6	42.6
China	–	–	5.7	8.5	4.5	5.4
Hong Kong	10.8	5.6	5.5	6.0	6.0	5.0
Korea, Rep of	5.7	5.1	8.8	10.9	10.8	6.7
Taiwan Prov.	6.6	6.9	9.5	11.4	11.2	7.6
Others	15.7[c]	17.7[c]	13.9	6.3	12.0	17.8
Latin America	6.9	2.8	1.6	2.0	1.7	1.4
Middle East	0.6	0.6	0.2	0.7	0.1	0.1
Africa	0.5	0.3	–	0.2	–	–
All countries	100.0	100.0	100.0	100.0	100.0	100.0
Sectoral distribution						
Primary[d]	4.3	2.9	2.2	2.3	2.5	1.9
Manufacturing	31.5	34.3	44.8	46.6	44.1	44.6
Food	3.8	4.3	3.9	4.5	3.3	4.0
Textiles	1.9	2.5	3.9	2.0	3.2	5.0
Lumber, pulp and paper	1.4	1.0	1.2	0.8	1.1	1.3
Chemicals	2.8	3.1	3.1	3.2	3.4	2.8
Iron, steel and non-ferrous metals	2.8	2.6	4.5	2.2	4.2	5.6
Machinery	10.5	12.0	17.5	21.9	18.4	15.3
Others	8.4	8.7	10.8	12.0	10.4	10.5
Services	64.2	62.8	53.0	51.1	53.3	53.5
Construction	2.2	1.7	0.9	0.5	0.6	1.2
Commerce	44.7	41.9	19.3	23.2	17.6	19.0
Services	7.5	7.4	9.0	9.2	9.2	8.9
Others	9.8	11.8	23.8	18.2	26.0	24.4
All industries	100.0	100.0	100.0	100.0	100.0	100.0

Notes:
[a] Based on number of new equity investment cases.
[b] For 1974 and 1975, only from April to December.
[c] Includes China.
[d] Agriculture, forestry and fishery, and mining.

Sources: Small and Medium Enterprise Agency, *Chusho Kikyo Bakusho* (*White Paper on Small and Medium Enterprises*) (Tokyo, Okura-sho Insatsu-kyoku, various issues).

was only 0.04 per cent of all SME assets – 1/23 of the degree of internationalisation of large firms in 1983[30] (Table 2.15). However, internationalisation is being undertaken by both small and large firms,[31] and the pace of internationalisation by SMEs is faster in the 1980s than in the 1970s, as indicated by the increased share of small and medium-sized TNCs in total FDI (Table 2.12).

However, a different picture emerges if one takes the ratio of foreign sales to total sales. This ratio is higher for SMEs than for large firms, at 25.6 per cent and 15.6 per cent, respectively, in 1988.[32] Based on the firms' projections, these numbers were expected to rise to 39.4 per cent and 21.3 per cent, respectively, by the early 1990s. The higher SME ratio may simply be the result of relatively small-scale operations by the parent company, or it may indicate the importance of foreign operations in the strategies of SMEs once they establish their foreign affiliates. The results thus depend on the criterion used to measure internationalisation.

In the services area, using the ratio of foreign stock equity and loan investments to total corporate assets yields similar degrees of internationalisation for SMEs and large firms. The transport equipment industry has the highest degree of internationalisation across all firms, since in this field SMEs are accompanying their clients, automobile makers, worldwide due to the 'drag effect'. SMEs are responding to their clients' request to maintain consistent quality and specifications of products and to prevent possible 'hollowing out' caused by clients' moving production abroad. Japanese SMEs that are now producing automobile components and space parts are also hoping to enter the United States to serve the Big Three United States automobile manu-facturers (Ford, General Motors and Chrysler). During 1983–6, Japa-nese parts components' SMEs established 41 subsidiaries and joint ventures in the United States, which is the same number as for the entire period up to 1982.[33]

Although the total number of affiliates owned by Japanese SMEs is expanding, the average number of foreign affiliates remained constant at 1.2–1.3 during the mid-1970s to mid-1980s. In contrast, the average number of foreign affiliates of large TNCs expanded to 5–6.[34] This suggests that for SMEs, the increase in the number of foreign affiliates is due to new entrants whereas for large TNCs, it is existing firms that are expanding their foreign affiliate network. As of March 1984, 90 per cent of SMEs with foreign affiliates had on average only 1 to 2 affiliates while one-half of large TNCs had more than 3 foreign affiliates.[35]

Table 2.14 Regional and sectoral distribution of Japanese FDI by size of firm, cumulative, 1977–86[a], %

Region	Primary[b]		Manufacturing		Services		All industries	
	SMEs	Large firms	SMEs	Large firms	SMEs	Large firms	SMEs	Large firms
Developed countries	1.4	2.3	12.9	14.5	45.0	39.0	59.2	55.8
North America	0.7	1.4	10.3	9.5	38.4	22.2	49.4	33.1
Europe	–	0.1	2.3	4.5	5.1	13.2	7.3	17.8
Oceania	0.7	0.8	0.3	0.5	1.5	3.6	2.5	4.9
Developing countries	1.5	1.8	22.0	18.0	17.3	24.5	40.8	44.2
Asia	0.9	0.8	21.2	15.7	14.7	16.3	36.8	32.8
Hong Kong	0.1	–	2.4	0.8	4.5	5.0	7.0	5.9
Korea, Republic of	0.1	–	4.6	2.5	0.9	0.9	5.6	3.4
Taiwan Province	0.1	–	6.0	3.5	1.8	1.3	7.9	4.9
Others	0.6	0.8	8.2	8.9	7.5	9.1	16.4	18.7
Latin America	0.5	0.7	0.7	1.9	1.9	5.4	3.1	8.0
Middle East	0.1	0.1	0.1	0.1	0.5	1.2	0.6	1.3
Africa	–	0.2	–	0.3	0.2	1.6	0.3	2.1
All countries	2.8	4.0	34.9	32.5	62.3	63.5	100.0[c]	100.0[d]

Notes:

[a] Based on number of new equity investment cases, from 1977 to 1986, calendar year for SMEs and fiscal year for large firms. On approval/notification basis. As notification criteria of investment value have changed from more than 3 million yen to 10 million yen since April 1984, the data is not consistent before and after 1983. As there are no data on foreign direct investment cases by large firms, estimation was made in a following way. Cumulative number of new equity investment of all firms as of fiscal 1976 is subtracted from that of fiscal 1986. Then, cumulative number of new equity investment of SMEs is subtracted from this number.

[b] Agriculture, forestry and fisher, and mining.

[c] Absolute number is 3529.

[d] Absolute number is 5616.

Sources: Small and Medium Enterprise Agency, *Chusho Rigyo Hakusho* (*White Paper on Small and Medium Enterprises*) (Tokyo, Okura-sho Insatsu-kyoku, various issues), and Ministry of Finance, *Zaisei Kinyu Tokei Geppo* (*Monthly Report of Fiscal and Financial Statistics*), no. 305 (September 1977) and no. 428 (December 1987).

Table 2.15 Japan: stock of equity and loan investment[a] as percentage of total assets of firm, FY 1980 and FY 1983[b]

	Equity and loan investment stock by small and medium-sized TNCs as % of total assets of all SMEs		Equity and loan investment stock by large TNCs as % of total assets of all large firms		Equity and loan investment stock by all TNCs as % of total asset of all firms	
	1980	1983	1980	1983	1980	1983
Primary	0.03	0.10	2.8	8.3	1.2	3.5
Agriculture, forestry & fishery	0.02	0.06	5.8	4.5	1.1	0.8
Mining	0.06	0.18	2.0	9.3	1.3	6.0
Manufacturing	0.06	0.19	1.2	1.3	0.9	1.0
Foods	0.06	0.03	0.4	0.4	0.2	0.3
Textiles	0.08	0.06	3.4	2.4	1.3	1.4
Lumber, pulp & paper	0.01	0.01	1.8	0.8	0.9	0.4
Chemicals	0.05	0.36	1.6	0.7	1.4	0.7
Iron & steel	0.03	0.20	1.1	1.3	1.0	1.2
Non-ferrous metals	0.01	0.05	1.0	0.7	0.9	0.7
Non-electric machinery	0.04	0.01	1.2	1.2	0.8	0.7
Electric machinery	0.15	0.14	2.0	2.2	1.6	1.9
Transport equipment	0.02	3.94	1.8	3.3	1.5	3.4
Precision machinery	0.15	0.08	1.6	0.9	1.0	0.6
Coal & oil products	–	–	–	0.4	–	–
Others	0.04	0.03	0.5	0.8	0.2	0.4
Services	0.01	0.51	0.5	0.5	0.4	0.5
Construction	–	–	–	0.1	–	0.1
Commerce	0.01	0.62	0.9	0.9	0.7	0.8
Services	–	0.05	–	0.3	–	0.2
Others	–	0.67	0.1	0.2	–	0.4
All industries	0.03	0.04	0.8	0.9	0.6	0.7

Notes:
[a] In addition to equity investment and loan investment, Japanese FDI includes payment to establishment and expansion of branches and purchase of property. Purchase of property, however, is not counted as FDI since December 1980.
[b] Based on the sample sizes (in all industries) of 399 for 1980 and 487 for 1993 for small and medium-sized TNCs, 892 for 1980 and 673 for 1983 for large TNCs, and 1291 for 1980 and 1160 for 1983 for all TNCs.

Sources: Ministry of International Trade and Industry, *Dai Ii-kai Kaigai Jigyo Katsudo Kihon Chosa: Kaigai Toshi Tokei Soran* (*The 1st Basic Survey on Overseas Business Activities: Statistical Compilation of Overseas Investment*) (Tokyo, Toyo Hoki Shuppan, August 1983), Tables I–15 and I–21, pp. 94–5 and 100–1; *Dai Ni-kai Kaigai Jigyo Katsudo Kihon Chosa: Kaigai Toshi Tokei Soran* (*The 2nd Basic Survey on Overseas Business Activities: Statistical Compilation of Overseas Investment*) (Tokyo, Keibun Shuppan, August 1986), Table I–18, pp. 62–3; Ministry of Finance, *Zaisei Kinyu Tokei Geppo* (*Monthly Report of Fiscal and Financial Statistics*), vol. 355 (November 1981) and vol. 390 (October 1984).

Technical licensing by SMEs has also grown since the early 1980s. Royalty receipts amounted to 9.4 billion yen (about $40 million) in fiscal year (FY) 1983, a 24-fold increase over FY 1974 and an eight-fold increase over FY 1980.[36] The share of SMEs in total royalty receipts was 10 per cent in FY 1983 compared to 1–2 per cent in previous years. This upward trend holds even if adjusted for currency valuation and inflation and reflects increased technology exports by SMEs. The explosion of technology exports by SMEs in FY 1983–4 turned the technology trade balance into surplus for the first time (17 billion yen in FY 1983 and 18 billion yen in FY 1984).[37] This was particularly notable since the total value of technology exports had never surpassed that of technological imports.[38] During FY 1985–7 the share of SMEs in technology exports was 17.6 per cent if assessed by the number of contracts and 4.0 per cent in terms of value.[39] The number of technological licensing contracts by small and medium-sized TNCs was about 1/17 that of large TNCs by March 1984 (Table 2.16). In services, more licensing contracts were concluded by SMEs than by large firms. In terms of destination, SME licensing contracts are primarily with their own foreign affiliates rather than with other foreign producers, in contrast with large TNCs. This seems to suggest that SME FDI may be a more limited means for technology transfer. Since SMEs have on average only 1–2 affiliates and FDI is a relatively new phenomenon for them, they are more likely to restrict their technology and other resources to their own affiliates than are large, well-established TNCs.

The United States Dimension

Size of firm is an important determinant in FDI for United States TNCs. The larger the firm, the more likely it is to invest abroad (Table 2.17). This is the result of a very large domestic market that does not reach a saturation point easily, and so SMEs are not put under pressure to internationalise. Comparisons of data between 1977 and 1982, the only years for which statistics are available, indicate that the share of small and medium-sized TNCs in United States FDI was very low and actually declined, if measured in terms of number of TNCs and their assets.[40] In 1977, about two-thirds of TNCs in manufacturing were firms with assets less than $100 million (Table 2.18). However, only 6 per cent of total TNC assets were concentrated in these firms. In 1982, those TNCs accounted for 42 per cent of the number of parents and only 2 per cent of total assets in manufacturing.[41] Small TNCs in

Table 2.16   Japan: no. of technology licensing contracts by small and medium-sized TNCs and large TNCs, March 1984[a]

Region	Primary	Manufacturing	Services	All industries
Developed regions[b]				
Small and medium-sized TNCs	–	39	24	63
	(–)	(17)	(3)	(20)
Large TNCs	2	753	14	769
	(2)	(134)	(3)	(139)
All TNCs	2	792	38	832
	(2)	(151)	(6)	(159)
Developing regions[c]				
Small and medium-sized TNCs	1	39	4	44
	(1)	(17)	(3)	(21)
Large TNCs	9	1008	12	1029
	(9)	(342)	(2)	(353)
All TNCs	10	1047	16	1073
	(10)	(359)	(5)	(374)
World				
Small and medium-sized TNCs	1	78	28	107
	(1)	(34)	(6)	(41)
Large TNCs	11	1761	26	1798
	(11)	(476)	(5)	(492)
All TNCs	12	1839	54	1905
	(12)	(510)	(11)	(533)

Notes:
[a] Based on the sample sizes (in all industries) of 478 for small and medium-sized TNCs, 668 for large TNCs and 1146 for all TNCs.
[b] Europe, North America and Oceania.
[c] Africa, Asia, Latin America and Middle East.
Figures in parenthesis are the number of technological licensing contracts with their foreign affiliates.

Sources: Ministry of International Trade and Industry, *Dai Ni-kai Kaigai Jigyo Katsudo Kihon Chosa: Kaigai Toshi Tokei Soran (The 2nd Basic Survey on Overseas Business Activities: Statistical Compilation of Overseas Investment)* (Tokyo, Keibun Shuppan, August 1986), Tables 1-46-1–1-47-3, pp. 90–92.

Table 2.17 United States: shares of parent[a] in total population of firms, by size of employment, 1977, %

Industry	Total	Size classes				
		1–10	*11–100*	*101–1000*	*1001–10 000*	*Over 10 000*
In number of parents						
Manufacturing	0.7	0.004	0.1	4.5	45.3	87.9
Trade	0.02	0.003	0.03	1.3	10.7	47.1
All industries	0.1	0.003	0.05	2.9	38.2	87.2
In number of employees						
Manufacturing	54.8	0.005	0.2	21.3	55.3	90.3
Trade	14.5	0.004	0.07	2.3	13.2	63.4
All industries	16.1	0.004	0.1	5.5	48.6	98.1

Note:
[a] Non-bank parents of non-bank affiliates. Parents whose foreign affiliates' total assets, sales, or net income were each less than 90.5 million, numbering 1175, are excluded from the survey. Thus, the share for smaller firms is presumably underestimated.

Source: Obie G. Whichard, 'Employment and employee compensation of US multinational companies in 1977', *Survey of Current Business*, vol. 62, no. 2 (February 1982), Table 5, pp. 44–5; US Department of Commerce, Bureau of the Census, *General Report on Industrial Organization: 1977 Enterprise Statistics* (Washington DC: US Government Printing Office, April 1981), Table 3, pp. 146–229.

services, particularly insurance, real estate and non-banking finance were the exception in terms of numbers, but were overshadowed in value of assets by large TNCs. With regard to employment, in 1977 one-half of TNCs in manufacturing were firms with less than 1000 employees, but they accounted for only 3 per cent of total employees.[42] In terms of numbers of TNCs, SMEs actually decreased by about one-third during this period.

To examine whether this declining internationalisation continued into the 1980s, a more restricted sample of 21 SMEs has to be used. The ratio of foreign sales (excluding exports) to total sales yields a declining trend: 27.4 per cent in 1980, 23.5 per cent in 1985 and 17.6 per cent in 1987.[43] Even if the 1987 figure is revised for United States dollar devaluations, it does not reach previous levels. During the period 1980–7, total sales grew by 9 per cent annually, while foreign sales grew by only 4 per cent annually. The same picture holds for large TNCs.

Table 2.18 United States: distribution of and changes in no. and total assets of parent, by size of total assets of parent, 1977 and 1982[a]

Industry	Total		Size classes							
	No.	Total assets (billion dollars)	under $10 million		$10–$100 million		$100 million–$1 billion		Over $1 billion	
			No.	Total assets	No.	Total assets	No.	Total assets	No.	Total assets
						(%)				
			1977 distribution							
Petroleum	158	218.8	13.9	–	29.1	1.0	36.7	8.6	20.3	90.4
Manufacturing	1841	633.4	17.7	0.3	46.8	5.2	27.4	26.6	8.1	67.9
Finance (except banking), insurance and real estate	600	379.9	70.8	0.1	9.7	0.6	11.2	6.9	8.3	92.4
Other industries	826	311.1	27.7	0.3	43.2	4.5	23.0	21.0	6.1	74.1
All industries	3425	1543.2	29.3	0.2	38.6	3.3	23.9	18.1	8.2	78.4
			1982 distribution							
Petroleum	143	486.6	4.2	–	15.4	0.2	42.7	6.2	37.8	93.6
Manufacturing	1215	1017.7	3.8	–	38.0	2.1	39.8	16.3	18.4	81.5
Finance (except banking), insurance and real estate	232	677.2	51.3	–	7.3	0.1	16.8	3.0	24.6	96.9
Other industries	520	560.2	11.5	–	35.0	1.5	35.8	11.8	17.7	86.6
All industries	2110	2741.7	10.9	–	32.4	1.2	36.4	10.3	20.2	88.5

Changes between 1977 and 1982

Petroleum	−15	+267.8	−9.7	–	−13.7	−0.8	+6.0	−2.4	+17.5	+3.2
Manufacturing	−626	+384.3	−13.9	−0.3	−8.8	−3.1	+12.4	−10.3	+10.3	+13.6
Finance (except banking), insurance and real estate	−368	+297.3	−19.5	−0.1	−2.4	−0.5	+5.6	−3.9	+16.3	+4.5
Other industries	−306	+249.1	−16.2	−0.3	−8.2	−3.0	+12.8	−9.2	+11.6	+12.5
All industries	−1315	+198.5	−18.4	−0.2	−6.2	−2.1	+12.5	−7.8	+12.0	+10.1

Source: Betty L. Barker, 'A profile of US multinational companies in 1977', *Survey of Current Business*, vol. 61, no. 10 (October 1981), Table 6, p.49; Obie G. Whichard and Michael A. Shea, '1982 Benchmark survey of US direct investment abroad', *Survey of Current Business*, vol. 65, no. 12 (December 1965), Table 7, p. 46.

Note:

[a] Data are for non-bank parents of non-bank affiliates. In these years, parents whose foreign affiliates, total assets, sales, or net income were each less than $0.5 million in 1977 and were each less than $3 million in 1982 are excluded from these surveys. The number of omitted parents was 1175 in 1977 and 1412 in 1982. Thus, in each year, smaller TNCs are presumably underestimated, and this is probably more significant in 1982 as the cut-off point was raised.

Data on the 108 largest United States TNCs shows the foreign sales ratio declining from 33.1 per cent in 1980 to 25.4 per cent in 1985.[44] However, it must be noted that although foreign sales ratios exhibited a downward trend, their absolute levels remain quite high. Moreover, the turnaround in FDI flows since 1986 has most likely restored the pace of internationalisation, although its effect is not yet seen in the sample.

The European Dimension

The bulk of FDI by European TNCs is accounted for by large TNCs. Cross-country and cross-regional comparison are made difficult by differences in data availability and definitions. Data from the United Kingdom for 1981, if SMEs' FDI is defined as FDI less than £2 million, suggests that there were 1000 small and medium-sized TNCs accounting for 66 per cent of total TNCs and owning 25 per cent of foreign affiliates (2276) but only 0.8 per cent of total net assets of all United Kingdom foreign affiliates (£226 million) (Table 2.19). The data also shows that the share of small-scale investment projects in the total has been declining in importance. TNCs which made foreign investments of more than £100 million increased their share in total number of parents by 3.6 percentage points, their share in total number of affiliates by 19.3 percentage points, and doubled their share of total book value of foreign affiliates to 72 per cent during 1974–81. The absolute number of SMEs with FDI also declined during this period (Table 2.19) as did the average value of net assets of their foreign affiliates, from £0.4 million in 1974 to £0.2 million in 1981. By contrast, in large TNCs (over £100 million net assets) not only did the absolute number of TNCs and their affiliates increase from 15 and 906 respectively in 1974 to 65 and 2068 respectively in 1981, but the average value of their foreign net assets also grew from £242 million in 1974 to £315 million in 1981. The higher transnationalisation of large firms is also confirmed by data for the 24 largest firms, which indicates that their share of foreign sales in their total sales increased from 46 per cent in 1976 to 52 per cent in 1985.[45]

There is as yet no official aggregate data on SME TNCs in other European countries. Comparisons can only be made on the basis of limited sample surveys. In France, one survey of 2000 TNCs engaged in technology transfer showed that 90 per cent (1800) were SMEs.[46] Another sample based on 413 firms gives a different picture: of companies with less than FF 20 million of capital only 11 per cent

Table 2.19 United Kingdom: FDI by size^a, 1974–81, %

FDI size^b (to million)	No. of enterprises			No. of overseas affiliates			Book value of FDI		
	1974	1978	1981	1974	1978	1981	1974	1978	1981
Under £1	67.1	68.2	50.3	24.7	19.7	18.0	2.9	1.7	0.3
1 –2	8.9	7.8	16.0	6.8	4.1	7.0	2.4	1.3	0.5
2 –5	8.7	7.4	11.7	9.9	6.2	9.1	5.1	2.7	1.6
5 –10	6.6	5.0	5.0	9.6	6.5	5.2	8.3	4.1	2.1
10 –20	3.5	3.9	4.2	10.5	10.5	7.5	8.4	5.7	3.4
20 –50	2.6	3.7	5.4	13.5	14.1	12.7	14.6	12.0	8.7
50 –100	1.8	1.8	3.2	15.9	11.9	12.7	22.4	12.7	11.7
100 –150		1.1	1.1		9.9	5.6		13.4	6.6
150 –200	0.8	0.5	1.0	9.2	6.1	5.9	35.9	8.5	9.4
Over 200		0.7	2.3		10.9	17.0		37.9	55.7
Total	100.0	100.0	100.0	100.0	100.0	100.0	100.0	100.0	100.0
(Absolute figures, numbers and billions of pounds)	(1798)	(1891)	(1509)	(12 303)	(14 193)	(9092)	(10.1)	(19.2)	(28.5)
Under £2 million	76.0	76.0	66.3	31.4	23.8	25.0	5.3	3.0	0.8
Over £2 million	24.0	24.0	33.7	68.6	76.2	75.0	94.7	97.0	99.2

Notes:
^a Excludes oil companies, banks and insurance companies.
^b Size of book value of net assets attributable to United Kingdom enterprises.

Source: Department of Trade and Industry, *Business Monitor*, MA4/M4, *Census of Overseas Assets 1974, 1978* and *1981* (London, Her Majesty's Stationery Office, 1978, 1981, 1984), tables 5, 12 and 12, respectively.

were TNCs, whereas of companies with capital of at least FF 500 million, 82 per cent were TNCs, whereas of companies with capital of at least FF 500 million, 82 per cent were TNCs in 1974.[47]

With regard to the Federal Republic of Germany, one study indicates that 27 per cent of parent companies were SMEs (less than 500 employees) accounting for only 14 per cent of employment in developing country affiliates, 18 per cent of employment in affiliates in NICs, and 21 per cent of employment in developed country affiliates.[48] According to another survey of TNCs from the Federal Republic of Germany, non-equity forms of investment are gaining in popularity among all TNCs. The survey, undertaken in 1985, predicted a decrease in the use of equity forms relative to non-equity forms of FDI by both large and medium and small TNCs over the period 1984–8 (Table 2.20).

In Italy, the available sample is a survey of 211 TNCs in 1987 (Table 2.21). According to this sample 60 per cent were SMEs (less than 500 employees) owning 29 per cent of total foreign affiliates, but accounting for only 7 per cent of all foreign affiliate employment and only 6 per cent of all foreign sales. Among SMEs, firms with 200–499 employees were the fastest growing group with respect to foreign affiliate employment and foreign sales (Table 2.21). These are mid-sized specialised firms producing niche products internationally for world markets. Their size is beneficial both from the perspective of relatively adequate internal resources and not-too-large or complex management hierarchy. In terms of ownership, about one-third of foreign affiliates of small Italian TNCs (less than 200 employees) were majority-owned, in contrast with 70 per cent of large TNC affiliates (more than 1000 employees).[49] Mid-sized firms are the exception: 58 per cent of their affiliates were majority-owned, higher than the next category of firm size (500–999 employees).

The sample for Sweden was based on 118 TNCs in 1978, of which 64 were firms with less than 2000 employees, accounting for less than 3 per cent of total value added.[50] The top 20–30 TNCs dominate virtually all spheres of economic activity. The only comparative figures for R&D intensity shows that R&D intensity by small Swedish TNCs (less than 200 employees) is one-half that of medium TNCs (200–999 employees) and one-fourth of large TNCs (more than 1000 employees).[51]

Western Europe is not only the largest home region for SMEs but also the largest host region (Tables 2.8–2.9). Due to the impending unified market of 1992, Western Europe is attracting FDI by SMEs both from within and without. SMEs, like large firms, want a presence in the European Union (EU) before 1992 to retain their markets there. Some United States SMEs (e.g. Digital Microware Co., Filament Fiber

Technology Inc., Holland Hitch Co., Neoterik Health Technologies Inc., etc.) have established production plants in Western Europe while others (e.g. Checkpoint Systems Inc., Extrel Corp., E-Z-EM Co, Gerber Alley Co., etc.) have set up and/or strengthened sales offices to offer better service networks.[52] Joint ventures are also in evidence but SMEs' general strategy in the EU seems to be to concentrate on cooperation agreements with EU companies, rather than to make independent investments in equipment and buildings.[53]

2.5 IMPLICATIONS FOR DEVELOPING COUNTRIES

SMEs in their roles as sub-contractors, independent niche producers, and small producers serving local markets, contribute significantly to the health of their home and host economies. Currently, the bulk of their activities are in developed economies and thus the benefits of employment, technological innovations and foreign exchange generation are confined largely to developed economies. However, the data analysed so far indicate that SMEs are increasing their investment in developing countries – particularly Japanese SMEs.

Part of the explanation for this trend is changes in investment regulations and incentives by developing countries in the 1980s that are more favourable to SMEs. In Indonesia, for example, regulations on minimum investment (at least United States $1 million) by foreign firms were abolished in 1988. Malaysia and Thailand have no minimum levels for FDI. In the Republic of Korea minimum levels of FDI were reduced from $500 000 to $100 000 in 1980 and in the case of joint ventures with Korean SMEs were further reduced to $50 000 in 1986. Chile also lowered its minimum investment level from $100 000 to $25 000 in 1986. Other incentives specifically directed at SMEs are speedier approval (Mexico) and tax incentives (Cameroon, Sri Lanka, Zaire).

In analysing the contributions of SMEs to host countries' economies, it is difficult to make a comparative analysis due to lack of data. Section 2.2 established that SMEs do create more jobs per unit of capital than large firms, due to their labour-intensive processes. Japanese data seem to indicate that Japanese small and medium-sized TNCs are more labour-intensive and create more jobs than large Japanese TNCs. The labour–capital ratio of Japanese small and medium-sized TNCs is higher than that of large TNCs – 15 per cent higher in manufacturing, 161 per cent higher in services, and 32 per cent higher in all industries for

Table 2.20 Federal Republic of Germany: foreign involvement of manufacturing TNCs, by employment size and country group,^a 1979–83 and 1984–8, %

Forms of investment	Past 5 years (1979–83)						Following 5 years (1984–8)					
	Developed countries		Developing countries		Eastern block countries		Developed countries		Developing countries		Eastern block countries	
	A	B	A	B	A	B	A	B	A	B	A	B
Equity form	53	88	13	38	–	–	29	52	10	24	–	–
Equity investment:												
Less than 50% equity share	7	12	7	9	–	–	2	8	3	5	–	–
More than 50% equity share	14	27	2	8	–	–	4	10	1	3	–	–
Establishment of subsidiaries, branches and sales offices:												
Joint ventures	3	10	2	7	–	–	6	9	4	6	–	–
Wholly-owned	29	39	2	14	–	–	17	25	2	10	–	–

Non-equity form	34	56	16	34	13	19	42	51	25	34	15	19
Licensing consignment to foreign enterprises	16	30	7	19	5	11	19	23	9	17	5	10
Co-production with foreign enterprises (includes processing consignment)	9	17	6	9	6	5	12	17	9	10	7	6
Other forms of co-operation without capital involvement	9	9	3	6	2	3	11	11	7	7	3	3

Notes:
[a] Survey by IFO-Institut in 1983. Numbers do not add up to 100 per cent owing to multiple answers. Excludes chemical industry.

A = Enterprises with 1–499 employment (256 enterprises).

B = Enterprises with more than 500 employment (414 enterprises).

Source: Manfred Berger and Luitpold Uhlmann, *Auslandsinvestitionen kleiner und mittlerer Unternehmen: Eine Uhbersuchung über des Auslandsinvestitions potential kleiner und mittlerer Unternehmen*, IFO – Institut für Wirtschaftsforschung (Berlin, Duncker & Humblot, 1985), Table 11, p. 56.

Table 2.21 Italy: characteristics of TNCs by size of parents and number of overseas affiliates, 1987, %

Employment size of parents	No. of TNCs		Foreign affiliates					
			Number		Employment		Turnover	
	No.	Annual rate of change 1985–7	No.	Annual rate of change 1985–7	No.[a]	Annual rate of change 1983–6	Value[a]	Annual rate of change 1983–6
1–99	15.2	2.5	6.3	–6.0	0.7	21.9	0.7	75.4
100–199	19.0	..	8.3	..	1.4	..	1.1	..
200–499	26.1	8.0	14.2	–0.5	5.4	48.5	4.4	112.2
500–999	10.4	–16.2	6.3	–23.8	1.5	–30.1	2.2	17.2
1000–1999	10.4	3.4	7.2	10.4	3.7	24.4	3.3	49.9
2000–9999	10.9	–20.6	11.8	20.4	8.9	21.7	8.4	34.2
More than 10 000	3.8	..	44.5	..	78.3	..	79.7	..
Total[b]	100.0	0.5	100.0	8.1	100.0	21.5	100.0	36.7
(Absolute number)	(211)		(678)		(321 802)		(52 723 billion lire)	
1–499	60.2	..	28.8	..	7.4	..	6.2	..
More than 500	35.5	..	69.9	..	92.3	..	93.6	..

Notes:
[a] Data for 1986.
[b] Includes private investors.

Sources: Sergio Mariotti, "Italian inward and outward direct investments: A new pattern of internationalisation", *Rappor to Interno n. 89–014*, Dipartimento di Elettronica-Politecnico di Milano (January 1989), Table 3; Juan Carlos Del Bello and Alejandro Ramos, *Caracteristicas Etructurales y Expansion Reciente de la Inversion Directa Italiana en el Exterior*, DT 05/88 (Buenos Aires, Centro Economia Internacional, December 1988), Table 12, p. 24.

FY 1983.[54] Foreign affiliate data indicate that the average labour–capital ratio of SME affiliates is three times higher than that of large TNCs, both in manufacturing and in services in 1987.[55] SMEs are better able to use the relatively less sophisticated production and management skills available in developing countries, since SMEs' production processes and marketing methods tend to be simpler than those of large TNCs. However, conditions differ from country to country. Inefficient allocation of production factors and lack of local input and resources can sometimes be a greater barrier to SMEs than to large firms. Another barrier to SMEs is factor-price distortion: in developing countries the market price of labour is higher than its shadow price and that of capital is lower than its shadow price, thus encouraging capital-intensive projects.

Adaptation to home/host country differences in scales, factor endowments and technical capabilities is also undertaken by small and medium-sized TNCs. In some cases, they are more willing than large TNCs to undertake adaptive efforts. For example, in the case of Japanese companies, small and medium-sized TNCs accepted local labourers from developing countries for training in Japanese companies at a higher rate than large TNCs during 1978–84 (except 1981 and 1983).[56] About 63 per cent of Japanese small and medium-sized TNCs had given training to local employees in Japan by 1988.[57] In Kenya, Argentina and Brazil, small and medium-sized TNCs also show an ability to accept change and modify production processes to suit local conditions.[58] Responsiveness to local realities may also be the result of another factor: that SMEs are more likely than large TNCs to initiate FDI at the request of the local government. Japanese small and medium-sized TNCs cited host country requests as the main reason for investing more than twice as often as large TNCs (18.2 per cent for small and medium-sized TNCs as opposed to 8.0 per cent for large TNCs).[59]

Developing countries are also taking an increased interest in developing their own SMEs. In Singapore, the Small and Medium Enterprise Division was created in 1985 as part of the Economic Development Board to help Singaporean SMEs become internationally competitive. In Thailand, the Industrial Finance Corporation directs development assistance from Japan's Overseas Economic Cooperation Fund and the United States Agency for International Development towards loans to local SMEs. In the Republic of Korea, SMEs are beginning to acquire advanced technology. Between 1983 and 1987, of 741 joint ventures with foreign firms, 608 were with SMEs. In terms of new technologies and techniques introduced into the economy, the share of SMEs in registering imports of technology increased from 34 per cent (1962–83) to

42 per cent (1984–86).[60] Developing countries are also interested in encouraging SMEs in their role as sub-contractors, complementing the work of large enterprises or large business groups that play the dominant role in leading the economy to international competitiveness.

At this stage, more data on SMEs worldwide and on a standardised country-by-country basis is required to be able to make meaningful comparisons. Data on SMEs also needs to be collected by product or classes of products as does data on the downside of SMEs – greater risks of bankruptcy and greater administrative costs to governments for attracting, registering and monitoring SME projects.

The most important implication for developing countries of the increased activity of small and medium-sized TNCs is that small and medium-sized TNCs increase the alternatives available for the transfer of productive resources and thus strengthen the negotiating position of developing countries.

Notes

1. A definition of SMEs is very difficult to make because of the impossibility of drawing a clear dividing line between SMEs and large firms and the lack of consistent, clear-cut criteria across nations. The criteria vary from size of employment, to size of assets, to size of capital invested, making international comparisons impossible.
2. For example, see United Nations Centre on Transnational Corporations (UNCTC), *Transnational Corporations in World Development: A Re-examination* (United Nations publications, Sales No. E.78.II.A.5, 1978), pp. 51–3 and *Transnational Corporations in World Development: Trends and Prospects* (United Nations publication, Sales No. E.88.II.A.7, 1988), Ch.II.B, pp. 36–8.
3. Canada, the United States, Japan, Austria, Belgium, Denmark, Finland, France, the Federal Republic of Germany, Ireland, Italy, Netherlands, Norway, Sweden, Switzerland, the United Kingdom, Australia, New Zealand.
4. Table 2.1 shows that in all categories, share of the number of enterprises (or establishments), share of employment, share of value of sales, share of value added, SMEs have a relatively more important role than large firms in well over half the countries surveyed.
5. The results of Table 2.3 can be extended to other countries, although the exact labour–capital ratio varies from country to country. In France, for example, the labour–capital ratio was 12 per cent higher in SMEs (less than 499 employees) than larger firms in 1983. See Institut National de la Statistique et des Etudes Economiques, *Annuaire statistique de la France, 1987* (Paris), p. 366.
6. US Small Business Administration, *The State of Small Business: A Report of the President, 1988* (Washington, DC US Government Printing

Office, 1988), Table A.25, p. 137. Data based on establishments.

7. This finding is contradictory to Birch's findings, which argue that small firms create jobs mainly by forming and large firms grow primarily by adding new branches and facilities. See David L. Birch, 'Down, but not out', *Inc.* (May 1988), pp. 20–1 and 'The hyping of small-firm job growth', *The Wall Street Journal* November 8, 1988, p. B1, which quotes Birch's figures.

8. Small and Medium Enterprise Agency, *Chusho Kigyo Hakusho (White Paper on Small and Medium Enterprises), 1986* (Tokyo: Okura-sho Insatsu-kyoku, June 1986), Table 1-2-14, p. 62.

9. *Chusho Kigyo Hakusho*, Table 4-2-6, p. 215.

10. US Small Business Administration, *The State of Small Business: A Report of the President, 1985* (Washington, DC: US Government Printing Office, May 1984), pp. 125–31.

11. Roy Rothwell, 'Small firms, innovation and industrial change', *Small Business Economics*, vol. 1, no. 1 (1989), pp. 51–64. The same results hold in the ratio of innovation share to employment share.

12. Examples include Bizerba (weighing equipment), Hauser (electronic control systems), Bogen (magnetic decoding devices) and Feldhues (meat processing). See 'Happy mediums' and 'West Germany's shy wealthmakers exposed', *The Economist* (24 September 1988), pp. 18 and 83–4.

13. Z.J. Acs and D.B. Audretsch, 'Innovation in large and small firms: An empirical analysis', *American Economic Review*, vol. 78, no. 4 (September 1988), pp. 678–90.

14. For calculation purposes, the same time period as Table 2.7 has been used. However, for France, the Netherlands and Norway this may be too short an interval for conclusive results.

15. Quoted in 'Small businesses aren't so little when it comes to role in exports', *The Wall Street Journal* (August 18, 1989), p. B2.

16. *The Exporter*, vol. 9, no. 9 (January 1989), pp. 4–5.

17. For the United States case, see US Small Business Administration, *The State of Small Business: A Report of the President, 1984* (Washington, DC: US Government Printing Office, 1984), pp. 300–14.

18. T.W. Sharkey, J.-S. Lim and K.I. Kim, 'Export development and perceived export barriers: An empirical analysis of small firms', *Management International Review*, vol. 29, no. 2 (1989), pp. 33–40. This study is based on small firms (employment less than 500) in Ohio, United States.

19. In Italy 'artigianato' employed 2 730 635 persons (21 per cent in total employment) in 1 180 710 enterprises (41.5 per cent in total enterprises) in 1981, in France there were 795 370 'entreprises artisanales' (27.9 per cent in total enterprises) as of 1 January 1986, and in the Federal Republic of Germany only in manufacturing 1 363 000 persons were employed in 'Handwerk' (19.6 per cent in total employment), producing the value of DM 159 659 million in sales (11 per cent in total sales) in 1987.

20. Based on data from eight countries (Australia, Austria, Canada, the Federal Republic of Germany, France, Japan, the United Kingdom and the United States), Spearman's rank correlation coefficient indicates 0.54, which is statistically significant. The real growth rate of *per capita* manufacturing value added is for the period 1970–82. Manufacturing value added

data is from World Bank, *World Development Report 1987* (Washington, DC 1987).

21. P. J. Buckley, G. D. Newbould and Jane Thurwell, 'Going international – The foreign direct investment behaviour of smaller UK firms', University of Reading, *Discussion Papers in International Business Studies*, no. 41 (July 1978), p. 9. The data is based on 43 firms.

22. This database defines small and medium-sized TNCs as those with less than 500 employees in all sectors including services. This differs from the definition used in Section 2.2, where SMEs in wholesale trade are defined as firms with less than 100 employees, and retail trade as those with less than 50 employees. Banks, insurance and other financial companies are currently excluded. Principal sources are international corporate directories, including *Who Owns Whom* (London, D&B International), *Kompass Directory* and various national directories.

23. In Japan, manufacturing SMEs are defined as firms with less than 100 million yen in capital and less than 300 employees. In wholesale trade, SMEs are firms with less than 30 million yen in capital and less than 100 employees while in retail trade and other services, SMEs have less than 10 million yen in capital and employ less than 50 people.

24. In Africa, Japanese SMEs have more affiliates than do European SMEs, however, these affiliates are disproportionately concentrated in countries like Liberia that offer 'flags of convenience'.

25. These companies are: Kasho Co. Ltd, Rikio, Shinko Kogyo Co. Ltd, Swany and Tabai Espec Corp. of Japan, Electro Kinetic Systems Inc., and Primages Inc. of the United States and Grorud Jernvarefabrik A/S of Norway.

26. Calculated from UNCTC, Billion Dollar Club Database. Data are for 1987. Services TNCs are excluded.

27. Average employment for a manufacturing SME is 268, while that for services is 220.

28. Based on the comparison between Table 2.11 and outward FDI stock data in six countries (Canada, the Federal Republic of Germany, Japan, the Netherlands, the United Kingdom and the United States). The shares of developed countries in FDI stock of six countries (in United States dollar terms) were 68 per cent in primary, 76 per cent in manufacturing and 73 per cent in services in 1984.

29. Small and Medium Enterprise Agency, *Chusho Kigyo Hakusho (White Paper on Small and Medium Enterprises), 1988* (Tokyo, Okura-sho Insatsu-kyoku, May 1988), Table 2-1-31, p. 52.

30. Stock of equity and loan investment in MITI's TNC survey is based only on the companies which responded to its questionnaire and excludes other components of FDI which are payment to establishment and expansion of branches and purchase of property (though purchase of property is not counted as FDI since December 1980). This stock data is thus assumed to be lower than FDI stock.

31. MITI's TNC survey (quoted in n. 34–36) suffers from some deficiencies. First of all, it does not cover all TNCs. In terms of number of parents, the 1980 survey covers 43.1 per cent and the 1983 survey covers 38.3 per cent. Figures on both small and medium-sized TNCs and large TNCs respectively are therefore, underestimated. It is presumed that large TNCs

tend to respond more to the MITI survey. Secondly, as the coverage ratio varies from survey to survey, accurate comparison between surveys is impossible. In fact, figures for FY 1986 indicate that the shares of equity and loan investment stock in total assets of firms are 0.01 per cent for small and medium-sized TNCs, 0.6 per cent for large TNCs and 0.5 per cent for all TNCs in all industries. The decreased shares in FY 1986 are due to the smaller number of TNCs covered. In the 1986 survey only 117 small and medium-sized TNCs and only 482 large TNCs responded to the questionnaire on stock of equity and loan investment. As the number of TNCs surveyed in FY 1986 is too small compared to the previous surveys, the results of this survey are not presented. The 1986 survey was from the Ministry of International Trade and Industry, *Dai San-kai Kaigai Jigyo Katsudo Kihon Chosa: Kaigai Toshi Tokei Soran (The 3rd Basic Survey on Overseas Business Activities: Statistical Compilation of Overseas Investment)* (Tokyo, Keibun Shuppan, May 1989).

32. Small and Medium Enterprise Agency, *Chusho Kigyo Hakusho (White Paper on Small and Medium Enterprises), 1989* (Tokyo, Okura-sho Insatsu-kyuoku, May 1989), Table 1-2-1, p. 54. Based on the survey of about 430 firms undertaken in December 1988.

33. *Shukan Toyo Keizai* (Tokyo, 21 November 1987), Table, p. 67 and *Ekonomisto* (Tokyo, 16 December 1985), Table, p. 127.

34. Ministry of International Trade and Industry, *Wagakuni Kigyo no Kaigai Jigyo Katsundo (Japanese Firms' Overseas Business Activities)* (Tokyo, various issues).

35. Ministry of International Trade and Industry, *Dai Ni-kai Kaigai Jigyo Katsudo Kihon Chosa: Kaigai Toshi Tokei Soran (The 2nd Basic Survey on Overseas Business Activities: Statistical Compilation of Overseas Investment)* (Tokyo, Keibun Shuppan, August 1986), Tables 1-12-1 and 1-12-2, p. 69.

36. Ministry of International Trade and Industry, *Wagakuni Kigyo no Kaigai Jigyo Katsudo (Japanese Firms' Overseas Business Activities)*, The 5th Survey (Tokyo, Okura-sho Insatsu-kyoku, October 1976), Table 27, p. 28, *Dai Ii-kai Kaigai Jigyo Katsundo Kihon Chosa: Kaigai Toshi Tokei Soran (The 1st Basic Survey on Overseas Business Activities: Statistical Compilation of Overseas Investment)* (Tokyo, Toyo Hoki Shuppan, August 1983), Tables 1-39-1 – 1-39-3, pp. 114–17 and *Dai Ni-kai Kaigai Jigyo Katsudo Kihon Chosa*, Tables 1-40-1–1-40-3, pp. 82–5. As noted in n. 31, figures are not total receipts by all small and medium-sized TNCs, but are based on the number of TNCs responding to the survey (467 in 1974, 408 in 1980 and 478 in 1983 responded, but it is not certain how many of those responded to this particular questionnaire).

37. Small and Medium Enterprise Agency, *Chusho Kigyo Hakusho (White Paper on Small and Medium Enterprises), 1986*, Table 3-3-2-1, p. 191.

38. Even for some large TNCs such as Fujitsu Ltd, Matsushita Electric Industrial Co. Ltd and Mitsubishi Electric Corp., technology imports are larger than exports. For Hitachi Ltd, technology exports and imports were almost balanced in 1986. *Nihon Keizai Shimbun* (Tokyo) (6 October 1987) p. 11.

39. Small and Medium Enterprise Agency, *Chusho Kigyo Hakusho (White Paper on Small and Medium Enterprises)* (Tokyo, various issues) and

Statistics Bureau, Management and Coordination Agency, *Report on the Survey of Research and Development* (Tokyo, various issues).

40. As parents whose foreign affiliates' total assets, sales, or net income were each less than $0.5 million in the 1977 survey and were less than $3 million in the 1982 survey are excluded, numbering 1175 and 1412, respectively, the importance of smaller TNCs is presumably underestimated in each year. Although this is probably more significant in 1982 as the cut-off point was raised from $0.5 million to $3 million, the result still holds. If the number of omitted parents were included in the smallest category of distribution size (under $10 million), the number of TNCs in this category would be 2177 in 1977 and 1643 in 1982 in all industries. The total assets of these omitted parents are not available.

41. In terms of asset size, $25 million could be the cut-off criterion between SMEs and large firms. See United States Small Business Administration, *The State of Small Business: A report of the President, 1982* (Washington, DC: US Government Printing Office, March 1982), Table 1.6, p. 51.

42. Obie G. Whichard, 'Employment and employee compensation of US multinational companies in 1977', *Survey of Current Business*, vol. 62, no. 2 (February 1982), Table 5, p. 44–5. Firms with employment size 500–999 are categorized as large–small firms.

43. The companies examined here are as follows: Anderson Jacobson, Inc., Consolidated Fibres Inc., Continental Information Systems Corp., Electronic Assoc., Electro-Biology Inc., Ferrofluidics Corporation, General Microwave Corporation, Hadson Corp., Health-Mor Inc., Ingredient Technology Corporation, Intelligent Systems Master LP, International Totalizator Systems, Lawter International Inc., Learonal Inc., Medex Inc., Qantel Corp., Seal Incorporated, Thompson Medical Company Inc., Triton Energy Corporation, Wainoco Oil Corporations, Wilshire Oil Company of Texas. The level of employment in these companies was less than 500 in 1987–8. Throughout this period (1980–7) foreign sales data are available for 17 out of 21 companies. Thus, the figures are based on these firms. The ratio of foreign assets to total assets is available for 14 companies throughout this period. The figures on this are 34.6 per cent in 1980, 23.9 per cent in 1985 and 26.2 per cent in 1987. It should be also noted that the sample size is too small to draw a definite conclusion.

44. Data for large TNCs are from UNCTC, Billion Dollar Club Database. There seems to be an exception to this. For example, based on the survey of companies of the American Business Conference (ABC), the share of foreign sales grew from 10.4 per cent in 1981 to 13.2 per cent in 1986. Member companies of ABC are high-growth (three times faster than the rate of the economy plus inflation) and mid-sized (revenues between $25 million and $2 billion) companies. For further details see American Business Conference, *Winning in the World Market*, report by McKinsey & Co., Inc. (Washington, DC, November 1987) and *The Challenge of Global Competitiveness: Views of America's High Growth Companies* (New York and Washington, DC, February 1987), 'A portrait of America's new competitiveness', *The Economist* (4 June 1988), pp. 57–8.

45. Calculated from UNCTC, Billion Dollar Club Database.

46. Gilles Y. Bertin, *Transfer of Technology to Developing Countries by*

France's Small and Medium-sized Enterprises, UNCTAD/TT/84 (Geneva: UNCTAD, 1986), p. 6

47. Julien Savary, *Les Multinationales Françaises* (Paris: IRM, 1981), pp. 35–51.
48. Gunter Kayser and Uwe Schwarting, 'Foreign investments as a form of enterprise strategy: On the results of a survey', *Intereconomics* (November/December 1981), p. 295. This survey is based on parent companies owning 654 foreign subsidiaries.
49. Segio Mariotti, 'Italian inward and outward direct investments: A new pattern of internalisation', *Rapporto Interno n. 89-014*, Dipartimento di Elettronica-Politecnico di Milano (January 1989), Table 4.
50. Erik Hörnell and Jan-Erik Vahlne, *Multinationals: The Swedish Case* (New York, St Martin's Press, 1986), pp. 27–9. TNCs here are defined as an industrial enterprise with at least one manufacturing subsidiary abroad.
51. Hörnell and Vahlne, Table 7.1, p. 85.
52. 'Should small US exporters take the big plunge?', *Business Week* (12 December 1988), pp. 64–8, 'Small US firms, awaiting 1992, set up shop in Europe', *The Wall Street Journal* (April 20, 1989), pp. B1 and B2.
53. Stanley Crossick, 'Comparative assessment of the impact of 1992 on SMEs and MNCs', *European Affairs*, no. 3 (Autumn 1988), pp. 83–95.
54. Ministry of International Trade and Industry, *Dai Ni-kai Kaigai Jigyo Katsudo Kihon Chosa*, Tables I-3 and I-42, pp. 52–3 and 86–7. Figures are based on 487 small and medium-sized TNCs and 674 large TNCs. However, in the primary sector, the labour–capital ratio is neglible for small and medium-sized TNCs. For definition of small and medium-sized TNCs and large TNCs, see n. 23.
55. Parents and foreign affiliates whose lines of business and host countries are the same or similar between small and medium-sized TNCs and large TNCs are chosen. Thus, typical niche producers which do not have competitors are not included. However, if the labour–capital ratio is calculated based on the average employment and average capital of 103 foreign affiliates, rather than the average of the labour–capital ratio of each foreign affiliate, the labour–capital ratio of foreign affiliates owned by small and medium-sized TNCs is higher only in services but not in manufacturing. This results from large variances in capital–labour ratios in these foreign affiliates. Data compiled from Toyo Keizai Shimposha, *Gyoshubetsu Kaigai Shinshutsu Kigyo Soran (Japanese Multinationals Facts and Figures, Sectoral Edition), 1988* (Tokyo, 1988). In this calculation, small and medium-sized TNCs are defined as those whose employment is less than 500 regardless of sector.
56. Small and Medium Enterprise Agency, *Chusho Kigyo Hakusho (White Paper on Small and Medium Enterprises), 1986*, Table 3-3-2-6, p. 193. Base year is 1977.
57. Small and Medium Enterprise Agency, *Chusho Kigyo Hakusho (White Paper on Small and Medium Enterprises), 1989*, Table 1-2-7, p. 60.
58. UNCTAD, *Impact of Technology Transfer by Foreign Small and Medium-sized Enterprises on Technological Development in Kenya*, UNCTAD/TT/85 (Geneva, 1987), Chapter III. J. Campos, S. Feldman and E. White, *Implications of the Transfer of Technology by Small and Medium-sized*

Enterprises for the Economic and Technological Development of Developing Countries: A case study of the Metalworking industry in Argentina and Brazil, UNCTAD/TT/69 (Geneva: UNCTAD, 16 December 1985), Chapter III.

59. Small and Medium Enterprise Agency, *Chusho Kigyo Hakusho (White Paper on Small and Medium Enterprises), 1988* Table 2-1-25, p. 49.

60. Il-Hwan Kim, 'Small and Medium Enterprises in Korea', Korea Exchange Bank, *Monthly Review*, vol. XXII, no. 7 (July 1988), Table 9 and 10, pp. 11 and 12.

3 Policy Implications

Jaime Campos, Javier Cardozo,
Alejandro Herrera, Eduardo White and
Marcelo Sierra

The findings and lessons that come out from this study go beyond the realm of 'academia'. We think that a series of suggestions as to new approaches and policies regarding the international transfer of technology can be derived from the experiences analysed. This chapter is devoted to a presentation of some of the referred suggestions with the expectation that the effort so far conducted can be also translated into ways and means according to which developing countries can make more efficient use of an up to now largely untapped 'reservoir' of technological assets.

3.1 THE POTENTIAL OF SME CONTRIBUTION

The first point to emphasise from the outset, is that this research has showed that small and medium-sized firms based in developed countries are in a position to transfer their know-how to developing countries. This outcome was far from obvious when this IDRC-funded project began. The first reaction of some colleagues when the project was being designed was of scepticism as to the possibility of getting off the ground a research endeavour which implied identifying and surveying a significant number of cases of SMEs with operations in developing countries.

Few studies had been made prior to the present one that have focused on non-traditional sources of technology from the viewpoint of developing countries. The main approach to technology transfer issues is still one based on the assumption that large transnational corporations (TNCs) are the only agents really worth taking into consideration. The first broad policy implication that comes out from this report is thus that SMEs constitute sources of know-how which developing countries should take seriously into consideration.

The fact that an agent which was until now excluded from the perceived possibilities for developing countries has demonstrated that they can perform a role in the international mobilisation of technical knowledge

71

leads to the conclusion that the international market for those assets is not so constrained as is frequently portrayed. In turn, this means that the traditional perspective according to which developing countries look at the supply market for technology should be significantly altered in order for them to understand that they will gain much in the process if they broaden that view to include agents such as SMEs.

Putting SMEs into the picture of the international market of technology implies for developing countries adding thousands and thousands of firms to the 'roster' of potential suppliers. Just to give an idea of orders of magnitude, it is appropriate to recall that the total number of manufacturing SMEs in the United States approached 340 000 in 1982. The significance of this figure is better understood if one recalls that most of the literature on transnational corporations has been based on a very limited number of firms. For instance, Vernon's (1971) influential study on the subject singled out 187 US manufacturing firms as pertaining to his definition of a multinational enterprise (MNE).

It would be, of course, a gross simplification to think that taking the potential role of SMEs more seriously into consideration means visualising their contribution in terms of substituting that performed by large firms, and particularly, that of transnational corporations. In fact, in many situations, SMEs and large firms do not compete, since they are established in different sectors, or the former operate as subcontractors of the latter.

3.2 'AUTONOMOUS' AND RECIPIENT-COUNTRY-DRIVEN SMEs

At the same time, it is important to recall – as this study has showed – that regarding the transfer of know-how to developing countries it is possible to differentiate among various types of strategies of SME involvement. Some of these are similar to that depicted in the literature on TNCs, while others are typical of SMEs. An important conclusion is that learning to distinguish among those categories helps to design useful policies to deal with those firms.

Some SMEs prior to their operation in developing countries could be correctly labelled 'SME multinationals'. These firms differ from typical TNCs in the absolute value of their sales, assets or employees, but operate in several countries as the latter do, have a strategy of internationalisation which includes a division of labor among its different affiliates, carry on efforts of R&D at its headquarters and transmit those results to its subsidiaries according to a worldwide strategy, proceed to take the maximum possible benefit of intra-affiliate trade, etc. Some of these firms are world leaders in their product segments and are responsible for a large percentage of their total industry sales.

On the other hand, this study found that SMEs with few antecedents as regards internationalisation did also participate in ventures in developing countries, but usually with the help of a pre-existent recipient firm. Many of those SMEs had no clearly defined strategy as to their international expansion, and reacted to an outside proposal. Although these two ideal types clearly simplify the variegated phenomenon studied, they are a useful departing point to organise the presentation that follows.

Those SMEs with an autonomous drive towards internationalisation become interested in operating in developing countries because of factors which have also been identified in studies on TNCs. For some of them the risks of losing an important export market, or of establishing themselves in high-growth economies, or of operating in a large close economy which cannot be supplied through exports, or of re-exporting from the recipient country, etc. justify the involvement.

But at the same time the evidence suggests that overall macroeconomic conditions seem to be more critical at the time of an SME decision to go overseas than it is for TNCs. SMEs have, by definition, a reduced managerial staff and most decisions are taken by the owners themselves or by a couple of chief executives. The capacity of these people to understand and analyse a variety of data on various alternative markets into which to operate, is limited. Explicitly or not, countries which do not offer a reasonably stable macroeconomic environment tend to be eliminated as potential areas of investment earlier in the selection process than do those that fulfil that criteria. High inflation-prone countries – like some in Latin America, for instance – are *ceteris paribus* less attractive for SMEs than others in which prices are more stable.

The same can be said with regard to the stability of the policies followed with respect to foreign investment, foreign trade regimes, capital movements, etc. No doubt those countries that appear in the perception of SMEs as following a more erratic behavior at this respect will tend to be replaced earlier in the selection process. Furthermore, since SMEs control more limited resources than TNCs, the risks involved in a foreign operation are higher. It is reasonable then, for those firms to minimise those risks by devoting their scarce managerial, technical as well as financial resources to projects in 'safer' recipient countries.

It could be suggested then, that recipient developing countries who cannot in the short run offer a stable macroeconomic environment, should devise mechanisms through which they can diminish, at least partially, the risks perceived by SMEs. One instrument is for them to sign bilateral agreements with certain developed countries according to which they grant special treatment to small investors. These guarantee schemes, if properly advertised and if possible backed by developed country institutions, could lead SMEs to take those markets seriously into consideration. One can envisage that the costs of these initiatives will be low given the amounts of the investments usually made by SMEs, and surpassed by the benefits of the mobilisation of know-how both for supplier as well as for recipient economies.

Another mechanism which can be used, in this case by several developed countries, is to ease the effort and reduce the perceived risk of SMEs by providing them with the financial and technical support of specialised institutions. Particularly among some European countries, certain development finance organisations exist with the aim of helping SMEs willing to operate in developing countries. There is no doubt that the latter should look for ways of benefiting from their existence, a fact which, at least from the information gathered from this survey, is not occurring.

But the impression commanded by this survey is quite pessimistic as to the influence that specific inducements can have over SMEs' foreign investment decisions. Unlike TNCs, which can take time and resources to negotiate a special deal with a host country government, SMEs are seldom in a position to afford that effort unless it is really necessary. At the same time, SMEs rarely can come up with a project big enough to attract the special attention of the local government, and as a result it is not so easy for them to obtain beneficial treatment.

It is also important to recall that SMEs, including those that have already expanded internationally, usually have a more limited presence overseas than TNCs. When a typical TNC analyses an investment in a given developing country it usually already has similar ventures in various developed and developing countries. For an SME, the probability of being in a similar situation is lower. The number of alternative markets for new operations is typically smaller for a TNC than for an SME, and this fact also contributes to the latter being more selective.

In addition, there is a lower ceiling for SMEs' than for TNCs' internationalisation. The former's capabilities are, by definition, more limited than the latter's, and thus they are constrained to operate in a smaller number of foreign countries. This fact suggests, again, that developing countries interested in attracting SMEs should understand clearly that for these firms many other alternative markets are usually available, and that they are frequently not in a position to spend time and resources to alter the negative impact of the macroeconomic environment through a 'package' of incentives specially designed for them.

As indicated above, the other 'type' of SME studied in this report can be depicted as one which has transferred its technology at the request of a recipient firm and which has no or only a very vague strategy as regards its operations in foreign markets.

The experience of these firms indicates that the transfer of technology overseas does not necessarily have to follow all stages of a given sequence. In fact, much of the modern thinking on the internationalisation process is based on the notion that firms gradually become familiar with foreign markets first through exports, then by opening up sales agencies abroad, followed by the celebration of licensing agreements and, finally, by the establishment of production joint ventures or wholly-owned subsidiaries. At the same time, this process usually is supposed to begin with operations being advanced in other developed countries and only late spilling over to developing countries.

This report has showed that many SMEs which were approached by recipient firms had no international experience prior to transferring their know-how. Firms in developing countries could obtain those resources, although their suppliers had not yet carried out a complete cycle in the process of internationalisation.

For developing countries, the first obvious implication is that they should try to look for ways of benefiting in a systematic manner from these sources of technology. A first step in this respect is for them to have access to data banks which could provide information as to SMEs which fulfil certain criteria. It is clear, as already stated, that not all SMEs can be realistically considered to be potential suppliers. Some of them are too small or lack the minimum resources needed to participate in a foreign venture, whatever the assistance they might obtain from the recipient itself or from other sources such as their home governments. Thus such a data bank would be useful only if it included data on SMEs which controlled those resources.

This remark must be emphasised. In fact, developing countries should take into consideration that the gap between the absolute total number of SMEs and the number of them that are in a position to transfer know-how internationally is extremely large. To single out the latter firms is the challenge that any useful data bank has to meet.

Some developed countries – such as Germany, Finland, Sweden, the Netherlands, etc. – have organisations that provide disaggregated information on SMEs to interested firms in developing countries. UNIDO has also established different offices in several developed countries with that aim. But unfortunately these institutions seemed to be rarely approached by the latter. In fact, in this survey no recipient firm that had looked for a foreign technology and finally settled an agreement with an SME had used their services.

In part this result is linked with the unawareness of developing country firms on the existence of those institutions. No doubt much has to be done on the part of developed and developing countries to disseminate among recipient firms information as to the services offered by those entities, and the ways of approaching them. But the impression conveyed from the evidence is that the lack of utilisation of those organisations has a deeper cause: the particular features of the procedure typically employed by developing country firms to select their suppliers of technology.

Developing country firms which decided to approach SMEs to acquire know-how from them rarely undertook first any extensive survey of potential suppliers. Some of them were already related to the SME through commercial links, and usually just went on to deepen that relationship. But in those cases in which no links existed, the selection was strongly based by the preference for SMEs of a given developed country or, at most, of a small group of developed countries.

Cultural, historical and geographical reasons are, of course, behind this trend. Rarely, in fact, will a recipient firm feel the need to go ahead with an in-depth survey of diverse suppliers in different countries, since usually it has the knowledge and sometimes some personal contacts in given developed countries. It is natural that it sticks to those countries – or regions of them – to select the supplier. Furthermore, from this survey it emerged that many of the selected SMEs were world leaders in their respective industries and only when the preferred suppliers were not in a position of transferring their know-how did recipients carry out a detailed analysis of alternatives.

3.3   THE NEED TO SUPPORT RECIPIENT FIRMS

Different implications can be derived from what has been said above. On the one hand, recipients could be helped if they could approach given institutions which could enlarge their horizon of potential suppliers. Developing country firms interested in importing technology would gain much if they could have access to information on the con-

figuration of the supplier market they are interested in. By this procedure, these firms would probably come to know that their initial preferences will not always suit them best.

On the other hand, it is probably unwise, at least at this point, not
to take seriously the cultural and historical features of the countries
involved, and particularly of the entrepreneurs involved as an important
factor that may be crucial in allowing an initiative to take off. In fact,
it should not be forgotten, as this study has shown, that SMEs and
also many potential recipients in developing countries are managed by
a limited number of persons, and that a deal among these firms – be it
a licensing agreement or a joint venture – will be more easily settled
if a good communication and understanding is nurtured among the
persons in charge of advancing the crucial decisions. It is in this light
that agreements of a bilateral nature between countries with strong
cultural and historical ties aimed at promoting entrepreneurial cooperation
appear a useful initiative.

But from the point of view of developing countries, taking into account these last type of SMEs as potential suppliers of technology has
other implications. It means looking at the market for know-how in a
manner quite different from that which is most frequent. More specifically, the implication for those countries has to do with a new perspective according to which, at least for a series of international
transactions relating to technology, there is no sense in paying attention only to the supply side of those ventures. The characteristics and
resources of the demand are as important. This means that a view of
the market for technology which is a simple extension of the models
used in economics in relation with goods or factors of production (i.e.
capital and labor) is insufficient.

The important point to stress here is that to carry out certain initiatives, the distinction between supply and demand blurred the fact that
the recipients' capabilities to absorb the SMEs' know-how were a crucial aspect for the implementation of the project. In other words, without their active participation those ventures would not have been realised.

This view of the international transfer of technology according to
which recipients are not seen as passive takers, nor mainly as importers but also as 'active absorbers' of know-how has at least three significant consequences in terms of policies. First, and most obvious,
this vision entails the need for developing countries to place particular
stress on the building up of domestic firms' capabilities, since without
a minimum technical base those firms will not be in a position to seek
and assimilate foreign know-how. This report has confirmed that

familiarity with manufacturing techniques is a necessary requirement for a firm to be in a position of importing foreign know-how. Experience with at least some in-house simple R&D is also important.

Secondly, the vision leads to a change in the policies regarding technology imports followed by some developing countries. In fact, although clearly much less popular than in the past, some of those countries still consider that to increase the negotiating stance of recipient firms, and to reduce the costs of those imports, governments have to give their attention only to regulating the modalities assumed by those transactions. This has been the main policy implemented by India in the 1980s, for example.

As has been pointed out by Scott-Kemmis and Bell, this policy was based on the assumption that recipients had no, or very limited, knowledge of what they were importing, and suppliers were particularly interested in entering through licensing a large domestic market otherwise closed for them (Scott-Kemmis and Bell 1988). The recent empirical evidence suggests that this vision does not capture many of the initiatives being advanced. The impression conveyed by the study on India – as well as this one – is that in many instances it is the recipient firm who is the interested party regarding the possibility of importing a given know-how, and also the one which is in a better negotiating position, particularly when the supplier is an SME.

Finally, the vision implies that developing country governments should put into practice mechanisms through which they can effectively aid their domestic firms in the process of searching, selecting and absorbing imported know-how. In other words, as in other areas of economic policy, governments should abandon their preference – when it is still observed – for a protectionist stance as a unique mode of approaching the issue of technology imports, and give more attention to the support of those domestic firms – particularly so those of small and medium size – which are interested in importing foreign know-how.

3.4 MOBILISING INTERNATIONAL RESOURCES

Many developing countries are going through a period of deep change in their economic policies. In general, the new policies put forward imply, among other things, lowering import barriers and severely reducing public sector outlays. As a result of these measures, the degree of freedom to conduct industrial policies has been significantly reduced, since tariff protection has lost (or is in the process of losing) much of its practical relevance, and governments are in no position to provide incentives to given manufacturing sectors or individual investment projects (usually established in certain backward regions).

An intelligent use of the existing sources of technology in the world, and particularly of SMEs, is an instrument to fulfil some – but obviously not all – of the objectives traditionally aimed at by industrial policies in developing countries. More specifically, there is ground to suggest that – with the help of developed countries – the former could design channels and fora through which domestic firms could select and meet entrepreneurs from SMEs in order to implement projects. These projects will help upgrade the skills of recipient firms, increase their competitiveness and, given the large export propensity of SMEs such as those included in this study, allow them to reach foreign markets with their products.

Developing countries should design special campaigns to attract SMEs to their markets. These promotional efforts should be specially tailored for each developed country and, particularly, for each given industrial sector, taking into consideration that usually the more salient potential suppliers have a significant participation in their domestic markets. These initiatives have to reach the entrepreneurs directly and the host country should be 'advertised' in a simple and reliable way. Again, to be effective, these initiatives should be based on a deep knowledge of the peculiarities and changes that are going on in given industrial branches of developed countries, in order to present the advantages of the potential recipient country in relation with them.

On the part of developing countries, several beneficial features of SMEs as suppliers of technology can be singled out. From the fact that because of their size they rarely become involved in difficult or conflicting situations *vis à vis* host governments, their more flexible stance relative to TNCs with respect to the control of a venture in a host country, their possession of know-how such as that related to the production of customised goods which would not be easily obtained otherwise, etc. But in terms of this chapter's purpose, it is particularly appropriate to underline the finding from the survey according to which most SMEs had a high export propensity. This entails that, contrary to well publicised preconceptions, SMEs are in a position to transfer the capabilities needed by recipients to export. At a time of severe balance of payment restrictions, this possibility appears as particular attractive for most developing countries.

It is important to underline in dealing with this subject that SMEs should not always be seen as the better option as suppliers of technology.

In fact, in some industrial branches SMEs do control know-how that are *a priori* not appropriate for developing country conditions. The advantages, as well as the drawbacks of these firms should thus be analysed in each case. Furthermore, it would be sad if developing countries began to confer on SMEs all sorts of positive attributes which are not empirically justified. A naive view according to which 'small is – always – beautiful' in the terrain of international technology transfer does developing countries a great disservice.

At a more concrete level of analysis, it should be recalled that smaller firms, in contrast to large firms, usually face more difficulties in mobilising financial resources for investing in projects overseas. They normally appear less credit-worthy than TNCs from the point of view of banking institutions. An investment overseas – particularly the establishment of a production facility – usually also implies a much larger relative effort (in terms of its overall assets) for an SME than for a TNC.

Obviously, this constraint that SMEs usually experience is particularly sensitive for many developing countries going through severe balance of payments restrictions. The fact that in many instances projects in developing countries with SME participation require a domestic capital contribution is a feature which makes those firms less attractive than larger firms, which are in a position of performing the direct investment by themselves.

Some developed countries have created financial institutions with the aim of supporting their home-country SMEs in their overseas operations. They participate as a minority shareholder in the recipient firm, and in this way help the SME (as well as their developing country partners) to raise additional financial resources from the capital markets. Also, when needed, they provide guarantees by which those firms can obtain loans from commercial banks. There is no doubt that every effort that developed countries make regarding an increase in the capitalisation of those entities is very helpful for the internationalisation of SMEs, and of course for recipient developing countries.

This field is one in which international or regional public investment banks such as the World Bank, the Inter-American Development Bank, The African Development Bank, etc. could play a direct role or – probably more appropriate – through their affiliates which deal specifically with the financing of the private sector. This possibility would be clearly in the interest of developed and developing countries alike.

3.5 OVERCOMING SME LIMITATIONS

Small and medium-sized firms from developed countries operate in a tight industrial network. This means that in terms of a standard input–output table, most of the cells in those countries are occupied. In other words, a given firm can rely strongly on the market since most of its requirements regarding specific parts or components can be purchased through it. If needed, subcontractors can also be approached to handle the manufacturing of those goods which cannot be bought directly, from the 'shelf'.

When it comes to operating in a developing country, some of the required inputs cannot usually be obtained so easily. Frequently they are not produced locally, and importing them is not always a feasible alternative. As a result, to carry out a project in a developing country, a SME faces severe obstacles which are not easily solved. In contrast, TNCs are, if necessary, in a position to modify the industrial environment in which their affiliates operate. SMEs have not the resources nor the political or economic influence to adopt similar behaviour, and so these firms are much more dependent on the overall industrial development of the host country.

This conclusion is relevant since it points to a very important limitation of SMEs. In particular – and the empirical evidence supports this statement – these firms normally encounter serious obstacles to operating in countries with a very weak industrial sector. Thus, as a whole, SMEs do not appear as easily available potential suppliers of technology, at least in the short and medium run, for the *least* developing countries.

From scant evidence derived from the case study and information obtained from some developed country organisations devoted to the promotion of developing country operations of SMEs, it appears that these firms experience changes in their positions in their home country markets more frequently than TNCs. As a result, when this occurs, these firms tend to reduce their commitments in their foreign ventures. It is interesting to stress that these changes are not necessarily caused by bad performance. On the contrary, given SMEs' limited financial and managerial resources, it is not difficult to verify that when a growth opportunity emerges at home these firms are not always capable of maintaining their presence overseas. Of course, this is a more probable outcome in cases in which SMEs participate as minority shareholders in a joint venture, or as licensors.

Most firms from developed countries have not participated in ventures abroad. Operations of this type are viewed as intrinsically risky for them. It is safe to say, that once SMEs go ahead with such projects, the experience gained makes them much more inclined to participate in other similar initiatives. Particularly if they are in a position of increasing their technological competence – for example, through learning from the recipient experience in using its know how – as well as deriving income (from royalties, etc.) which would not have been possible otherwise. In other words, internationalisation can be viewed also as a learning process.

From this perspective, the first project overseas carried out by an SME will necessarily imply larger relative costs than the ones that follow. From a social benefit point of view then, it seems reasonable to suggest that developed and developing countries would gain if some mechanisms were devised to put down the private costs of the first international involvements of SMEs. In this vein, focused "advertising" campaigns such as the ones mentioned above could well be tackled by both types of countries with the help of some international organisations: other actions, related in this case with the transfer of technology as such, can also be implemented.

SMEs' technological capabilities should not be equated with SMEs' technology *transfer* capabilities. The control of know-how does not assure a similar capacity to transmit it overseas, particularly to firms in developing countries. Given their usual lack of experience regarding international production operations, SMEs tend to have weak transfer capabilities. Engineering and consulting firms appear as useful agents that can help SMEs overcome these constraints. But again, the evidence from this survey suggests that these firms have very rarely hired their services. It is clear that much has to be done to convince potential supplier firms of the need to benefit from the advice of specialised undertakings, governmental efforts through which both types of firms may obtain the needed technical support at a reduced price may lead manufacturing firms to decide to approach those entities.

In order to participate in a foreign production venture, SMEs need to perform a series of operations aimed at formalising their know-how, together with dispatching to the host country technicians familiar with it, and/or being in a position of receiving the recipient firm's personnel to deliver to them the relevant skills. Carrying out these tasks usually entails not insignificant costs for these firms, particularly when they have to face their first technology transfer experience. Ways of easing those efforts should be advanced by the governments of both home and host countries. There are probably at least two concrete mechanisms which could be used at this respect. The first one has to do with the assistance of certain technical organisations from industralised countries to help formalise the know-how controlled by SMEs. The second deals with the need to reduce the costs associated with the training of personnel and the dispatching (either way) of engineers and technicians through the utilisation for that purpose of the resources that are controlled by national and/or international organisations devoted to the diffusion of technical knowledge.

Part II

Technology Suppliers

4 The Case of Canada

Jorge Niosi

4.1 INTRODUCTION: TECHNOLOGY TRANSFER, SMEs AND MULTINATIONAL ENTERPRISES

Received wisdom (and theories) associate foreign operations with large enterprises. Only large firms have the resources – technological, human, financial or other – to undertake the risky and costly endeavours of international technology transfer and foreign investment. This conventional belief is based on several major facts. In the first place, large enterprises, based in industrialised countries, were the first to launch international activities, from the late nineteenth century. Small and medium-sized enterprises (SMEs) followed only later, often well after the second World War. Secondly, large enterprises are much more visible than SMEs; most often they are publicly owned; their huge size makes their international moves evident and they often become the object of wide debate and public policy. This is not the case with SMEs; smaller firms are often privately owned and controlled, they carry reduced amounts of resources across borders and hire few worker in the host country; often associated with local partners and devoid of well-known trademarks, they are much less visible than large firms. Finally, large enterprises can undertake international operations in many different developed and developing countries, while SMEs often spill over the frontiers into neighbouring (mostly developed) countries and seldom undertake more than three or four international operations at the same time.

However, some of the most dynamic SMEs from developed countries have been transferring technology and organising foreign subsidiaries and joint ventures with increasing frequency since the 1950s and 1960s. The evidence is still scarce and fragmentary, but the trend is well established and documented. While large enterprises still constitute the majority of the foreign direct investment (FDI) of all developed countries, a wide variety of small and meduim-sized firms are developing an international strategy. The conditions for this trend are, of course, the dramatic improvement in international transportation and communications that has taken place in the last forty years, the increase and liberalisation of world trade during the post-war period, and the rise of new industries such as electronics, plastics and bio-technology, in which SMEs can thrive and develop side by side with large enterprises, and often compete with them.

. Theories on multinational corporations, even if based on evidence collected on large enterprises, can provide useful starting points for understanding the international activities of small and meduim-sized firms. The industrial organisation approach associated with Hymer (1976), Kindleberger (1970), Caves (1982), Buckley and Casson (1976) emphasises size, but also the possession of technological assets (and thus some level of product differentiation and oligopolistic market position) as determinants of foreign direct investment (FDI) and technology transfer. SMEs often possess some kind of exclusive technological assets (patents, technical know-how and highly qualified human resources) that is considered a pre condition for the internationalisation of manufacturing firms. These assets, often based on internal reasearch and development activities (R&D) give some SMEs an oligopolistic position on the domestic market, and confer on them the same kind of advantages that large enterprises utilise in their international operations.

The product cycle theory of Vernon (1966, 1971, 1977), adopted and developed by Wells (1972 and 1983) and Knickerbocker (1973), among others, associates foreign activities with the oligopolistic market situations created by innovative firms in the large, affluent markets of the developed countries, specially the United States. These firms go abroad in order to protect their product innovations once technology becomes standardised and competitors from other developed countries can adopt it and copy the new product. Later, however, FDI by the original innovators can seldom stop the entry of newcomers from among the followers in other developed countries, and a new wave of investments takes place, this time towards a cohort of late industrialising countries. Thus, FDI in the product cycle approach appears as a defensive strategy by creative firms trying to extend through time the technological rents stemming from their innovations. This pattern can also be applied to innovative SMEs, even if the theory was originally conceived in order to explain the international expansion of large firms.

In their foreign operations, firms use the resources they can more easily gather from their environment. The factor endowment theory associated with K Kojima (1978) and T Ozawa (1979), but also with the synthetic or eclectic approach adopted by Dunning (1979) argues that firms that are active in FDI and technology transfer intensively use the factors that their home countries possess, be it qualified labour, abundant capital, expertise linked to the transformation of particular natural resources or other.

An enterprise can serve foreign markets either by exporting from its home country, producing in the host country through subsidiaries or affiliates (FDI), or transferring technology to an independent firm already operating in the host country. Most firms prefer the first alternative, but exports can become difficult or impossible to undertake because of protectionist policies of the importing nation or one factors such as distance or lower labour or resource costs in the client country. In such cases the exporter would probably prefer to invest and control its technological, marketing or organisational assets through a subsidiary. Theories on multinational corporation insist on the fact that large enterprises have a strong preference for 'internalising the market' of their assets, through the creation of subsidiaries and by controlling the use of their technology and other critical productive facilities. But this second alternative can also become difficult to implement, either because of legal requirements in the host country (legislation prohibiting wholly-owned subsidiaries or even minority affiliates, government inducements to technology transfer, etc.) or economic obstacles (strong internal competition by established firms, high fixed costs of creating a foreign subsidiary, management shortages of the exporter, etc.). In this case, a situation equally more common with SMEs, the innovating enterprise has no alternative but to transfer its technology (or any other asset) to an independent firm in the host country, usually by licensing.

4.2 APPROPRIATE TECHNOLOGY AND SMEs

Since the 1960s a major debate has divided the literature on technology transfer: the issue of the appropriateness of the technology transferred in North – South transactions. By 'appropriateness' the authors mean different things, but there is a semantic agreement centred around the notion of small-scale (thus best suited to the smaller markets of developing countries), labour-intensive and capital saving (thus best suited to the factor endowment of developing countries. Small and meduim-sized enterprises of industrialised countries might be more adequate suppliers of appropriate technology than large, often multinational, corporations, where technology is best adapted to large markets, being capital-intensive and labour-saving.

The arguments in favour of the transfer of appropriate technologies were developed among others, by A Sen (1962), C Wolf and S Surfin (1965) and N Jéquier and G Blanc (1983). Appropriate technologies would need less adaption to the market size and factor endowments of developing countries, they would facilitate the progressive entry of developing countries into the industrial world, they would necessitate less geographical displacement of populations, and they would be easier to learn and master by a low-skilled labour force. A whole movement of appropriate technology centers was created in industrial and Third World countries, with the aim of scanning and developing this kind of technologies.

A Hirschman (1959), A Emmanuel (1981) and C Stewart and Y Nihei (1987) argued against appropriate technologies. In the first place, less developed countries are not very capable of adapting any technology, and thus using the best available technology without adaptation would be the best possible choice. Secondly, in the contemporary open world economy the size of the market is not a major constraint: developing countries must produce for export if they want to develop a sustainable industrial base; using the most productive technologies is the best bet given a competitive world markets. Thirdly, managerial and technical skills are also lacking in developing countries. The multiplant (and eventually multifirm) structure suggested by appropriate technology theories could disperse these scarce skilled workers among far too many productive units. Fourthly, the scope of appropriate technologies that can compete with the most advanced ones, employed in industrialised countries, is very restricted: they can be found only in agriculture, transportation, construction and some particular industries. They cannot sustain long-term industrial development. Finally, in today's industrial structure of developed countries, most SMEs fall into two groups: either they are suppliers and subcontractors to large multinational corporations (such as automobile producers, or electrical and electronic equipment manufacturers) or they are specialised high-technology firms (in industries such as electronics, medical equipment, special machinery producers or chemical and allied products), with marked R&D strategies, and a large share of the world market, either through exports or foreign affiliates. Even in 'traditional' industries such as textiles, apparel, or shoe manufacturing, new technologies are increasingly using a highly-skilled labour force. In other worlds, most SMEs are not potential suppliers of appropriate technologies for the developing world. And new technologies acumulated by SMEs are not suitable for the developing countries factor endowment.

The issue of technological appropriateness *stricto sensu,* however, does not exhaust the analysis of SMEs as an alternative channel of technology transfer to developing countries. Smaller firms may be more adequate when dealing with LDCs because of other considerations: their reduced size and less abundant resources give them less bargaining power against larger firms from newly or semi-industrialised countries; their organisation is more flexible, and thus better suited to developing countries' markets; and the amounts of capital, technology and skilled labour used in their operations is smaller, and thus more affordable, for the host firm.

4.3 CANADIAN SMEs IN FOREIGN TECHNOLOGY TRANSFER

Canadian SMEs have been entering international markets probably only since the end of the Second World War. The only exception to this rule seems to be the United States market, where some Canadian SMEs were already operating in the inter-war period (Marshall, Southward and Taylor, 1936). These smaller enterprises were active in pulp, paper and wood sectors, in fabricated metal products and in the food industries and probably numbered no more than 20 in total. Geographical, cultural and economic proximities explain the choice of the American market as the first foreign experience of these early ventures.

In the post-war period the United States remains by far the most common destination of Canadian manufacturing FDI by SMEs. The industrial spectrum of these involvements has grown wide as Canadian manufacturing has attained some level of maturity. Europe is the second destination of Canadian FDI by smaller manufacturing firms, both chronologically and in terms of the number of firms. Canadian SMEs' involvement in Third World countries started probably in Mexico, Brazil and India. While evidence is scarce, these smaller firms may have entered the developing countries through two different routes. Some of them started producing in Third World countries as suppliers or sub-contractors of large Canadian multinational enterprises, either in mining, manufacturing or foreign utilities (Niosi,1982). Others became involved in foreign operations, directly or indirectly, as a consequence of the Canadian government aid programmes (Colombo Plan in Asia since 1960, Canadian International Development Agency since 1969). Some evidence of this is provided by the *Directory of Foreign Collaborations in India* (1981), listing foreign investment and technology transfer cases by country and year of the agreement. The first Canadian collaboration took place in 1953, and the first technology

Table 4.1   Direct overseas investment outstanding, end 1984

Country	Amount (US$ billion)	Share %
USA	233.4	42.5%
UK	85.3	15.5%
Japan	37.9	6.9%
West Germany	36.6	6.7%
Canada	31.3	5.7%
Netherlands	31.2	5.7%
Other	93.3	17.0%
Total	549.0	100%

Source: JETRO: *White Paper on Overseas Investment* (Tokyo, 1986).

transfer agreement by a Candian SME in 1955. By 1965, no more than 10 Canadian manufacturers of small and medium size were listed in this source as having transferred technology to Indian firms.

Most SMEs in industrialised countries do have an international strategy and do not consider the possibility of exporting, setting up foreign subsidiaries or selling technology abroad (White and Campos, 1986). This also applies to Canadian SMEs. The proportion of Canadian manufacturing SMEs with either foreign investments or technology sales is probably one per cent. *Statistics Canada* reports nearly 40 000 manufacturing SMEs in the country, and no more than 400 of them have some FDI or technology transfer, including approximately 150 in the Third World.

However, an increasing number of Canadian manufacturing SMEs, are going abroad, not only for the export of products, but for more sophisticated technological agreements as well. Our interviews have confirmed the increased involvement of Canadian manufacturing SMEs as exporters of technology through different contractual forms.

Some figures on Canadian FDI can help us to tackle more precisely the scope of the problem. First, Canada has become in recent years the fifth largest international investor, after the United States, the United Kingdom, Japan and West Germany (see Table 4.1).

Canadian direct investment abroad (CFDI) is largely concentrated in developed countries, particularly in the United States. In 1983, according to the latest figures from *Statistics Canada*, 67 per cent of all CFDI, and 63 per cent of CFDI in manufacturing was located in the United States (*Statistics Canada*, 67–202, 1988). Developing countries only host 15 per cent of all CFDI.

Table 4.2   CFDI by manufacturing enterprises, by size of investment, 1985

	$million	$million
Small firms (0–9.9)	253	551
Medium firms (10–24.9)	37	569
Large firms (25 and over)	70	24 175
Total	360	25 295

Source: Statistics Canada, Balance of Payments Division, special tabulation (1988).

A second tabulation gives us the distribution of Canadian manufacturing firms abroad, based on the size of investment, used as the only available proxy of the size of the investing firm. Table 4.2 shows that some 290 manufacturing firms had foreign investments under C\$25 million in 1985. These were probably the Canadian SMEs with foreign direct investments. If the geographic distribution of these investments is similar to that of the overall CFDI, then 15 per cent (or some 44 firms) are located in the Third World.

4.4   RESEARCH AND METHODOLOGY

This study was part of a larger research project on the export of technology by manufacturing SMEs from the seven largest developed countries (the United States, Japan, West Germany, France, Italy, the United Kingdom and Canada) to some of the largest and/or most dynamic developing countries: India, Korea and Singapore in Asia; Argentina, Brazil and Mexico in Latin America. Three industrial sectors were targeted: electronics, fabricated metal products, and chemicals. These sectors were believed to hold the largest potential for international technology transfer.

The survey population was obtained through the national registers of technology transfer: those of the India Investment Center, the Instituto Nacional de Propiedade Industrial (INPI) of Brazil, the Instituto Nacional de Tecnologia Industrial (INTI) of Argentina, etc. They provided us with lists of Canadian companies having transferred technologies to these target countries. These were complemented with data from the Canadian Agency for International Development (CIDA) to which some Canadian SMEs had applied for assistance. In addition several bilateral chambers of commerce and private consultant firms in Toronto

and Montreal provided some cases. Nearly 100 companies were reported to have transferred technology to the target countries, but less
than 75 of them were in the size and industries chosen.

The next problem was to track down in Canada, the relevant SMEs.
Nearly 30 had disappeared either because of bankruptcy, change of
name, change of address or absorption by another firm and could not
be found. Six enterprises were in other industrial sectors (food processing,
textiles, apparel, wood products); this subset was taken out of the sample,
but their small number confirmed the adequateness of the industrial
choice. Eight companies were located in remote places and five others
refused to be interviewed. We were left with 27 companies located in
Vancouver (four cases), Calgary (three), Edmonton (One), Windsor
(one), Burlington (one), Brantford (one), Toronto (eight), Ottawa (one),
and Montreal (seven). These 27 cases constituted our sample. The population and the sample did not contain a single company in the Maritimes.
We believe the sample to be representative of the target population.

From a sectoral point of view, six companies were in the electronics
industry, two in chemical products and the other nineteen in fabricated metal products, including machinery (electrical and non-electrical), auto parts, electric products and miscellaneous metal products
such as valves.

The questionnaire consisted of 91 questions, mostly closed and easy
to interpret by the responding executives. The interviews, except for
two, were done personally by the researcher.

4.5   THE RESULTS

Brief Portrait of the Transferring Firm

The average Canadian firm having transferred technology to the target
LDCs was 24 years old. Only two of them were founded before the
Second World War. This average firm had 150 employees in Canada
and its domestic sales were C$28 million (or US $ 22 million) in
1987. These two measures of size, however, hide large differences. In
terms of employees, for instance, a majority of SMEs (17) were under
the average of 150 employees, only two had 500 employees or more.

Exports were a large percentage of sales (58 per cent) of our average enterprise and its markets were diversified, including both developed
and developing countries. Only one firm indicated no exports at all.

The SMEs' annual growth rates for the last five years was high:

nearly 18 per cent, but seven firms, all linked to the energy industry, reported no growth at all for the period.

The sampled firms were very active in R&D. 23 of them were engaged in R&D activities. The average firm dedicated 8 per cent of its sales to R&D, but there were, as expected, wide industry differences: in electronics the non-weighted average was 19 per cent, while in chemicals it was 11 per cent, and infabricated metals only 4 per cent.

On average the Canadian SMEs had launched four new products in the last two years, and had asked for three patents in Canada in the last four years. Interestingly enough, eight enterprises declared that they did not believe in patents, and that a trade secret was the best way of appropriating their technology. Again, there were marked industrial differences: chemical and electronic firms launched more new products (an average of six in the last two years) and asked for more patents (an average of seven for the only three firms in these industries that asked for patents).

The typical firm had only one plant in Canada. Only six enterprises had more than one plant. A slight majority of the firms (52 per cent) operated their plants under custom-order production, while 30 per cent produced in short series and the other 18 per cent produced batches for an anticipated demand; no firm showed continuous production.

The SMEs' plants were larger than the average Canadian plant in their respective industries (48 per cent), while in some other cases they were the only producer in Canada (16 per cent), in only 26 per cent of cases was their plants smaller than the average Canadian plant. Conversely, 70 per cent of SMEs indicated that large foreign plants (in the United States, Europe or Japan) were larger than theirs.

The sampled enterprises typically occupied a large portion of the Canadian market for their products. The average for our sample was 46 per cent. This finding shows that some of the Canadian SMEs were small oligopolists in their particular market niches, thus supporting the 'industrial organisation' approach of Hymer, Caves and Knickerbocker. However, six of the SMEs did not know their share of the Canadian market (but generally believed it to be fairly small), and four others reported no Canadian sales at all for some or all of their product lines.

The Average Transfer: Univariate Analysis

The majority of the firms interviewed had transferred their technology more than once. The average number of transfer cases was three. Again, this average hides important differences. 10 firms (37 per cent) had only one experience in international technology transfer, while the 17 other SMEs had between two and 14 transfer experiences.

Among the 88 technology transfer transactions completed by the SMEs, 30 were the object of in-depth analysis (three firms responded to two different cases of transfer in the target countries). Over the 30 transactions, Indian firms were the recipients of the largest number of transfers: 14 cases (or 47 per cent), followed by Korea (five cases or 17 per cent), Brazil (four cases or 13 per cent), Mexico and Singapore (three cases or 10 per cent in each country), and Argentina (one case or 3 per cent). The initiative came most often from the SMEs (16 cases or 53 per cent), while in the remaining cases it was the host country firm that searched for a Canadian supplier. However, the country distribution of the initiative shows important differences: in India, most of the transfers took place because of a local firm's initiative (nine cases of 14) and similarly, all the Korean cases were the result of Korean initiatives; while in Latin America and Singapore almost all the transfers took resulted for a Canadian SMEs initiative.

Typically, the Canadian SME motive for the transfer was to secure a foothold on a foreign market or to increase exports from the home market. In only two cases, one in India and one in Korea, was the main motive to export from the developing country. Again, when asked why the country was selected for the technology transfer, by far the most important factor mentioned was the growth respects of the LDC domestic market. This finding is in line with that of other studies on the export of technology by SMEs: demand-related and aggressive strategies (attraction of external markets, entry in new markets) prevailed over supply-related and 'defensive' considerations (such as securing raw materials, preserving market shares or anti-risk diversification) (White and Campos, 1986, p. 91). In this respect small and medium-sized firms differ from large, multinational corporations, with more diverse motivations.

At the time of the technology transfer, most of the Canadian SMEs were not exporting to the relevant developing country (11 cases), or their exports were below 5 per cent of their sales (12 cases). In only seven cases were exports to the developing country above 5 per cent of the SMEs sales. This distribution occured because most transfers were to highly protected markets, like India, Korea or Brazil, which the SME could only penetrate by creating a subsidiary (wholly-owned or joint venture) or by transferring its technology to a local firm. This result suggests that the product-cycle pattern (that starts with exports to the recipient country, followed by sales subsidiaries, then production in the host country) may not apply to SMEs.

In 20 cases (67 per cent), Canadian SMEs preferred a technology agreement without equity involvement. The reasons mentioned were the high costs of equity participation in terms of capital, personal time of the SMEs' officers and communications. Local legislation forbidding wholly-owned subsidiaries, risk and management difficulties of foreign ventures in developing countries were also mentioned as reasons for arm's-lenght transactions. In this dimension, Canadian SMEs more closely resemble the Italian or German SMEs, than American or Japanese ones, where a majority of firms prefer equity investments abroad instead of pure technology agreements (Berger and Uhlman, 1984; Onida, *et. al* 1985; Ozawa, 1985; White and Feldman, 1982; see also chapters 7 and 8 in their volume).

However, among the SMEs with equity involvement nine cases under study involved joint ventures with local partners, and one Canadian enterprise had a wholly-owned subsidiary in a developing country. The greater frequency of joint ventures to wholly-owned subsidiaries, however, reflects host-country preferences rather than the Candian firm's choice. All the SMEs with joint ventures mentioned government restrictions as the main motive that drove the SME to choose this kind of arrangement instead of an outright subsidiary: five of the joint ventures were in India, three in Mexico and one in Brazil, all countries that at the time, either forbade or discourage wholly foreign subsidiaries. The only wholly-owned subsidiary was in Singapore, a country with few restrictions on foreign investment. Clearly, several Canadian firms would have preferred a greater degree of control over their foreign investment, but were dissuaded by local legislation.

All the joint ventures were established through the incorporation of new companies in the host country. In half of the 10 cases in which the Canadian SMEs had an equity participation, they did not receive any assistance from government or private agencies. In the other five cases CIDA, Canadian banks or the local government were mentioned. Technology was the most common kind of resource (nine cases) that the Canadian SME contributed to the foreign subsidiary or joint venture; capital goods were also mentioned in six cases, foreign exchange in five, and technical assistance in three.

In most of the situations under study, 21 cases (or 70 per cent), the Canadian enterprise did not know the local firm at the start. When it did, it was typically a customer or the local sales agent. To get in contact with the local firm, where no previous relationship existed, different channels were used: in four cases the Canadian SME searched alone for a local partner (through newspaper ads or chambers of commerce); in eight other cases the initiative was taken by the host firm; intermediaries (other firms, CIDA) put the two firms in contact in the remaining six cases. Typically, the Canadian SME did not look for a different partner when contacted by a local firm, of having been introduced to a local enterprise by an intermediary. The position, prestige, experience or technological capacity of the recipient firm were by far the main reasons mentioned by the Canadian SME in selecting or accepting the local firm. In seven cases, the SME signalled that in hindsight it had selected the wrong local partner; we will come back to this point later, in order to explain these unsuccessful ventures.

What kind of technology did the Canadian SME transfer? 13 cases out of 30 (43 per cent) involved plant design technology, 19 (63 per cent) involved process technology, and all the SMEs (100 per cent) transferred product technology. How did the transfer occur? In all cases blueprints, designs or drawings were mentioned as vehicles; technical assistance was given in 28 cases, critical parts or components were exported in 19 cases (63 per cent), and special equipment in 15 cases (50 per cent).

In 17 cases the majority of the items were prepared or modified for the specific technology transfer under study. Technical training took place in both the host firm and the Canadian SME, the most common situation being the dispatching of Canadian personnel (one to three persons for several weeks) and the receiving of several (again one to three) employees of the host-country firm in Canada for several weeks. Very seldom was any other training involved, either formal or in-house.

The host-country plant was most often smaller than the Canadian plant (17 cases out of 28 or 61 per cent), seldom the same size (three cases or 11 per cent) and not uncommonly larger (eight cases or 29 per cent). The equipment was in the majority of cases (20 out of 28 or 71 per cent) similar to the one used in the Canadian plant; in two cases it was more modern, and in six other cases it was simpler and/ or less advanced. Consistently, labour costs were not a significant factor in the choice of equipment in 23 cases, and products were similar to those produced in Canada in 24 cases.

In half of the transactions studied, the Canadian SME was more diversified than the host-country firm, while the other 14 cases were equally divided between those with the same level of diversification, and those with a less diversified home-country firm. Two firms were not manufacturers.

Only four Canadian subsidiaries reported that they strategically allocated more mature products to their lot partners. All the others mentioned that they transferred their best current technology to the local enterprise. As to the technical capabilities of the recipient firm, in most cases (66 per cent) the Canadian SME considered that the local firm was able to make some adjustments to the technology they had received, but only in 13 cases was the local recipient able to design new goods from the basic technology. Moreover, there were no more than seven cases in which the Canadian respondant thought that the local firm was capable of transferring the technology to other firms.

The picture that emerges from the preceeding paragraphs is one of a typical Canadian SME 'codifying' and preparing its know-how for the technology transfer, but without introducing significant alterations to the technology as such: the same equipment was generally used and products were, more often than not, similar to the Canadian ones. The recipient was often active in the 'scaling down' of the plants, or in the reorganisation of its plant in order to adapt it to shorter production runs or to the intermediary goods or machinery availble in the host country, or in the simplification of the products for the host country.

Canadian SMEs invest in or transfer their technology to developing countries through autonomous moves; they are not often subcontractors to large multinationals: only three cases were registered of small firms following large ones; of which in two cases, the initiative came from engineering firms (for which the SMEs were subcontractors), and in one case from a large aluminum producer.

The Agreements

Four options were offered: patents, trademarks, know-how and technical services. Know-how was by far the most common item of the transactions (26 cases or 87 per cent), followed by technical services (18 cases or 60 per cent), patents (40 per cent) and trademarks (37 per cent). The agreement was usually registered with the host government except in Singapore (there is no such a register) and in one case in another developing country. In (12 cases out of 30 (40 per cent), the two parties had to modify the agreement as a consequence of govenrnment pressures. Local legislation on equity distribution and royalties, and bureaucratic red tape in the host countries were the most common items of difficulty in the negotiations. The negotiations took an average of one year, with some cases being settled in one or two weeks, and others lasting up to three years. The agreements had very different durations. 12 of them (40 per cent) were open; for the others the average duration was six years. In those cases in which the original agreement had expired, eight were not renewed and four were renewed.

Royalties on sales was the most common form of payment that was agreed upon between the parties; it appeared in 57 per cent of the cases. Most often, however, it was combined with other forms of payment, typically lump sums (seven cases), dividends (five cases) and the pricing of the components or technical services provided by the Canadian SME (three cases). The average royalty was 5 per cent, but in several cases they were sliding percentages over time. In five cases (17 per cent) the Canadian enterprise was paid entirely through the pricing of parts or components sent to the developing country. In four cases (13 per cent) the payment was exclusively a lump sum paid by the recipient firm on the signature of the transaction. Dividends were the only form of payment in only two cases. In one case a lump sum plus the price of the components and parts was the stipulated payment form. And in 14 cases the local firm had to buy parts, components or other inputs from the Canadian enterprise or from other sources stipulated in the contract.

In the overwhelmingly majority of cases, the agreement had a restricted scope in terms of markets: the recipient was most often restricted to the local market (16 cases or 53 per cent), although in some other cases a few neighbouring countries were added (nine cases or 30 per cent). Only three cases contained no export restrictions. Again, this strongly suggests that market penetration was the main motive of the Canadian SMEs. One firm interviewed declared that exporting through the licencee in a developing country was the main motive of the technology agreement. Four other firms had some hopes of exporting through their minority joint ventures in the developing countries.

Typically, the recipient was free to introduce improvements or modify the technology (22 cases or 73 per cent). As market restrictions impeded the local firm from competing in foreign countries with the exports of the Canadian SME, these improvements could not constitute a potential threat to the licencor.

Further Relations Between the SME and the Host Firm

After the initial technology transfer most host firms (23 or 77 per cent) did not employ any officer of the Canadian enterprise, a result which is in line with the type of transaction (technology agreements with no equity investment) that constitutes the majority of the cases. However, the links between the Canadian enterprise and the host firm were not broken after the first transaction: only five SMEs reported having discontinued their assistance to the recipient company. New product design was the most common technological assistance that the Canadian SMEs provided to the recipient firms; it was mentioned in 14 cases; quality control assistance (11 cases), marketing support (10 cases), process engineering (10 cases), and management organisation (eight cases) were also mentioned. This assistance was most frequently provided at the request of the recipient on a case-by-case basis (12 cases), rather than programmed in advance (six cases), while some clauses on eventual future assistance by the Canadian SME were already included in the agreement in six other cases.

Nearly half of the Canadian firms (13 cases) increased their exports to the developing country after the technology transfer. But very few of them (three out of 28) imported either products or components from the recipient firms. This is consistent with the market penetration strategy that was mentioned previously as the most important motivation of Canadian SMEs.

When evaluating their experience retrospectively the Canadian firms found that the greater appropriateness of their technology was their main competitive advantage with regard to other foreign or local competitors 21 firms (or 70 per cent) chose this option; other advantages mentioned frequently were their willingness to adapt the technology to local conditions (17 cases or 61 per cent), better proprietary technology (10 cases), lower overall costs (10 cases), better organisation and management (eight cases or 20 per cent), previous experience in similar projects (eight cases), and Canadian government inducements (seven cases).

The overall evaluation of the project by the responding firms show that for eight of them the transfer surpassed their objectives, for 14 objectives were met and for seven others objectives were not achieved (One firm answered that it was too early to evaluate the results.) Again, we find here several successful and unsuccessful stories that we will evaluate later. Most firms found that the experience had had some beneficial effects on their technological or managerial capacities (60 per cent), while the remaining 40 per cent did not find any positive feedback gain from the experience. However, 24 of them (80 per cent) wanted to expand or continue their involvement in the host country, another indicator that, on the whole, the experience was largely fruitful.

Finally the most important and frequent problems mentioned by the Canadian SMEs in the technology transfer were language barriers, distance and communications (10 cases), government red tape in the host

Table 4.3   Countries having received technology from Canadian SMEs, number of cases

India	16
Brazil	9
China	9
Korea	9
Mexico	7
USA	5
Australia	3
Colombia	3
Singapore	3
Indonesia	2
Japan	3
South Africa	2
Venezuela	2
UK	3
Other	9
Total	88

country (nine cases), poor management of recipient firms (five cases), and lack of funds of host enterprise (five cases). However there was a marked country distribution of the perceived problems. Government bureaucracy (slow approval of the agreement or of necessary imports) was signalled eight times as the main problem in the care of India, while it was noted only once as the main problem in Mexico and in Brazil. Language and communication problems were again signalled five times in India as the major problem, and three times in Korea. In Brazil, local government restrictions on royalties and imports, and lack of marketing capabilities of the host firm were the main problems, while in Mexico poor management was noted twice as the main problem.

Choice of Countries and Timing of the International Transfer of Technology

The 27 SMEs interviewed referred to 88 cases of transfer, although the bulk of the interviews was focused on 30 experiences, some information was gathered on 88 transactions on the basis of a question summarising the overseas involvement of the firm.

The first item it is worth reporting is the choice of countries. As was previously pointed out, Canadian SMEs transferring technology to developing countries do not often sell it in industrialised countries. Table 4.3 synthetically presents the most frequent countries mentioned.

Table 4.4   Time distribution of the transfer cases, 1970–88

Before 1970	15
1970–9	15
1980–8	58
Total	88

Table 4.5   First foreign experience of Canadian SMEs

India	11
Brazil	3
Australia, Mexico, Singapore	
Korea and USA (each)	2
Argentina, UK and Portugal (each)	1
Total	27

India is by far the most important destination of Canadian technology, with Brazil and China following. An important difference among the three countries is worth mentioning. While India and Brazil are traditional buyers of Canadian technology, the first transaction in China was only reported in 1983. This country might become the most important importer of Canadian technology in the next few years. Only 12 cases out of 88 (14 per cent) mentioned a transfer to more developed countries like the United States, the United Kingdom, Japan, France or Germany. Our group of companies differs markedly from the vast majority of Canadian SMEs, that are selling technology and/or investing in the United States and the BU.

Table 4.4 shows the rapid emergence of Canadian SMEs as technology suppliers to the Third World. Almost two thirds of the transactions were concluded in the 1980s.

It was impossible to find a definite sequence of Canadian transfer to developing countries; India was the first experience for many of the 27 SMEs, the other countries following far behind (Table 4.5). For the 11 firms having started in India, this was their only experience; the four others followed by technology sales in Brazil, Indonesia, Japan and Venezuela.

Another definite pattern emerges from the analysis of the origins of the initiative of the 88 cases. Summarising the pattern, one could say

Table 4.6　Exports and no. of transfers

| | | Exports (as % of sales) | |
		54% +	Less than 54%
No. of transfers	1–3	8　(53%)	11　(92%)
	4+	7　(47%)	1　(8%)
	Total	15　(100%)	12 (100%)

Fisher Test 0.097.

that Canadian SMEs typically take the initiative towards Latin America (all the cases in the region but one occurred after a SME proposal), while Korea, Australia and New Zealand are demanding Canadian technology (all the transfers towards these countries took place after the host firm's initiative). The Indian and Chinese cases are equally divided between those with host-country initiative, and those started by SMEs proposals.

Bivariate Analysis: Some Tentative Explanations

Due to the small number of cases, multivariate analysis was excluded, and only a few bivariate correlations were calculated. Percentage differences and the Exact Fisher Test for small distributions were used.

Number of Transfers

The average number of technology transfers by the firms interviewed was three. Some characteristics of the SMEs were associated with the number of transfers. The exports behaviour of the SME was the most important of these. The companies with the largest number of transfers were also those with a larger percentage of exports to sales (Table 4.6). This is the only relation that passes the Exact Fisher Test. The younger and smaller chemical and electronic enterprises seem more prone to sell their technology overseas than the more traditional firms in the fabricated metals industries; however, the statistical test did not confirm the relationship, partly because the numebr of cases was too small.

Choice of Forms

The type of arrangements concluded is linked in the first place with the origins of the initiative and, secondly, with the politics of the host

Table 4.7   Origins of initiative and choice of contractual form

Form	Initiative	
	Host firm or both	Canadian SME
Technical agreement	13 (87%)	7 (47%)
Joint venture or subsidiary	2 (15%)	8 (53%)
	15 (100%)	15 (100%)

Fisher Test: 0.043.

country more than with any other variable. Size, age and industry were eliminated as possible conditions of the choice of arm's length transactions versus subsidiaries or affiliates. The origins of the initiative was crucial in the choice of contractual forms. Again, this relationship is significant, according to the Fisher Test. When the initiative came from the host-country firm (11 cases) or from both the recipient and the supplier (two cases), the result was most likely a technological agreement with no equity involvement; when the initiative came from the Canadian SME, the result was most often a joint venture or a wholly-owned subsidiary (see Table 4.7).

The relationship between country and type of arrangement was also strong: 36 per cent (10 cases) of the 30, transfers took place between enterprises having some ownership link but there are some visitor by host country. All the technology transfers to Mexico were with the minority joint ventures of the Canadian firms; 36 per cent (five out of 14) of those to India went through joint ventures, 33 per cent of those to Singapore, 25 per cent of those to Brazil and none of those to Korea and Argentina. The political framework was probably the key factor here: Mexican laws imposed, more than those of other countries, the organisation of joint ventures by foreign SMEs and joint ventures were always controlled by local partners.

Successful Transactions

What were the conditions of success for the Canadian enterprise? Success of failure was measured on the basis of question 85; 'How did the results of the project in [the target country] compare with the initial objectives?' Three options were offered: they surpassed, met or did not reach the objectives. The first and second choices were qualified

Table 4.8   Quality of host-firm management, and success

	Management	
	Poor	*Fair*
	0	22
	4	3
Totals	4	25

Fischer Test: 0.002.

as success and the third as failure. Only seven transfers out of 30 were unsuccessful (23 per cent), or this measure.

Several variables seemed associated with success. The most important of these was the quality of the management of the host-country enterprise. Using question 88 (problems encountered in the project), we observed that poor management of the host country firm was always linked to failure, but that it was not the only condition of failure (see Table 4.8). Other variables seemed also to be linked with success or failure, but did not pass the requirements of the Fisher Test. Size of the Canadian enterprise was one of these variables. The chances of being unsuccessful were double in the smallest firms (1–100 employees) than in medium-sized enterprises (101–500 employees). The country of destination was probably another important variable. India seemed a safer place (two unsuccessful cases out of 14 transactions or 14 per cent of failures) than East Asia (two failures out of eight transfers or 25 per cent); the riskier place was Latin America (three unsuccessful cases out of eight or 38 per cent).

Other variables seemed less evidently associated with success or failure: government incentives by home-country agencies (Table 4.9), age of the Canadian SME, type of transaction involved (technology agreement, joint venture or wholly-owned subsidiary) or industry.

Adaptive Efforts

Six transfers (out of 30) or only 20 per cent were involved in some degree of product adaptation. There was no relation between the size of the SME and adaptive efforts, or between the host country and product adaptation. Industry seemed a more important factor: almost all adaptive efforts, at the product level, were concentrated in the fabricated metal industry (see Table 4.10): equipment and machines, both elec-

Table 4.9   Canadian government aid, and success

	Aid	
	With	*Without*
Success	9 (69%)	13 (76%)
Failure	3 (25%)	4 (24%)
Neither	1 (6%)	–
Total	13 (100%)	17 (100%)

Table 4.10   Industry and product adaptation

		Industry		
		Chem.	*Elec.*	*Fabr. Met.*
Product adaptation	No	3 (100%)	5 (83%)	16 (76%)
	Yes	–	1 (20%)	5 (25%)
Total		3 (100%)	6 (100%)	21 (100%)

trical and non-electrical, constituted the bulk of these adaptations. (This relationship, however, does not pass the Fisher Test when chemical and electronic companies are put together.)

Adaptive efforts were more substantial in the use of equipment: nine SMEs signalled differences in equipment between home- and host-country firms. However, a closer look at the data shows that some of the differ- ences (two cases) were due to an upgrading of the Canadian equip- ment after the initial technology transfer. In one case the host-country equipment was more advanced than that of the supplier. In the six other cases the equipment used in the host country was, from the start, different from that used in Canada. In all cases it was simpler: usually, the host country firm (India in six cases, Brazil in one) had to rely on older and more labour-intensive equipment: numerically-controlled machines, computer-aided design, electronic testing equipment and other more sophisticated machines were lacking in the host country. The strong relation between destination and equipment adaptation is prob- ably linked to Indian and Brazilian trade policies, forbidding the im- port of any product that can be either produced in the country or replaced by domestic goods (see Table 4.11).

Table 4.11   Host-country and equipment adaptation

		Host-country		
		India	*Brazil*	*All other*
Equipment Adaptation	Yes	6 (43%)	1 (25%)	–
	No	8 (62%)	3 (75%)	12 (100%)
Totals		14 (100%)	4 (100%)	12 (100%)

Table 4.12   Size of Canadian SME and equipment adaptation

Size of Canadian SME	
1–100 empl.	101–500 empl.
2 (11%)	4 (45%)
17 (89%)	5 (55%)
19 (100%)	9 (100%)

Fischer Test: 0.064.

The size of the Canadian SME was also related to equipment adaptation: medium-sized Canadian companies were more likely to use more complex equipment and adapted this more often than small firms. (Here the statistical relationship was significant using the demanding Fisher Test, see Table 4.12).

4.6   TWO CASE STUDIES

Two short case studies can illustrate the typical cases found in the survey. They operate in the industries in which most firms of the sample were active, and are located in the two cities where most companies were interviewed.

Company A: A Machinery Producer

This company is a diversified wire machinery manufacturer founded in the 1960s and located in Toronto. In its early years and up to the

1970s, it was linked to a specialised Canadian steel producer, but then it became autonomous and started its international development. It bought one machinery manufacturer in the United States, then acquired minority control positions in one company in each of Mexico and Brazil. It transferred its technology to each of those companies. Its production is custom-order, and its market is the world (95 per cent of customers are outside Canada) with strong positions in the North American and largest Latin American markets and marketing outlets in Europe. In-house R&D (12 per cent of sales, a record for the industry) is complemented with international cross-licensing agreements in order to maintain its technological edge.

Company B: An Electronic Producer

This is a specialized telecommunications producer formed in the early 1980s from a foreign subsidiary purchased by its Canadian executives. It is located in a Montreal suburb. Although it has only 250 employees, it is now the world largest supplier of point-to-point microwave digital radio systems. A public company, it has grown at a very rapid pace. Producing in batches for an expected demand, exports account for more than 80 per cent of the company's sales. The company bought its basic technology from the mother foreign company and, though intense R&D (16 per cent of sales go to R&D) it came to the forefront of this specialised technology. Its product gives radio service to remote and thinly populated areas, connecting the isolated users with the conventional telephone network. This technology has proved useful in many developing countries; in three of them Company *B* has signed technology agreements with local firms in order to produce some of its equipment.

4.7 CONCLUSION

While Canadian SMEs with international strategies are mostly involved in industrialised countries, mainly the United States, a subset of these firms are active in LDCs. India seems by far the most important destination of Canadian technology transferred by SMEs, followed by Latin America and East Asia. The adoption of an international strategy by Canadian SMEs seems a rather new phenomenon, rapidly evolving since the late 1960s and 1970s.

The picture that emerges from our study is in line with previous surveys on the international strategies of small and medium-sized manufacturing firms. The SMEs that participated in the study were strongly technology- and export-oriented. They usually performed R&D, regularly launched new products, and asked for patents (or protected their innovations through secrecy). All of them were in the fabricated metals, electronics and chemical products industries, in which technology plays an important part among the resource inputs; very few firms (which were not interviewed) were found in the food, textiles, clothing and furniture industries. These findings are all consistent with the Hymer–Kindleberger–Caves approach to international business, but also, to a lesser extent, with the product-cycle hypothesis.

At least half of Canadian SMEs could be described as small oligopolists, occupying a large proportion of the domestic market in their respective market niches, thus bringing, again, some confirmation to the industrial organisation approach to foreign investment and technology transfer.

A few firms followed the export–sales agent–direct investment sequence predicted by the product cycle theory. However, most SMEs opted for the creation of subsidiaries or for technology transfer, because they met barriers in particular developing countries while they were looking for new exports markets. Canadian SMEs showed no particular inclination to use the most abundant Canadian resources, as predicted by the factor endowment theory of international operations.

The majority of Canadian SMEs exported to more than one country, and transferred their technology more than once, thus showing a marked international strategy. Typically, Canadian SMEs preferred exports to foreign direct investment. It was the recipient countries' legislation (tariff, restrictions to equity participation and control by foreign firms) that often forced them to organise minority joint ventures or arm's length agreements with host-country firms. The origins of the initiative was the most important factor affecting the choice of transfer forms. When the intiative came from the host-country firm, the outcome was most often a technology agreement without equity involvement; the opposite happened when it was the Canadian SME that took the initiative, thus confirming the preferences suggested above.

India and Latin America are the most important destinations of the SMEs technology. Canadian firms are oriented towards Latin America and India, but the dynamic countries of East Asia are actively demanding their technology.

Product technology was the most common type of technology transferred. It was the object of the agreement in all the cases. However, only six cases involved product adaptation. Almost all of them were in the fabricated metal; industries. Process technology and plant design technology were numerically less important. As to equipment adaptation, it also only took place in a few cases; it was linked to the need of using the machinery and electronic equipment that was available in the host country. All the cases of different equipment were in India (except for one in Brazil) and most of them had medium-sized Canada firms as sellers, probably reflecting the fact that larger Canadian SMEs own more modern equipment, not available in the host country (due to restrictions).

Most transfers were successful from the point of view of the Canadian firm. The unsuccessful firms were most often the small firms with less than 100 employees. These firms were probably less able to find reliable partners, and had less resources to invest to make sure that the transaction went smoothly. As for the destination, Latin America seemed slightly riskier than East Asia, and India had the best chances of success for Canadian exporters of technology.

Some theories on multinational corporations proved partially useful for understanding the international operations of small and medium-sized manufacturing firms. The industrial organisation approach is probably the best suited in the respect: Canadian SMEs had very often some 'special assets' (new products, or new processes) that gave them industrial strength both in the Canadian market and abroad. The product cycle theory seems less suited to the understanding of the foreign activities of SMEs. The sequence of their foreign undertakings do not correspond to the one predicted by the product life thesis: technology transfer occurred with countries where exports were negligible or non-existent. However, Canadian SMEs were often innovators in their own market niches, and started their international expansion by exporting their specific products. Finally, the factor endowment thesis does not explain all the firms we studied: their products did not reflect Canada's relative endowments.

In the light of this study, one is forced to conclude that all theories on multinational enterprises suffer, when applied to SMEs, from a major inadequacy: they were conceived for large enterprises, that have the resources to 'internalise' the technology market, and thus create subsidiaries abroad. The international operations of SMEs, with less resources and economic power, are more often confined to trading their technology through arm's length transactions and/or minority joint ventures. Also, SMEs are more prone to comply with existing legislation than to try to shape it, the institutional framework of the host country (tariffs, legislation on royalties and foreign investment) is much more restrictive for them than for large transnational firms, often able to negotiate on equal (or even favourable) terms with host-country governments. Theories of multinational corporations can only provide a starting point; the full understanding of the international strategies and operations of small and medium-sized firms will need the development of new theories based on much more solid and complete empirical evidence.

Our empirical evidence tends to dismiss some of the appropriate technology arguments. Not only do Canadian manufacturing SMEs not tend to invest in developing countries, thus bringing an indirect but important refutation of the appropriate technology theories, but also the most active of these SMEs do not own 'appropriate' technology, in the sense that it is small-scale, easy to absorb and capital-saving. Most of our SMEs were in sophisticated machinery, electrical and electronic, chemical or plastic product, with narrow niches and large shares of the world market to there sides. They had high sales or employees and were very active in R&D. Their products are not substitutes to those supplied by large multinational corporations, but complementary to them. In the few cases when some adaptation had taken place, the SMEs had arranged all the adaptation that was needed.

However, the Canadian SMEs were probably more adequate partners of LCDs firms than larger corporations. Their scale of production is generally smaller than that of large MNCs. Their organisation and technology (most usually batch or custom-order production) is simpler and more flexible, and thus easier to assimilate and adapt. With fewer resources to invest, they are less able to 'internalise' the technology market, and they lose some technological rents to host firms. The host-firm technological disadvantage is less pronounced in dealing with SMEs than with larger multinationals.

5 The Case of France

Michel Delapierre

5.1 INTRODUCTION

For several decades, the main concern of governments, bankers, managers and business analysis when dealing with industrial structure has been focused on the big corporation. Size was the key to competitiveness at the firm as well as at the national level. Industries were evolving into oligopolies, based on the mass production and mass consumption of standardized goods. The multinationalisation process was considered as directly related to the growth of national oligopolistic firms.

However, since the beginning of the 1970s small and medium-sized enterprises (SMEs) increasingly came to front stage. They first appeared as were innovators, in opposition to large corporations more eager to maintain their oligopolistic rents. In the 1980s it was the contribution of SMEs to employment which was put forward. Finally the SME is presented today as a highly flexible and adaptative structure, particularly suited to operate in a turbulent and risky environment.[1]

The last period has then seen, in nearly every country in the world, the creation of specialised public administrations and the launching of specific programmes devoted to the promotion of small and medium-sized enterprises. Simultaneously, the fast introduction of new technologies has enabled the growth of a host of new business ventures in traditional, oligopolistic industries as well as in new, emerging sectors. In the last 15 years, more than 600 biotechnology companies have been formed, mainly in the United States.[2] This new image of the SME, innovative and adaptive instead of lagging and clumsy, leads to its frequent presentation as an epitome of the industrial strategies suited to the new business environment.

The qualities attributed to the SME from developed countries may help to explain the emphasis put on their actual on potential role as an alternative technology source for developing countries. The involvement of SMEs in the transfer of technology to LDCs can be approached from a double perspective.

SMEs as such, have many working characteristics close to those prevailing in developing countries, such as limited assets and small

113

scale of production. Furthermore, their size, relative to their partners allows more speedy and open negotiations and ensures a greater openness to local requirements, SMEs may thus be identified as the most suitable suppliers of technology to industrialising countries' firms, to the extent that they appear to share similar conditions of operations.

Developing countries, on the other hand, could consider SMEs as the more dynamic part of the emerging new industrial system, sources of the most innovative products and production processes. They could provide them with the latest technologies, access to an international competitiveness on world-wide markets.

Such a twofold approach may appear a paradox. SMEs are singled out as purveyors of technology simultaneously for their similarities with enterprises and industrial structures of developing countries and for their capacities to initiate the emergence of new high-tech sectors, world-wide. This paradox reflects the contradictions increasingly arising today between the structuring of national industrial systems and the building of transnationalised industries.[3]

This chapter deals with the first aspect of SMEs, their ability to provide an alternative technology source for developing countries to large multinational corporations. It is based on the presentation of the available evidence from the French case. In some concluding remarks we will, however, try to address the second aspect, SMEs in the new forms of competition based on technology in transnationalized industries.

5.2   SMEs IN THE FRENCH INDUSTRIAL STRUCTURE

To present figures on SMEs is a nearly impossible task. First of all, statistical sources are quite often missing, small firms by far outnumber large corporations and lack of data accuracy increases with the size of the population surveyed. Furthermore, a dynamic analysis of SMEs in a national industrial structure is made difficult to the extent that the population of firms is not a stable one, new firms constantly appear and existing ones disappear. This could be taken into account as a natural life cycle phenomenon, but it is made more complex by the fact that a successful SME may eventually become a large corporation and leave the category. Data on the evolution of performance of SMEs as a group is also difficult.

Secondly, the category of SME itself can secondly be questioned. A given firm, according to its sector of operation, may appear large or small. Software companies with an employment of 500 people are large corporations while a 1000 people car manufacturer is small. Also, the yardsticks used to define a SME are generally not consistent, size categories built from employment, sales or assets do not give the same classification of firms. Absolute size may not be relevant to discriminate between small and large enterprises.

The SME label, thirdly, encompasses an heterogeneous group of firms as far as their general strategy and their situation within the competitive context of their industry is concerned: some of them are mainly subcontractors for large companies, others are highly specialized innovators and leaders in their niches. It is, therefore, difficult to talk about SMEs as a uniform and well-defined type of enterprise. It is in particular obvious that SMEs can be found in many different kind of activities, from agriculture to industry, through services and retailing companies, involving completely different types of know-how. In order to focus on the transfer of industrial technology, know-how related to the design, production and commercialisation of manufactures, this chapter will deal with industrial SMEs.[4]

SMEs and French Industry

French industry in 1986 encompassed 32 902 industrial corporations with over 10 employees, of which 31 198 were enterprises employing between 10 and 499 people.[5] Table 5.1 shows that SMEs as a whole, represent 95 per cent of the total number of manufacturing corporations, 49 per cent of employment, 39 per cent of total sales and, for companies of more than 20 employees, only 30 per cent of investments. They are less capital-intensive than their large counterparts.

The population of SMEs has been relatively stable – there were 32 476 in 1978. SMEs, despite the attention they presently command, cannot be considered a new phenomenon. A study on a sample of 1300 corporations found that 49 per cent of them had been created before 1960, 26 per cent between 1960 and 1976, 15 per cent between 1976 and 1981, 5 per cent between 1981 and 1984 and 5 per cent between 1984 and 1987. A breakdown by industry would, however, show a different picture. A survey of SMEs in the telecommunication industry, the high-tech sector, has noted the relative youth of French SMEs, many of them having been created after 1975, compared with their German competitors.[6] On the whole since 1984 creation of new enterprises has increased from a low 17 320 incorporations in 1983 to 22 300 in 1986. Furthermore the number of the smallest SMEs, the 20–49 people category, has slightly increased since 1978, from 12 226

Table 5.1 Structure of French industry by firm size, 1986

Size	No. of firms Nb.	(%)	Employment 100	(%)	Sales Billion F.	(%)	Investment Billion F.	(%)
10–19	10143	31	154	4	63.5	3		
20–49	12563	38	412	12	186	8	6.3	7
50–99	4324	13	310	9	148.5	7	5.6	6
100–199	2540	8	357	10	183.5	8	6.3	7
200–499	1628	5	501	14	298	13	11.9	12
Sub-total	31198	95	1735	49	878	39	30.2	31
500 and more	9182	3	1752	30	1311	50	65.3	60
Out of range	786	2	27	1	53	2	0.9	1
Total	32902	100	3514	100	2243	100	96.4	100

Note: Out of range firms are mainly contracting companies.

Source: Ministry of Industry, SESSI (1988).

to 12 563, while every other category has shown a small reduction, which means that if new incorporations concern very small companies and failures hurt bigger ones, the economic impact is not equivalent.

SMEs therefore, quite often operate in conjunction with other larger firms. They are part of an industrial fabric and rely on their relationships with other corporations for their inputs as well as the sales of their output, which often need to be subsequently incorporated with other parts in final goods (see Table 5.2).

The contribution of SMEs to French industrial R&D is relatively limited, as Table 5.3 indicates. A survey made in 1985 by the French Ministry of Research showed that 0.4 per cent of SMEs with 10–49 employees had at least one equivalent full-time post devoted to R&D. The proportion then increased from 4 per cent of firms in the 50–199 employees' bracket to 18.8 per cent for companies in the 200–499 range. The figure for the larger firms was 50.4 per cent.[7]

SMEs of more than 20 employees have consistently raised their share of total industrial employment from approximately 37 per cent in 1973 to 40 per cent in 1978 and 45 per cent in 1986, which sustains their reputation as job-creators.

The major involvement of SMEs compared to large firms, as Table 5.2 indicates, is focused on consumer goods and their minor one on equipment goods. While they account for 61 per cent of the total value added in consumer goods, their share falls to 26 per cent in equipment goods. A more detailed breakdown of SMEs by size shows a similar

Table 5.2   Breakdown of value added by type of goods manufactured, 1986, %

Type of firm	Types of goods		
	Consumer	*Equipment*	*Intermediate*
SME	37	28	35
Large firms	16	54	30
Total	24	44	32

From Ministry of Industry, SESSI (1988).

Table 5.3   R&D spending, by firm size, 1985

Size of employment	R&D/Sales	
	Whole industry (%)	*Firms doing R&D (%)*
under 50	0.1	12.3
50–199	0.4	
200–499	0.1	4.6
500–999	1.9	
1000–1999	1.6	3.5
over 2000	5.1	6

Source: Ministry of Industry, in J. TILLAC, 'L'economie française souffre-t-elle d'une insuffisance de la recherche?', *Journal Officiel, Avis et Rapports du Conseil Economique et Social*, Session de 1989, séances des 25 et 26 avril 1989.

distribution among industry groupings, there is no specific pattern of specialization among them according to size at that level of aggregation. SMEs, therefore, may be considered as more likely holders of technologies suited to the manufacture of consumer goods rather than equipment goods, which may raise some questions about their relevance as suppliers of technology for industrialisation purposes.

Relative size seems, however, to play a significant role as far as their relation to customers is concerned. One out of two SME is working with a contractor and the smallest ones are relying on subcontracting for the largest share of their sales, from nearly 50 per cent for enterprises employing 20–49 people, to 16 per cent for 200–499 firms.

In 1985 1102 SMEs declared themselves to be conducting continuous R&D activities, accounting for 13.4 per cent of total in-house R&D by French corporations and benefiting from only 6.9 per cent of public R&D funding.[8]

Such research seldom leads to a real technological breakthrough. According to a 1981 survey, only 7 per cent of innovations made by a sample of 750 SMEs having made a significative innovation in the last five years were considered a real break-through, while 52 per cent of the cases were described as 'major innovation', 32 per cent marketing-related and 20 per cent technology-related, and 41 per cent were considered as an improvement.[9] According to these figures, SMEs may thus, be characterised more as holders of mature and well-established know-how than producers of new technologies.

It seems however, from other studies on industrial innovation that the distribution by type, namely commercial or technological nature, does not significantly differ between SMEs and large firms.[10] Such an orientation of R&D is not a specific feature of SMEs.

Internationalisation of French SMEs

Internationalisation has always been associated with large corporations, endowed with sufficient financial means and seeking to further increase their sales by looking abroad, beyond their national markets. SMEs as a whole indeed are much less involved abroad than the biggest firms.

The share of exports to total sales shows a close relation to firm size. While all manufacturing enterprises in 1986 had an export to sales ratio of 27.5 per cent, SMEs had a ratio ranging from 9.7 to 21.3 per cent, increasing with size category, while large firms' exports were reaching a third of their total sales. Once again, however, aggregated figures hide contrasting individual situations: if nearly every large corporation is exporting, many SMEs have no foreign sales while some of them are very large exporters, 60 per cent of SMEs have nearly no exports, while in 1986, 1150 SMEs exported for over 50 per cent of their total sales. According to a 1981 survey of French SMEs, for 32 per cent of them the market was local or regional, it was national for 38 per cent and for 30 per cent their market was European or world-wide.

French SMEs' international involvement is even less prominent as far as other forms, FDI and licensing, are concerned. Figures on stock of foreign assets as well as licensing operations by firm size of French companies are lacking. The UN Centre on Transnational Corporations, however, estimates that 1600 French SMEs have affiliates or licensees abroad.[11] A survey made in 1978, stated that approximately 1000 French SMEs had taken part in transfers of technology to developing countries.[12] Furthermore, such approximations are based on the number of

Table 5.4   Share of exports in total sales, by firm employment size, 1986, %

Size	Exports/Sales before taxes
20–49	9.7
50–99	13.5
100–199	18.7
200–499	21.3
Total SMEs	16.7
> 500	33.9

Source: Ministry of Industry in SESSI (1989).

operations engaged in, they may be inflated to the extent that many firms have more than one licensing agreement or affiliate abroad. The actual proportion of SMEs with assets or licensing agreements abroad may be somewhat smaller.

As far as the geographical scope of the general study is concerned, in mainly Latin American and Asian recipient countries, French SMEs are not very well represented.[13] Their main areas of expansion are constituted by the nearer regions, in terms of geographic as well as cultural proximity: French-speaking Africa and Middle East, Asean countries and the 'four dragons' are hosting less than 1 per cent of the total worldwide French foreign direct investment compared to 4.5 per cent for Italian direct assets, 5 per cent for the United Kingdom and 6 per cent for the Federal Republic of Germany.[14] A. Weil and G.Y. Bertin found that more than 50 per cent of technology transfer operations took place in African and Middle Eastern regions. Another survey made on the new forms of investment and focusing on joint ventures, and therefore including equity participations, conducted between 1981 and 1983, has shown that 74 per cent of cases, for manufacturing corporations, were in African and Middle Eastern countries, against 11 per cent in Latin America and 15 per cent in Asia where India and China had the lion's share.[15]

In an increasingly transnationalised economy, nationality of firms may be hard to define and it is more and more difficult to identify the population of true French SMEs. A fair proportion of small and medium-sized enterprises operating in France are in fact majority or minority affiliates of foreign corporations as shown by Table 5.5.

As the main trends in multinationalisation may lead one to expect, the share of foreign affiliated firms increases with their size. However nearly 10 per cent of French SMEs and a quarter of their sales are

Table 5.5   French companies with foreign participation,[a] 1 January 1986, in % for each class

Size	No. of firms	% of sales
20–49	5.2	8.9
50–99	11.7	17.7
100–199	18.0	27.7
200–499	25.2	34.0
Over 500	35.4	28.6

Note:
[a] Companies with 20% and more foreign participation.

Source: Ministry of Industry, SESSI (1988).

controlled by transnational corporations. The very notion of a 'French' SME has therefore to be questioned. It may nevertheless be noted that SMEs seem to resist to foreign penetration more strongly than their larger domestic counterparts.

To summarise this schematic presentation of French SMEs, one must note some of their characteristic features. First of all, SMEs are highly integrated within their national industrial structure, they are part of an interrelated fabric and depend heavily on their immediate environment for their day-to-day operations, from input supplies to output deliveries to prime contractors or business customers. Secondly, they constitute an extremely heterogeneous category, including traditional subcontractors working with stabilised know-how and high-technology enterprises with a huge relative level of R&D expenses and corporations entirely focused on the national market while others are heavily involved abroad, mainly through exports. Their role as an alternative source of technology to developing countries may therefore differ notably according to their sectoral and individual specificities.

5.3   FRENCH SMEs AS AN ALTERNATIVE SOURCE OF TECHNOLOGY FOR DEVELOPING COUNTRIES: THE AVAILABLE EVIDENCE

The direct analysis of the actual involvement of French SMEs in the transfer of technology to developing countries has encountered several practical difficulties. First of all, cases involving French SMEs, particularly bearing in mind the necessity to construct samples of firms belonging to a limited array of industries for generalisation purposes, have been relatively hard to find. As we have mentioned previously there are few of them with operations in the countries within the scope of our study. They were, in many cases, hard to identify and locate from the recipient countries themselves. Furthermore, on many occasions French SMEs were quite often affiliates of large industrial groups and could not be included in our population of cases. Secondly, the localisation in France of some firms, was not always possible to the extent that the high rate of mortality of this type of corporation implies that many of them no longer existed or had been bought or merged with others, and were therefore no longer registered under their previous name. Thirdly, unlike large firms which have their headquarters concentrated in a few large cities, SMEs are scattered all over the country out of easy reach without involving high travel expenses. Last but not least, their time resources are very scarce and many requests for an appointment were turned down.

In the course of the study, 75 small and medium-sized companies were solicited by mail and telephone calls for direct interviews; only firms which gave a positive answer were visited. In several instances firms (the name of which had been provided by correspondent teams in developing countries) stated that they had no activity in any LDC.

This extremely limited sample cannot be utilised to support any valid general statement on the experience of technology transfer by French SMEs. The information they provided was, however, supplemented through interviews with an industrial federation, the Electric and Electronic Industries Federation, FIEE, and by findings from surveys and studies previously conducted on their behalf or with their support. Data were also drawn from two previous global analysis of the role of French SMEs in technology transfer to developing countries, namely the reports by Weil in 1978 and by Bertin in 1986.

Presentation of the Sample

The nine French SMEs which are engaged in transfer of technology operations abroad and agreed to be interviewed were long-established firms (see Table 5.6). The youngest was created in 1963, the oldest in 1912, six out of the nine were incorporated before 1990. Their size brings them into the middle of the range, which does not come as a surprise considering their maturity; only one has less than 100 employees.

The firms of our sample are typically companies with narrow areas of specialisation. They usually occupy more than 50 per cent of their

Table 5.6   The sample, by size and date of creation

Company	Creation	Employment
A*	1920	350
B	1948	150
C	1949	230
D	1950	215
E	1932	840
F	1953	330
G	1963	130
H	1958	80
I	1912	480

Note:
* Names have been omitted for confidentiality purposes.

Source: Author's interviews.

domestic market for the product line related to the operation to transfer of technology. However they do not belong to international oligopolies, their share of the world market is quite often negligible. In only two cases were the firms declared to be the world leader in their field. Such a strong position is, in the majority of cases, related to a high level of R&D spending, well above the figures previously quoted for French SMEs as a whole. Furthermore, the average R&D to sales ratio of 4.6 per cent of SMEs of the 50–500 employees range, actually undertaking research and/or development, is somewhat lower compared with the levels reached by several companies in our sample, as shown by Table 5.7.

The corporations from our sample obviously belong to a subset of the population of French SMEs. They hold strong positions in their national markets and sustain it through a high level of R&D (more development than research). Four of them had deposited more than 20 patents in the last five years. Their technological sophistication may be highlighted by the nature of their mode of production which appears to be more generally for custom order than for expected demand. They seem to be operating in national rather than transnational markets. Their position on the world markets is quite often negligible. They are, however, large exporters, with an export to sales ratio close to 50 per cent on average, compared with the 16.7 per cent for the whole population of French SMEs. They are therefore not entrenched on their domestic market, and are willing to expand their activities into the outside world.

Table 5.7 Main features of companies in the sample, for the product lines concerned in the transfer operation

Company	R&D/sales domestic market	Share of share %	Export share of sales	World market share
A	1	50	55	Negligable
B	NA	80–50	–	Negligable
C	8	90–40	>40	Negligable
D	–	50	20	Negligable
E	>1.2	25	50	Leader
F	5	50–40	>30	5%
G	5	100	60	5%
H	8	10–25	70	2–20
I	>3.5	100	70	50

Source: Author's interviews.

The international orientation of the companies from our sample is also demonstrated by the high level of foreign implantation, totalling 29 affiliates, 10 joint ventures and 29 licensing agreements. It shows a strong preference for equity control over other forms of investment. In the majority of cases, the first activation was to secure a foothold in the local market. There is only one occurrence where re-export to the French or a third country market was a primary consideration. The international investment strategy remains market-driven, and does not usually to lead the implementation of an international division of labour within the firms.

Factors and Motivations

Access to the market is the first and main motivation of French firms, large or small, to engage in foreign operations. According to the study conducted by Bertin, such a reason is even stronger in the case of SMEs than of big companies.[16] When countries in the field of study are taken into account, 10 cases have been documented, one firm having provided information on two operations. The cases divide equally between Latin America and Asia. This shows a bias in favour of Asian-related cases, with in particular three transfers to Korea. Keeping in mind the limitations accruing from the small number of firms in our sample, a schematic characterisation of host countries may be attempted. Operations in Latin American countries have been originated either by an outside proposal or by protectionist measures against imports. Growth prospects of the local market are more systematically put forward for implantations in Asian countries. This could indicate a more cautious and defensive approach of Latin American countries and a more aggressive one toward Asian NICs by French SMEs.

It is important to note at this stage that the motive of exploitation of a technical advance was stated in only one case, concerning an affiliate in Brazil. It is almost never mentioned in answers to Bertin's questionnaire, despite the explicit wording of one of his questions. In another questionnaire to SMEs, in 1982, only 12.5 per cent of responses stated it as an outcome from their activities of technology transfer.[17] While SMEs are approached by foreign firms searching for technology or know-how, they are often not aware of the value of their knowledge *per se*, and still think in terms of products.

A study of a sample of 20 companies from electric and electronic industries and including the major manufacturers as well as some SMEs, found that pure transfer of technology, i.e. licensing, is always made out of necessity rather than by first choice.[18] This is quite in tune with the fact that licensing is often presented as the only alternative left to a market-driven company whose exports in the country are restricted and who does not have the financial resources for a direct investment or does not want to commit them for that purpose. Technology licensing, does not, therefore usually generate a strong flow of exports. Further evidence, from the electric and electronic industries study and from our own interviews is given by the large number of cases where the initiative for the transfer comes from the foreign partner rather than from the French firm, particularly when the host country is a relatively small one, with a narrow domestic market base.

The selection of countries of installation and of local partners does not seem to follow a rigid screening procedure. A feasibility and/or market study prior to any decision was mentioned only in cases of operations in Asian countries. Latin America appears a familiar type of business environment for firms in our sample. Moreover the French corporation usually had had previous relations with its local partner. The two only exceptions are to be found in Mexico. Mexico is also the only other country, with India, where the French firms had exported before creating an affiliate, a joint venture or concluding a licensing agreement. Furthermore, no other country was usually considered as an alternative for the delocalisation. In other words, companies from our sample do not seem to be ready or able to devote much time and effort to a world-wide screening of opportunities for foreign operations. In many cases, our respondents stressed the narrowness of their business segments to justify their ability to pinpoint the best international opportunities from easily available information. For one of them, a supplier of equipment to car manufacturers, 'clever daily reading of the *Financial Times* is the best market study we can find'. In such conditions, the bandwagon effect is a powerful means of host country identification and selection. SMEs therefore are probably induced to follow leaders which may quite often be large multinationals. A more detailed analysis would open to them some other areas of international expansion well attuned to their own specificities.

Local partners may be either companies engaged in the same lines of business or firms seeking to diversify. This last situation is often found in Korea. Host partners in every case from our sample are much smaller, 10 times on average, than their French counterpart. Their manufacturing activities are however often more integrated, generally due to the lack of availability of inputs or spare parts in their domestic market. But they have a lesser degree of product differentiation, they concentrate on less sophisticated products. Despite their smaller size, they quite often use the same type of equipment as their French partner or another company. There is thus in many cases a relative disequilibrium between the French and the host-country SME. The companies from our sample are in a position of strength in the French market, of which they usually hold a dominant share. They also manage to enter into agreements with foreign firms smaller than themselves in order to keep the dominant relationship.[19]

Mode and Content

SMEs, when they cannot penetrate a Third World market through exports, show a strong preference for licensing over direct investment. In some cases, however, such as Korea and sometimes Brazil, they will rather chose the joint venture route. The advantages of licensing lie mainly in cost minimisation, companies are not able or willing to commit their limited financial resources to far away and unknown environments. For Korea and Brazil, domestic firms' strategies and government export promotion policies are seen as constituting potential competitive threats. French corporations fear that the local licensee will eventually become a strong competitor on their own markets, at home or in third countries. An equity participation is then sought out, in order to control the operations of the local firm.

The licensing agreement is then seen, from the French entreprise's perspective, as a long-lasting relationship, royalties are more frequent than lump-sum payments, the agreement is continuously renewed when it expires, particularly to provide the persisting use of brand names. The foreign partner is thus integrated, like a relay or replace unit, within the licensor's operations. In every case but wholly-owned affiliates there is a formal technology agreement between the French SME and its foreign partner, which often covers the whole range of activities from patents to technical services and when it is not global in scope always includes brand names and know-how, the most valuable assets of the French firm.

It is not possible to draw any strong evidence on the actual level of difficulties encountered by SMEs in dealing with their partners and from government interventions during the negotiations, to the extent that only successful cases have been scrutinized. Abortive discussions have not been analysed. It has been, however, frequently stated in our interviews that, thanks to the local partner having taken the initiative, discussions were not difficult and any problems which may have arisen with local administrations were easily resolved by the partner himself. The form of involvement which was first considered was eventually implemented and few modifications were introduced at the request of the local government. Problems had in fact arisen in some cases, later on, with the red tape necessary to ensure actual financial returns.

The negotiation period is often quite short, 6 months or even less, with one case but needing 3 years to be settled. Help from the French or local authorities is seldom acknowledged. One case, however, is worth mentioning, where the Korean government showed their interest in the deal, stating they would consider the French joint venture for their export promotion programme.

The transfer of technology is mainly made through the sending of plans and the provision of technical assistance. In a fair number of cases some critical components are also supplied in order to ensure a good product quality from the very beginning. The prime objective is not to ensure a captive flow of exports from the technology supplier, only in one out of two cases of transfers operated in part through the sending of key components did the agreement state a compulsory purchase of goods from the licensor by the licensee. One must not forget that the investment or the licensing agreement is in many instances justified by protectionist policies which preclude imports of goods.

The main vector of transfer is nevertheless formed by the transmission of knowledge. Assistance is of a technical nature – that is, information on product specificities and manufacturing processes, with sometimes some help with commercial operations. Training is often extremely limited. Rather than sending scarce engineers to the host's premises, the French firm receives trainees from the foreign partner in its own plant. Training periods are generally limited to a few months. This has two consequences. First of all, it implies that the local partner must have a good technological capacity, prior to the transfer itself. He can thus acquire the relevant skills without straining the thin human resources of the licensor. The local partner's capacity to absorb know-how has been stressed by each of our respondents. It may also help explain the fact that the initiative often comes from the recipient firm, and the straight forward nature of negotiations. It further implies that the technology transferred consists rather in well-mastered, mature, know-how. A short stay of skilled operators of the plant in France is usually enough to pass on the necessary practical knowledge which is not fair removed from their own capacities.

The second consequence is that the products and processes which are transferred cannot be very significantly transformed or adapted by the French firm. According to the MRE/FIEE study and our own interviews, products are seldom modified and increasingly world-wide standards are enforced upon national markets in developed as well as developing countries. The main adaptions concern the manufacturing processes.

Modification of manufacturing processes stems mainly from three types of constraints. The first arises from the local availability of equipment goods. In some cases, when equipment manufacturers are world-wide companies, often multinationals, the question of equipment choice does not occur and the same is used in both partners' plants. Whenever there are local equipment manufacturers, the host country may request the utilisation of local suppliers. The second constraint stems from specificities of local inputs. They may have to be purchased locally due to high transportation costs from remote countries and public import policies. In several cases, also, the lack of local inputs, inputs which are found by the French SME for its own operations in France through subcontractors, have to be manufactured by the partner in the developing country. The difference in the industrial structure of the two countries, therefore, accounts for the higher level of vertical integration of the host-country firm. The third motive for production process adaptation lies in end-market specification. The smallest production series may request slightly different manufacturing processes. A more limited range of products, mainly restricted to lower-end goods, may allow the use of less sophisticated and flexible manufacturing equipment. The distribution of final demand may be more oriented toward less technology-intensive products, requiring less up-to-date equipment.

Last but not least, the big industrial customers, particularly in the case of intermediate goods, may have their own specific requirements. Some French SMEs, as previously mentioned, are working as subcontractors. In some instances, they may have followed their multinational contractors abroad, in other cases their partners in developing countries are in touch with other contractors who may have specific demands. The adaptation is then sometimes made in cooperation with the French licensor and the local customer of its licensee. In the majority of cases, where an adaptation of the production process appears necessary, however, the local firm is in charge of it, with limited assistance from its French counterpart. This gives further evidence on the necessary preliminary level of skill requested from the recipient in order to ensure a real transfer of knowledge.

In the majority of licensing agreement cases, French SMEs do not express the fear of helping to create a future competitor. When that risk is felt, the firm turns down the proposal or manages to form a joint venture instead. Such an absence of fear is sustained by the remoteness of the host countries in the cases under study; their markets seem out of the direct reach of the French firms. The feeling of security is also sometimes strengthened by the relative technological gap which persists, or is maintained, between the two partners. According to the French firm, such a gap is due both to the necessity to transfer only well-mastered and established technology for the sale of efficiency and the state of development of the host-country market. It must, however, be noted that the high level of skill of the foreign firm has, in several instances, given it the ability to grow level with its industrialised country partner, and the relationship could then evolve toward a more real partnership.

Evaluation

It would be extremely presumptuous to try to give an overall estimation of the results of technology transfers from the exclusive perspective of the French company. One must therefore keep in mind that only one aspect of the results of transfer of technology operations will be given here.

From the French SMEs' point of view it can be said, first, that successful operations actually exist; every survey of French corporations experienced in this field states that many firms declare themselves ready to engage in further operations on the grounds of their previous satisfactory experience.

More generally, French SMEs express mixed feelings about transfering technology to foreign firms. Not every venture can be said to have been a success. Problems can arise from several sides. For the French firms, first of all, some put the emphasis on their lack of specific resources. They cannot devote enough engineers' and managers' time to the operation. Hence, they do not pay frequent visits to the developing country's firms, nor host many missions from them. Links between partners may rapidly weaken after the relatively more intensive period of the initial transfer, and the agreement be put to sleep or on hold.

For the partner, specifically in the case of Korea, language and culture are often mentioned as major hindrances. The local partner is not always considered in isolation. The MRE/FIEE study states that French SMEs from the electric and electronic industries put great emphasis on the local industrial fabric and human resources. It is recognised that the level of capacity of the local partner will largely depend on its infrastructural environment. This kind of preoccupation may be more prominent from the point of view of SMEs which are not very integrated and know the importance of a tight fabric of suppliers and customers in their own domestic market. In the majority of situations, however, the technical skill level of the foreign firm is recognised and is said to play an important role in the success of the operation. Their level of competitiveness is rated as fairly good, helped sometimes by the international prestige drawn from a relationship with the French company. For Latin American host countries, administrative interference, mainly on financial matters, is always highlighted, but it does not seem to preclude any transfer of technology.

The last success factor relates to the local market. Transfers of technology are linked to the effective penetration of the developing country market by the products concerned. As the main motive for the transfers is commercial, success is measured by growth of final sales, which depend on the local economic situation. In recession periods, royalty flows dry up and disappointment grows from the French company is side. One can then see, from French SMEs' reaction to sales figures, that the commercial motives for technology transfers translate into a commercial yardstick of their outcome. No other type of impact on the French company has been ever mentioned, in particular no technological feedback has been experienced or expected, despite the not infrequent assertion that the foreign counterpart had reached a level of technological capacity which enabled it to make adjustments to the technology, and even to design some new products from it.

The focus on results and rewards, read from a commercial perspective, may also help to explain the country classification made by French SMEs and which does not significantly differ from the hierarchy established by multinational enterprises. It goes without saying that the attractiveness of the European market, and of the North American one for the most technologically advanced firms, predominates. Developing countries as a whole, come second. As far as they are concerned, a first level of distinction is made according to their national market size. India, China, Brazil and Mexico are thus singled out. A second level is slowly appearing now, which deals with export capacities. Korea, Brazil and also Mexico for its proximity to the United States, are mentioned as possible export bases for their respective geographic areas. For every other country, French firms have to be subjected to strong pressure from would-be partners before considering any operation. Many general campaigns designed to promote the establishment of technical or commercial relationships with countries outside this short list have been met with a total lack of interest from French SMEs, and large firms as well.

A Bilateral Industrial Cooperation Programme: The Case of APRODI

APRODI, the Association pour la Promotion et le Développement Industriel, is a private association jointly created in 1969 by the French Ministry of Industry, the permanent assembly of chambers of commerce and industry, the national council of employers (CNPF), and the national confederation of small and medium sized entreprises (CSPME). It has engaged since the mid-1970s in the promotion abroad of French companies, first through specific missions, then in 1984 permanent offices were opened in foreign countries to foster international business cooperation. The first offices were set up in Korea and Mexico, followed later by Spain and Portugal and, in 1988, by Haïti and Quebec as launching bases toward the North American market.

As far as Third World countries are concerned, Korea is at present the best working case. The French and Korean governments have jointly decided to set up a programme of transfer of technology between the two countries. The programme is implemented by APRODI in France and the Korean Small and Medium Industry Promotion Corporation (SMIPC). SMIPC is a rather large organisation with approximately 150 consulting engineers, several technical training centres, which manages a special industrial zone for SMEs near Seoul. It systematically monitors a nucleus of 9000 Korean SMEs, out of a total population of

30 000 and has selected a smaller group of 300 firms which constitute the 'Promising Companies' eligible for international cooperation. There is one APRODI staff member posted within SMIPC, who works with three Korean colleagues and benefits from the assistance of two members of the French cooperation services. A staff of two work in France for the programme.

APRODI, in France, is in charge of the identification and selection of partners on request by SMIPC as well as the transmission to SMIPC of demands from French firms looking for a Korean associate. It does not intervene in purely commercial operations and concentrates on agreements leading to local manufacturing with French technologies.

The first partnerships were initiated by Korean companies. On reception of a request, the French expert based in SMIPC goes to the Korean firm to help it define a detailed demand. Then the search for a partner may be started in France. In the beginning, APRODI relied mainly on information provided by industries federations; it has now built its own portfolio of contacts of more than 600 companies. Except in cases where it prepares a business trip by a representative of the Korean firm willing to choose himself a possible partner, APRODI singles out a unique candidate for its ability to meet the demand and its readiness to engage in a cooperative venture.

A second type of partnership starts with the exchange of information by the two companies and the preparation of a meeting. Each of them visits the other in its own country. Important efforts are devoted to cultural briefing and awareness-building at this stage. APRODI and SMIPC then take the would-be partners through negotiations and contracts up to the final signature of the deal.

French companies may either hire APRODI assistance and consulting services on a yearly subscription basis or pay on a case-by-case basis in two instalments, the first at the signature of the preliminary protocol and the second one at the conclusion of the definitive agreement.

Up to 1986 APRODI had participated in the establishment of 52 contracts, of which 13 were joint ventures and 12 licence agreements. Since 1984 half of the French FDI in Korea has been chanelled through joint ventures in which APRODI was involved.[20]

If, from the Korean side, the APRODI-SMIPC programme is devoted to the promotion of technology transfers to SMEs in relation to the SMIPC mandate APRODI does not restrict its interventions to French SMEs, in fact in only half of the cases the French partner which has been selected by APRODI was a SME.

Accumulated experience shows that mature technologies are the most likely to be transferred. Korean companies are looking more for products than for technologies *per se*. Price still supersedes quality or product sophistication on the Korean market which is generally singled out for the cooperative venture, and therefore the more traditional and well-established technologies of the French partner are eventually selected.

From the available, if rather limited, evidence it is possible to discern some characteristic features of French SMEs involved in transfer of technology to Asian and Latin American developing countries. First of all, they are often well established, medium-sized corporations with several decades of activity behind them. They have a good experience of the outside world through exports and foreign investment mainly to and in industrialised countries. They are leaders on some of their market segments in France, often through custom-made products for which narrow market segmentation exists. This implies, lastly, that they have a good technological capacity, based on relatively high R&D to sales ratio and a strong manufacturing and design know-how. They often face much bigger competitors, Japanese and US firms, on world markets and need to find some partners in order to expand their activities abroad. Their visibility on the French market and their size have attracted the interest of SMEs from developing countries willing to acquire technologies without falling into the grasp of large multinationals.

The weakest industrial infrastructure of many developing countries makes more difficult the introduction of an SME technology without any adaptation to a new more complex type of industrial environment; the absence therefore, of a strong local competition does not mean that developing countries can provide an easy ground for expansion for companies unable to stand the reinforcement of competition in their home market. On the contrary, a strong technological capacity is needed to penetrate the tougher environment of the Third World.

5.4 ALTERNATIVE INTERNATIONAL STRATEGIES FOR FRENCH SME AND POTENTIAL ROLE IN THE TRANSFER OF TECHNOLOGY

When dealing with the international transfer of technology, two aspects must be simultaneously taken into account, the internationalisation process in relation to national industrial policies and the role of technology within competitive strategies of firms.

Transnationalised Industries and National Industrial Systems

International operations of manufacturing SMEs, including exports, licensing and FDI, seem to follow two types of strategies.[21] The first is based on the successive penetration of national markets. Local partners or affiliates are given the task of occupying the biggest share possible of their domestic market, acting as agents for the mother company. The strategic rationale of each of the sister corporations is based on its adjustment to the specific characteristics of its country of incorporation. Some product and manufacturing process adaptation can hence, be undertaken in order to fit the local environment better.

The second strategy is adopted by more global, truly multinational corporations, operating within world-wide industries where international standards of products and processes predominate. These firms tend to organize their production on a world-wide basis with an international division of labour between specialised units. Local affiliates or partners act as workshops. Their output is not only sold on their national market but also exported to their broadest geographic area, Asia in the case of Korea, the United States for Mexico, possibly Latin America for Brazil.

French SMEs mainly follow the first option. It could be stated that their strategies can be characterised as traditional international strategies. They follow the same cycle of development as their larger counterparts, the MNEs, starting from a commercial perspective of national markets' penetration before entering more production-based strategies. Along their path of growth they would eventually reach the global stage of the real multinational, meaning that a successful SME is bound to evolve into a bigger MNE.

SMEs, as well as bigger firms, are faced in developing countries with a set of contradictions. On the one hand they operate in a given national environment, with its specific industrial structure. On the other hand, they are more and more subject to world-wide products and processes standards stemming from the pattern of operations of increasingly transnationalised industries. The two systems, the national and the transnational, work according to their own characteristics, their own rationale. Every industrial activity is located both in a national structure and in an increasingly transnationalised industrial environment; it can therefore be subject to contradicting mechanisms.

The present relationship of developing countries' SMEs with their French partners may help to illustrate such a situation. Developing countries are trying to acquire technologies from abroad and to adapt them to their domestic conditions of operation. The national rationale is therefore put forward. French SMEs are also ready to transfer their knowledge to the extent that its utilisation will be restricted to the host-country market. The national rationale therefore holds. The contradiction arises when the producer of technology has to engage more heavily in the innovation process which is made increasingly compulsory by its growing multinationalisation and international exposure. Firms have to enter transnational competition. The partner from the developing country is therefore, at risk, either of falling behind and experiencing a deepening technological lag, or trying to catch up. The catch-up strategy will imply an international involvement, to find inputs, equipment and external outlets, thus becoming a competitor to its supplier of technology. The latter would not accept this, and will either tighten the restrictive parts of the licensing agreements or reject any further partnership proposal.

Strategic Role of Technology

Companies are nowadays operating in a turbulent world. Stable traditional oligopolies are destabilised by the exacerbation of world-wide competition and by the irruption of newcomers, related to the introduction of new technologies.[22] In this new type of turbulent environment, acquisition and mastering of knowledge has become a major factor of competitiveness, R&D spending is increasing in order to keep pace with accelerating product life cycles. Publicity expenses are rocketing to ensure a fast introduction and rapid acceptance of new products. Management techniques are increasing in complexity and require growing amounts of information to be processed to define and implement quick-reacting strategies. Corporations have to be permanently on the move and cannot exploit so easily their previous rents under the protection of entry barriers built on economies of scale; flexible manufacturing techniques now allow cost efficient customisation practices.

With the introduction of new types of goods, industries boundaries are becoming blurred. Traditionally independent activities such as telecommunications and data processing or chemicals, pharmaceuticals, food processing and biotechnology are converging, even merging. Technologies and know-how are spreading horizontally across industries. Corporations continuously restructure and reorganise their scope of activities moving the borders of their industries and taking part in the permanent reclassification of competitors' categories and listings. Products themselves are taking more and more the form of complex systems, incorporating various devices bearing upon distinct technologies. Innovations subsequently appear more often at the component level, allowing a fast and continuous evolution of the final, systemic, good.

Large enterprises try therefore to design new organisational structures based on the networking of relatively small specialised units. These units can be put to work in parallel, to explore several products or market orientations simultaneously in order to select more rapidly the most promising one or to proceed at the same pace as the design and development by specialised teams of complementary elements to be eventually assembled into finished complex goods.

SMEs find new areas of activities as technological mavericks. They engage in contractual relationships with big companies which do not necessary intend to swallow them for fear of dismantling their generic form of operation and disbanding their teams of high-tech researchers. In such an environment a vast majority of Third World countries could find themselves in an awkward situation. They see their role as providers of raw materials or cheap labour force decreasing, in the face of the development of new materials substitutes, the introduction of more service-based goods and the generalisation of automated manufacturing processes. Only a small number of NICs can imitate the pace of the leaders, the others will be left for behind in the accelerating race for new technologies.

It would be extremely presumptuous to offer definitive solutions to such a contradiction. To conclude, I will thus only draw some lines of thought and discussion.

First of all, from the developing countries' standpoint, a shift of perspective from products to technologies could be favoured. Partners could be identified for their technological potentials rather than their product portfolios. In that case horizontal, transindustrial transfers could be privileged. Partners would not immediately appear as competitors or potential competitors on the end-products markets. Furthermore, faced with large MNEs eager to invest on their territory they could try to make a selection within the incoming candidates. With SMEs, the first question is to identify them in their country of origin, then select a local potential partner and try to bring them together. Such a policy requires the preliminary acquisition of screening capacities on a more minute level than when dealing with multinationals and implies a deeper form of cooperation between industrialised and developing countries' public administrations, as shown by the Franco–Korean industrial cooperation programme.

Secondly, a real kind of partnership could be developed. It should be a technological partnership in which each participant's share of R&D directed toward a common goal. It is striking to note that French SMEs never quote a technological spin-off from their technology transfers to developing countries. This implies that, from their point of view, the operation is not technology-driven. The transfer operation may therefore become marginalised if there is no commercial outcome from the venture. Cooperative R&D is obviously extremely difficult to organise between remote units. The development of fast and relatively cheap communication devices and channels could however, facilitate the establishment of strong links between research groups. It would, furthermore, break the relative isolation of developing countries' scientists and give them the opportunity to interact permanently with their colleagues elsewhere in the world.

The last consideration deals more with the specific situation of French SMEs. They are facing strong competition from other firms from developed countries, mainly the United States and Japan. The outcome of that competition will be the establishment of world-wide standards of products and processes. These standards will be set by the leading firms, resting on their national base of competitiveness strongly supported by their national governments. French corporations by themselves, like corporations from developing countries, cannot pretend to impose their own standards on transnationalised industries. Alliances are necessary in order to build real capacities to participate, at the world level, in the standard-setting process. The launch of huge European R&D programmes follow that kind of strategy. Developing countries could ask for some access to these programmes for their own firms. They could also try to convince French SMEs to engage with their own, into technological cooperation directed toward the design and development of innovative products, explicitly suited for specific utilisation in the developing countries themselves. These goods could find large markets in which they would escape from the present competition from world-wide standardised goods, more attuned to the environment of the industrialised countries in which they have been designed. SMEs may appear more suited to such a kind of venture, they may be more interested in the sometimes more limited domestic markets than larger, multinational, companies.

It must, however, be noted that governments in some instances may tend to favour big corporations as suppliers of technology. As we have previously mentioned, huge multinationals are more visible and are easier to identify than small very innovative firms. Moreover, French authorities themselves have often demonstrated a clear preference for the main national industrial groups over the smallest companies when selecting national participants to international cooperation programmes. SMEs are there considered weaker entreprises. It is feared that their lack of resources, staff and financial, could lead them to withdraw at the first obstacle, which would injure the reputation of the national industry as a whole. Security is preferred to risk by public authorities and this, again, leads to a selection of countries eligible for industrial cooperation on the sole basis of their attractiveness to the larger companies.

It is obvious that such policies in order to be implemented should be matched by specific sets of measures in the developed countries themselves; cooperation has to be sought and built at every level, public as well as private.

Notes

1. See CEDREI, *Alternative technology sources for developing countries: the role of small and medium-sized enterprises from industrialized countries.* Chap II (Buenos Aires), CEDREI, June 1986 (mimeo).
2. 'Special report on biotechnology', *The Economist* (30 April '92).
3. A preliminary attempt to delineate this paradox can be found in LAREA-CEREK, 'Les politiques d'industrialisation du Tiers-Monde face aux complexes industriels transnationalises', ATP du CNRS, 'Politiques et strategies de development dans le Tiers-Monde' (1986).
4. The French statistical apparatus distinguishes PMI – small and medium-sized industries – within the broader category of PME – small and medium-sized enterprises. The more detailed data avaiable deals with PMI.
5. Data from the Ministry of Industry and excluding agribusiness, housing, public contracting and energy, in SESSI, *L'etat des PMI* (Paris: Ministère de l'Industrie et de l'Arrangement du Territoire. La Documentation Française, 1988).
6. From Mackintosh Consultant France, quoted by A. Bucaille and B. Costa De Beauregard, *PMI, enjeux regionaux et internationaux* (Paris: Economica-CPE, 1987).
7. SESSI, *L'état des PMI.*
8. Cf C. Magaud, 'L'avenir de la politique de la Comaunauté Economique Européenne en matiere de science et de technologié', Rapport au Conseil Economique et Social, *Journal Officiel, Avis et Rapports du Conseil Economique et Social.* Session de 1988, séances des 26 et 27 Janvier 1988.
9. *Les petites et noyennes industries en 1981* (CEPKE, Paris: June 1981), in A. Bucaille and P. Costa de Beauregard.
10. See data collected by A. Pjallier, *L'innovation dans l'industrie: les enselignements* de quelques *enquetes* (CPE: Paris, 1984).
11. *Transnational corporations in world development. Trends and prospects* (New York: UN Centre on Transnational Corporations, 1986).

12. A. Weil, *Les transferts de technologie aux pays en développement par les petites et moyennes industries* (Paris: Ministére de l'Industrie, March 1980).

13. G.Y. Bertin, *Le transfort de technologie aux pays on développement par les petites et anyennes entreprises françaises* (Geneva: UNCTAD, 1986).

14. Marie-Pierre Subtil, 'La France et l'Asie Pacifique, Mieux vaut tard que jamois', *Le Monde* (20 Septembre 1989).

15. M. Delafierre and C.A. Michalet, *Les 'nouvelles formes d'investissement' dans les pays en dévelopment: le cas français*, Report for the OECE Development Centre (Paris, 1984) (mimeo).

16. See G.Y. Bertin, *Le transfert de technologie.*

17. The study was conducted by *HOCI* and published in its February 1982 issue.

18. H. Delacroix Saint-Cyr, *Le comportement des entreprises françaises du sectur électrique et electronique dans le domaine des transferts de technologie dans les pays en développement* (Paris: Ministère des Relations Extérieures/FIEE, June 1985) (mimeo).

19. One must, however, notice that if the host market is smaller than the French one, firms enjoying an equivalent dominant position on each of them will be of unequal size.

20. From interviews with APRODI. See also 'Les PMI au coeur de la coopération franco-coréenne', *Le Monde* (9 September 1988).

21. For a presentation of that typology see M. Delapierre and C.A. Michalet, *Les implantations étrangéres en France, Stratégies et structures* (Paris, Calmann-Lévy, 1976).

22. For a more elaborate presentation see M. Delapierre and L.K. Mytelka, 'Décomposition, recomposition des oligopoles', *Cahiers de l'ISMEA*, no. 11–12 (1988).

6 The Case of Germany

B. Nino Kumar and H. Steinmann

6.1 INTRODUCTION

The topic of this chapter is technology transfer by German small and medium-sized enterprises (SME.). In sections 6.1–6.3 we will attempt to give a short overview of the background. Two main themes are discussed in this context: (1) the extent of German technology transfer; (2) the official policy of the German government regarding technology transfer of SME to developing countries.

In order to be able to talk about technology transfer in a consistent manner and to be able to present figures, we need first to define the term. In the literature 'technology transfer' has been understood in various ways. The most commonly known meaning, which is also used here, refers to the exchange of tangible and non-tangible goods (technological hardware and technical and management know-how) within *equity* and *non-equity* forms of international cooperation. The value of technology transfer in the context of equity involvement is equivalent to the volume of *foreign direct investment* (FDI). This includes transfer of comprehensive property rights within long-term running businesses organised in the form of joint ventures or wholly-owned subsidiaries abroad. Based on property rights, this involvement implies direct influence and control of foreign subsidiary management.

The value of technology transfer in connection with non-equity cooperation is directly based on the worth of transferred know-how and technological hardware in the context of *contractual* cooperation. The main forms are: prospecting contracts, licensing and patent agreements, management and consulting contracts and coproduction (Oppenländer, 1985).

The figures available in Germany on the above two categories are aggregate data at the total industry level. The German Federal Bank (Deutsche Bundesbank) which computes and publishes these data provides no information according to size of firms by industry. It is therefore not possible to present a statistical picture of how SMEs in Germany are involved in technology transfer. However, some trends can be shown, based on various questionnaire surveys of international activities by German SMEs.

When we speak of SMEs a clear demarcation with large corporations must be made. Such delineations are always arbitrary in nature, depending on their purpose. It seems most useful for our study to draw the line based on an employment criterion and count only firms that have 50–1000 employees in the parent company as SMEs. This classification leaves out very small firms which most probably do not have any international potential anyway. On the other hand it excludes larger companies who behave differently based on resources, equity and other factors.

6.2   VOLUME OF TECHNOLOGY TRANSFER

With Equity Involvement: Direct Investments

FDI by German industry has been on the rise for more than a decade. After a rather long period of abstinence and reservation due to historical reasons (Kumar and Steinmann, 1978) German industry has only now made up its lag; Germany is currently a leading nation with large foreign industrial assets and activities.

As Table 6.1 shows, the total volume of German FDI was over DM 164 billion at the end of 1988. During the past four decades the major portion of the investment has been in developed countries. In recent years the balance has shifted even more in favor of industrialised countries, as one can easily see from Table 6.1. Out of all countries the United States has been the most attractive host nation to German investors and very high growth rates have been recorded.

Within developing countries Brazil has always been the leading recipient of German FDI. Recently there has been a negative trend, however, with quite a number of divestments which has meant that FDI stock has stagnated over the the last three years (Table 6.1). Among other developing countries included in this study Argentina and Mexico also have a substantial amount of German FDI. Latin America on the whole is the most attractive region outside Europe and North America for German industry. The main reasons for this seem to be the growing market prospects and the greater cultural affinity as compared to Asian or African countries.

As can be expected, investment in the secondary sector accounts for the major portion 7 total FDI, with the tertiary sector (services) coming up fast (table 6.2). Within the industrial sector, the chemical branch has traditionally been the leading investor. This top role can be ex-

Table 6.1   Volume of German FDI, by regions/countries, billion DM, 1983 and 1988

Region	1983	1988	
Total	101.6[a]	164.2	
All Developed countries:	75.50 (74%)	134.0	(82%) (+77%[b])
EC	30.8	51.6	(+68%[b])
USA	25.1	54.6	(+117%[b])
All developing countries:	26.10 (26%)	30.2	(18%) (+16%[b])
Argentina	1.56	2.08	(+33%[b])
Brazil	7.20	7.56	(+0.05%[b])
India	0.215	0.227	(+0.06%[b])
Korea	0.084	0.253	(+201%[b])
Mexico	1.45	2.179	(+50%[b])
Singapore	0.627	0.766	(+22%[b])

Notes:
[a] Figures are rounded up.
[b] Change over 1983.

Source: Compiled from past numbers of '*Runderlaß Außenwirtschaft*' (Bundeswirtschaftsministerium).

plained by various factors. For instance, because of historical and other reasons the German chemical industry has traditionally been very R&D-intensive (Kumar and Steinmann, 1978). This has shortened the life cycle of many chemical/pharmaceutical products on the one hand, and contributed to creating world-wide competitive advantage on the other. Both these processes are well known to correlate positively with FDI (Vernon, 1966; Hymer, 1976). The German electrical industry has followed a similar route and recently FDI by the automobile industry has also picked up, albeit for different reasons. The iron and steel industry could never compete with the leading branches, perhaps because of easier access to and faster standardisation of underlying technology, which reduced its international competitive advantage.

As elsewhere, FDI by German industry has traditionally been the domain of large corporations. The chemical and electrical industries are especially dominated by large companies; and firms like Bayer and Siemens set the pace in foreign investment as early as the turn of the century.

Direct investments by German small and medium-sized firms on a scale worth mentioning are a relatively recent phenomenon dating back to the mid-1970s. Although traditional concepts of FDI theory have

Table 6.2   Volume of German FDI, by important branches of industry, billion DM[a], 1983 and 1988

Branch	1983	1988
Total	101.6[b]	164.2
Industrial sector	72.6 (71%)	106.8 (65%)
Services	25.9 (25%)	50.9 (31%)
Others	3.1 (4%)	6.5 (4%)
Chemical industry	13.9 (19%)[a]	19.2
Eletrical	9.4 (13%)	14.3
Iron/Steel	5.9 (8%)	6.87
(Mech.) engineering	8.3 (11%)	11.0
Automobile/parts	8.8 (12%)	15.0

Notes:
[a] Change over 1983.
[b] Figures are rounded up.

Source: Compiled from past numbers of Runderlaß Außenwirtschaft (Bundeswirtschaftsministerium).

applied to the internationalisation of German SMEs, the accents have often been different. For instance, it has been shown that explicit trans-action costs and control motives as suggested by the internalisation concept apply less than considerations in connection with competitive advantage and oligopolistic reaction (Kumar, 1988).

As mentioned earlier, there are no specific micro-data available on German FDI according to firm size. Various studies conducted on a sample basis suggest that on the whole about one-quarter of the total volume of German FDI may be accountable by SMEs. Of course, some differences according to host country and branch of industry must be taken into consideration. The most common sector represented is mechanical engineering and machinery. Other prominent branches are electrical/electronic components, automotive accessories and precision tools. (Kumar, 1987; Berger and Uhlman 1984; Steinmann *et al.*, 1977).

Regionwise, SME have much the same pattern as German industry as a whole (Table 6.2). In the mid-seventies Brazil attracted a big number of small and medium-size subcontractors of large German firms who had settled in that country earlier in the decade in the wake of its import-substitution policy (Wasner, 1985).

Table 6.3   Income received for licences, patents and processes from abroad, by region, million DM and %, 1965–83

Region	1965	1973	1977	1983
All countries	301 (100)	576 (100)	778 (100)	1313 (100)
Industrialized countries	212 (70.4)	413 (71.7)	565 (72.6)	1128 (85.4)
Deveoping countries	83 (27.6)	146 (25.3)	142 (18.3)	128 (9.8)
Socialist countries	6 (2.0)	19 (3.3)	71 (9.1)	57 (4.3)

Source: Deutsche Bundesbank; Oppenlände, 1985.

Non-equity Involvement

Statistical data pertaining to different forms of non-equity contractual involvement is very sparse since there is no systematic registration required of such businesses. The only reliable indication of how much know-how German industry has transferred abroad on a contractual basis is in terms of *income* received for licences, patents and processes from outside the country.[1]

As we can see from Table 6.3, income from the industrialised countries makes up the major portion and their importance has risen since 1965. On the other hand, the relative role of developing countries has considerably diminished as compared to previous years. This finding suggests that developing countries are losing their relative share as recipients of German technology.

Looking at Table 6.4 we find that, as in the case of direct investment, the most important branch for German technology transfer is the chemical industry which accounts for almost 39 per cent of all income received from abroad.

The relative importance of this branch of industry is, however, bigger in the developing countries. The metal-producing and metal-working industries and the electrical sectors follow.

Table 6.4 Income received for licences, patents and processes from abroad, by main branch and region, million DM and %, 1983

Branches	Industrialized countries	Developing countries	Socialist countries	All countries
Chemical	431.3 (84.6) (38.2)	72.3 (14.2) (56.6)	5.9 (1.2) (10.4)	509.5 (100) (38.8)
Metalworking and metalproducing	331.7 (86.3) (29.4)	18.4 (4.8) (14.4)	34.3 (8.9) (60.2)	384.4 (100) (29.3)
Electrical/ Electronic	235.5 (88.1) (20.9)	21.6 (8.1) (16.9)	10.1 (3.8) (17.7)	267.2 (100) (20.3)
Precision tools/ optical, etc.	5.1 (68.9) (0.4)	0.1 (1.4) (0.1)	2.2 (29.7) (3.8)	7.4 (100) (0.6)
Food/ foodstuffs	22.6 (96.2) (2.0)	0.8 (3.4) (0.6)	0.1 (0.4) (0.2)	23.5 (100) (1.8)
Other manufacturing	32.6 (84.2) (2.9)	5.3 (13.7) (4.1)	0.8 (2.1) (1.4)	38.7 (100) (2.9)
Other sectors	69.6 (84.4) (6.2)	9.3 (11.3) (7.3)	3.6 (4.3) (6.3)	82.5 (100) (6.3)
Total	1128.4 (85.9) (100)	127.8 (9.7) (100)	57.0 (4.4) (100)	1313.2 (100) (100)

Source: Deutsche Bundesbank; Oppenländer, 1985.

Development Trends

According to a study by Ifo-Institute, German industry in the past has preferred direct investment to non-equity forms of cooperation. However, in the future the weight will most probably shift to the latter type of international involvement (Berger and Uhlman, 1984). In Figure 6.1 one can see that this change of preference is ascertained for investments in the industrialised and developing countries alike. In the latter, non-equity cooperation will be the dominant pattern.

As Table 6.5 shows, this trend towards more non-equity involvement in the future is somewhat stronger among smaller firms. Relatively more larger firms are keen to reduce cooperation with majority ownership in the future than smaller firms.

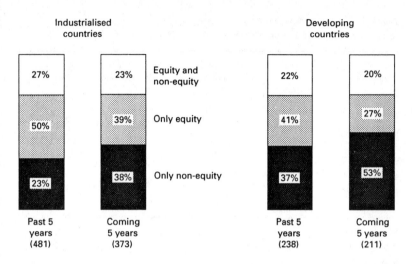

Figure 6.1   Perspectives of equity and non-equity international cooperation of German industry, 1983 (N = No. of responding firms), per cent of N

Source: Oppenländer (1985).

The general impression is that in the light of past experience both developing host countries as well as the cooperating firms from Germany have revised their preference for equity involvement. For both, there have been problems in the past resulting from collision of different interests. Future strategies will therefore aim to keep the stakes involved within limits so as to reduce conflict potential.

6.3   GERMAN GOVERNMENT POLICY OF TECHNOLOGY TRANSFER OF SME TO DEVELOPING COUNTRIES

General Policy

The general policy of the German government is to foster equity and non-equity cooperation between German firms, especially SMEs, and parties in the developing countries. To ensure this, a number of objectives are pursued: (1) promotion of competitiveness of German (small and medium-sized) firms in foreign markets; (2) growth of trade relations with developing countries; (3) support of the market economy in the third world; and (4) use of free enterprise as development agent (BMZ, 1985).

Table 6.5   Perspectives of equity and non-equity cooperation of German firms in developing countries, 1983 (N = 670)

Type of cooperation	During the past 5 years		In the coming 5 years	
	A	B	A	B
	(% of N)		(% of N)	
Pure licensing	7	19	9	17
Coproduction	6	9	9	10
Other non-equity	3	6	7	7
Equity:				
Up to 50 %	7	9	3	5
Over 50 %	2	8	1	3

Notes:
A = Firms with below 500 employees.
B = Firms over 500 employees.
(Sum does not add up to 100 % because of cooperation in other regions not shown here.)

Source: Berger and Uhlman (1984).

Special attention is given to the promotion of activity of German SMEs. Three main arguments serve as orientation for this focus (Kitterer *et al.*, 1983):

- *Promotional worthiness*: the activity of SMEs is seen to be more compatible with development goals and general conditions of the Third World than larger multinational enterprises (MNE)[2]
- *Promotional need*: SMEs have a greater deficit of resources needed for activity in developing countries than MNEs
- *Promotional possibility*: the State is in a better position to assist SMEs than MNEs.

Aid Framework and Programmes

Based on the above goals and considerations the German Federal Government has developed an extensive aid framework for German SMEs in their endeavor to establish equity and non-equity cooperation in Third World nations. The main feature of this framework is aimed at reducing *economic* and *political risk* through specific measures providing:

- Reliable *information* about potential host-countries
- *Management consultancy* on the situation in developing countries (including search for local partners)
- *financial* credit facilities at reasonable terms
- State *guarantees* and sponsorships
- *tax* reductions and exemptions.

The assistance that SMEs can expect varies according to the risk of involvement. Assistance is generally largest when smaller German firms venture into Least Less Developed Countries (LLDC).

Various measures are made available through different *aid-programmes*. One such provision is the so-called *'Subsidiary-Programme'* ('Niederlassungsprogramm'). The Federal Development Ministry (BMZ) grants financial credits to companies with an annual turnover of less than DM 200 million for the purpose of establishment, expansion or acquisition of subsidiaries in developing countries. Terms of credit are: 2.5 per cent p.a. for subsidiaries in LLDC and 3.5 per cent p.a. for activities in other developing countries payable for a maximum of 15 years. The maximum sum that can be granted per firm is DM 2.5 million. During 1985 a total sum of DM 30.7 million was provided to firms. For 1986 the sum was raised to DM 36 million (BMZ, 1985).[3]

6.4 METHODOLOGY

In this part of the paper the experience of German SMEs in carrying out technology transfer to developing countries is analysed. The analysis draws on our empirical study of 13 German SMEs that were identified (by CEDREI) as having technology transfer agreements with firms in Argentina, Brazil, India, Mexico, Singapore and South Korea (recipient countries). The firms were interviewed by the authors in spring/ summer 1988 on the basis of a questionnaire developed by CEDREI for administration to suppliers of technology.

Our sample includes a total of 20 cases of technology transfer, since some of the 13 firms had more than one operation in the recipient countries. The case data has been aggregated to present an overall picture. If and when variances between individual cases are of importance (for instance according to recipient countries), they will be pointed out.

Obviously, the sample may not suffice to give results representative of the total universe of German SMEs engaged in technology transfer operations overseas. Nevertheless, apart from giving a picture of the

Table 6.6　Size of German firms in the sample, 1988

No. of employees	No. of firms (N = 13)
50 – 250	4
251 – 500	6 (2)
501 – 750	3 (2)

Note:
( )-members of a group of companies.

sample, the results do have a heuristic function of generating hypotheses. The presentation and analysis of data is undertaken within the frame of reference which underlies the questionnaire.

6.5　CHARACTERISTICS OF THE TECHNOLOGY SUPPLIERS (SAMPLE FIRMS)

Some Basic Characteristics

Not all firms in our sample complied strictly speaking to our definition of SMEs. As Table 6.6 shows, all firms were compatible regarding number of employees, but not all were independent of the companies.

- Branchwise, the sample showed a clear concentration of firms in the *capital goods industry*, especially in the metalworking sector, e.g. machinery industry (6 out of 13), where German SMEs traditionally enjoy international comparative advantage. On the supply side the firms' markets were considered to be concentrated rather than competitive.
- *Specialization in market-niches*: out of 13 companies nine had made-to-order production with a high degree of flexibility for customers' individual needs.
- *Level of technology*: all firms considered their technological standards to be somewhat higher than the average domestic and international level.
- *R&D*: the majority of the SMEs examined had relatively high R&D expenditures. Out of the 13 firms 11 had been able to register their own patents in the past 5 years (Table 6.7 and 6.8).
- *Goals and objectives*: most firms (nine out of 13) in the sample were growth-oriented, with a 5–10 per cent increase in sales vol-

Table 6.7   Intensity of R&D Activity, 1987

Ratio of R&D to sales (%)	No. of firms (N = 13)
Up to 3	5
3 – 6	5
More than 6	4
Not available	3

Table 6.8   No. of registered patents in the last 5 years, by firm size, 1987

Size (employees)	0	No. of patents 1 – 3	4 – 10	above 10	Total (N = 13)[a]
below 250		3	1		4
251 – 500	2		2 (1)	1	5
501 – 750		1 (1)		2 (1)	3

Note:
[a] 1 missing.

ume in the past 5 years. This level exceeds the average growth rates of German industry.
• *Size of firms*: within the range of SMEs examined, firms were on the larger side.
• *Export performance*: all companies had export ratios of over 40 per cent of total sales, 5 firms had more than 60 per cent.

Summarising, SMEs in the sample basically belong to the metalworking industry and have a specialised product programme catering for market niches. There is an indication that this competitive advantage is based on R&D which relative to SMEs in general is quite developed, even though somewhat haphazardly organised. Furthermore, these SME are by and large growth-oriented and can generally back on export experience when going in for direct investment or non-equity technology transfer. These characteristics suggest a considerable internationalisation potential of the SMEs in the sample.[4]

International Disposition and Orientation

With the above-mentioned corporate background we can expect the firms in the sample to show a substantial disposition towards more intensive modes of foreign activity than mere exportation, including for example, different forms of technology transfer. We have some indication of our expectations regarding their international orientation. For instance in terms of the *duration* of possible international involvement more than half of the firms examined had started operations prior to 1975.

International disposition is also demonstrated by the fact that in the majority of responding firms (11 out of 13), as well as recorded cases (12 out of 20), foreign technology transfer involvements were based on *self-initiative*. In the remaining few firms and cases (two and eight) proposals from outside (customers, clients, etc.) were responsible for the decision to look abroad. This somewhat defensive attitude was justified by the respondents on grounds of lack of information and general scarcity of resources.

In line with the general growth objectives of German SMEs in the sample as reported earlier, the main driving force behind the initiative to look abroad in terms of technology transfer were potential growth prospects, together with profit expectations (in nine out of 20 cases). Other motives mentioned in the literature, such as defending existing markets, risk diversification, availability of government incentives or taking advantage of lower production costs abroad did not play significant role. One may say that responding German SMEs by and large demonstrated an orientation which could be characterised as rather 'aggressive'. This disposition is known to facilitate expansion overseas (Aharoni, 1966).

Corresponding to this 'aggressive' disposition of the SMEs is their risk-taking behaviour as demonstrated by two phenomena: first, most firms (eight out of 13) had begun their operations abroad with equity forms of technology transfer. Given the scarce resources of SMEs one would have rather expected an incremental approach in developing the activity by starting off with less risky non-equity forms and gradually increasing commitment as market knowledge is gained (Johanson and Vahlne, 1977). Apparently, the firms were open minded and confident enough towards international activity to risk an intensive involvement abroad right away. Many firms had in fact preferred to take an opposite path than what might be expected from the risk standpoint: they began first with equity ventures and continued in later stages with non-equity forms.

The second observation in this respect is that most firms in the sample (seven out of 13) had begun their first foreign operations in developing countries rather than in familiar developed countries. Remarkably,

Table 6.9 Choice of organisational form of technology transfer, by host country, 1987

| Country/ Form | Non-equity: technology agreement only (e.g. licensing) (N = 10) | Equity involvement | | Total |
		Minority joint venture N = 8	Wholly-owned subsidiaries N = 2	(N = 20)
Brazil	2	3	2	7
South Korea	5	1	–	6
Mexico	–	2	–	2
India	1	1	–	2
Argentina	2	–	–	2
Singapore	–	1	–	1

those SMEs that did begin first in developed countries were the larger ones in the sample. Apparently, the smaller firms are less risk-averse and also somewhat more predisposed (flexible) towards activity in developing countries.

These few indicators give us the idea that the German SMEs in our sample have by and large an international orientation: this is an important corporate characteristic that will enable us later to explain the technology transfer process.

6.6 THE ORGANISATIONAL FORMS OF TECHNOLOGY TRANSFER AND THEIR DETERMINANTS

The first phase of the technology transfer process refers to the choice of form of involvement regarding equity or non-equity operations. Table 6.9 shows the pattern that was established among the sample firms. We can see that both organisational forms, i.e. non-equity and equity cooperation, are equally present (10 each). Only with regard to the recipient country was there an uneven distribution. In the Brazilian sample firms with equity participation dominate, whereas among the firms engaged in Korea non-equity forms are in a majority. Most of the equity operations in the sample are in minority joint venture form, with only 2 firms having wholly-owned subsidiaries in Brazil.

As shown in Table 6.10, most of the Brazilian operations date back to the years 1971–5, when direct investments in that host country were

Table 6.10   Year of first technology transfer, by host country

Country	Year of operations began 1971–5	1976–80	1981–5	Since 1986	Total (N = 20)
		(No. of cases)			
Brazil	5	1	1	–	7
Korea	–	1	4	1	6
Mexico	1	–	1	–	2
India	–	–	1	1	2
Argentina	–	1	1	–	2
Singapore	–	–	1	–	1

strongly propagated (Wasner, 1985). On the other hand Korean and most other operations are relatively recent, since there has been a shift of preference in both German industry and the host countries from equity to non-equity forms of technology transfer.

Our sample shows that among the 10 equity operations eight were *greenfield ventures*; only in 2 cases in Brazil were investments made in existing companies. This pattern incidently seems typical of the international operations of German SMEs elsewhere, where for various reasons preference is given to new establishments instead of acquisitions (Kumar, 1987; Steinmann *et al.*, 1977).

According to our framework we can assume that the choice of the organisational form of technology transfer is influenced by relevant corporate characteristics. The main connection found in our sample is between what we have previously called international orientation of the firms and their choice of organisational form (see Table 6.11).

Very clearly most of the respondents who were growth-oriented preferred to choose equity forms of technology transfer. Since half of the cases with equity participation in our sample are situated in Brazil (Table 6.9), there is a strong influence of prospects in this particular market on choice of organisational form. Obviously, the factor of *control* underlying equity participation is seen as a necessary condition for achievement of growth goals. Nonetheless, most technology suppliers did not insist on full control. On the contrary, many firms themselves stressed the advantages of minority joint ventures in the recipient countries (e.g. because of a lack of local market knowledge).

As can be further seen from Table 6.11, in all eight cases where respondents were pushed to look abroad by outside proposals (e.g. by foreign customers), non-equity organisational forms of technology transfer

Table 6.11　International motivation and choice of organisational form

Indicator of international orientations: driving force to go abroad	Equity arrangements		Non-equity forms	Total
	Wholly-owned (No. of cases) (N = 10)	Joint ventures	E.g. licensing, contracts (No. of cases) (N = 10)	(N = 20)
Growth and profit prospects	1	6	2	9
Attractive proposal from outside the firm	–	–	8	8
Others	1	2	–	3

(e.g. licensing) were selected. The main factor underlying this connection according to the respondents was the relatively low risk attached to this type of involvement. Whenever firms themselves did not take any initiative to scout abroad, they felt neither capable nor keen to go in for high-risk strategies. Furthermore, non-equity arrangements were generally accompanied by relatively liberal agreements, for instance the freedom to sell identical products to third parties in the same host country.

There also seems to be a relationship between *age* of established operations and choice of organisational form. The older operations are more organised as equity forms, the recent ones as non-equity ventures. This connection is especially to be seen in the context of past industrialisation policies in Brazil and the influx of FDI to that country on one side, and recent Korean economic development and the general shift of preference to non-equity cooperations among German SMEs on the other.

Apart from the above-mentioned factors there does not seem to be any evidence in the sample that other corporate characteristics such as R&D activities, product lines or export sales had any notable impact on choice of organisational form of technology.

Table 6.12   Previous relationship with partner, by form of involvement

Form of technology transfer	Previous relationship (No. of cases)		(Total) (N = 18[a])
	Yes	*No*	
Non-equity (e.g. licensing)	4	6	10
Equity: Joint ventures	1	7	8

Note:
[a] No. of cases with partnerships (i.e. excluding 2 cases of wholly-owned recipients)

6.7   IMPLEMENTATION OF TECHNOLOGY TRANSFER

How Prepared are SMEs for Implementing Technology Transfer Projects?

Because of systemic weaknesses like lack of international experience and information, scarcity of qualified personnel and so on, SMEs generally find implementing their foreign projects a difficult task (Braun, 1983). The problems to be solved require a certain amount of familiarity with the environment and issues of the project. Firms which have had the chance to get themselves acquainted beforehand will find implementing the project easier. So before we analyse the implementation phase of the technology transfer process, we will briefly discuss how prepared German SMEs in our sample were for their ventures abroad. We have indication for this in connection with three issues.

First, we can assume that *previous relationships* with local partners give the SMEs opportunity to get acquainted with the problems to be solved. As shown in Table 6.12, in most cases (13) where SMEs chose forms of partnership (i.e. all organisational forms of technology transfer except fully-owned subsidiaries) there had been no previous relationships with the eventual partner. In cases of non-equity cooperation there had been relatively more previous contacts than in cases where SMEs went in for joint ventures. As mentioned earlier, non-equity cooperations in our sample had generally been 'triggered off' by outside proposals which apparently came from acquainted parties who later became partners in the ventures.

Out of the seven cases where SMEs established joint ventures without previous contacts, five had to search for their partners themselves after they had decided to invest. In the remaining two cases the German SMEs were approached by local firms not known to them until that point. In all cases the most important criteria for selection of the partner were its experience and reputation in the local market. Mutual respect and the fact that the potential partner had prior experience with a German collaboration were also factors which were mentioned as important for partner choice. So, summarising, we can see that SMEs in most cases could hardly count on previous relationships with partners for assistance while building up technology transfer ventures abroad.

Second, SMEs have generally had the opportunity to prepare themselves for foreign operations by getting assistance from government and private agencies. In Germany and in most recipient countries there are several Federal and State aid programmes specially designed for SMEs' direct investments abroad. Further, most banks, consultants and Chambers also offer assistance. However, as our findings show, in none of the 10 cases in our sample of equity operations abroad did the SMEs avail themselves of any concrete government or private assistance. In one or two cases the firms just sought some *general information* from consultants, banks and the Chamber of Commerce.

These results are quite representative of the general picture among German SMEs, who are either unaware of various aid programmes or hesitate to use them because they fear the administration involved (Kumar and Steinmann, 1985). Furthermore, the experience which German SMEs have had with government programmes has not always been good (Kayser *et al.*, 1981).

On the other hand, as our findings show, SMEs in our sample have always approached recipient-country agencies for support in settling down there. But only in two cases was the assistance obtained worth mentioning: a machinery joint venture in Singapore was given 'pioneer status' which meant receiving tax exemption for 5 years. A wholly-owned manufacturer of machinery in Brazil also obtained tax reductions.

Third, there is evidence from other studies that *export activities* in a country prior to establishment of local operations there are helpful in getting acquainted with the environment and therefore getting prepared for implementation of technology transfer (Aharoni 1966; Steinmann *et al.*, 1977). Although most SMEs in our sample are generally export-oriented, only in one case did exports to the potential recipient country exceed 5 per cent of annual output. In most cases the export volume was below 5 per cent. In fact in seven cases there were no

Table 6.13   Category of technology resources transferred

Resources	No. of cases (N = 20)[a]	
Foreign exchange	3	
		(equity
Capital goods	6	ventures)
Technology (intangible know-how, etc.)	20	(equity and non-equity ventures)

Note:
[a] Sum greater than *N* (multiple answers).

exports to the particular recipient countries prior to establishment of local operations at all. This is surprising since a step-by-step approach is usually practised and propagated, especially for SMEs in order to benefit from learning effects and keep down risk (Steinmann *et al.*, 1977). The relatively minor importance of export activities in the recipient countries in most cases can also be seen from the fact that in only seven cases did SMEs maintain their own sales representatives or sales offices there. In the other cases, exports were organised directly from the home office.

Summarising all three points we can conclude that most German SMEs in the sample were not well prepared for implementing their technology transfer operations in the developing countries. This statement is also supported by the finding that in 14 out of the 20 cases no systematic market survey or formal feasibility studies were reported prior to the establishment of operations in the respective countries.

Content and Mechanism of Technology Transfer

At the beginning of the implementation phase the relevant issue is *what* should be transferred within the frame of the organisational form, and *how*. Table 6.13 shows that in all cases technology in the form of know-how was considered to be the most important resource for transfer. Foreign exchange and capital goods were imported by SMEs involved in equity transfer; intangible technology was transferred within both equity and non-equity deals.

Looking at the content of transferred intangible technology in detail, three main elements are relevant (Table 6.14): *plant design technology* (layout, building, infrastructure, etc.), *process know-how* (organisation of production line, planning of material flow, quality control, etc.) and

Table 6.14   Nature of know-how transferred, by organisational form

Elements of know-how	Non-equity: e.g. licensing (No. of cases)	Joint ventures	Equity: Wholly-owned subsidiary	Total (N = 20)[a]
	Organisational form			
		(No. of cases)		
Plant design technology	1	2	2	5
Process technology	6	8	2	16
Product technology	10	8	2	20

Note:
[a] Sum greater than *N* (multiple answers).

product technology (choice of materials, product design, new product know-how, etc.). Looking at the results according to the organisational forms there is confirmation that wholly-owned subsidiaries are the most comprehensive form of technology transfer, combining all three elements.

A question closely related to technology content is through what *mechanism* are the elements under consideration transferred. Here focus is on the medium of transfer. By far the most important one used by German SMEs in the sample are blueprints, drawings, designs and technical assistance (Table 6.15). The use of special equipment as a transfer medium in more equity ventures than in non-equity is compatible with the higher capital goods export in the former. The export of 'critical parts' was pertinent only in cases relating to ventures in Brazil (equity) and in Korea (non-equity). In both instances, the main purpose was to upgrade quality and reliability of local production.

Our findings show that the single most important mechanism is 'technical assistance' in the form of training of personnel, training programmes, personal assistance in assembly, etc. This is a clear indication that both the German suppliers and recipients of technology see personal transfer through which human capital endowment can be improved as the basic element of the transfer process.

The main mode of technical assistance followed was training key employees of the recipient firm. In most case, training was conducted in the supplier's company in Germany followed by assigning supplier

Table 6.15   Mechanism of know-how transfer, by form of involvement

Mechanisms	Organisational form			
	Non-equity:	Equity:		
	e.g. licensing (no. of cases)	Joint ventures	Wholly-owned subsidiary	Total
	(N = 10)	(no. of cases)	(N = 10)	(N = 20)[a]
Blueprints/ drawing/designs	10	8	2	20
Technical assistance	9	8	2	19
Special equipment	2	4	–	6
Exports of 'critical' parts	4	2	2	8

Note:
[a] Sum greater than *N* (multiple answers).

Table 6.16   Location of technical training of recipient firm's employees by form of involvement

Location	Organisational form			
	Non-equity: e.g. licensing (no. of cases) (N = 10)	Equity:		
		Joint venture	Wholly-owned subsidiary	
		(no. of cases) (N = 10)		Total (N = 20)[a]
At the recipient's firm	5	3	2	10
At the parent company	6	8	2	16

Note:
[a] Sum greater than *N* (multiple answers).

company expatriates abroad (Table 6.16). Practise of these modes was independent of the form of involvement, although joint ventures had a relatively greater tendency to use training in the parent company. Smaller firms preferred training in the parent company, whereas larger firms used both locations evenly.

Table 6.17   How modern is installed technology in affiliate?

Organisa-tional Form	How modern vis-a-vis home plant?				
	equal (less than 2 years behind)	2–4 years behind	5–10 years behind	more than 10 years behind	Total (N = 20)
	(no. of cases)				
Wholly-owned subsidiary	–	1	–	1	2
Joint venture	2	3	3	–	8
Pure licensing	3	4	3	3	10

Standardisation and Adaptation of Transferred Technology

Another basic question with which firms are faced while implementing technology transfer overseas is whether technology should be adapted to local conditions or be left standardised according to parent-company norms and practises.

Large MNCs have in the past often been criticised in connection with transfer of inappropriate technology which is capital-intensive, too big, and highly automated, to name only a few points (Kumar, 1982). On the other hand, SMEs are considered to be more flexible regarding adaptation of technology as and when required by recipient countries. In the following we shall discuss this issue in context, with the SMEs in our sample. To assess the adaptation issue, responding firms were asked to compare installed and transferred technology in recipient firms to technological standards in the home plant.

In most cases, responding SMEs felt that the overall general level of installed technology found in host-country companies as well as in the affiliates in the developing countries was obsolete and unmodern as compared to the technology in the home plant (Table 6.17). But mostly they expressed the opinion that it was adequate and adapted to local requirements. By and large there was no difference in this view with respect to the organisational form of the operations.

On the other hand, technology that was transferred by the German SMEs was considered by most respondents to be modern and similar (standardised) to the home-country level. This was the case with the transferred production and factory equipment as well as with products and product design.

In the small number of cases (four out of 20) where production and

Table 6.18   Size differential between recipient firm and German partner

Extent of differential in physical output	No. of cases (N = 20)
2–4 times smaller	4
5–9 times smaller	6
More than 9 times smaller	3
Not known to respondents	7

factory equipment was considered adapted, three factors were mainly seen to be responsible.

First, the size of the *production runs* in these particular recipient firms was much smaller than in the parent country (Table 6.18).

Second, in all four cases equipment was adapted to *lower labour costs* in the recipient country. This had mainly led to a lowering of the degree of mechanisation.

Third, in connection with all four cases respondents reported adaptation of equipment to a *greater degree of vertical integration* in foreign affiliates (Table 6.19). All the corresponding recipient firms were compelled by scarcity of good local suppliers to produce more components of the end product themselves than was the case in the German parent company. As a consequence, more and different plant equipment had to be installed.

Regarding product and product design, our findings show that in the majority of cases (15 out of 19, 1 is missing) similar or even very similar technologies were preferred. In connection with these 15 cases all respondents borrowed standard technology from the parent company and avoided adaptation as far as possible. The respondents were generally of the opinion that recipients basically wanted original products. As a matter of fact, in most cases only original products without modifications were considered competitive on local markets.

In the few cases where adaptation was undertaken, it was done because of local materials and components. For instance, a manufacturer of brake and clutch linings was using asbestos in its joint venture in India as a lining material. This was quite in line with local practice but very different from Germany where asbestos was forbidden by law. Specific demand requirements and climatic conditions were also mentioned as influencing factors for modification of product and product design.

Interestingly, in all cases where adaptations were reported, *made-to-order production prevailed.* On the other hand, where product stand-

Table 6.19 Comparison of vertical integration, supplier and recipient firm

Comparison	No. of cases (N = 20)
Greater at home	3
About the same	10
Smaller at home	5
Not known	2

ardisation was practised the recipient firms catered for the anonymous market. This is also an indication that local markets by and large preferred original product design.

Summarising the results, we find what at first sight might seem to be contradictory practice on part of German SMEs. On one side the general standard of technology in the recipient firms in most cases is perceived as unmodern and lagging behind the home level, however it is considered as being adequate according to local conditions. On the other hand the equipment and products transferred to the recipient firms are not adapted, but rather similar and standardised to parent-company norms.

This pattern suggests that German SMEs are not particularly keen and/or capable of modifying transferred technology to developing countries. Unfortunately, in most cases they apparently also do not seem to get much support from their local partners in solving this problem; they generally insist on getting the most modern technology, even though it may not be suitable to local conditions.

Supplier–Recipient Relationship in the Operation Phase

Parent companies require suitable mechanisms to control operations with respect to standardisation and adaptation strategies in their foreign operations. In previous studies several modes of control have been suggested and also found to be pertinent in practice. For instance short- and long-term exchange of staff between parent and foreign subsidiary has been generally found to be a good method to diffuse central policies and philosophy among local employees, and hence to enforce standardisation (Steinmann and Kumar, 1984).

Looking at our findings, we see that the *long-term assignment* of parent-company expatriates in the recipient firms was quite rare (only in four out of 20 cases). Among these four cases there were two joint ventures in Brazil, one a manufacturer of foundry auxiliary materials,

Table 6.20   Short-term exchange of staff

Direction of exchange	Frequency of exchange (no. of firms: N = 20)		
	None	*Once a year*	*1–2 times annually*
Parent-company staff in recipient firms	6	4	10
Local personnel of recipient firms in supplier companies[a]	6	6	8

Note:
[a] In 2 cases, visiting had not yet begun.

the other of industrial pumps who employed German engineers. One joint venture producing knitting and crocheting needles in Mexico had a German plant manager and finally one non-entity operation in Brazil employed about 10 German engineers and managers. All four were among those ventures which were using more standardised production equipment and product design rather than adapted technology.

Astonishingly, there was no German staff assigned to the two fully-owned subsidiaries in Brazil. This could, of course, be connected with the fact that both Brazilian subsidiaries had enough time to train local staff according to central policies. On the other hand our findings with respect to adaptation of transferred technology showed that these two Brazilian subsidiaries were among those few operations which were using adapted production equipment rather than standardised technology.

As far as short-term exchange of staff between supplier and recipient company is concerned, we see (Table 6.20) in most cases that there was a mutual exchange of staff. We also find that visiting was common among those cases where standardised equipment and product design prevailed. This may be a hint that exchange of visits increases influence of supplier firms in recipient firms.

Another important way for parent companies as suppliers of technology to maintain their influence in the recipient firms is to continually *reinforce technology transfer* with new content. The initial technology package is usually not sufficient to keep up bargaining power *vis-à-vis* the recipient firm for a long period of time. Reinforcement strategy has been found to be especially effective in joint ventures (Kumar, 1975).

Our findings in this respect show (Table 6.21) that in most cases

Table 6.21   Technological assistance to recipient firm after start-up of operations, by form of involvement

Type of assistance given	Wholly-owned subsidiaries	Joint ventures	Non-equity: Licensing	Total (N = 20)
		(No. of cases)		
No assistance at all	–	–	4	4 N = 16ᵃ
Process engineering	1	8	4	13
New designs (products)	1	6	3	10
Quality control	1	6	2	9
Management/ Organisation	1	8	1	9

Note:
ᵃ Sum > *N*, multiple responses.

(16 out of 20) assistance was given even after start-up of operations. We have no information as to how long afterwards assistance was offered. But we can assume that it was partly assistance in the initial stage in order to facilitate start-up, partly assistance at a later stage in order to update technology.

The most frequent technological assistance given was in the field of process engineering followed by new product designs. All joint ventures and wholly-owned subsidiaries had been given further technological assistance. In all four cases where no new transfer was granted this referred to non-equity ventures. In three of the latter cases involving licensing arrangements in the field of resistor units, switch gear cabinets and chemical products further technology transfer was considered economically unfeasible in the light of their limited involvement. In the fourth case (referring to a Korean licencee in the machine-tool sector) further support was denied by the German supplier because of 'unfair behaviour of the recipient' in passing over know-how to unauthorised parties.

None of these four firms belonged to the category of suppliers that had indicated adaptation in production equipment and product design *vis-à-vis* standardisation. This gives a hint that in these cases the *initial* technology transferred sufficed to exercise continuous influence needed for standardization. Reinforcement of technology transfer does

Table 6.22 Exports to recipient country since start-up of operations, by size of the German SME

| Trend of exports | Size of supplier (employees) | | | |
	Up to 250	*251 to 500*	*501 to 700*	*Total (N = 20)*
Increased	–	1	2	3
Decreased	2	1	–	3
No change	3	8	2	13
Not available	1	–	–	1

not seem to be very important among these German SMEs as a mechanism for controlling operations in recipient firms.

A further mode to maintain scope of standardisation in the recipient firms is through *intersubsidiary exchange* of components and materials. Intensive transactions undoubtedly enhancing the potential of unifying operations across borders are in themselves an indication here (Kumar, 1987).

According to our interviews trade of finished products and parts (as an indicator of interchange) between supplier and recipient firms on the whole remained unchanged after the beginning of operations in the latter companies. As Table 6.22 shows, exports from supplier firm to the recipient country[5] remained on the whole constant. In three cases, reports dropped to nil. All these recipient firms were organised as joint ventures and the German suppliers belonged to the smaller companies in the sample. But there were also three cases with significant export increases. These involvements were all arm's length technology agreements with Korean firms where the German suppliers belonged to the largest companies in the sample. On the other hand, imports from recipient firms were in most cases of no importance. Only in two cases (out of 20) did supplier firms import goods from recipient companies. Regarding the role of intersubsidiary trade as a control mechanism we have an indication that all supplier companies where exports had increased and where imports had begun belonged to the category of firms that had similar production equipment and product design in their recipient companies. The preparedness of supplier companies to import from recipient firms especially gave the former an influence over the latters' technology and production.

Finally, the most direct method to influence operations of foreign subsidiaries is through control of their annual *budgets and plans*. According to our interviews, in nine out of 10 cases with equity participation, supplier firms admitted that budgets and plans of their joint ventures and wholly-owned subsidiaries had to get their consent. Two of these instances belonged to the group of four cases where adaptation in production equipment was practised and one to the group of four where product modification was undertaken. The rest belonged to the category where technology in the recipient firms was standardised, which indicates that there may be some influence exerted through annual budgets.

This analysis has shown that in most cases the German SMEs in the sample maintained relationships to their recipient firms which allowed them to exert some influence on their activity. Although assignment of expatriate personnel is not practised in most cases (probably because of personnel shortage), it is a strong means to enforce standardisation of technology. Direct influence through control of annual budgets is also a mode which German SMEs adhere to. On the other hand, securing influence through continuous technology transfer and through intersubsidiary trade are less important, perhaps because these modes are less developed among the sample firms.

Technology Agreement

According to our interviews and also previous studies (e.g. Kumar, 1975), German SMEs with international experience generally place two requirements on technology agreements: (1) the terms and conditions should safeguard their interests; (2) the administrative procedures in setting the contract should not put strain on their resource. We shall now look into these issues.

First, the terms and conditions of the agreement must allow for *long-term participation and protection* of interests on foreign markets. All technology transfer projects, even if they are on an arm's length basis, must be treated as an integral part of the total business of the technology supplier and, as such, given a specific role to play within its total activities with respect to product programme, profits, market share and so on. It seems that this issue is especially crucial for SMEs since they do not possess many foreign operations – on the average only one or two – and therefore each one takes a prominent place and has an important contribution to make.

In our sample, technology agreements with partners had been made in 18 cases (out of 20; in the remaining two cases no formal agreements were laid down since these were wholly-owned ventures). Table 6.23 shows on what issues agreements were made. As might be

Table 6.23 Issues of technology agreement, by type of technology involvement

Issue	Non-equity: locally-owned licensee etc.	Equity: joint ventures	Total (N = 18)[a]
	(No. of cases)		
	(N = 10)	(N = 8)	
Patents	2	1	3
Trademarks	3	6	9
Know-how	10	8	18
Technical assistance	7	5	12

Notes:

N = Excluding 2 wholly-owned subsidiaries.

[a] Sum > N, multiple responses.

expected, basic know-how was the object of agreement in every one of the 18 contracts. On this basis, the suppliers were able to make themselves indispensible and therefore laid good foundations for long-term cooperation and presence on the market. In all 18 cases recipient firms were free by contract to improve or to modify the received technology. However, as we have seen previously, supplier firms have a certain control over the recipients so that changes in know-how and technology were almost always subject to careful examination in order to avoid incidents of inferior quality that might prove harmful to suppliers' reputation.

The fact that agreements on *trademarks* played a greater role in joint ventures than in non-equity ventures indicates the stronger perceived need of German supplier firms to put clear limitations *vis-à-vis* equity partners. Apparently the fear that trademarks would be misused was greater in joint ventures than in non-equity cooperations.

Other points in the technology agreement through which German SMEs establish and protect their long-term interests in the recipient markets are *duration* and *geographical scope* of activity. Half of the contracts were laid down for 5 years (nine cases), in two cases (comprising a manufacturer of household-cleaning products and a manufacturer of pumps) the duration was 10 years. Further in seven (out of 18) cases there was no time limitation, the period of cooperation was open. Here we see that these companies followed long-term interests in capturing a foothold in the respective markets. In most of the cases where contracts were limited, a renewal of the agreement had not been considered as yet. In the sample there was only one case where the agreement had been renewed in order to update supplied technology. Another firm had applied for renewal of its contract in Brazil, but was denied this by the Brazilian government. All together, German SMEs give the impression that with the contracted duration they are interested in securing a long-term foothold in the local and regional market. In fact in only a single case, that of a manufacturer of switch gear cabinets with a licensee in Argentina, did the respondent clearly desire withdrawal due to bad economic conditions.

Many previous studies have reported conflict between cooperation partners with respect to exports to third country markets (Kumar, 1975). Local partners at times wish to supply to regional markets (sometimes due to the pressure of the local government to increase exports), whereas the foreign technology supplier firm often controls these particular markets within its global strategy from the parent company (or other foreign units). Such conflicts can be avoided by fixing the geographical scope of recipient firms by contract. In our sample, this was done so in 16 out of 18 cases, whereby in five of these cases the scope was restricted to the local market only; and in 11 cases limitations applied to a number of specified regional areas. For instance, most of the licensees in Latin America were allowed to export to specified countries in this region or within the whole continent. In the case of an Argentinian and Brazilian licensee, in fact, exclusive representation for Latin America was granted. In one joint venture in Latin America there existed two agreements on this item: an official contract without any export restrictions, and an unofficial one in which the partners had decided on the restrictions among themselves.

All of the five cases with limitation to local markets were non-equity arm's length technology agreements, three of them in Korea, are one each in India and Brazil. Apparently the size of the local markets justified the limitation. The Korean partners were rated as technologically quite developed, which could create a 'threat of soliciting in unauthorised markets'.

A further point in the technology agreement which helps to bind the recipient firms' activities to the total perspective of the supplier's business is the clause regarding sales of components to the former. In 16 out 18 cases such purchases were fixed by contract. In most cases, the main motive was to deliver components not available at all or in the desired quality in the recipient country. In this way, the recipient firm was dependent on the technology supplier who could thus also follow 'world-wide standard' product and quality strategies.

Table 6.24 Form of payment laid down in technology agreement, by form of organisation

Form of payment	Non-equity: licensing (N = 10)	Equity: joint ventures (N = 8)	Total (N = 18)[a]
Solely as percentage of sales	4	5	9
Lump-sum and percentage of sales	3	2	5
Payment included in price of components	3	–	3
Man-hours	1	1	2
Information not available	–	1	1

Note:

N = Excluding two wholly-owned subsidiaries.

[a] Sum > N, multiple responses.

The *forms of payment* stipulated in the contracts indicate also German SMEs' desire to bind recipient firms on a long-term basis within their global activities. Table 6.24 shows that basically payment was transacted through methods which allowed for participation in a running business. Outright sale of technology with one lump-sum compensation was not considered by any respondent for any involvement. This strategy was followed in equity and non-equity ventures alike. The only difference worth mentioning is that in three cases of non-equity involvement transfer-pricing in connection with components sales was also practised as a method of payment. This practice was apparently difficult to get accepted by partners in joint ventures.

The second requirement experienced German SMEs place on technology agreements is that their settlement must not put strain on firms' resources. Most SMEs with activities in developing countries complain heavily of bureaucratic hurdles and 'red tape' that must be overcome before agreements are finalised. This puts a heavy strain on companies' resources which they cannot afford (Kumar, 1975).

According to our findings, a certain amount of administrative procedure could indeed not be avoided by SMEs in our sample. In all but one case, the agreements had to be authorised by local governments of the recipient countries. In five cases the government authorities created problems with proposed agreements and the firms had to modify the draft contracts. All these firms, however, were the smaller firms in the sample with little or no foreign experience. Perhaps some assistance at this stage would have helped to avoid some problems.

Negotiations with the respective recipient partners took between two days (with an Argentinian licensee of a branded product in the field of household cleaning) and 30 months (with a Korean licensee of brake and clutch linings). There were some difficult items in the negotiations, too. Two firms pointed out that payment modalities of their Korean licensees had created problems because their partners refused to abide by accepted international practice. Other German firms cited the duration and the geographical scope of the agreement as difficult items, and two firms had problems with setting the amount of royalties and the down payment. The overall impression is that administration and bureaucracy needed to finalise collaboration contracts remains within acceptable limits. There seems to be little difference in procedures and time required according to the mode of technology transfer. Smaller and inexperienced suppliers of technology are at a disadvantage, which calls for assistance from government and private agencies at this stage.

6.8 SUCCESS AND APPRAISAL OF TECHNOLOGY TRANSFER OPERATIONS

The Pattern

In this final section we shall look at the success of German operations. As mentioned earlier, the success of technology transfer should be looked at from the point of view of both the technology supplier and technology recipient. However, due to lack of space and information only the former's success and appraisal is reported here.

From the point of view of the German SMEs, we measured success on the basis of a goal attainment criterion. Our findings show that in most cases (11 out of 20) the goals and expectations placed on the respective technology transfer projects by the supplier firms had either been met fully (six) or were even surpassed (five) by the achieved operations. In five cases, the original goals had not been fulfilled, and concerning the remaining four projects respondents could not give a reliable opinion because the activities were very recent. We can say that on the whole the results indicate successful operations.

This opinion is also supported by further evidence that in 18 out 20 cases supplier firms expressed plans to either expand (seven) or at least continue (11) operations in the present manner. Only in two cases was termination an issue. In one case, the German SME complained about the unfair behavior of the Korean partner regarding secrecy of know-how. In the other case a manufacturer of switch gear cabinets had earlier, in 1984, terminated part of its collaboration with an Argentinian partner because of serious problems concerning the amount of the licence fee and its transfer to Germany.

Given the choice, supplier firms in seven of the 10 cases of equity participation would rather have reinvested profits in their respective foreign projects than repatriate them to the parent company. In fact, only in one case did the supplier firm insist on continual repatriation; in another two German companies the choice depended on circumstances. This again shows that, by and large, respondents were satisfied with their projects in the developing countries.

In several previous studies (German) SMEs have reported *learning effects* resulting from foreign activities as one of the important motives for setting up operations abroad (e.g. Kumar, 1987). Due to lack of experience SMEs more than large MNES hope to improve their competitive advantage with the help of feedback from foreign operations.

In our sample, beneficial feedback was reported in six out of 20 cases. However, all responding firms agreed that their present involvement abroad gave them valuable experience for entering into new foreign ventures in the future. From this point of view their present activities 'could also be considered as fruitful'.

Influencing Factors

According to various studies of international companies, the success of international operations can be connected broadly with three major categories of influencing variables (e.g. Fayerweather, 1978; Daniels and Radebaugh, 1986): (1) the characteristics of the foreign subsidiary; (2) the characteristics of the parent company, and (3) the environmental conditions of host or recipient countries. In the following, success is discussed under these aspects as far as possible for the small sample of 20 cases.

In connection with the characteristics of the foreign affiliates, the most important variable in our study is the *organisational form* of technology transfer. The influence of this variable must be seen primarily in conjunction with the property control paradigm. Equity ventures offer suppliers of technology more possibilities to influence operations than non-equity projects. On the other hand, the former require relatively large amounts of resources, perhaps more than SMEs can afford.

Table 6.25 Success from the point of view of German SMEs, by organisational form, 1987

Success criteria	Non-equity: licensing only (No. of cases) (N = 10)	Equity: Joint venture	Equity: Wholly-owned subsidiary (No. of cases) (N = 10)	Total (N = 20)
Results surpassed goals expectations	2	3	–	5
Results met goals/ expectations	5	–	1	6
Results didn't meet goals/expectations	1	3	1	5
Too early to judge	2	2	–	4

Table 6.25 shows how the choice with respect to equity and non-equity forms relates to our findings of success. An observation worth mentioning, perhaps, is that in four out of the five cases where results did not meet expectations, equity participation was the form of involvement. Looking at it from another angle we note that most of the non-equity operations (seven out of 10) can be considered as successful. On the other hand among the 10 cases of equity participation five were unsuccessful, and there were no fully-owned subsidiaries among those cases where expectations had been surpassed. All told it seems that *non-equity involvement* is the more successful mode of technology transfer in developing countries. Apparently, control connected with equity ventures is either unnecessary for success (or may be even a hinderance!); of course control is exercised through other means with non-equity projects, e.g. via agreements. In any case equity presence does not seem to be a *conditio sine qua non* for successful technology transfer.

A major success factor in connection with corporate characteristics of the parent company are their *competitive advantages*. Such skills are an important base for internationalisation. As we reported earlier, firms in our sample seem to possess some potential in this respect.

Table 6.26 shows in detail the competitive advantages which investigated firms claimed to possess *vis-à-vis* their national and international competitors in the recipient countries. 'Better proprietory technology' is the basic know-how transferred, and the most important

Total 6.26 Perceived competitive advantage of German SMEs in recipient country, by type of involvement

Competition advantages (vis-à-vis) local competition)	Non-equity: licensing only (no. of cases) (N = 10)	Joint venture	Wholly-owned subsidiary (no. of cases) (N = 10)	Total (N = 20)[a]
Better proprietary technology	6	7	–	13
Better appropriateness of technology	3	5	–	8
Previous experiences in similar projects	3	1	1	5
Better organisation and management	1	4	–	5
International prestige	1	1	2	4
Willingness to adapt technology to local conditions	2	–	1	3

Note:
[a] Sum greater than *N* (multiple answers).

factor which was equally present in both equity and non-equity forms of involvement. A certain relationship to success of operations can be seen in the sense that in all but one cases where goals were met, better proprietary technology was also found to be present. This result confirms the importance of some specialised know-how for starting and running successful projects abroad. With respect to the other items of competitive advantage, no other definite success relationships are apparent.

Influence of *international experience* and company size on success has also been reported elsewhere (e.g. Kumar, 1987). In our sample, however, most responding firms denied the importance of *small size* for success. The smallest company in the sample considered its size as a possible factor responsible for its unsuccessful experience in Argentina. On the other hand, the two largest respondents thought that their successful operations abroad were to some extent influenced by the fact that they belonged to the category of SMEs. Whereas in the case of the smallest firm small size apparently had a negative influence, in the two latter cases it affected operations positively.

In contrast to size, *international experience* of the parent company

Table 6.27   Success from the point of view of German SMEs, by recipient country, 1987

Success criteria	Brazil	Korea	Mexico (No. of cases)	India	Argentina	Singapore	Total (N = 20)
Results surpassed goals expectations	2	1	1	–	–	1	5
Results met goals/ expectations	2	3	–	–	1	–	6
Results didn't meet goals/ expectations	3	–	1	–	1	–	5
Too early to judge	–	2	–	2	–	–	4

seems to have a somewhat more consistent effect. In half of the cases (10 out of 20) the German supplier firms perceived international experience as having a positive influence on the success of their operations. In one case a supplier said lack of foreign experience was responsible for unsuccessful operations.

Finally, we have to investigate the influence of conditions in the recipient countries on success of operations. We can assume that most SMEs will find it especially difficult to cope with environmental influences in developing countries since these are very different to the home country. German SMEs have in the past therefore always shown a preference in establishing operations in countries which are familiar in culture and economy dimensions, European Market countries and the United States (Steinmann *et al.*, 1977; Berger and Uhlman, 1984).

Table 6.27 shows how success of sample firms is spread according to recipient countries. Although, of course, the number of cases is too small to allow statistical analysis, we can observe that in all five cases where goal expectations were not met, location of operations was in Latin American countries. The cases of successful operations were distributed evenly on a regional basis.

The type of environmental problems encountered are shown in Table 6.28. Some interesting findings are that mentality and cultural problems were only encountered in forms of involvement where cooperation with local partners was existent. Apparently these problems were experienced in connection with mentality conflicts with foreign partners. However, such cultural conflicts do not appear to be so relevant for success: administrative and economic conditions were reported as negative

Table 6.28　Main environment problems for German SMEs in recipient country, by type of involvement

Problems	Non-equity: licensing only (no. of cases)	Equity Joint ventures (no. of cases)	Equity Wholly-owned subsidiary (no. of cases)	Total (N = 20)
Mentality/ culture	4	3	–	7
Regulations concerning foreign involvement and bureaucracy	2	1	–	3
Import restrictions	–	1	–	2
Infrastructural facilities	–	2	–	2
Socio–political and economical situation	–	–	1	1
No major problems	4	–	–	4

influences on success only in connection with projects in Brazil and Argentina; and difficulties in connection with infrastructural facilities (e.g. water, electricity supply, telecommunication) were encountered only in (joint venture) operations in Brazil and Mexico. Most of the cases that reported *no* problems (three out of four) were located in Korea. As all of these four cases apply to non-equity ventures, we can suggest that these forms of involvement have lesser environmental problems than equity ventures. This also could be an explanation for more success among non-equity projects, as reported earlier.

To summarise the findings, we can conclude that in most cases of technology transfer German supplier firms seem to be quite satisfied with the outcome. Non-equity ventures appear to have better conditions for successful operation than equity cooperations. The main factor contributing to success seems to be the competitive advantages of supplier firms in basic technological know-how. Administrative and infrastructural problems encountered in Latin American countries seem to be important handicaps that impede successful operations.

Notes

1. This is also not a very accurate measure for non-equity involvement since licence contracts may also be settled alongside equity participation. But since the compensation within the latter is mostly on the basis of dividends, we can assume that most of the income shown is in the context of non-equity cooperation.
2. For detailed treatise of this relationship, see Steinmann *et al.* (1981).
3. For details on this and other various programmes see BMZ (1982).
4. Due to space limitations we cannot go into these relationships, e.g. between R&D and direct investments, or between specialisation and direct investments, but these connections are well known in the literature.
5. Exports to the recipient country can be taken as an indication of exports to the recipient firm.

7 The Case of Italy

Anna Falzoni and Gianfranco Viesti

7.1 INTRODUCTION

This chapter will try to assess the characteristics and importance of Italian small and medium-sized firms in the technology transfer to developing countries.

The first part of the chapter gives some information and short comments about the importance and the role of SMEs in the framework of Italian industry. In particular, sections 7.2 and 7.3 will focus on the quantitative weight of SMEs in Italian industry, their sectoral specialisation, their innovative behaviour and their export activities.

The aim of sections 7.4 and 7.5 is to present data, collected from different sources, regarding international technology transfer activity of Italian firms, with special reference, when the data is available, to SMEs behaviour. Section 7.4 mainly deals with non-equity technology transfer; it refers to technological balance of payments as well as the 'technical assistance' data collected by Italian official statistics. Section 7.5, in contrast, is devoted to the analysis of equity ventures, presenting data referring to foreign direct investments (FDI) of Italian firms.

The second part of the chapter presents a first assessment of behavior and performance of Italian SMEs in their technology transfer operations to developing countries. The analysis is both based on the findings of previous studies (Onida *et al.*, 1985 and Onida and Viesti, 1988) and on the results of 12 new cases analysed in the framework of the CEDREI project. Section 7.6 focuses on the general approach to technology transfer of Italian firms, and on forms and content of this kind of operations. Finally, Section 7.7 summarises the whole experience and presents some conclusion about the effects, on a micro and macro level, of technology transfer operations of SMEs to LDCs.

7.2 THE ROLE OF SMALL AND MEDIUM-SIZED FIRMS IN ITALIAN INDUSTRY

In the whole of Italian industry, SMEs play a larger role than in any of other main industrialised countries. Taking into account all the firms with more than 20 employees,[1] the beginning of the 1980s, was 99 employees, compared with 160 for France, 192 for the United Kingdom and 205 for the Federal Republic of Germany. In a larger international comparison, Italy and Japan clearly emerge as the countries in which smaller firms employ a larger part of industrial workforce as opposed to FRG and the United Kingdom who show the opposite behavior. In the latter countries, around half of industrial employment is concentrated in firms with more than 500 workers; in the former ones, the percentage is between 15 and 20.

Italian small firms increased their importance during the 1970s. The average size of enterprises fell as their share of total workforce increased. The gap between SMEs and larger firms, in terms of productivity and capital endowment, narrowed. Since 1979–80, the picture has somewhat changed. All economic indicators show that Italian larger firms have gained momentum again, recording better performances than SMEs. This is not to say, of course, that SMEs performance has been bad, even if on a micro level there are signs of increasing problems for smaller enterprises in maintaining their performance. As a whole, Italy remains characterised by a crucial role played by SMEs, but with a growing weight of larger groups.

There is a clear interplay between the presence of small firms and the industrial composition of Italian manufacturing. Industries such as metal products, mechanical engineering, precision instruments, textiles, clothing and shoes, leather, wood and furnitures show very high percentage of industrial value added being produced by firms with less than 200 employees (see Table 7.1 and 7.2); of course, the presence of small firms is much lower in industries in which economies of scale play an important role, such as transportation equipment and steel. There are two major poles of specialisation. SMEs cluster in all the mechanical industries (especially non-electrical). The typical Italian small firm of this kind is a highly specialised, 'niche', producer of a very focused range of goods; organised on a very flexible basis, so to be able both to meet specific customer needs and to exploit the growing cycles of domestic and international demand; able to generate incremental innovation, that is, to improve continuously its products and thus to compete on their quality and performance.

Table 7.1   Italian industrial value added: breakdown by firm size, 1973 and 1985, percentage values[a]

ISTAT Code		1973			1985		
		20–100	100–200	>200	20–100	100–200	>20
22	Steel	6.9	4.2	88.9	14.0	9.5	76.5
24	Building materials	31.3	14.1	54.6	39.6	17.9	42.5
25	Chemicals	9.8	9.5	80.7	16.7	12.5	70.8
26	Fibres	0.2	0.8	99.0	2.1	0.8	97.1
31	Metal products	43.0	17.7	39.3	52.9	18.3	28.8
32	Mechanical engineering	28.0	17.1	54.9	35.4	18.1	46.5
33	Computers & office automation	0.8	0.6	98.6	1.0	0.7	98.3
34	Electric and electronic materials	11.9	8.0	80.1	17.6	10.0	72.4
35	Road vehicles	3.6	2.6	93.8	7.7	5.8	86.5
36	Other transportation equipment	8.2	3.9	87.9	9.8	4.1	86.1
37	Precision instruments	35.9	19.9	44.2	35.5	16.1	48.4
41	Food[b]	28.2	10.9	60.9	38.9	13.6	47.5
42	Sugar, sweets, alcohol, beverages	16.7	12.7	70.6	22.7	12.3	65.0
43	Textiles	27.5	14.7	57.8	46.1	20.1	33.8
44	Clothing and shoes	47.3	18.9	33.8	69.2	21.3	9.5
45	Leather	35.5	17.6	46.9	52.0	17.9	30.1
46	Wood and furnitures	58.4	19.2	22.4	70.3	18.5	11.2
47	Paper and publishing	26.0	12.1	61.9	30.8	13.0	56.2
48	Rubber, plastics	22.6	12.3	65.1	41.5	16.2	42.3
49	Miscellaneous	41.2	22.1	36.7	68.6	13.1	18.3
	Total	22.6	11.7	65.7	30.0	13.3	56.7

Notes:
[a] Firms with less than 20 employees are not covered in this ISTAT survey.
[b] Except items listed as 42.

Source: Barca (1988), based in ISTAT data.

A large share of SMEs manufacture traditional consumer products. Some of them are the main representatives of the so-called 'Made in Italy' style: fashionable and well designed goods, with a market positioning towards the richest segments, strong effort in process innovation, and international strategies mainly based on non-price factors. Others are more 'traditional', offering cheaper goods, competing more on price, producing in a less automatised way, facing the problems of less and less competitive labour costs.

Table 7.2 Industrial composition of value added for size groups of firms, 1980 prices, percentage values[a]

		20–100		100–200		>200	
ISTAT code		1973	1985	1973	1985	1973	1985
22	Steel	2.1	2.5	2.5	3.8	9.3	7.1
24	Building materials	9.5	7.9	8.3	8.1	5.7	4.5
25	Chemicals	3.5	5.9	6.6	10.0	10.0	13.3
26	Fibres	0.0	0.1	0.1	0.1	1.4	1.5
31	Metal products	15.8	11.0	12.6	8.6	5.0	3.2
32	Mechanical engineering	12.1	11.3	14.3	13.1	8.2	7.9
33	Computers & office automation	0.1	0.1	0.1	0.2	2.1	7.2
34	Electric and electronic materials	4.6	6.5	6.0	8.3	10.7	14.2
35	Road vehicles	1.5	1.7	2.0	2.8	12.7	9.9
36	Other transportation equipment	0.8	1.1	0.7	1.0	2.9	5.0
37	Precision instruments	0.8	1.6	0.9	1.6	0.3	1.1
41	Food[b]	5.1	5.4	3.8	4.3	3.8	3.5
42	Sugar, sweets, alcohol, beverages	3.4	3.0	4.9	3.7	4.9	4.6
43	Textiles	10.2	10.5	10.6	10.3	7.4	4.1
44	Clothing and shoes	1.5	1.9	1.2	1.3	0.4	0.1
45	Leather	7.8	9.0	7.4	6.9	3.5	2.7
46	Wood and furnitures	8.2	6.9	5.2	4.1	1.1	0.6
47	Paper and publishing	6.5	6.6	5.9	6.3	5.3	6.4
48	Rubber, plastics	4.8	5.7	5.1	5.0	4.8	3.0
49	Miscellaneous	1.7	1.4	1.8	0.5	0.5	0.2
	Total	100.0	100.0	100.0	100.0	100.0	100.0

Notes:
[a] Firms with less than 20 employees are not covered in this ISTAT survey.
[b] Except items listed as 42.

Source: Barca (1988), based on ISTAT data.

A peculiar feature of the organisation of the production in some of these industries is the high geographical concentration of firms in very small areas, the so-called 'industrial districts' (see for example Sabel and Piore, 1987; Becattini, 1987). This kind of spatial organisation does give competitive advantages to firms due to external economies:

they mainly arise from the availability of highly-skilled workers and the speed of diffusion of technical information, through informal channels such as personal contacts, labour mobility and imitative behavior.

Among the largest OECD countries, Italian R&D expenditures are by far the lowest as a percentage of GNP. Though growing very fast, the R&D expenditures over GNP ratio was 1.4 per cent for Italy in 1985, compared to 2.2–2.3 for France and the United Kingdom and 2.7–2.8 for FRG, the United States and Japan. This is both due to a different industrial composition (that is, an over-representation in Italy of industries with a lower R&D ratio, such as traditional sectors) and a lesser effort of research in more innovative sectors. Taking into account the G-7 countries, Italy accounts for around 7 per cent of total product while generating only around 3 per cent of R&D expenditures. In this general framework, SMEs seem to have a lesser emphasis on R&D than larger enterprises. Data on patents registered in the United States shows how firms with less than 1000 employees cover a very small share of the total, major exceptions being mechanical engineering and metals (Ministero dell'Industria, 1988).

A survey performed by ISTAT on the diffusion of technological innovation in manufacturing firms (with more than 20 employees) showed that only two-thirds of small (20–100 employees) firms introduced an innovation in the first half of the 1980s as compared to 85 per cent of larger (more than 200) ones. For one out of two small firms, innovative behavior was associated with the purchase of new capital goods, while for only a minority of SMEs was innovation associated either with real R&D activities (7 per cent) or design and project commitment (23 per cent) (see Table 7.3). These data picture SMEs as incremental innovators: that is, firms able to utilise innovations coming from outside, often incorporated in capital goods, to improve both production processes and final goods. Competitive strengths and shortcomings, of a large share of Italian SMEs stem directly from these points: flexibility in organisation and ability to adapt to change; organisational modelling with the goal of reducing costs and improve efficiency; understanding of customer needs, supply of products of good quality level, often in very specific and limited market niches.

7.3 SMES IN ITALIAN EXPORTS

The Italian exporting pattern can be summarised with the help of Table 7.4, showing the share over total OECD exports.[2] Among indus-

Table 7.3 Innovative activities of Italian firms, % firms performing different innovative activities, by firm size

	R&D[a] (1)	Design[b] (2)	Capital goods and components[c] (3)
Firm size (employees)			
20–49	7	23	44
50–99	12	33	51
100–199	18	43	57
200–499	28	48	59
500 and over	39	62	60

Notes:
[a] Percentage of firms performing direct R&D activities.
[b] Percentage of firms performing design and project activities.
[c] Percentage of firms introducing innovation via acquired capital goods, components and material.

Source: ISTAT (1986).

trialised countries Italy clearly has an unusual trading behavior:[3]

- In traditional consumer goods, Italy achieves the position of a main OECD exporter, with substantial shares of world markets and very large trading surpluses, mainly competing with non-OECD producers
- In mechanical industries, Italy also enjoys a good export standing, as one of main world exporters
- The picture of 'scale-intensive', large oligopolistic industries with important multinational activity, is quite mixed: a general weakness in chemical products, a small share of export of cars, together with better standing in household appliances
- Lastly, worse indications come from hi-tech sectors, in which Italy shows under-the-average percentage shares of world markets and, in several industries, a weak competitive position.

Industrial export propensity (export/production) similarly, differs widely, being higher that the 25 per cent average in sectors like mechanical engineering, textiles–clothing and leather–shoes and lower especially in all food products. Four-fifths of Italian exports are directed towards more advanced markets: intra-EU trade obviously has a special role (56 per cent). Developing and CMEA areas account for the remaining fifth: their role much was higher (35 per cent in 1981), in connection

Table 7.4	Italian exports, 1987, ranking by Italy/OECD percentage share[a]

Industry	Value of Italian exports (million $)	Italy/OECD % share
Shoes	5 290	50.1
Travel goods	833	42.2
Clothing	9 013	26.3
Leather	1 814	25.9
Furniture	3 623	23.9
Sanitary equipment	882	19.4
Textiles	7 321	14.3
Building materials	4 300	11.9
Metal products	4 450	11.4
Other mechanical (non-electrical)	8 076	11.0
Miscellaneous	6 452	10.9
Mechanical engineering	7 965	10.6
Machine tools	1 862	9.9
Rubber	1 313	8.7
Wood	504	6.9
Steel	4 114	6.7
Plastics	2 869	6.7
Electrical engineering	5 833	6.1
Pharmaceuticals	1 183	5.2
Organic chemicals	2 262	5.0
Engines	2 314	4.8
Other chemicals	879	4.0
Road vehicles	8 732	3.9
Office machinery	2 852	3.9
Optics, photo	914	3.8
Precision instruments	1 286	3.7
Paper	1 451	3.6
Cosmetics	403	3.5
Non-ferrous metals	1 049	3.4
Dyes	411	3.3
Other transportation equipments	1 563	3.1
Inorganic chemicals	508	3.0
Fertilisers	200	2.8
Telecommunications	1 395	2.6
Total	103 916	7.6

Note:
[a]	Food and petroleum derivatives are excluded.

Source: OECD.

with the boom of the OPEC markets. Since 1981, the weight of LDCs has been continuously and rapidly shrinking, with the 1987 data being 16 per cent. Among LDCs, major shares are accounted for by African (especially Mediterranean) and Middle Eastern (oil-producing) countries. In 1987, the large and fast-growing markets of Far East Asia still received less than 3 per cent of Italian total manufacturing export, while Latin American countries received 1.5 per cent, historical low.

In this general framework, small firms account for a significant share of Italian export. In 1987 registered 78 800 firms were exporting less than 5 bn lire of goods each,[4] their cumulative exports summing up to 32 per cent of the total. This share remained basically unchanged during the eighties. They have a lower export propensity than larger firms: the export/production ratios were (1985) 21.5 per cent for firms in the 20–99 employees class, around 25 per cent for 100–500 employees firms and 27 per cent for larger firms; all these ratios have been growing during the eighties. Half of the 'smaller' exporters of 1987 proved not to have exported every year in 1982–7: that is to say that an important share of them is not constantly present on international wmarkets. Finally, smaller firms show a larger propensity to export towards larger neighbouring markets, especially EU ones. Their relative participation in trade with LDCs is lower than the average; the role of developing.

7.4 ITALIAN TECHNOLOGY TRANSFER: THE QUANTITATIVE FRAMEWORK

Data on the Italian Technological Balance of Payments (TBP)[5] are available from 1956, but only since 1972 have they become sufficiently detailed to offer a more faithful picture of the phenomenon. Moreover, since 1979, data also include 'non-connected technical assistance' (NCTA), which concerns teaching and professional training, feasibility and market studies, the preparation of technical plans and drawings, the institution of manufacturing controls, etc. TBP data, even though collected on firm bases, are not available for any firm size breakdown; therefore only the general framework will be presented below.

The Italian TBP has shown a constant deficit (Table 7.5), as have most of the industrialised countries, except the United Kingdom and the United States. As the relative position of several net technology-acquiring countries has changed over the years (in the case of Japan the receipts/payments (R/P) ratio greatly improved), for Italy, the R/P ratio has shown some signs of improvement, moving from an average

Table 7.5 Italy: technological balance of payments, non-connected technical assistance, R&D expenditure in industry and direct investment, billion lire, 1980–7

	1980	1981	1982	1983	1984	1985	1986	1987	1980–3	1984–7	1980–7
Technological balance of payments (TBP):											
– Receipts	191.6	225.4	217.0	224.8	289.6	275.3	326.4	389.9	214.7	320.3	267.5
– Payments	543.5	647.9	808.4	911.5	989.7	1042.4	1056.3	1021.1	727.8	1027.4	877.6
– Balance	–351.9	–422.5	–591.4	–686.7	–700.1	–767.1	–729.9	–631.2	–513.1	–707.1	–610.1
– Receipts/payments ratio	0.35	0.35	0.27	0.25	0.29	0.26	0.31	0.38	0.30	0.31	0.31
Non-connected technical assistance (NCTA):											
– Receipts	485.3	793.5	1022.5	1157.6	1305.9	1642.2	1474.9	1639.0	864.7	1515.5	1190.1
– Payments	473.9	740.0	1082.9	1276.4	1596.1	1885.1	1969.5	2086.6	893.3	1844.3	1388.8
– Balance	11.4	53.5	–60.4	–118.8	–290.2	–242.9	–494.6	–447.6	–28.6	–368.8	–198.7
– Receipts/payments ratio	1.02	1.07	0.94	0.91	0.82	0.87	0.75	0.79	0.99	0.81	0.90
R&D expenditure in industry	1710	2286	2790	3440	4128	5201	5946	7240	2556.5	5628.8	4092.6
Foreign direct investment:											
– to Italy from abroad	816	1629	1464	2499	2758	4182	6572	6430	1602.0	4985.5	3293.8
– from Italy to abroad	896	2514	2716	3769	4091	4360	4974	4646	2473.8	4517.8	3495.8
TPB payments/R&D (ratio)	0.32	0.28	0.29	0.26	0.24	0.20	0.18	0.14	0.29	0.19	0.24
NCTA payments/R&D (ratio)	0.28	0.32	0.39	0.37	0.39	0.36	0.33	0.29	0.34	0.34	0.34
TBP and NCTA payments/R&D (ratio)	0.59	0.61	0.68	0.64	0.63	0.56	0.51	0.43	0.63	0.53	0.58

Source: Sirilli (1987) and for 1987 data author's calculations, based on ISTAT, UIC and Bank of Italy.

value of 24 per cent in the 1970's to 31 per cent in the 1980s. The ratio between TBP payments and R&D expenditures has constantly decreased since 1982. The internal innovation effort, in fact, has grown at a greater pace than expenditures to acquire technology from abroad (Table 7.5).

The structure of Italy's TBP, like that of other European countries, supports the hypothesis that Italy is a technology 'transforming' country. The technology is acquired from the technologically advanced countries, primarily the United States and the major European countries, which in the 1980–7 period accounted for more than 85 per cent of the payments on the average, and sold both to OECD and developing countries. But single LDCs, though they play a significant role as a whole, are only occasional purchasers of Italian technology, while the OECD countries provide the continuity of receipts. In the 1980–7 period, the principal sources of Italy's TBP receipts were Europe and the United States, with an average share of 70 per cent (Table 7.6).

Payments are dominated by the purchase of licences,[6] which between 1980 and 1987 accounted for around 60 per cent of the total, followed by payments for technical assistance and know-how (19 per cent). On the receipts side, these items have respectively a share of 26 per cent and 43 per cent, followed by designs (15 per cent) and patents (7 per cent). A cross-analysis of the breakdown by type of operation and by geographical origin/destination of payments and receipts indicates that Italy tends to be relatively dependent on the more advanced OECD countries for the purchase of licences and patents (items for which there are significant deficits), while it has the most important flows of receipts from the transfer of know-how and technical assistance, with a higher presence of receipts from countries of more recent industrialisation. Additional information in this regard can be derived from the breakdown of NCTA by geographical area, which shows that areas generally marginal in terms of international technology flows, such as Africa, are important destinations of this kind of services (Table 7.7): this would seem to suggest the existence of a correlation between the sale of industrial plant abroad, particularly to the LDCs, and NCTA.[7]

In the eighties, manufacturing industries showed a substantial deficit, though improving in recent years. Largest receipts generally come from textiles, clothing and shoes, motor vehicles (thanks primarily to the presence of FIAT) and pharmaceuticals. Substantial deficits typify the high-technology sectors such as electronics and telecommunications and chemicals.

Table 7.6 Italy: technological balance of payments: receipts by type of operations and partner country/area, million lire and % values, 1980–7, year average

Types Country/Area	Patents		Licences		Trade marks		Designs		Inventions		Know-how and Technical Assistance		Total	
	Value	(%)	Value	(%)	Value	(%)	Value	(%)	Value	(%)	Value	(%)	Value	(%)
EUROPE	11 100	59.3	36 212	52.5	9 098	46.4	22 057	53.8	1393	56.8	53 018	45.3	132 879	49.7
of which: EU	5 595	29.9	27 155	39.4	5 698	29.1	12 849	31.3	1276	52.0	27 151	23.2	79 943	29.9
Socialist Countries	248	1.3	2 731	4.0	107	0.5	3 913	9.5	20	0.8	10 078	8.6	17 097	6.4
UNITED STATES AND CANADA	2 507	13.4	18 189	26.4	5 374	27.4	5 761	14.0	537	21.9	22 053	18.8	54 423	20.3
JAPAN	2 099	11.2	6 404	9.3	3 920	20.0	1 865	4.5	128	5.2	2 715	2.3	17 132	6.4
OCEANIA	53	0.3	310	0.4	45	0.2	1 155	2.8	63	2.6	1 483	1.3	3 110	1.2
TOTAL OF ABOVE	15 759	84.2	61 115	88.6	18 437	94.1	30 838	75.2	2121	86.4	79 269	67.7	207 544	77.6
LATIN AMERICA	606	3.2	2 221	3.2	514	2.6	1 044	2.5	86	3.5	8 322	7.1	12 793	4.8
of which: BRAZIL	229	1.2	176	0.2	65	0.3	390	0.9	1	0.0	2 447	2.1	2 621	1.0
ARGENTINA	150	0.8	717	1.0	59	0.3	101	0.2	38	1.5	1 197	1.0	2 261	0.8
AFRICA	604	3.2	1 364	2.0	181	0.9	3 724	9.1	33	1.3	15 844	13.5	21 749	8.1
DEVELOPING ASIA	1755	9.4	4 256	6.2	479	2.4	5 395	13.1	213	8.7	13 333	11.4	25 431	9.5
of which: CHINA	125	0.7	183	0.3	55	0.3	199	0.5	14	0.6	2 923	2.5	3 499	1.3
ASEAN	867	4.6	770	1.1	13	0.1	66	0.2	106	4.3	835	0.7	2 823	1.0
HONG KONG	109	0.6	256	0.4	122	0.6	37	0.1	0	0.0	291	0.2	718	0.3
SOUTH KOREA	144	0.8	181	0.3	105	0.5	1 499	3.6	57	2.3	710	0.6	2 696	1.0
INDIA	15	0.1	1 263	1.8	19	0.1	739	1.8	10	0.4	2 340	2.0	4 386	1.6
TOTAL DEVELOPING COUNTRIES	2 965	15.8	7 841	11.4	1 174	5.9	10 163	24.8	332	13.6	37 499	32.0	59 973	22.4
GRAND TOTAL	18 724	100.0	68 956	100.0	19 611	100.0	41 001	100.0	2454	100.0	117 018	100.0	267 518	100.0

Source: Author's calculations, based on DIC data.

Table 7.7 Italy: non-connected technical assistance: receipts by partner country/area, million lire and % values, 1984–7, year average

Country/Area	Value	%
EUROPE	820 278	54.1
of which: EEC	617 085	40.7
Socialist Countries	33 279	2.2
UNITED STATES and CANADA	219 898	14.5
JAPAN	12 663	0.8
OCEANIA	8 249	0.5
TOTAL OF ABOVE	1 061 088	70.0
LATIN AMERICA	70 670	4.7
of which: BRAZIL	21 014	1.4
ARGENTINA	7 052	0.5
AFRICA	247 992	16.4
DEVELOPING ASIA	135 756	8.9
of which: CHINA	5 464	0.4
ASEAN	7 011	0.5
HONG KONG	1 384	0.1
SOUTH KOREA	2 885	0.2
INDIA	17 224	1.1
TOTAL DEVELOPING COUNTRIES	454 418	30.0
GRAND TOTAL	1 515 519	100.0

Source: Author's calculations, based on UIC data.

In OECD countries, multinational firms play a decisive role in determining TBP balance.[8] As far as Italy is concerned, in 1980 purely domestic companies were responsible for around 70 per cent of both payments and receipts, while the Italian multinationals were responsible only for 3 per cent of the payments and 22 per cent of the receipts, a much smaller share than those found in the other most industrialised countries (see Scarda and Sirilli, 1982). It may be hypothesised, however, that this share has increased in recent years following the increase of the internationalisation process in Italian firms, which will be discussed in greater detail below.

7.5   FDI AND JOINT VENTURES

Whatever standard is used to measure foreign direct investment (FDI), Italy still appears to play a minor role as international investor compared

Table 7.8   FDI by major home countries, US$ million and % shares 1970–86

Home country		Foreign direct investment	Share on the total G-7 countries	Share on export
Italy	1970–4	237	1.54	1.31
	1975–8	306	1.18	0.74
	1979–82	925	2.41	1.24
	1983–6	2.155	4.78	2.71
Germany	1970–4	1.344	8.73	2.57
	1975–8	2.552	9.88	2.33
	1979–82	3.897	10.13	2.29
	1983–6	5.379	11.92	2.86
France	1970–4	571	3.71	2.05
	1975–8	1.467	5.70	2.47
	1979–82	3.128	8.13	3.16
	1983–6	2.850	6.32	2.77
United Kingdom	1970–4	3.006	19.53	10.92
	1975–8	4.560	17.65	8.53
	1979–82	10.773	28.02	10.99
	1983–6	10.949	24.27	10.98
United States	1970–4	8.686	56.42	15.29
	1975–8	13.529	52.38	11.21
	1979–82	12.896	33.54	6.28
	1983–6	12.178	26.99	5.51
Japan	1970–4	1.042	6.77	2.93
	1975–8	1.937	7.50	2.70
	1979–82	3.683	9.58	2.83
	1983–6	7.578	16.80	4.17
Canada	1970–4	508	3.30	2.07
	1975–8	1.479	5.73	3.45
	1979–82	3.151	8.19	4.67
	1983–6	4.032	8.94	4.79

Note: Data includes reinvested profits for France, Germany, the United Kingdom and the United States.

Source: Bank of Italy, *Annual Report* (1987). Calculations based on IMF data, *Balance of Payment Statistics* and *International Financial Statistics*.

with the leading industrial countries, but is rapidly catching up. In the last few years the trend of Italian FDI showed a considerable upswing: a structural change in the internationalisation process of Italian industry (Table 7.8).

Table 7.9 Geographical distribution of FDI among developed countries and LDCs by selected home countries, % values

Share of: Home countries	Years	Developed countries	LDCs	
Italy[a]	1985	51	49	employees[b]
	1987	67[d]	33	employees[c]
United	1975[f]	79	17	stock of FDI
States[e]	1986[f]	75	22	stock of FDI
Japan[e]	1975	33	67	stock of FDI
	1986	42	58	stock of FDI
Germany[e]	1976	70	30	stock of FDI
	1985	79	21	stock of FDI
United	1974	79	21	stock of FDI
Kingdom[e]	1984	84	16	stock of FDI

Notes:
[a] Manufacturing, oil and mining industries.
[b] Based on MITA database (Onida and Viesti, 1988).
[c] Based on REPRINT database (Mariotti, 1989).
[d] Europe, North America and Japan.
[e] Primary and manufacturing sectors.
[f] Data do not add to 100 per cent because unspecified countries are included in the total.

Source: Onida and Viesti (1988), Mariotti (1989a) for Italy; official data for other countries.

Until the eighties, one of the main features of the geographical distribution of Italian FDI certainly was the interest in LDCs. The comparison with geographical distribution of FDI of the main investing countries (Onida and Viesti, 1988; Mariotti, 1989), shows that, besides Japan, no other home country had such a high share of its investment in LDCs (Table 7.9). The most recent data nevertheless show that the geographical composition of Italy's FDI is becoming more and more similar to that of the other advanced countries. In the latest period Italian investment in OECD countries has reached its maximum.

Operating subsidiaries in LDCs were mainly established before 1975 (Onida and Viesti, 1988). Thereafter Italian interest in these areas declined, in line with the orientation of the whole of international investors. The weight of the debt burden and reactions to the problems it has raised, made it clear that growth prospects in LDCs had to be revised, at least for a few years, leading to a reduced relative attractiveness of these countries to international direct investment flows (OECD, 1987; UNCTC, 1988).

Italian presence in developing areas shows a polarisation towards Latin America. In 1987 about 11 per cent of sales of foreign subsidiaries and 21 per cent of their workers, were registered in this area. Within Latin America, Brazil is the first recipient country. The share of African countries is lower, and decreasing in last years due to divestments in the oil industry. Affiliates located in Asia are concentrated in the manufacturing sector; their global importance is very small though increasing: about 3 per cent of employees.

The significant share of Latin American countries can be explained by considering their linguistic and cultural affinities with Italy, the past emigration flows towards this area, the size of its main markets and the expectations held in the 1960s and 1970s regarding their growth. The importance of the Italian presence in the Latin American subcontinent is further evidenced by a comparison of market shares acquired through exports with those achieved through direct investments. While in 1983 the former far exceeded the latter (as affiliates' sales revenues) in every other area (whether developing or industrial), the contrary happens in Latin America. Total sales of manufacturing affiliates of Italian firms are almost twice as large as exports from Italy (Onida and Viesti, 1988).

Italian FDI is highly concentrated on specific manufacturing sectors – automotive, rubber, and mechanical industries above all. In some of them the majority of investment is concentrated in developed countries: food and beverages, office machinery and data processing and basic chemicals. Some others grew especially in LDCs: in addition to the mining industry (largely concentrated in Africa), clothing, metalworking (prevailing in Latin America), oil products, pharmaceuticals and cars.

The reality of Italian multinationals is dominated by two different groups. On one side there are the larger groups, which account for half of the foreign affiliates, but for some 90 per cent of the total sales and of the number of employees abroad; on the other side, there are more than 100 small firms with less than 500 employees that make up the biggest group of investors. These firms have about 200 manufacturing affiliates in foreign countries. The value of their investment is very small if compared with the average value of the stakes owned by the larger groups, but nevertheless significant if related to the size of the Italian parent: they account for about 8 per cent of the total sales and employees abroad (Table 7.10). It is worth noting that, in

Table 7.10 Italian FDI by parent company size, end 1987

SIZE (employees)	Parent companies		Foreign affiliates		Employees		Sales	
	No.	(%)	No.	(%)	No.[a]	(%)	billion lire[b]	(%)
Private investors	9	4.27	9	1.33	721	0.22	62	0.12
1–99	32	15.17	43	6.34	2 143	0.67	387	0.73
100–199	40	18.96	56	8.26	4 356	1.35	587	1.11
200–499	55	26.07	96	14.16	17 443	5.42	2 316	4.39
500–999	22	10.43	43	6.34	4 738	1.47	1 155	2.19
1000–1999	22	10.43	49	7.23	11 859	3.69	1 749	3.32
2000–9999	23	10.90	80	11.80	28 539	8.87	4 445	8.43
> 10000	8	3.79	302	44.54	252 003	78.31	42 022	79.70
Total	211	100.00	678	100.00	321 802	100.00	52 723	100.00

Notes:
[a] Employee data refer to 1986.
[b] Sales data refer to 1986.

Source: Mariotti (1989a), based on database REPRINT, R&P and Politecnico of Milan.

Table 7.11　Affiliates, by parent company equity stake and size, end 1987, % values

Size (employees)	Equity stake		
	> 50%	<50%	Total
Private investors	44.44	55.56	100
1–99	30.23	69.77	100
100–199	35.71	64.29	100
200–499	58.33	41.67	100
500–999	48.84	51.16	100
1000–1999	69.39	30.61	100
2000–9999	76.25	23.75	100
> 10 000	70.86	29.14	100
Total	62.39	37.61	100

Source: Mariotti (1989a), based on database REPRINT, R&P and Politecnico of Milan.

recent years, the group of investors from 200 to 500 employees' firms has increased its role in the internationalisation process, as shown by the shares of sales and employees abroad. This is principally the result of the growing competitiveness of their products in some specific niches of international markets.

Foreign operations are relatively more important for small firms; in 1985 employment in foreign countries (including employment in minority-owned affiliates) was more than 50 per cent of domestic employment for 40 per cent of SMEs. The average value for firms with more than 500 employees was 20 per cent (Onida and Viesti, 1988). However, one should take into account both the small size of small firms' employment in Italy and the relevance for these SMEs of labour-intensive ventures in developing countries.

Minority and 50 per cent joint ventures are very important in the Italian experience. In 1987, about 38 per cent of all affiliates (accounting for 30 per cent of employees and 24 per cent of total sales) were less than 51 per cent owned (Table 7.11). In an international comparison only Japan behaves similarly. In recent years, however, majority and 100 per cent investments have been growing faster than minority and 50 per cent joint ventures. The propensity to invest in joint ventures depends upon firm, industry and host country-specific factors (Dunning, 1988). The relevance of joint ventures appears clearly linked with geographical location of investment: in developing countries, and particularly in Asia and Africa, minority joint ventures with local firms are very common. A strong reverse correlation exists between the investing firm's size and the propensity towards joint ventures (Table 7.11). There is a sort of 'minimal scale' needed to implement and manage majority or wholly-owned foreign subsidiaries. Small firms go multinational with less experience in managing foreign operations and less financial resources than their competitors; moreover the very financial effort needed for investing abroad can exceed the economic possibilities of small firms. And the small firms have the greatest propensity to invest in LDCs.

7.6 TECHNOLOGY TRANSFER BY ITALIAN SMES TO DEVELOPING COUNTRIES

The following pages present an assessment of the behaviour and the performance of Italian SMEs in their technology transfer operations to developing countries. The analysis is based both on the findings of previous studies (Onida *et al.*, 1985 and Onida and Viesti, 1988) and on results of 12 new cases analysed in the framework of the CEDREI project[9] (Table 7.12). Reference will be made to the 'average' behaviour of the 'average' Italian small firm, as seen above. As a matter of fact, the kind of pattern described has been found in the largest majority of cases analysed, even if differences can be obviously found in specific experiences. The identification of a general behaviour may nonetheless be useful to highlight the implications of the process.

The approach to technology transfer of Italian firms appears to be mainly 'market-oriented', responding to the need for increased penetration on international markets. The cooperation with the LDCs partner is by and large viewed as a mean to enter their market via export from home country and new production arising abroad.

'Supply-related' determinants of these international operations, ranging from the desire to locate some manufacturing facilities abroad either to decrease production costs (especially labour), or to secure access to raw materials and energy sources are less important, as clearly emerged from a study on the whole of Italian firms behaviour abroad (Onida and Viesti, 1988).

This holds particularly true for firms operating in traditional consumer industries and in the mechanical engineering: their operations, which account for a significant share of total cases, are mostly due to the desire for increasing foreign market penetration. The small size of

Table 7.12 Twelve cases of technology transfer by Italian SMEs

Italian firm	Size (employees)	Industry	Exports to sales ratio	Main countries/areas of destination of exports	Internationalisation process (no. of agreements)	Partner nationality	Case under study Year	Form of technology transfer
1 SITI SpA	350	Kilns & complete plants for the ceramic & metallurgical industry	60%	Far East – China	more than 15	Brazil	1970	Wholly-owned subsidiary
2 OCN PPL SpA (ex Pietro Pontiggia)	600	Machine tools	30%	Europe	4	India	1986	Licensing
3 WELKO INDUSTRIALE SpA	200	Kilns & plants for the ceramic industry	90%	• Africa and Far East in the past • China and Soviet Union in the future	more than 2	Brazil	1960s	Joint minority-owned venture
4 DALTON SpA	54	Auxiliaries for leather tanning & textile industries	15–20%	Europe, S. Korea, Israel, Morocco, Egypt	2	India	1988	Technology agreement
5 SECIFARMA SpA	78	Bulk pharmaceutical chemicals	92%	United States and Europe	1	India	1980s	Technology agreement
6 CARABELLI SpA	566	• Mercerized & dyed cotton yarns • Socks & pantyhoses • Natural & man-made fibres	8%	Europe	1	S. Korea	1985	Technology agreement

7 PIACENZA 1733 SpA	abt 200	• Fabrics, woven of sheeps or lamb's wool or of fine animal hair 70% • Yarn of wool or animal hair	Japan and Europe	3	S. Korea	1984	Technology agreement
8 ZEGNA BARUFFA LANE BORGOSESIA SpA	1300	• Yarn of wool 42%	Japan, Europe and United States	3	S. Korea	1983	Technology agreement
9 TECNOGAS SpA	500	Static and multifunction ovens 70%	Europe (mainly United Kingdom and France)	12	Singapore	1980	Joint majority-owned venture
10 GIESSE SpA	180	Window & door frames, parts of aluminium 10%	Africa and Middle East	1	Argentina	1981	Technology agreement
11 VIBRAM SpA	240	Rubber soles for footwear market 65%	Europe and United States	7	Argentina	1960s	Licensing
12 BALLESTRA SpA	700	Know-how & plants for the chemical industry (oil & detergents) 99%	World	3	India	1985	Licensing

most firms and their relative shortage of financial and managerial resources, the availability at home of very skilled workers, the growing importance (especially in the 80s) of efficiency-increasing investments at home, and the need for close contact with their customers and suppliers, are all important factors in discouraging international redeployment of production (Onida *et al.*, 1985, Ch. 5).

In cases where cost pressure is strong enough to motivate foreign production (and their number has significantly grown in the 80s), this is alternatively made by the establishment of wholly-owned subsidiaries or by subcontracting agreements, with a low content of technology transfer. An important feature that often completes the market-orientation strategy is the desire to overcome protectionist barriers. Factors linked to the total or partial lapse of the possibility of exporting to important markets or the willingness to expand towards 'closed' countries clearly affect many firms' decisions to transfer their technology to LDC partners.

In most cases, the process begins with the request of the partner, actively seeking technology: in almost all the deals concerned, the first step was made by LDC firms. It is worth noting that in a survey of Italian firms' international cooperation (CESPRI–CESAG, 1988) it clearly emerged that, on the whole, and particularly in cases of agreement with OECD partners, the initiative for the deal either was taken by the Italian firms or a common interest of the two partners was noted.

The fact that in the technology transfer operations with developing countries the initiative of the deal was taken by the LDC firm can be explained by two main reasons. Very often, in cooperative agreements among firms involving a transfer of knowledge, it is the (potential) recipient firm of a technology who is more interested in the deal. It may have a better knowledge of the potential application of the technology in a new economic context, that is, of the gains that may be created. It may, for example, have 'market' assets (knowledge of the market, production units, commercial network), which may be complementary (Teece, 1986) to the technological knowledge, allowing a better evaluation of the results of the cooperation.

This behavior is also due to the asymmetry in the importance of this kind of deals for the two partners. On the one side, for the LDC partner, the new technological package may allow a substantial upgrading of technical level of production and, in some cases, the very production of goods for which a new market is envisaged. On the other side – and this is an important issue – Italian firms may in most cases foresee only a limited and uncertain inflow of royalties. Not surprisingly the interest for the deal increases as far as additional (or new) export to the market in question can be seen by the Italian side. And, of course, this becomes more important still when traditional export strategies are not possible at all, due to the existence of tariff and non-tariff barriers to trade.

Despite the previous statement, it would be incorrect to define Italian SMEs, in their relationships with LDCs, as passive, only waiting for incoming proposals. For sure, they are not 'global scanners'. They do not systematically study all world market opportunities, analysing what kind of strategy (direct investment, licensing, export) they could adopt, as large multinationals usually do. Limited information, lack of human resources, lack of experience, fear of risks, all factors typically linked to their size, generally do not allow such behavior. Moreover, their 'technology' is rarely incorporated in patents, designs or formulae, typical results of R&D activities which are relatively easily transferred and that usually motivate an active search for sale possibilities by their owners who want to transfer them. Discussing the content of the technology transfer by Italian SMEs (see below), it will clearly emerge as usually quite complex, in some cases designed ad hoc ('custom-made'). SMEs appear well able to take advantage of unplanned opportunities, adjusting their strategies to the requests of possible foreign partners.

A kind of 'entry barrier' to technology transfer seems to exist. In fact, as the first (generally unplanned) operation is concluded, firms usually adopt a more interested approach, more actively seeking for international cooperation. What happens is a sharp reduction of transaction costs of international technology transfer (Williamson, 1975) as the main outcome of the first operation:[10] the learning of 'which' and 'how' to transfer their know-how, experience acquired in the personal and technical contacts, knowledge of different managerial cultures, ability to 'translate' their 'technology' in a written or oral form available for people external to the firm, ability to manage foreign legislation and regulations, and so on. All this leads to a substantial learning of how-to-transfer-technology, showing the potential gains and reducing the risks and cost of such operations.[11]

All the firms who successfully concluded their first deal were much more interested in repeating their experience, and actually signed more cooperation agreements with LDCs. Almost all the interviewed firms stated that the first operation was 'more difficult and more risky', and that after its conclusion they had learned a lot about the way of implementing such a deal. The first experience appears a key issue in the promotion of technology transfer. Firms that have already concluded international operations usually need information about new possible ventures: they are able to evaluate their interests and to proceed with the deal. For firms with less, or no international experience, this is absolutely not enough: they are not able to evaluate possible gains and losses, they do not have the managerial and technical time or human resources even to study the possibility. They need more than information.

The empirical evidence of cases under study, confirmed by the results of works such as Onida *et al.* (1985) and Onida and Viesti (1988), shows that 'non-equity' forms are the most frequent contractual solution adopted by Italian SMEs transferring technology by LDCs. Several factors may explain this behaviour.[12] On the side of the firm, non-equity forms sharply reduce investment outlays and the risks involved; this holds particularly true as far as small firms are concerned, whose global amount of financial resources to be invested is quite limited. Moreover, in the case of several LDCs the risks of direct investments increased during the 1980s, due to the worsening of their financial and economic situation.

Non-equity forms permit a more flexible strategy, reducing the global risks and enhancing the possibilities for the firm going international to withdraw from the deals.

This behaviour is also due to technology import policies of some countries (i.e. India and S. Korea) characterised by the careful management and control over the process of importing and assimilating technical knowledge via selective use of FDI and non-equity forms complemented by the development of indigenous technological capabilities.

For smaller firms the importance of cooperating with a local partner is very important. Both via joint equity ventures (as seen above SMEs show a larger proportion of joint ventures over their total foreign investments) or, more frequently, by non-equity agreements, smaller firms try to benefit from the skills and the knowledge of their partner. In a sense, there is always an exchange of 'complementary assets': even when the deal involves a 'pure' transfer of technology, some knowledge is acquired from the partner in exchange; when the deals are more articulated, this exchange is richer and more complex.

In the experience of Italian firms, this usually means taking advantage from a better knowledge of the partner country's economic environment, a larger understanding of market dynamics, as well as the partner's relationship with the political and social institutions and with the labour market.[13]

One more factor appears to be specifically relevant in the cases of SMEs agreements in developing countries. In all the cases, Italian SMEs have a multi-domestic international strategy instead of a global one (as in Porter, 1985). That is, they face any single foreign market in a unique way, without any particular relationship with their behavior and operation in other markets. All foreign operations are in connection with the home country alone; their development and success have little if any relationship with that of other activities abroad. This is clearly linked with the foreign market-orientation of the deals: the foreign production should all be addressed to the local market, no flow of components, parts, semi-finished products goes from any foreign location to others or to the parent company. This clearly reduces the need for a closer control both on the quality and on the amount of the foreign location production, with possibly no conflict of interest among different foreign ventures if they effectively work for their own local or neighbouring markets.

This approach has specific advantages as well as disadvantages. Among the latter one should notice that when the technology is transferred to a smaller developing country, and the recipient firm is not allowed to create its own foreign market (e.g. regional), the deal may rarely be seen as important for the transferor, due to its very size, with possible implications on its commitment to effective technological acquisition and development.

Some evidence has been found of a sort of development cycle of foreign presence, a path going from exporting to licensing a local producer to direct investment. In some instances (a clear example is given by a shoe components producer), a reverse pattern can be seen: the license is used as a risk-minimising first approach to the market, followed by direct exports in case of success. However, the choice of mode of entry and stay abroad seem to have motivations that may change over time, but not necessarily towards a more direct presence. Moreover, one should never forget the idea of these firms as deeply different from global scanners and planners. They act in a world of very limited information; they do not have any network of sources of information regarding possible operations; nor do they have people working on strategic planning and/or evaluation of different possibilities. The elements of the choice among different modes of operating in LDCs do appear much more an *ex post* rationalisation than any real description of the selection process.

The proposals of the deals coming from abroad usually suggest a specific kind (or a limited range) of contractual solutions, leaving SMEs with a real possibility of choice which is narrower than a theoretical approach could suggest.

The theory of international growth of firms underlines the risks of dispersion of firm's competitive advantage through the licence of technology, highlighting the noticeable advantages, from this point of view, of completely internalised strategies of international expansion. For interviewed firms operating in traditional sectors and machinery manufacturing this, though important, does not seem crucial in determining either choices of internationalisation or the decision to sign a non-equity agreement with an independent firm. They have relatively little fear of losing their own competitive advantages through the giving up of know-how. As seen above, their advantages are often dynamic through time; they are often linked to the firm's home location, as the availability of a skilled work force with good knowledge of product and process; to the commercial integration with technologically advanced suppliers of machinery; to their ability in offering products characterised by a quality–cost mix which is more effective than that of competitors. As far as quality is concerned, they are tied to elements of image, fashion appeal and trade mark.

The key competitive factors seem related to the whole knowledge of the firm: the continuously evolutionary interplay among technical improvements, organisation and human capital. In investment goods, giving way to a flow of subsequent incremental innovation both in final products and in the process of production; in traditional consumer goods in the ability of producing and offering on the market through appropriate channels diversified and fashionable goods. So, the rate of appropriability of their 'technology' is quite high, as far as we define their technology in a large sense as above. Uncodified and very complex competitive assets, much more than specific product design, patents, formulas, can really be acquired by their partner only via a long learning process.

Finally, in any case, it is the firm that ultimately decides the nature of know-how to be transferred: it can protect itself from imitation by shaping and limiting the technological package. Not surprisingly, in many cases of technology transfer under scrutiny, it is not technology in a narrow sense, but more general 'manufacturing ability' to be transferred. Especially in traditional industries, such as textiles, cooperation agreements include a large amount of know-how:

- *Process know-how*: advice on the kind of machinery to be bought (and their sellers), organisation of production so to increase produc-

tivity, improvement of partner's reliability on the market via quality controls, time planning of production and sales, and so on;
- *Product know-how*: choice of raw materials, training of personnel, improvement of design, manufacture of new products so to increase the commercial range.[14]

In mechanical engineering the process is similar, even if it appears more closely centered on specific product know-how: new machines to be produced locally, often importing some key components from Italy. Here again, the emphasis is on the attainment of a higher level of product reliability.

In a 1986 survey[15] an estimate of the importance of the different channels in the sale of technology was given: know-how and technical assistance scored the highest, followed by licences and design; lesser weight was attributed to patent and trade marks.

In a general evaluation of the level of technology transferred to LDCs, the firms stated that it can be considered as standard, not particularly different from that used at home. This is related to both the need for a sufficient quality of technical organisation and product design for an effective transfer of manufacturing ability and to the fear of losing 'technological secrets' that has already been pointed out. No major modification of technologies for their implementation abroad is generally reported.

Technical assistance in general terms is obviously a crucial element that must be added to the export of components, to plant design, to the advice in the organisation of both the production process and the firm as a whole. In traditional industries (e.g. textile manufacturing), the advice on the supply of the machinery is very important, being process technological progress very often incorporated in the machinery bought. Training of the workforce clearly emerges as very important, since the possibility of the recipient firm becoming competitive is strictly linked to its ability to improve its human capital endowment. This is both true for managers and white-collar workers in general and for blue-collar workers.

The availability of skilled labour in the recipient country is clearly seen by Italian managers as one of the key features of the host economy that can determine in the first place the decision to cooperate with a LDC and later the success of the venture.

Royalties are the most common form of payment for the technology, often associated with lump sums. Lump sums are intended to cover the costs of initial technology transfer, seen by firms as the minimum goal to be achieved by the agreement to avoid financial losses.

The royalties constitute a payment reflecting the use of the technology, generally connected with the technological assistance supplied by the firms to the recipient company after implementation. But there are not only financial gains. Most contractual agreements foresee the import of components from Italy by the recipient party, usually for the whole period of the deal. There are two main reasons for this: on the one side, it can be true that some components may be more economically imported from the transferor than produced locally, either because they are too 'sophisticated' or because there are scale returns at home. On the other side, it is clear that Italian firms, in this way, secure for themselves an important export outlet. The gain they reach via export is in many cases more important than that associated with the inflow of royalties and a lump sum.

As Italian SMEs involved in non-equity agreements cannot have full control over some choices concerning major management issues, the agreements on market outlets are crucial. In a multidomestic, market-oriented, export-centred international strategy it is of the greatest importance not to create, via a licensee's activity, any damage either to direct exports from the home country or to the production of other international partners. So a clause limiting LDC partner sales to its own domestic market, often allowing export only to the neighbouring countries, is very often imposed.

Product quality controls are also among frequent contractual conditions. Especially when the trade mark used is the Italian one (this is often the case in the mechanical engineering), the supplier of know-how is interested in associating its name with a quality level that is similar to its own, so to keep open any possibility of direct export or of expanding its presence in neighbouring countries. In cases where the transferor fears the risk of a loss of the technology package supplied, conditions regarding controls on diffusion are imposed.

The SMEs' overall evaluation of the results of technology transfer operations is positive. The indicators of the success of the agreement most frequently mentioned are the increasing trade penetration on partner's and neighbouring markets, consistently with their market-oriented strategy, the creation of a regular flow of royalties and the acquisition of international experience.

However, as in general for every cooperative agreement among firms, one has to keep in mind that the reported 'success' by one partner not necessarily means the same success rate for the other. The technology has been transferred and paid for: but has the recipient firm effectively learned how to use (and improve) it in its production?

Some cases of partial success or complete failure were recorderd on the Italian side. In recent years, in particular, some planned operation of technology transfer were not implemented at all: the worsening of the economic situation in the host countries caused a strong reduction of the potential domestic demand so to discourage the agreement coming to reality. Among the cases of failures, the reported causes were very varied. Generally speaking, three main areas of problems can be recalled:

- Low commitment on the side of the transferor, probably due to the very limited importance that was attributed to the deal. This led to a very limited interaction among partners, without any particular assistance after the first transfer of know-how.
- Lack of experience in technology transfer, leading to incorrect evaluation of some of the elements of the agreement: wrong evaluation of the ability of the partner, limited skill in the transfer of knowledge, etc.
- Differences in managerial attitudes with the partner. Difficulties sometimes arise not only in the choice of the partner and in the definition of the programmes, but also in the negotiating and final operating phases of the activities.[16]

The future amount and quality of technology transfer by Italian smaller firms to developing countries is clearly linked to their ability to recover from general economic recession, and in particular to stimulate their internal demand for both capital goods and consumer products.

The bad macroeconomic conditions, weakness of demand and limitations in import policy, that have characterised many developing countries in the 1980s have a negative effect on the technology transfer strategies of developed countries' smaller firms. As far as Italian ones are concerned, some factors that may nonetheless stimulate these operations are among the following.

- First of all, many SMEs who actually export only towards large European neighbouring countries (as the majority of them do) may be always interested in increasing their *foreign outlets*, involving themselves in operations towards LDCs. These, though small in size, are in any case 'additive' for them.
- Protectionism on the side of LDCs continues to be a strong incentive to technology transfer, as the only possible key to open closed markets. Anyway, it is not the solution *per se*: firms must perceive

not only that it is the only way of entering the market but also that
it is possible and worthwhile.

- International competition has a stimulating effect: 'marginal' or uncertain operations can be done also because of the perception that
  some other OECD competitor suppliers will otherwise take the place
  of the firm.

- Major possibilities obviously emerge in better-performing non-OECD
  countries, such as Far Eastern ones. Many of the general conditions
  that have been mentioned as obstacles to technology transfer do not
  hold true for them. Moreover they are expressing a strong demand
  for foreign technology in industries which are upstream of their already developed sectors: machineries for traditional consumer goods
  are a clear example.

- Finally, in traditional industries there is a growing evidence of Italian firms changing their perception of some developing countries:
  seeing them not only as potential market but also as low-cost suppliers of goods. Some of them are implementing a new international
  division of labour, based more on an intra-industrial specialisation
  than on an inter-industrial one: that is transferring not only mature
  industries to LDCs, but only some part of them (competing more on
  labour costs and prices) keeping at home some other large segments
  and competing more on non-price factors.

7.7 EFFECTS AND IMPLICATIONS OF TECHNOLOGY
TRANSFER FOR DEVELOPING COUNTRIES

This final section presents some comments on the possible effects, and
their magnitude, of the technological learning and competitiveness of
the recipient developing countries.

To begin with, three general problems will be briefly presented: the
possible trade-off between technology acquisition and balance of payments performance; the issue of 'unpackaging' the foreign contribution; and the issue of the scale of operations.

As it has been stressed several times in previous sections, most of
the cases of technical cooperation with LDCs were decided by Italian
firms on the basis of their interest in those markets. They expected to,
and actually did, receive earnings from the operations via both royalties and increased (or new) exports. Moreover, they generally prohibited autonomous export by their partner in order not to create real or
potential competition for their products on other markets. In the ma-

jority of cases, they seemed to have little or no interest in experiences such as export processing zones: Italian SMEs prefer to manufacture by themselves, at home, the goods they sell on international markets.

It is difficult to state the net effect of these operations on the balance of payments of recipient countries; in some cases, they may create a new national production which substitutes for previous imports. A key issue is that increased technological capabilities may allow autonomous exports in the future. Nonetheless, in such a deal, there may be in the short term a trade-off between balance of payments constraints (lump sum and royalties for the technology, need to pay for import related to the transfer, clauses forbidding export) and know-how acquisition.

The implications of this trade-off are clear: shortage of funds for investments (in foreign technology) and the need to limit imports due to macroeconomic constraint, or to the debt service burden, may impede the innovative progress of the industry, decreasing its future competitiveness and creating a very dangerous vicious cycle.

The second issue to be briefly commented on is 'unpackaging'. The most relevant aspect of a policy of 'unpackaging' foreign technology transfer is the separation of foreign 'packages' into different elements, importing only some of them. In particular divorcing all the technological elements (know-how and capital goods), to be imported, from ownership and management, that should be local. A trend of thought, especially at the beginning of the 1980s, suggested 'new' forms of foreign ventures in developing countries, as opposed to the classical behavior of multinational enterprises to operate via fully-controlled subsidiaries. The new forms should be non-equity contracts and joint ventures, with shared forms of management and control on manufacturing activities. The package linked to foreign direct investments in this way is divided into possible different sources for technology (foreign) and capital (national). Generally speaking, SMEs can be suitable partners for such deals: they are willing to transfer their know-how without taking the direct management of the ventures, with its financial costs. The experience of Italian firms is very often similar to this pattern.

But again macroeconomic constraints seem to raise a trade-off. Traditional FDI tends to exclude local firms from direct control of operations, reducing their technological and managerial learning but creating an highly desirable inflow of capital. New forms, in absence of third, financing parties, may lead to a more effective local participation but create the need for raising funds locally.

The firms in our sample reported several instances in which they were asked to take a direct financial share in the recipient venture. Italian engineering firms are often also asked to capitalise their earnings from the supply of turnkey plants and participate in their management. Of course, shared forms of financial investment and control could be desirable, such as equity joint ventures, to meet both needs. But one should keep in mind that joint equity does not necessarily means joint management, control and power: and the problems recorded in cases of wholly-owned foreign ventures can be also found in ventures with a local nominal equity share.

The third issue regards the scale of operations. Smaller firms, much more than larger multinational corporations, may be interested in smaller projects in developing countries, due to their very size. The revenues coming from such ventures can be marginal for large companies but very interesting for smaller ones. Generally speaking, SMEs may also possess technological capabilities better suited for smaller, more flexible projects.

In the 1980s, the large flow of mega-industrial and infrastructural projects in developing countries that characterised previous periods was sharply reduced, due both to lack of resources and to different industrial policies in some countries. In this environment SMEs' contribution can be important, giving birth to a new flow of smaller, more financiable, projects.

One crucial question remains open: are these smaller-scale operations effectively competitive on an international standard or are they, because of their size, ineffective in reaching economies of scale and therefore not competitive on the markets?

All the previous issues are more or less based on one key question: is technology transfer effective? Balance of payments problems are mitigated as firms get more and more competitive; local capital is repaid by a stream of earnings; smaller firms can be very competitive in world market niches.

This topic will now be elaborated on the basis of both the experience of Italian smaller firms and from a more general viewpoint.

The effectiveness of a technology acquisition can be seen from three main points of view:

- The ability to choose the right technology
- The ability to acquire it
- The ability to use (and improve) it

These elements will be now discussed in the light of the role that smaller firms can play, as transferor, in this process.

The first point is: what technology? It is often difficult to discriminate between smaller firms and large multinational corporations on the basis of which of the two generally owns a superior technology. Given different industrial, technological and national characteristics both kinds of firm can have the right know-how to be transferred. It is difficult to state that smaller firms *per se* normally have a technology which is more suitable to be transferred to developing countries. In some industries, due both to static and dynamic economies of scale, smaller firms are clearly backward; in others (capital goods industries offer clear examples) smaller firms may be on the technological frontier. A technological policy that discriminates between foreign contributors depending only on their size does not seem reasonable.

An interesting, and quite widespread, difference among different firms in terms of their size can be on the contrary seen if technology is seen as organisation and entrepreneurship. Larger firms tend to have organisational schemes that fit poorly with the reality of industries in developing countries. The ability of using, coordinating and improving the work force skills which are available in LDCs, the ability of creating (changing) managerial roles and managers suited for them, the intelligent, flexible and efficient use of scarce technical and human resources, the ability to create excess resources and use them for a steady growth: all this knowledge, which is crucial in LDCs, can be probably found more often (but not only) in smaller firms. They can be used to face and solve these problems and have developed organisational schemes and procedures, routines, which are useful and that can be transferred, modified if necessary, to developing countries firms.

Other topics are then linked (but not discussed here) to the question of the choice of know-how: how to discover who possess it; how to evaluate its importance before engaging in the deal; how to create competition, if possible, among different suppliers; what basic knowledge is needed to start a process of technological acquisition, given that it is neither a public good nor a simple, standardised item on sale in the market at arms' length prices.

The second point (how to acquire it) rises two main issues: the effective willingness of the partner and the time horizon of the deal.

Why should a firm give away a part of its technological knowledge? Basically, to gain something in exchange. Money, lump sums paid for, is a good reason; but a lot of firms are searching (also) something else: experience, knowledge, market access. A very frequent case is the transfer of technology in exchange for (money and) market access: developing countries firms usually have a key competitive asset to exchange in their better knowledge of their own and neighbouring markets.

In any case, transferor firms must have a specific interest in the deal, something they are willing to exploit or acquire; possibly, not only money, that can theoretically be acquired everywhere. Something that drives their interest in a good progress, of all the phases of the transfer. For developing countries' firms, and governments, it is very important to understand why are they giving their technology and if the strategic goals of the transferor are compatible with the ones of the transferee.

This turns out to be a very important issue. Especially where SMEs are concerned several cases of technology transfer end unsatisfactorily because of the low interest, and commitment, of the transferor. SMEs usually have a lesser degree of strategic planning than larger firms; they can get involved in contracts which they later discover to be not fruitful for them; they can fear the risk of financial losses or desire to withdraw because they did not earn the expected returns as soon as they thought.

One of the keys of the success of a technological acquisition, especially where SMEs are concerned, is that the transferor must perceive a clear interest in the cooperation.

The other key is the time horizon. When the relationships among the partners are more similar to a simple sale of technology (a package of know-how acquired spot, without any further contact with the transferor) the conditions for the success are more stringent. The technology must be simple in its comprehension, and use, well codified; the transferee must already have all the complementary skills to use it. This is quite frequent: buying the rights of a patent, a licence to manufacture following a well-defined process, the use of a trade mark. Depending upon these conditions, buying a technology 'on the market' can be very successful.

But in several instances, especially where SMEs are concerned, it is not so easy. The application of the know-how must be tested, if necessary it has to be modified, the work force must be trained, the organisation modified. Again, when in the technological package there is also 'manufacturing ability' and organisational expertise, time is needed for an effective interaction of the new knowledge with the existing organisation and 'routines' of the firm.

The acquisition, the real learning and implementation of a new know-how needs time, interaction among partners, trial and errors. And the ability to *learn* a technology must be transformed into the ability to *use* it. When a new process is introduced it must work, possibly as well as in the supplier. The competitiveness of the transferee must be increased.

But what happens when time passes? In some cases, nothing: the know-how (a chemical formula) remains as such: if you have learned how to use it, your competitiveness is increased. But most technologies are constantly increased by a flow of incremental modifications, constantly improved without any evident new breakthrough.

Three cases are then possible:

• The transferee continues to use the original know-how as such, and its competitiveness steadily declines
• The transferee is able to receive from the transferor a continuous flow of information (often after a time lag) regarding its improvements
• The transferee is able to improve the technology by itself.

The first case is frequent. Is technology transfer a success? For the OECD firm, possibly 'yes'; for the LDC firm, possibly 'no'. Even if the know-how has been effectively transferred, and acquired, it has produced no modification in the status of the firm: the reasons for searching help abroad will last.

The second case is the case of common success. The transferor finds its own interest in continuing the relationships: be it the size and growth of the market concerned, the importance of the royalties, the interest in the new applications made by the partner. The learning by cooperating increases as long as cooperation goes on. The transferee is not autonomous yet: but its competitiveness increases.

The third case is obviously both the most difficult and interesting for developing countries; most of the fast growing developing economies have relied on a mix of imported technology and original improvement. But discussing all its conditions and implications is well beyond the goal of this chapter.

SMEs can be suitable partners for second-case relationships: due to their size and resources, they can find use in continuing the cooperation with a partner, operating in joint venture in some parts of the world; if the partner proves to be efficient in manufacturing and able in selling the constant stream of royalties may be preferable to the risk of investing alone; especially if the partner provides not only money, but also a significant flow of information both on process (e.g. a specific range, a different factor intensify in production) and products (modification for different markets, marketing techniques), cooperation could be on both sides the first best. LDC firms may also become the most efficient source of certain components or products, complementary to those of the transferor for their cost and quality. In other cases, the complementarity may be geographical, given its ability in selling in certain markets or the problems for SMEs of implementing their own commercial network all over the world. This is especially the case in which not only technical knowledge is transferred, but also 'manufacturing ability' and organisation.

Notes

1. Because of the statistical methods applied by ISTAF (the Italian National Institute of Statistics) in its surveys, we will often exclude in this chapter firms with less than 20 employees from our coverage.

2. Food products are excluded due to the difficulty of separating agricultural and industrial products in OECD, SITC II, data. Italy does not perform well in foodstuff export, except for some specific products (wine, pasta etc.). Petroleum derivates are also excluded from Table 7.4.

3. For a more detailed analysis, see F. Onida, 'Patterns of International Specification and Technological Competitiveness in Italian Manufacturing Industry', in Onida and G. Viesti (1988).

4. Here we refer to 'small' firms in terms of their export volume: clearly, large firms with a very low export propensity can be included in this number. These data may approximate the phenomenon fairly well.

5. The TBP is one of the indicators of international technology transfer. It represents currency transactions related to the purchase and sale of patents, licences, trademarks, designs, inventions, know-how, and technical assistance. TBP data, though they are the most direct measurement of technological flows between countries, must be interpreted with caution, because they fail to register some operations such as the payment of R&D contracts abroad, services connected with the sale of industrial equipment and all those exchanges of technology which escape measurement because they give rise to no financial payment. Furthermore, TBP is influenced by the foreign investment activity of firms. Transactions between parent companies and subsidiaries, in fact, often reflect economic and financial conditions rather than technological relations, since they are affected by problems linked to transfer of profits, fluctuations in the exchange rate, the existence of particular tax regulations and the location of international holding companies.

6. In Italian TBP, licenses are defined as the authorisation granted by the owner of a property right (patent, trade mark, design, etc.) to somebody to use the object of the property right.

7. It should be pointed out, however, that the content of NCTA, which has represented increasingly important values, far outstripping the payments and receipts of the TBP (Table 7.5), is still rather ill-defined, and it is

difficult to determine how much technology is actually transferred through this item. A survey by the CNR, in fact, shows that in reality part of the transaction registered in it should be considered without any technical or technological content (such as services of an administrative and organisational type, generic consultation studies, etc.) (CNR, 1988).

8. Countries with a large share of foreign subsidiary companies see their balances worsen for this reason. About 80 per cent of the payments by the United Kingdom and the Federal German Republic, for example, are effected by subsidiaries in favor of their foreign parent companies. In both countries, independent companies show a positive balance, which only in the case of the United Kingdom was large enough to exceed the negative effect produced by the subsidiaries of multinationals (CNR, 1989).

9. Firms interviewed generally employ less than 500 employees and operate in traditional consumer goods industries (textiles–clothing, leather–foot-wear), chemicals and machinery manufacturing.

With respect to recipient developing countries, the technology transfer cases refer to Argentina, Brazil, India, South Korea and Singapore, and are mainly characterised by non-equity forms. Data regarding new cases are tabulated in Table 7.12).

10. Buckley and Casson (1987) presents the idea of decreasing transaction costs in repeating the deal with the same partner.

11. This may be seen as a typical learning-by-doing process (Malerba, 1988) in which the firm is able to create a new internal routine to cope with this kind of market transaction (Nelson and Winter, 1982).

12. For a more detailed discussion of factors influencing the international strategy choice, see Onida and Viesti (1988), Ch. 5.

13. For a general discussion of advantages arising from cooperative ventures, see Viesti (1988).

14. The experience of downstream traditional consumer goods in transferring upstream process technology is noteworthy.

15. The survey (Sirilli, 1986) covered 76 cases of technology transfer, to both DCs and LDCs.

16. Moreover, as technology transfer is also based on close personal relationships between partners' management, the substitution of the managers of the recipient firm during the agreement's operating life led in some cases to incomprehension and failure.

8 The Case of Japan

Terutomo Ozawa

Things – economic phenomena – change so rapidly in Japan these days that what are at the moment considered the most up-to-date developments are doomed to be outdated practically overnight. In 1985, I completed a report on Japan's small multinationals for UNCTAD[1] and thought I had captured the latest developments so that there would be no immediate need to update my analysis for a while, but my more recent trips to Japan have made me realise that more exciting changes are in the making in Japan's small business sector, along with its large business sector – especially under the pressure of the ever-soaring yen, the pressure that has been letting market forces dictate the course of the Japanese economy in an unprecedented fashion.

Overseas direct investment is made in response to – and as a direct function of – both the 'push' effect at home (generated by rapid technological progress, a saturation of the domestic market, a rise in wages, etc.) and the 'pull' effect from the host countries (caused by availability of low-cost labour or raw materials, economic growth, special governmental incentives, etc.). The greater the combined forces generated by effects, the more extensive – and the more intensive – a country's overseas direct investment. This phenomenon can be clearly observed in Japan's present rush to overseas markets via direct investment.

8.1 RECENT PATTERNS AND CHARACTERISTICS

Pervasiveness and Vigor of Japan's Small Industry

A surprisingly large number of small-scale manufacturing units exist in Japan. One might expect that the rapid modernisation of Japanese industry, spawning gigantic corporations such as Toyota, Hitachi, Matsushita, Nippon Steel and other globally-known enterprises which take the dominant positions on *Fortune*'s lists, would have reduced the room for the existence of small firms. On the contrary, they are thriving as vigorously as ever.

Indeed, in the early post-second World War period the small business sector was regarded as the backwater of Japanese industry, a remnant of economic dualism, eking out its existence from the manufacture of low-quality unsophisticated products, mostly sundries and textiles, with the help of cheap labour. Its products, when exported, epitomised the then prevalent image of Japanese manufactures abroad as 'cheap and shoddy merchandise'.

Yet in the recent past Japan's small industry has been, all of a sudden, rediscovered – and indeed, touted – as a marvellously resilient and vital industrial segment without the contribution of which the phenomenal growth of the Japanese economy would not have been possible. Indeed, many of Japan's small and medium-sized enterprises (SMEs) began to thrive in new high-tech growth industries such as electronics, mechatronics, biotechnology, new materials, and other highly specialised fields, fields where the entry and competitive conditions are still in a state of flux.

The Ministry of International Trade and Industry (MITI) defines 'small and medium business units' in terms of number of employees and size of capitalisation (as far as manufacture is concerned, those enterprises with an employment of 300 or fewer workers or with a capital of ¥100 million or less). According to this definition of small and medium-sized manufacturers, in 1986, for example, this class accounted for as much as 99.5 per cent of the total number of manufacturing units (870 262 out of 874 471 units), 74.4 per cent of the total number of employees (9 920 555 of 13 341 836 workers), and 56.5 per cent of the total value added (¥50 488 billion out of Y89 294 billion.[2]

Yet this definition includes those small manufacturing units, which though physically separate, are actually owned and controlled by large firms – hence making the existence of small and medium enterprises somewhat over-represented. At the same time, however, MITI excludes those smallest units employing one – three workers.

Although some biases are thus inevitably introduced into statistics, the fact nevertheless remains that Japanese industry is still crowded by an amazingly large number of small and medium-sized enterprises. Other countries define this category of enterprises much more broadly. For example, the US definition uses the criterion of less than 2000 employees (see Gomes-Casseres and Kohn, Chapter 10 in this volume); the Singaporean definition less than 1000 employees (see Pang, Chapter 16); and the Korean less than 500 (see Lee, Chapter 14). If these other criteria were used, the size of Japan's SMEs as a whole would be much greater. Furthermore, there is no sign of their disappearance in Japan, despite the fear often expressed by policy-makers

who always see the rising tide of monopoly or oligopoly by large enterprises. Indeed, small firms multiply themselves more quickly than
large ones, though their demise may be equally as fast.

In fact, despite the 'high value' yen which wiped out the price competitiveness of Japan's small firms in the world market, they have swiftly
recovered from the currency blows and begun to thrive on the super
yen. Their economic health has been improving and showing remarkable strength and resilience; this is reflected by the small business
index prepared by Japan's Small Business Finance Corporation (see
Figure 8.1). Apparently they have succeeded in finding ways out of
the recession caused by the yen's appreciation and, as will be stressed
below, this has something to do with the technobiological dynamism
of the small industry sector.

Overseas Direct Investment

As already revealed elsewhere,[3] Japan's SMEs have been quite active
in direct overseas operations such as direct foreign investment (FDI),
technology licensing, and subcontracting. As shown in Table 8.1, their
overseas investments, in the neighbourhood of 40 per cent of the total
in terms of number of investments (counting those locally incorporated
ventures and acquisition of equity interests in existing local firms),
have been expanding phenomenally since 1985, along with those made
by large enterprises. (If the US definition, for example, is used, Japan's small industry's share in overseas investment will naturally be
much more considerable.)

The current outward move of Japan's small industry constitutes the
second wave, the first wave of its overseas advance having occurred
in the early 1970s when the yen began to appreciate sharply for the
first item in the post-war period (in the wake of the dollar's devalua-
tion *vis-à-vis* gold). The current wave is again closely related to the
yen's dramatic rise in value that began after the Plaza accord in 1985.

As far as manufacturing activities are concerned, the SMEs overseas investments are still – and particularly at present – heavily concentrated in Asia (see Table 8.2); in 1987, for example, 341 of 469
manufacturing ventures were made in Asia, notably in South Korea,
Taiwan, Hong Kong, and China, all Japan's neighbouring economies.
those made in Hong Kong and China are interrelated in many instances.
Investments by Japan's SMEs in China are the latest developments
designed to use low-cost labour and at the same time to establish a
foothold in China's future economic growth.

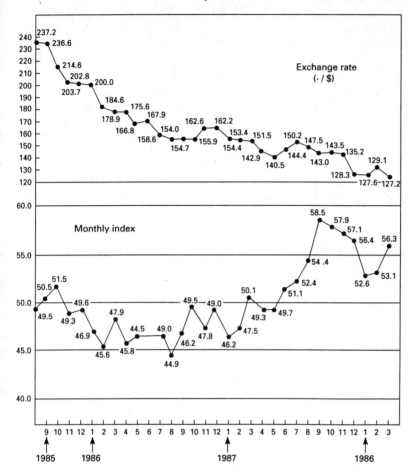

Figure 8.1. The rising yen and the economic health index of small business, monthly

Note: The index is prepared by Japan's Small Business Finance Corporation, based upon 800 small firms' condition relating to sales, profits, inventory, employment, etc.

Source: Shoko Sogo Kenkyusho, *Chusho Kigyo Shinjidai* (New Era of Small and Medium Enterprises) (Tokyo: Nikkan Kogyo Shimbundha, 1988), p. 10.

Table 8.1 No. of overseas investments by small firms, 1978–87[c]

No. of investment[a]	1978	1979	1980	1981	1982	1983	1984	1985	1986	1987
A By both large and small firms[b]	887	990	790	748	765	868	828	1023	1419	n.a.
B By small firms in all industries	306	437	326	336	247	306	312	318	599	1063
C By small firms in manufacturing	112	133	90	108	86	91	109	137	279	469
B/A (%)	34.5	44.1	41.3	44.9	34.8	35.3	37.7	31.1	42.2	44.1
C/B (%)	36.6	30.4	27.6	32.1	32.3	29.7	34.9	43.1	46.6	44.1

Notes:
[a] These investments consist of newly-incorporated overseas ventures plus new equity acquisition with management participation in local ventures.
[b] Investments by small firms include those made jointly with large corporations, as well as with individuals (non-corporate investors).
[c] Included are investments of more than ¥3 million before 1 April 1984, and of more than ¥10 million after 1 April 1984. Hence these two sets of figures are not strictly comparable.

Source: Small and Medium Business Agency, White Paper on Small and Medium Business Enterprises (Tokyo, 1988), p. 48.

Table 8.2 Overseas investments (newly incorporated ventures abroad and new equity acquisitions), Japan's small enterprises, 1987, by industry and region

	Asia						North America	Latin America	Europe	Middle East	Oceania	Total
	South Korea	Hong Kong	Taiwan	China	Others[a]	Total						
Manufacturing	96	30	91	30	94	341	99	3	19	0	7	469
Food	8	1	2	4	6	21	6	1	2	0	5	35
Timber/pulp	0	0	2	1	4	7	4	0	1	0	0	12
Textiles	2	7	3	7	7	26	7	0	1	0	0	34
Chemicals	6	0	10	3	7	26	8	0	2	0	0	36
Metals	5	6	12	4	13	40	4	1	0	0	0	45
Machinery	50	11	37	4	36	138	46	1	9	0	2	196
Sundries	25	5	25	7	21	83	24	0	4	0	0	111
Agriculture, forestry, and fishery	1	0	0	3	4	8	5	3	2	1	3	22
Mining	0	0	0	0	0	0	3	1	1	0	0	5
Construction	1	1	1	0	1	4	2	0	0	0	0	6
Commerce and services	17	33	27	15	29	121	346	11	30	0	53	561
Total	115	64	119	48	128	474	455	18	52	1	63	1063

Note:
[a] Africa is not listed because there was no new investment in 1987.

Source: Small and Medium Business Agency, White Paper on Small and Medium Enterprises (Tokyo, 1988), p. 40.

As before in the recent past, machinery is the sector in which Japan's Asia-focused investments most frequently originate (138 out of 341 new ventures), followed by sundries (83 new ventures).

Next to Asia, North America is the second most popular region in manufacturing; in 1987 it hosted 99 new investments. But North America is attractive particularly for small firms' overseas investments in the service sector (commerce, information gathering through branches, real estate, finance, leisure-related businesses, and other services). No less than 346 new ventures were set up in these service areas.

Motivation

The underlying assumption for our research is that small multinationals are different from their large counterparts in investment and business behaviours. Does firm size alone really matter as significantly as we postulate?

There are many other factors, however, that are closely interrelated with firm size or that may overwhelm the effect of firm size. If we are to gauge the role of firm size separate from all other factors, we need a vast amount of statistics and information.

Nevertheless, what limited amount of information we have (Table 8.3) may shed some light, if only partially, on the question. Spearman's rank correlation analysis on the relative importance of different motives between the small and the large Japanese firms (coefficient = 0.818) seems to indicate that there is, overall, not much significant difference between the two when it comes to a given set of possible reasons for overseas investments shown in Table 8.3. Both are equally influenced by the same set of motives as a whole.

Yet the rank correlation masks some important differences as far as certain specific reasons are concerned. For example, motive(2), 'Utilisation of low-cost labour in the host country' is among the top four reasons for both categories of firms (that is, not much difference rankwise), it is nonetheless significantly more important for the small Japanese firms (39.4 per cent) than for the large ones (22.3 per cent).

Another substantial difference is seen in the motive (3),'In responses local customer needs'. The small firms (38.2 per cent) appear to be investing more frequently in response to, or at least taking into consideration more often, the host countries' invitations than the large ones (8.0 per cent). This, however, may simply reflect the host countries' greater preference (hence more favourable welcome gestures) for small firms rather than the firms' responsiveness for such gestures itself.

Table 8.3 Major reasons for overseas investment, Japan's small and large multinationals, rank correlations, firm size and location of investment

Reasons	Small/medium firms	large firms	Asia	North America and EC
1 Promising local and neighboring markets	51.5% (1)a	54.3% (1)	60.0% (1)	53.8% (1)
2 Utilisation of low-cost labor in the host country	39.4% (2)	22.3 (4)	50.0 (2)	7.7 (10)
3 In response to local customer needs	30.3 (4)	33.0 (2)	22.0 (3)	41.5 (2)
4 Information gathering	27.3 (5)	23.4 (3)	20.0 (4)	27.7 (3)
5 Requests from the host country	38.2 (3)	8.0 (9)	10.0 (8)	6.2 (11)
6 To secure orders from parent companies and other established customers	15.2 (6)	21.3 (5)	16.0 (6)	26.2 (4)
7 To cultivate local markets	15.2 (6)	12.8 (8)	18.0 (5)	12.3 (7)
8 Low-cost raw materials in the host country	12.1 (7)	12.8 (8)	14.0 (7)	10.8 (8)
9 To avoid exchange risk	9.1 (9)	17.0 (6)	18.0 (5)	13.8 (6)
10 Favorable local tax treatment	9.1 (9)	5.3 (10)	8.0 (9)	4.6 (12)
11 Strengthening of financial functions (fund raising and investment)	9.1 (9)	11.7 (8)	6.0 (10)	12.3 (7)
12 To avoid trade friction	6.1 (10)	16.0 (7)	14.0 (7)	15.4 (5)
13 To secure technology	6.1 (10)	5.3 (10)	0 (11)	9.2 (9)
14 Other reasons	12.1 (8)	4.3 (11)	10.0 (8)	3.1 (13)
Spearman's rank correlation coefficient	0.818		0.702	

Notes: Since multiple answers are given, percentages exceed 100%.
a Ranking in parentheses.

Source: Compiled from the results of a questionnaire survey on the status of Japan's overseas ventures (December 1987) by Small and Medium Business Agency as presented in White Paper on Small and Medium Enterprises (Tokyo, 1988) p. 49.

Motive (12), 'To avoid trade friction' (6.1 per cent) than for the large ones (16.0 per cent), though this motive itself ranks relatively low for both (10th and 7th). A similar observation can be made about the avoidance of exchange risk as a motive. The large firms' greater export sales or import purchases (in absolute terms) are subject to much greater exchange risks, although the individual firms, whether large or small, differ greatly in export or import dependence and the foreign markets they deal with, hence they differ in evaluating exchange risks.

With respect to the motives (1), the 'Promising local and neighbouring markets', and (3), 'In response to local customer needs', the large firms appear to be more strongly motivated than the small ones (54.3 per cent v. 51.5 per cent and 33.0 per cent v. 30.3 per cent), though these two reasons are among the top motives for the both groups.

Motive (6), 'To secure orders from the parent companies and other established customers', seems not to be among the top motives – for both (the 6th ranking reason for the small firms and the 8th for the large ones). This result for the small firms is somewhat surprising, however, since it is often reported that Japan's small firms that serve as subcontractors are now following their parent firms or other major assemblers in tandem with the latter's overseas advances. Yet this tandem type of investment may also be reflected in such reasons as (1) 'Promising local and neighbouring markets,' (3) 'In response to local customer needs,' and (7) 'To cultivate local markets', for those components suppliers that are aggressive enough to go overseas are not really passive 'captive suppliers', but are rather the ones who are eager to expand their sales beyond their 'tied' markets and to capture new markets so as to make their total business large enough to justify direct overseas production. (As will be detailed below, many of them are Type C-2 small multinationals.)

Another important finding is the more pronounced difference we can detect between the host regions (Asia v. North America and the European Community, (EC)) with respect to the same set of motives. Unfortunately the statistics do not differentiate the investing Japanese firms in terms of size. Nevertheless, we can still appreciate the importance of considerably different location-specific factors between the two regions (i.e. different 'pull' factors) impacting on the investment motives of the Japanese firms, small and large alike.

Although Spearman's coefficient is a relatively high 0.702, there are, again, significant differences with respect to specific motives. Most noticeably, for example, motive (2), 'Low-cost labour in the host countries', is decisively a key factor in investing in Asia (50.0 per cent), as compared to North America and the EC (only 7.7 per cent). Given the fact that the small Japanese firms are more local labour resource-oriented in overseas investment than the large ones, this means that the former are naturally more attracted to other Asian countries than to North America or Europe.

Japan's investment in Asia as a whole also indicates the attractiveness of the growing local markets in the region – somewhat more strongly than its counterpart in North America and Europe, though motive (1), 'Promising local and neighbouring markets', is the foremost important reason for investments in these regions.

Thus the location-specific factors on the hosts' side, along with the investing firms' motives (which are the products of both firm-specific and their home location-specific factors), do interact and play decisive roles in producing differentiating characteristics of overseas investment, as emphasised in John Dunning's eclectic theory.[4]

8.2 TYPOLOGY OF SMALL MULTINATIONALS

Although we conceptually emphasise the differences between small and large firms as two distinct groups, there is equally a great diversity in organisational and operational characteristics among the small firms themselves. As I looked at a limited number (eight) of my own case studies and also at the existing case studies made available by Japan's governmental agencies,[5] I found it useful to classify Japan's small multinationals into four basic types, as summarised in Table 8.4.

Type-A (Traditional-type) Firms

Type-A producers manufacture low value added (low-tech), traditional light industry products with the conventional manufacturing processes that are highly intensive in the use of unskilled or semi-skilled labor.

The sweat-shop or cottage-industry image of small-scale workshops fits the basic nature of Type-A firms. This is exactly the type of small producers who were often found in the back alleys of Japanese industry in the pre-war days – and, in decreasing numbers, until the early 1970s. Their survival depended on the hiring of low-wage workers. The type of goods produced by this class of small producers were represented by such light industry manufactures such as low value added textiles, toys, umbrellas, and other sundries. They operated in fiercely competitive markets. Raw materials and other necessary inputs were,

Table 8.4 Classification of Japan's small multinationals in manufacturing

Type	Market characteristics	Subcategories	Direct overseas operations
Type-A Traditional (low-tech, cottage-industry-type) workshops	Light industry goods Food, toys, tableware, textiles, kitchenware, and sundries	A-1 Domestic market-oriented A-2 Export market-oriented	The major investors during the first wave of investments in Japan's neighbouring countries (1968–74) Some are now investing in China
Type-B Parts and components manufacturers	'Closed' or 'semi-closed' markets Long-term contractual arrangements	B-1 Captive suppliers B-2 Independent suppliers	Tandem investments, following their major customers Currently active investors 1985–)
Type-C High-tech (high value added) manufacturers	'Niche' monopoly or 'mini' oligopoly	C-1 High-tech product manufacturers Precision machinery Electric/electronics equipment C-2 High-tech process-using manufacturers	'Product-cycle' investors More and more oriented to advanced countries in overseas investment and licensing
Type-D Engineering and technical services firms	'Patent or know-how'-based monopoly or oligopoly	D-1 Semi-autonomous firms (spin-offs from large enterprises) D-2 Completely autonomous firms	Active in plant exports and overseas projects as organisers

in many cases, provided, and finished products were purchased, by some intermediaries, usually small trading companies and trade associations (or cooperatives).

This group of traditional small manufacturers, once so dominant in the Japanese industrial scene, has nearly disappeared in Japan. In fact, this industrial segment was among the first group of activities that were shed from and transferred by Japanese industry to lower labour-cost areas, first to Okinawa and then on to Japan's neighbouring low-wage countries in the late 1980s (when shortages of low-cost young factory workers were experienced for the first time in postwar Japan). Their overseas investments were usually assisted by trading companies:

In the beginning Japan's [small] enterprises concentrated their overseas [manufacturing] ventures in developing countries very close to Japan. Until 1970, for example, as many as 87.6 per cent of their ventures were located in the neighboring Asian countries or territories: those set up in Taiwan alone accounted for 43.9 per cent of the total. The Republic of Korea, Hong Kong, and Okinawa were other major host economies, together receiving 23.1 per cent (Japanese investments in Okinawa prior to its return to Japan in May 1972 were officially treated as overseas investment).[6]

During the 1951–71 period, these manufacturing ventures by Japan's SMEs numbered 436, but as many as 156 were in sundries, 72 in textiles, 28 in food, and 55 in 'electric machinery' but most in relatively standardised household electric appliances (such as irons, fans, radios, rice-cookers, and the like). 28 ventures in chemicals similarly involved the production of, *inter alia*, such simple products as ink, paints, and plastics.[7]

With the rise in wages in these neighbouring countries, many of them had to totally withdraw from these ventures or transmigrate to still lower labour-cost areas. But some have succeeded in growing into profitable corporations with significant product, process, and marketing innovations. Swany Corporation, a glove maker, is a prime example:

Swany, originally established in 1937 as a family-owned shop to manufacture gloves and incorporated in 1950, was one of several hundred small glove-makers who clustered together in a small rural town, Hiratori, on the island of Shikoku. In its heyday (1955–65) as many as 90 per cent of the townsfolk (totalling about 4000) were either directly or indirectly engaged in the manufacture of all kinds of gloves, from dress gloves to gardening gloves.

The labor shortages and wage hikes that began to occur in the 1960s put a squeeze on this local industry. The appreciation of the yen added difficulties, and the town's exports declined precipitously year after year.

To overcome rising labor costs at home and the appreciating yen, Swany chose the Masan Export Processing Zone in South Korea as the location of its first wholly owned manufacturing subsidiary abroad. It started out by employing as many as 450 workers. The unique feature of the factory was a conveyor system "contrived" and introduced by Swany to mass-produce gloves cost-effectively. This venture's earnings moved into the black after two years.

In fact, Swany's export sales expanded so rapidly thanks to the company's direct (not intermediated by trading companies) marketing strategy with big American merchandisers such as Sears Roebuck) that in 1976, it decided to open another wholly owned subsidiary in South Korea employing 300 workers. And this expansion was followed by the opening of a third subsidiary with a work force of 250 in the same host country. At the same time, Swany closed its three factories in Japan and ended up only with the home-office activities of product development, procurement, and quality and production controls.

The company, with a staff of only 50 people in Japan, now employs about 1000 local workers in its three factories in the host country. With an eye to further expanding sales in North America, Swany opened a New York office with a showroom and a sales staff of 10. It established a sales office in Canada in 1983. China and Sri Lanka are now considered the future possible sites for manufacturing investments.[8]

Some traditional small manufacturers (such as those of cast iron products) do still subsist in Japan, nowadays often relying on illegal foreign workers who come to Japan as tourists or students but seek employment for low wages. But the days of overseas investment by the traditional-type small firms seem to be over, simply because they have fast become nearly extinct in Japan. Many have failed, while some others have successfully moved into the new growth sectors.

Nevertheless, it is important to keep in mind that the traditional small manufacturers contributed enormously to Japan's early post-war exports of manufactures, earning the precious foreign exchange Japan badly needed. Throughout the 1950s this group of small manufacturers were Japan's star exporters, accounting for as much as 70 per cent of Japanese exports by marketing overseas labour-intensive light industry products such as textiles, Christmas decorations, toys, musical boxes, sports equipment, wigs, umbrellas, and a variety of other sundries.

Type-B (Parts and Components) Manufacturers

This group of small producers are the manufacturers of parts and components and other industrial-customer-specific intermediate goods. Two subgroups may be identified: Type-(B-1) and Type-(B-2). (B-1) are captive suppliers, 'captive' in the sense that all or the majority of their outputs are sold to one or two specific customers who are most likely to be large corporations.

In fact, Type-B-1 suppliers' customers may be their own major stockholders with the despatched executives on their management. But in many cases this captive type of supplier may be family-owned but have a long-standing business relationship with a certain major customer, almost as if they were an operating division of the latter.

In contrast, Type-B-2 suppliers are more independent in their business, catering to a much more diversified group of customers. Many even consciously strive to remain autonomous by avoiding dependence on a limited number of customers. They are quite willing to deal with as large a number of customers as possible, domestic or foreign, some of whom may even be each others' rivals.

By and large, the independent suppliers are more technologically sophisticated (frequently possessing a number of patents and significant firm-specific know-how) and more independent in research activity and more capable of developing new markets and distribution outlets than the captive suppliers.

These parts and components suppliers, Type-B-1 and B-2 alike, increasingly came into existence in significantly large numbers during the late 1950s and throughout the 1960s when Japanese industry shifted its structure away from light industry toward heavy and chemical industries, notably assembly-based ones such as shipbuilding, automobiles, and electric/electronics appliances and machinery. For example, some might have been small producers of light industry goods such as buttons, hoses, and simple metal flatware, but they quickly transformed themselves into suppliers of button-size terminals for electric appliances, specialised industrial hoses and belts for machines, and mechanical metal components.

The export share of small manufacturers in the traditional lines of light industry goods consequently declined to 60 per cent in 1958, 50 per cent in 1963, 40 per cent in 1969, and as low as 35 per cent in 1971. In the meanwhile, large corporations such as automobile makers took over the role of Japan's foreign exchange earners. Yet the inputs supplied by small producers were now exported indirectly in 'embodied' form in the large corporations' exports. Thus, although the share of small firms' direct exports dwindled to 30 per cent in 1980, for example, their indirect exports accounted for as much as 55.3 per cent of the total value of exports in the transportation equipment industry (automobiles, motorcycles, ships, and rolling stock).[9]

Indeed, pervasive subcontracting relationships came to be spun, crisscrossing Japanese industry. In 1982, 52.3 per cent of small manufacturers' total sales were accounted for by subcontracting; the ratio was highest in transport equipment (77 per cent), followed by electric machinery (76 per cent), precision machinery (68 per cent), metal products (64 per cent), and non-electric machinery (52 per cent).[10] These are the industries whose exports all recorded phenomenal growth throughout the 1970s.

Small industry's 'silent' contribution as efficient component suppliers to Japanese exports of high value added modern products are now recognised and they are sometimes described as Japan's kagemusha or 'shadow-samurai' industry. Without the help of this supporting industry, Toyota, Nissan, Sony, Matsushita, Hitachi, Mitsubishi or any other major Japanese corporations could certainly not have built their competitiveness in the world market.

Now that these major assemblers have begun to set up shop in those overseas markets where their exports are being replaced increasingly by local production, not only to avert protectionism but more importantly to become 'local' producers themselves, their suppliers are urged to make overseas investments. Some suppliers are finding it difficult to do so because of a limited overseas market, while others (particularly the Type B-2 whose customers are more diversified) are aggressively taking advantage of this new opportunity as a jumpboard to capture new markets overseas. (In my case studies, Kato Spring, Tokyo Byogane, and Takara are the Type-B-2 small multinationals.)

Type C (High-tech, High Value Added) Manufacturers

This third group of small manufacturers are those who have successfully transformed themselves from low value added traditional small workshops to technology-based, skill-intensive advanced producers. They are highly advanced either in terms of the products they are specialised in (such as sophisticated medical equipment, industrial measuring and monitoring devices, electronics products, machine tools, and other precision machinery) or in terms of the machinery, equipments, and methods they use although their products themselves may be rather standardised products (such as food, chemicals, household and electric appliances). In other words, the former's competitiveness derives mainly from *product innovations*, while the latter's from *process innovations* in a broad sense.

Type-C firms in turn can therefore be subclassified into Type-2 C-1 high-tech product manufacturers and Type-C-2 high-tech processors – using manufacturers of relatively standardised products (although the Type-C-1 producers are most likely process innovators as well).

Both Type-C-1 and C-2 small producers usually exhibit a very large market share, since their products are either highly specialised in technically specified lines of products (in the case of Type-C-1 producers) or extremely cost-competitive with the use of some unique methods of production involving firm-specific, often patented machinery, equipments, and tools.

The industry in which Type-C-1 producers operate may be described as 'niche' monopoly or 'mini' oligopoly ('mini,' since the term 'oligopoly', in the conventional sense, denotes the existence of a handful of large-scale corporations dominating a certain industry). On the other hand, the Type-C-2 small producers still operate in a highly competitive market, though their products are differentiated in reliability, design, delivery, services, etc.

Type-C firms are the most dynamic of them all. They are usually described as *venture businesses* in Japan. Their founders are often engineers, self-taught mechanics, or inventors, but al with entrepreneurial flair. They are aggressive risk-takers. These firms go overseas in search of not only markets but also new ideas. They are in many respects 'Schumpeterian entrepreneurs', driven by the founders' personal desires:

> First of all, there is the dream and the will to found a private kingdom, usually, though not necessarily, also a dynasty...Then there is the will to conquer; the impulse to fight, to prove oneself superior to others, to succeed for the sake, not of the fruits of success, but of success itself . . . Finally, there is the joy of creating, of getting things done, or simply of exercising one's energy and ingenuity.[11]

Type-C small producers are increasingly headed for advanced countries, i.e., the United Sates and Europe, not only because their technological superiority enables their overseas ventures to compete with local competitors but also because they can acquire new information from the advanced countries' markets.

Nac Ltd (in our case studies) is the prime example of a Type-C-1. It employs at home only 170 people but produces highly specialised products related to cinematography, videography, image creation, image instrumentation and remote sensing. Its products include rocket-tracing cameras and space video recorders, and a 360-degree shooting/projection system. Nac has only one wholly-owned overseas subsidiary, located in Singapore, which manufactures the parent company's 'relatively mature' lines of products such as high-speed cameras, analysis projectors, and film-motion analysers.

Another example of the Type-C-1 is Okazaki Works, a small producer of highly specialised thermoelectrometers with a capital of ¥49.5 million and an employment of 300. It purchased a small American thermoelectrometer maker, Ari Industries Inc. in 1980.[12]

The Type-C-2 can be illustrated by Iwasaki Co., a food wax-sample maker. In 1974, when Iwasaki received an order for 13 000 wax specimen of food to be displayed at the Chicago Industrial Science Fair, it decided to establish a factory in California, a wholly-owned subsidiary capitalised at $5 million (initially $30 000) and with an employment of 35 people. Iwasaki developed a unique process technology to make samples with polyvinyl chloride (heat-resistent, hence form-retaining) instead of paraffin was.[13]

Type-D (Engineering) Firms

Type-D are the engineering and technical service firms that have direct overseas operations in the form of licensing, technical service contracts, and/or manufacturing facilities.

Two subtypes can be identified. One, Type-D-1, represents those engineering firms that have been created by or spun off from large corporations as specialised units to market the parent companies' accumulated patents and know-how. This type of firm is frequently seen in the chemical or petro-chemical industry. Although these firms are wholly- or majority-owned by large corporations, they may be quite independent in management and business operations. (Chlorine Engineering Corporation in our case studies, a 100 man-firm owned by Mitsui Engineering & Shipbuilding Co. and Mitsui & Co., enjoys business autonomy, although it actively exploits its link with the Mitsui group in serving for overseas projects.)

The other subtype, Type-D-2, involves those engineering or technical services' firms that are totally autonomous in capital ownership and business operations without any special affiliation with large corporations. Some started out as manufacturing firms, but have transformed themselves into enterprises without manufacturing activities or with only production subcontracted to other firms. They specialise in research, development, and marketing or what may be identified as the corporate *brain* functions by licensing or farming out the *brawn* functions, both at home and abroad.

The Type-D-2 may be illustrated by Giken Engineering Ltd, a 110-man firm capitalised at ¥80 million and specialised in design engineering of a variety of mechanisms (such as micro-shafts) to be used for audio-cassette products. In addition to a number of subcontractors in Japan, it has joint ventures in Singapore and Taiwan, and a subcontracting arrangement with a local firm in Malaysia. Production of technologically advanced, sophisticated components are farmed out in Japan, while more standardised components are produced in these three Asian countries.[14] This organisationally advanced type of firm is now popularly identified as the post-industrial network or disaggregated company.[15]

The preceding classification of Japan's small multinationals into four basic types thus encompasses a whole spectrum of small firms ranging from the pre-modern traditional sweat-shops to the post-industrial network corporations. Indeed, Japan's small manufacturing sector has been structurally evolving from the traditional type, 'low-wage-worker sweat-shops,' to the kagemusha type of supporting industry, and now to the modern network type of corporations – with rapid technological progress as the underlying force for their competitiveness.

It is very important to keep in mind this dynamic structural evolution of Japan's small industry when we analyse the nature and patterns of their direct overseas operations. Any host country anxious to attract Japan's small businesses as investors must understand this changing diversity in the latter's industrial composition.

8.3 WHAT IS ACTUALLY TRANSFERRED

It is often claimed or presupposed that small multinationals transfer intermediate or 'appropriate' technology to the developing countries, technology that is not too advanced to be adequately transplanted onto local industry. Behind this belief is the idea that technology, if it is to be successfully transplanted, needs to be suitable for the relatively low level of the developing countries' absorptive capacity, and that small multinationals are less technologically sophisticated, using more labour-intensive processes than their large counterparts.

In this sense, small multinationals and the developing host countries are looked at as suitable partners. Technology transfers require an appropriate match between the level of technology supplied and the absorptive capacity of recipients. Overall, this generalisation may be true, but it is important to remember that so far as Japan's small multi-nationals are concerned, many of them have come to possess, as we saw earlier, some unique 'niche' technology and adopt highly sophis-ticated ways of organising production and marketing on a global basis. Their overseas operations may thus not meet the general expectation of some policy-makers in the developing countries. The stereotype image of small industry as the traditional cottage industry may be something for policy-makers to guard against.

The compatibility between small multinationals and the developing country can be examined within a framework of analysis presented in Figure 8.2 (p.231). It shows the possible interactions between the tech-nology suppliers' willingness and ability to transfer different levels of technological activity and the technology recipients' capacity to learn and absorb the knowledge and skills imparted.

On the supply side, it is important to look at technology not as a monolithic entity but as a continuum of knowledge and skills running from production-related information (shop-floor rudimentary industrial knowledge) to engineering/designing (knowledge needed to adapt, ad-just, and modify in accordance with specific conditions) to R&D capa-bility (the most advanced knowledge to beget new knowledge for commercial purposes). The supply of production-related basic infor-mation usually requires an organisational setting (i.e. shop-floor train-ing); it cannot be effectively transferred through such indirect (human contact-free) means of transfer as manuals and drawings. On the other hand, more sophisticated (e.g. patented) knowledge related to product- or process-specific engineering and designing can be supplied in or-ganisation-free form such as blue-prints, drawings, and other docu-ments (that is, through licensing agreements).

On the recipients' side, their capacity to absorb technology depends largely upon the existence of macro-level absorptive facilities. For example, when such basic infrastructural services as adequate and re-liable power supply are not available, as is the case with many devel-oping countries, transfers of technology, even that of the rudimentary type, are discouraged simply because foreign investors are wary of

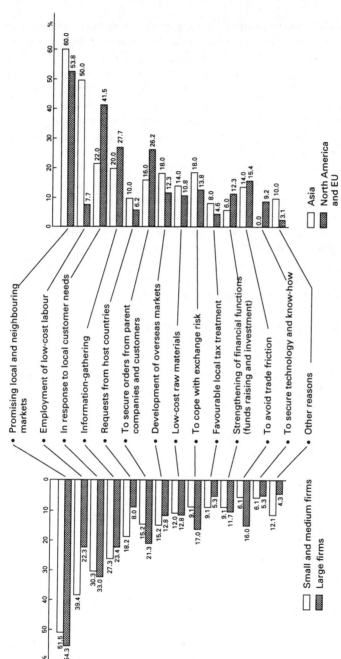

Figure 8.2 Major reasons for overseas investments by Japan's small and large enterprises.

Note: Since multiple answers are given, percentages exceed 100.
Source: A questionnaire survey on the status of Japan's overseas ventures (December 1987) by the Small and Medium Business Agency, as presented in its *White Paper on Small and Medium Enterprises* (Tokyo, 1988), p. 49.

making commitments to setting up local production. Low literacy and lack of basic arithmetic skills are certainly negative factors that reduce the recipients' capacity to learn industrial knowledge. Similarly, when the local supporting industry is underdeveloped, technology related to a vertically integrated process of production that requires intermediate inputs cannot be transplanted smoothly, although imports of those necessary parts and components may provide stopgap measures. (Indeed, this explains why the newly industrialising economies, in particular, are eager to attract small multinationals, since many of the latter are in the supporting industries.) Without an adequate local supply of scientists and engineers, the host country cannot expect to absorb the necessary knowledge for R&D activities.

Given the fact that the majority of Japan's small multinationals (mostly Type-A, Type-B, and Type-C-1) are usually heavily devoted to the shop-floor production end of the technology spectrum to remain competitive, while the developing countries' absorptive facilities are low, a configuration of technological transactions between the two parties is seen in the northwestern corner of the matrix in Figure 8.3. On the other hand, the corresponding relationship between small multinationals and the advanced countries is more oriented toward higher levels of technological interactions (i.e. more on the southwestern corner of the matrix).

What the developing host countries receive from Japan's small multinationals, then, are mostly basic shop-floor production technologies (assembly, fabrication, and processing skills that can be transferred to local employees through training).

This production-skill orientation means that what may be called 'human labor-embodied' technology is involved and that personnel training (on-the-job training of managers, foremen, and workers) is the key mechanism for transferring job-specific skills and know-how. Yet training is a form of investment in labour, involving risks, especially when local labour is footloose (i.e., highly mobile between firms). As I emphasised elsewhere,

> Human-labour-embodied technology and its transfer often tend to be given much lower priority than technologies that are physically-centered or non-human-centered, such as plant-embodied, input-embodied and product/process-embodied technologies, particularly in developing countries, perhaps because the latter yield immediately visible results. Moreover, human-labour-embodied technology is essentially internalized, not in the firm but in individual workers,

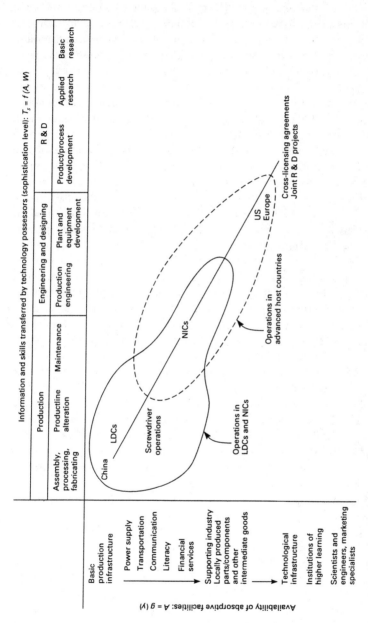

Figure 8.3 Multinationals and technical/technological activity configurations

that is, if workers quit, the firm loses such technology or, worse still, loses it to its competitors. Hence there is less incentives to emphasise the development of human-labour-embodied technology and much greater incentive to solve the productivity problem in terms of physically-centred approaches.[16]

Given the abundant supply of labour services in the developing countries which can be hired at relatively low wages, it is rather difficult to see local workers as suitable objects of investment.

Yet all the firms I interviewed pointed out the importance of, and their very active involvement in, in-house on-the-job training, either given to workers on the factory floor or given to a limited number of key personnel at the companies' home plant in Japan. In fact, the training-intensive feature of Japanese small firms' overseas operations is corroborated by studies made in the developing countries. For example, Pang and Paloheimo report that

> The dependence on home country training of local technicians is particularly strong among Japanese SMEs which like to ensure that local engineers and technicians are not only trained in technical skills but are also familiar with the management style and values of the head office. (see Pang and Paloheimo, Chapter 16, in this volume.)

Indeed, one company I interviewed (Kato Spring) even emphasises a holistic approach to technology transfers (transfers of 'socially desirable' ways of doing business) that includes not only the transfers of technical knowledge to factory workers but also the imbuing of local managers with the company's 'humanware-centered' managerial philosophy and corporate culture devoted to a harmonious fusion between the business success of an enterprise and the personal fulfilment of individuals.

In the host countries Japanese small multinationals' emphasis on in-house, on-the-job training is thus closely related to the wide practice of Japanese-style management in such forms as groupism and egalitarianism (e.g. rankless company cafeterias and parking lots, non-partitioned open-plan offices, and company-sponsored outings and parties), teamwork and participatory management (QC circles and the suggestion box system) and the seniority rules for wages and promotion (i.e. the reward system for company-specific, long-term skill formation).

Labor economists have already recognised the utility of Japanese-style management as an effective system of intra-company on-the-job training, an important factor for Japan's high growth of labour productivity in the post-war period.[17]

In general, the more assembly-oriented the local operation is and the more devoted to in-house skill formation via on-the-job training, the greater incidence of Japanese-style management in local ventures, if not in its 'raw' form but in modified form to suit local culture.

One problem often expressed by Japanese investors with regard to labor training is a frequent loss of trained workers to other firms. It is not clear, however, whether Japanese-style management encourages or helps alleviate this problem, since Japanese firms' emphasis on in-house training increases the rent embodied in local workers, yet at the same time the atmosphere of job security and paternalism associated with Japanese-style management (firm-specific acculturation) often serves as a strong inducement for workers to be loyal and stay with the company. Many of the firms I interviewed are of the opinion that they are usually able to reduce the rate of worker turnover considerably after a few years' operation. Yet the same phenomenon may equally occur at Western companies' overseas plants in the developing countries.

In short, what is transferred to the developing host countries by Japan's small multinationals in the form of industrial knowledge is basic production (assembly, processing, and fabricating) and machine maintenance skills taught to local workers. In some cases, the next higher rung on the technology ladder, engineering and designing, may be involved (see Nikki's operation in South Korea, and Chlorine Engineers' plant export in India in Chapters 13 and 14), but this seems to be as far as the technological interactions between Japan's small manufacturers and the developing host countries have gone.

At the time of factory construction, blueprints for a factory layout and design information for products and work processes and the like are brought in by Japanese engineer teams, but these types of technology transfers are one-shot deals and do not provide any significant opportunity for local engineers to learn from, especially when the venture is a start-up company wholly- or majority-owned by Japanese interests; in the first place, local personnel are not yet hired at such an early stage of investment.

Active v. Passive Participants

Related to the issues of what actually is transferred, and how effectively technology is indigenised is the relative aggressiveness of technology suppliers and recipients. In this connection, each side can be classified into two types, *active* and *passive*.

Examined in terms of this conceptual differentiation, a question of 'whether the technology supplied was modified and adjusted for local conditions' is less important than the questions, 'which side took the initiative to introduce the necessary modifications' and 'which side was actually involved in such modification efforts'. For obvious reasons, the learning-by-doing effect is related to the latter set of questions. I found that in the limited number of firms I interviewed, the Japanese suppliers were mostly the ones who practically did everything and were very active participants, whereas the local side remained largely passive (except Nikki's partner in South Korea). This may be due to the fact that Japan's macroeconomic push forces and the accompanying microeconomic (firm-level) determination for overseas expansion are much stronger than the macro–micro pull forces in the developing host countries. Again, one exception is South Korea, for which Lee reports:

As for the question who initiated the technological licensing, six replied that the recipients were the initiators while four replied that the suppliers were the initiators. For the remaining three cases, two firms responded that both the recipients and suppliers played equal roles. (See Lee, Chapter 13 in this volume)

In any event, the present pattern of technology transfers from Japan's small firms to the local community is certainly in sharp contrast with Japan's own experience with technology absorption and adaptation; Japanese firms have been very active recipients, while their technology suppliers in the West tended to be passive (imparting key technology mostly under licensing agreements with minimal technical assistance).

It may be generalised that the more actively both parties are involved, the more effective the process of technology transfers, though bargaining may be lively and intensive in strategic manoeuvring. On the other hand, if both parties are passive, third-party intermediation will be needed for an opportunity for technology transfer to be exploited. In the case of many small Japanese manufacturers who happened to be ignorant about foreign technology available and hence remained passive, general trading companies and their parent companies or affiliates frequently played a crucial role of intermediary between the Western possessors of technology and Japan's small industry.

8.4 CONCLUDING OBSERVATIONS

Market Share and Monopoly Power

One of the expectations about small multinationals on the part of the developing countries is that they are small, without much market power, and compete in a highly fragmented market, hence their entry into the local market enhances its competitive environment and does not threaten native enterprises.

Yet it is generally found that many small and medium-sized manufacturers that invest overseas often enjoy a very large market share at home; some therefore conclude that these small multinationals are after all no different from large multinationals, since the former also possess monopolistic market power. True, most of Japan's small manufacturers I interviewed have substantial market shares, even up to 90 or 95 per cent (as in the case of Newlong's bagging machines) at home.

But I have come to the conclusion that market share should not be interpreted as an indicator of monopoly power or concentration of economic power. For small manufacturers usually operate in a very narrow segment of a particular industry by catering for what may be called a 'niche market', a market segment left unserved or neglected by large manufacturers because of such a market's smallness (hence unprofitable and valueless for large-scale production by large firms). The more narrowly a product line is defined, the greater a market share of a particular firm becomes: there are not many firms that are interested in producing coffee-bagging machines in Japan.

Similarly, textiles include all sorts of clothing and fabrics, and specialised types of products such as children's mittens for skiing or gardeners' gloves may be produced by only a handful of small manufacturers. In fact, in order to survive small producers need to specialise in finely segmented lines of products which involve production in small lots but often in great variety. Thus a large market share does not mean so much monopoly or dominance (in the sense of exploiting scale economies and wielding economic power with towering dominance not only in a particular industry but also in the economy as a whole), but rather a high degree of specialisation and product differentiation. 'Niche monopoly' in a very small market cannot be equated with concentration of economic power.

Separation Between Ownership and Management

Many small manufacturers are owned by large corporations. Hence it is usually argued that these small subsidiaries should not be included when we study small multinationals, for they are in reality not small, being part and parcel of large corporations. Yet I have found that a company majority-owned by huge companies may have total autonomy in management (as is the case with Chlorine Engineers), hence any direct overseas operations (such as licensing and direct investment) are solely decided upon by itself without any interference from its majority owner. The latter's interest may only be in its subsidiary's profitability, not in its daily operations.

Indeed, nowadays Japan's large corporations spin off autonomously managed companies (subsidiaries) for the very purpose of 'slimming down' by delegating authorities completely to them. One economist describes this process 'quasi-disintegration'.[18]

'Small' Capital Requirement

Since by definition SMEs are capitalised at a small amount of capital (¥100 million or less in the case of Japanese small and medium-sized manufacturers), one may be tempted to argue that it is relatively easy to start such a business even in capital-scarce developing countries; hence small multinationals are welcome as a role model in the developing host countries. In this view, small manufacturers are assumed to be somewhat less sophisticated, simpler business entities than large manufacturers.

Yet, as seen above, Japan's small industry has gone through rapid structural changes from the traditional type of low-wage-based workshops to the crucial suppliers of parts and components for large-scale assemblers and most recently to the post-industrial knowledge-based firms. In some specific areas some are technologically more sophisticated than large corporations (as seen in our case study on Nac Ltd). In other words, a certain type (Type-C) of Japan's small manufacturers are becoming highly intensive in the use of *human capital* (employment of engineers and skilled technicians and R&D) if not in that of *physical capital* as usually defined. In fact, these small firms usually farm out production to their subcontracting subsidiaries, both at home and abroad, and concentrate on R&D., the result being not much change in their small capitalisation (at least on paper). It is thus important to realise that it is often misleading to judge the level of small manufacturers' industrial sophistication in terms of size of capitalisation.

How 'Small' are They?

Immediately related to the preceding observation is the question of how 'small' Japan's small firms are when some of them have manufacturing and service subsidiaries as their captive subcontractors. Swany, a glove maker often cited as one of Japan's 'Typical' small multinationals, operates with only 50 staff members and a capital of ¥170 million in Japan, but with more than 1000 workers in its South Korean factories. Is this company really 'small'? It is certainly so designated in Japan and is entitled for the government-sponsored special programmes designed to help Japan's small industry. Newlong Machine Works itself operates with 240 employees and ¥100 million capital, but has three manufacturing subsidiaries (with a total employment of 410) in Japan, and three overseas subsidiaries (with a total employment of more than 100).

As already pointed out, this type of 'small' enterprise is the vanguard of the post-industrial organisations characterised by division of corporate functions within a network of small 'separate' enterprises (satellites) surrounding the headquarters or 'brain function' company. They do not grow like the traditional companies that develop into multidivisional corporations. The 'network' corporations' growth is in part responsible for the existence of so many small production units in Japan.

Small Multinationals as Alternative or Complementary Technology Suppliers?

It is hypothesised that small multinationals are alternative – and more desirable than large multinationals – technology suppliers for the developing countries, since small ones suposely possess *intermediate* technology and create more employment opportunities because of their more labour-intensive operations.

I have already pointed out the advanced state of skills and technological assets possessed by certain groups of Japan's small multinationals and the strongly complementary characteristics of small firms' technology and product lines *vis-à-vis* those of their large counterparts.

In fact, I would argue that this complementary pattern has been particularly dominant in Japanese industry, since small manufacturers specialise in light industry consumer goods (Type-A) or in intermediate goods (parts and components) as suppliers for large corporations (Type-B) or in the high value added, 'niche' products that are left untouched by the latter because of the limited nature of the markets (Type-C and Type-D). Gomes-Casseres and Kohn's study on US small multinationals (Chapter 10 in this volume) seems to strongly indicate the complementary relationship, for the American small firms focus on 'products sold to industrial buyers'.

Moreover, different patterns and behaviours of overseas operations are discernible among the various types of Japan's small industry. Type-A products are now less and less manufactured in Japan as they are being replaced by imports; many of the Japanese Type-A producers have already moved to neighbouring countries, causing the first wave of overseas investments from Japan during the early 1970s.

It is Type-B small producers that are currently on the move toward overseas markets, riding – and causing a further surge – on the second wave of Japanese overseas investments. Some are investing in tandem with overseas investments by large multinationals who are now increasingly confronted with the problem of the local content requirements in the host countries. But, as pointed out earlier, many Type-B suppliers are serving aggressively not only their Japanese corporations but also Western multinationals as well as emergent local firms through direct local production in overseas markets. If the developing countries want to invite Type-B small multinationals, they should either first invite large multinationals in the assembly-based industries or encourage large domestic assemblers (as best exemplified by the Korean experience); 'tandem' investments by small multinationals then will follow.

Type-C small multinationals are an interesting group. Since their technological progress is very rapid, they soon make some of their own product lines 'outdated' for themselves to produce. Hence they may be interested in farming out those 'obsolete' lines to the developing countries (as is the case with Nac Ltd., which produces the 'mature' lines of cinematographic equipment). This is exactly in line with Vernon's product-cycle theory of overseas investment.[19] They are succeeding in generating the waves of new technology (mostly adding and combining functional improvements and new designs rather than Schumpeterian breakthroughs) one after another. To attract this type of small multinationals, the developing host countries need to have a good supply of engineers and training-effective workers and locational advantages as an export platform (as in Singapore).

Type-A small multinationals are perhaps intensive in the use of labour (for example, Swany's employment of more than 1000 workers in Korea, and a blanket maker who has only 165 employees in Japan but operates a 1200-worker plant in Thailand, a 1000-worker plant in Indonesia, and a 250-worker plant in Malaysia). But Type-B small multinationals are more dependent on automated production processes to ensure quality and delivery than on low-cost local labour; hence they are likely to be relatively capital-intensive. On the other hand, Type-C small multinationals are usually limited in output; their overseas plants are of small scale, employing from 20 to less than 100 local workers.

Notes

1. Terutomo Ozawa, 'International Transfer of Technology by Japan's Small and Medium Enterprises in Developing Countries', United Nations Conference on Trade and Development (Paris, 1985).
2. Small and Medium Enterprise Agency, Chusho Kigyo Hakusho (White Paper on Small and Medium Enterprises) (Tokyo, 1988), Appendix pp. 1–8.
3. Osawa (1985). Also see Terutomo Ozawa, *Multinationalism, Japanese Style: The Political Economy of Outward Dependency* (Princeton: Princeton University Press, 1979).
4. John H. Dunning, *International Production and the Multinational Enterprise* (London: George Allen & Unwin, 1981).
5. Small Business Corporation, *Chushokigyo Kaigai Shinshutsu Jireishu* (case studies on small and medium firms' overseas operations), SBC (Tokyo, 1986), and Japan Overseas Development Corporation, *Chushokigyo Kaigai Toshi Kyoryoku Shikin Yushi Jigyo Jireishu* (case studies on small and medium firms' overseas investment and loans from the cooperation funds) (Tokyo: JODC, 1984).
6. Ozawa (1985), p. 14.
7. Ozawa (1985), p. 62.
8. Ozawa (1985), pp. 45–7, and Small Business Corporation, pp. 5–6.
9. Small and Medium Business Agency, *Chushokigyo Hakusho* (White Paper on Small and Medium Business) (Tokyo: Government Printing Office, various annual issues.
10. Small and Medium Business Agency (1983), pp. 15, 71.
11. Joseph A. Schumpeter, *The Theory of Economic Development* (Cambridge, MA.: Harvard University Press, 1949), p. 93.
12. Small Business Corporation, pp. 63–4.
13. Small Business Corporation, pp. 77–8.
14. Shoko Sogo Kenkyusho, *Chushokigyo Shinjidai* (A New Era for Small and Medium Firms) (Tokyo: Nikkan Kogyo Press, 1988), pp. 44–52.
15. 'And Now, the Post-Industrial Corporation. It could farm out everything from manufacturing to billing', *Business Week* (3 March 1986). The article describes the evolution of the corporation from (1) 'owner-managed small companies' (1800), to (2) 'vertical' companies (that 'grow larger and hire more managers, each to oversee a stage of the chain from raw material

to finished product (1850), (3) 'divisional' large companies that are organised 'around a series of vertical chains of command to manage each
product, or group of related products, that the company makes' (1900),
(4) 'matrix' large companies 'with vertical structures to add a second,
informal reporting chain that links managers with allied responsibilities
or managers working together on temporary projects' (1950), and (5)
'network' companies that 'rely on other companies and suppliers to perform manufacturing, distribution, marketing, or other crucial business
functions on a contract basis' (2000).

16. Ozawa (1985), p. 19.
17. See, for example, Kazuo Koike, 'Human Resource Development and Labor-
    Management Relations,' in Kozo Yamamura and Yasukichi Yasuba, *The
    Political Economy of Japan, Vol. 1. The Domestic Transformation* (Stanford:
    Standford University Press, 1987), pp. 291–321. Also, Shinichi Ichimura
    (ed.), *Azia ni Nezuku Nihonteki Keiei* (Japanese-Style Management Takes
    Root in Asia) (Tokyo: Tokyo Keizai Shinposha, 1988).
18. M. Aoki, 'Innovative adaptation through the quasi-tree structure: An
    emerging aspect of Japanese enterpreneurship', *Zeitschrift für
    Nationalökonomie*, vol. (4, 1984), pp. 25–35.
19. Raymond Vernon, 'International Investment and International Trade in
    the Product Life Cycle', *Quarterly Journal of Economics*, vol. 80 (1966),
    pp. 190–207.

9 The Case of the United Kingdom

Peter J. Buckley and Hafiz Mirza

This chapter examines the role of United Kingdom small and medium sized enterprises (SMEs) in transferring technology to developing countries. After a brief review of the scale of foreign direct investment by United Kingdom SMEs in section 9.1 (details of non-equity foreign involvement is not consistently reported), the chapter summarises the cases investigated and offers an overview of the findings (section 9.2). The concluding section is followed by an appendix which includes an analytical summary of the 12 United Kingdom technology suppliers interviewed. This structure differs from that of the other chapters, but the intention is to permit an understanding of the behaviour of each supplier as a complete entity.

9.1 THE SCALE OF UNITED KINGDOM SME FOREIGN DIRECT INVESTMENT

In the case of United Kingdom foreign investors, according to the latest survey conducted in 1981, an estimated 1500 enterprises had 9100 foreign affiliates. Two-thirds of these foreign investors (i.e. 1000 firms) with net foreign assets of less than £2 million each accounted for 0.8 per cent of the total net book value of United Kingdom foreign direct investment (FDI) at the end of 1981 (*British Business*, 2 March 1984). This is in sharp contrast to the 34 enterprises with net assets of over £200 million each and 1550 overseas affiliates between which these accounted for 55 per cent of the total stock of British FDI.

When FDI in the United Kingdom is examined, it is found that about 3000 foreign companies had United Kingdom affiliates, and that three-quarters (2150) of these had United Kingdom affiliates with a book value of less than £2 million, accounting in total for 2.4 per cent of inward FDI in the United Kingdom (excluding oil, banking and insurance). In contrast, 21 foreign companies had assets valued at over £150 million in the United Kingdom, and these accounted for one-third of the total (*British Business*, 2 March 1984). Inward investment was less concentrated than outward: the 100 largest inward investors accounted for 60 per cent of total FDI; the 100 largest outward investors accounted for 80 per cent (again excluding oil, banking and insurance).

9.2   THE UNITED KINGDOM SUPPLIERS OF TECHNOLOGY: MOTIVE, MODE OF TRANSFER AND OVERALL EVALUATION

Table 9.1 shows a summary of the key features of the United Kingdom SME technology suppliers, covering location, industry sector, mode of technology transfer and employment (world-wide, in the United Kingdom and in host country, where available). The number of cases in each host country is shown in Table 9.2 and the mode of technology transfer in Table 9.3. The cases themselves are individually summarised analytically and appended at the end of the chapter (p. 252).

This section examines particularly the motives for SMEs undertaking technology transfer, the competitive advantages they possess, the international strategies which the firms followed, the organisational structure adopted in the recipient country and the technology transfer process. Table 9.4 summarises the main characteristics of the cases discussed below.

Motive

The sample of 12 cases splits exactly into two halves, with six cases having a proactive motive and the other six cases (four firms) being approached by an outside agency. Of the active market-seekers (the first group), two firms were also concerned to avoid tariff barriers which represents a secondary motive; and one firm was concerned to forestall the copying of its products (by entering a joint venture in Korea with one of its imitators!). Of those cases where the firms were approached, the approach was normally made by the ultimate licensee or partner; in only one case was another agency (a government body) involved. This contrasts with seven firms out of 43 responding to an outside approach in the Bradford study of United Kingdom first time foreign investors (Buckley, Newbould and Thurwell, 1988). the difference may be explained in terms of the nature of the host countries (psychic, geographic distance, etc.) and this would be consistent with the difficulties faced by smaller firms in scanning global horizons: foreign approaches reduce search costs and, of course, this in itself partly determines the type of technology transfer which eventually occurs.

Table 9.1   Interviews conducted: summary of UK firms

Case no.	Location	Industry sector	Mode of technology transfer[a]	Employment developing		
				Worldwide	UK	Host
1	Singapore	Speciality chemicals	Wholly owned-subsidiary	993	390	47
2	Korea	Consulting engineers mainly power equipment for vehicles – internal combustion engines	'Contractual joint venture'	545	545	NDE
3	Brazil	Textile machinery	Wholly-owned subsidiary	460+	460	few (start-up)
4	Singapore	Speciality chemicals	Wholly-owned subsidiary	1080	860	?
5	Korea	Specialised metal manufacture	Joint venture	?	519	?
6	Korea	Mechanical engineering	Licensing	200	200	NDE
7	India	Mechanical engineering	'Contractual joint venture'	200	200	NDE
8	India	Specialised instruments	Licensing	21	21	NDE
9	Brazil	Specialised instrument	Licensing	21	21	NDE
10	Korea	Mechanical engineering	Joint Venture	?	400	?
11	India	Motor vehicle ancillary plant	Turnkey	?	90	?
12	Singapore	Rubber products	(1) Joint venture (2) Wholly-owned subsidiary	?	550	?

Notes:
[a] As defined in the chapter.
NDE = None directly employed.
? = not known.

Table 9.2   Host country of UK SMEs

Republic of Korea	4
India	3
Brazil	2
Singapore	3
Total	12

Table 9.3   Type of technology transfer

FDI	6
of which:	
Wholly-owned subsidiary	(3)
Joint venture[a]	(3)
Licensing	3
'Contractual joint venture'	2
Turnkey project	1
Total	12

Note:
[a] One joint venture later became a wholly-owned subsidiary.

There is some confirmation of this hypothesis in the comments made by small firms. In the case of one 'reactive' case, for example, the firm in question already had a 'fanning out' strategy based on specific international locations – but an approach by a Korean company was from outside familiar markets and the technology transfer was handled directly from the United Kingdom, rather than by the Asia/Pacific center (based in Australia).

Competitive Advantage

The competitive advantage exploited by the SME is predominantly a unique (or at least a specialist) product, skill or brand name. This covers 10 out of 12 cases. The other two firms rely on the provision of cheap but effective equipment which they regarded as appropriate to the conditions of the host country. Both of these cheap equipment–suppliers were reactive in motive rather than market-seekers. This finding is in line with previous studies of actual investment by United Kingdom SMEs which were also active with specialist skills in niche markets (Buckley, Newbould and Thurwell, 1988). The considerable range of products, processes and skills which were the subject of technology transfer in the United Kingdom sample (see table 9.1 and Appendix), despite a deliberately restricted set of industries in the survey, suggests that the potential for transfer to developing countries is much greater than is often thought. Of course the level of industrial development of a recipient country may well generally determine which technologies can be absorbed, but what is more important is the sophistication and requirements of the recipient countries. The fact that relatively sophisticated technologies were being transferred (and absorbed by indigenous companies and local workforces) in the United Kingdom sample implies that the transfer of less advanced processes and skills takes different routes. This implication, if correct, suggests that a careful matching of route and type/level of technology transfer would aid in the success of the transfer process.

Strategy and Internationalisation

In general, companies with an active, market-seeking motive were more internationally experienced than the reactive group. None of the active group were making a first foreign venture, whereas three of the reactive group had no prior international ventures. Many of the active group could be considered to have a regional strategy, e.g. using Singapore as a base for activities in the Asean (or Asia Pacific) region. Companies with specialised skills to offer (for example, the company providing turnkey plant and related technology/skills), by contrast, looked for significant clients and tended not to have an integrated international strategy.

Technology Transfer Process

Tables 9.3 and 9.4 show the type, organisational form and range of the technology transferred in the United Kingdom sample. FDI accounted for a half of the cases, but three-quarters (including three 50:50 joint ventures) involved indigenous companies. This greater participation by local companies (as compared to the operations of larger multinationals) bodes well for the technology transfer process to developing countries and may explain the high success rate (see below). The range of the transfer varied from a relatively narrow focus on a single product or process to the transfer of a full package of a United Kingdom firm's technology and expertise. In the case of the two 'contractual joint ventures', and in a number of other cases, technology was specifically developed for the requirement of local markets or the recipient firm.

Table 9.4 Analytical summary of cases

Case no.	Recipient country	Motive	Technology transfer	Organisation	Competitive advantage	Transfer of technology; returns from venture
1	Singapore	Proactive market search	Narrow range limited technology cooperation	Autonomous subsidiary	Niche products	Highly successful transfer and returns
2	Korea	Client, full consultancy	As per agreement	Consultancy	Experience skills	Successful transfer and returns
3	Brazil	Followed competitor	Product and technology manufacture	Dependent subsidiary	Product	Start-up only
4	Singapore	Proactive market search	Technology skills	Autonomous subsidiary	Yes–specialist strategy	Highly successful transfer and returns
5	Korea	Avoidance of tariff, market	Production technology	50:50 JV	Potential specialised niche product	Successful transfer, but expansion limited by size of market
6	Korea	Approach by licencee (pull) later licences market	Full range transfer	Licence	Unique application of technology/ niche product	Highly successful transfer and returns
7	India	Approach by licencee	Joint development of product	Joint development	Unique application of technology applied to host country	Successful – achieved objectives

8	India	Approach by licencee and secure foothold	Product technology	Licence	Cheap and effective equipment	Successful transfer, but unsuccessful because markets failed to emerge
9	Brazil	Approach by licencee	Product technology	Licence	Cheap and effective equipment	Successful transfer and returns
10	Korea	To forestall copying of product	Product technology	50:50 JV Korean MD has casting vote	Control of customers world-wide – repeat buying	Successful transfer, but unsuccessful returns
11	India	Approach by local firm	Built plant for customer	Turnkey plant and training	Specialist skills in building and organising project and proprietary technology and international prestige	Successful transfer, but too soon (could have had greater returns)
12	Singapore	Approach by government agency	Product/ process skills	Dependent subsidiary	Product marketing, brand	Successful transfer, but moderate success in terms of return change from offshore production to servicing local market

Note: JV = joint venture.

A few words need to be said about the fact that the technology transfer processes (within the limits of specific agreements) were all deemed to be successful. Bearing in mind that companies with less favourable cases of technology transfer may have declined to be interviewed, it is clear that the nature of the firms and their relationships were of key importance. In four cases United Kingdom companies effectively 'transferred technology to themselves' because they established wholly-owned production subsidiaries (this includes one case which originally started as a joint venture). In the remaining cases there are a number of reasons promoting success: some recipient firms were large (e.g. members of Korean Chaebol industrial groups) or experienced in the appropriate industry; in a number of cases there was already a degree of familiarity between the source and recipient firm (e.g. former agent or customer, formerly linked in the same group, etc.) which aided in the design and implementation of the agreement; and, of course, in a number of cases the technology was being designed for the local recipients. With regard to the only two commercially unsuccessful cases it can be noted that both recipient firms were relatively small and unknown.

Of course, successful transfers (in the case of non-wholly-owned subsidiaries) are not necessarily to the advantage of the United Kingdom supplying firms and, where the transfer could affect them strategically, attempts were made to prevent, delay or restrict full transfer. Examples include trying to retain control of vital components or preventing a recipient company exploiting received technology in other geographic markets. These attempts appear to have been thwarted in most cases by large recipient firms using their economic muscle and legal skills; the difficulties besetting small United Kingdom firms in trying to put their tactics into force; the skills of host government departments vetting technology agreements; and, more generally, by the recipient firm (with appropriate aid) ensuring that the technology agreement was clear and well defined.

9.3 CONCLUDING REMARKS

This study of SME technology transfer from the United Kingdom covers four recipient countries: Korea, Brazil, Singapore and India. Our sample of 12 cases of technology transfer divides equally between equity (three foreign direct investment plus three joint ventures) and non-equity ventures (three licenses, two technology agreements and one turnkey venture).

Though small in number, the cases show a high degree of success from the point of view of the SME. This represents success in the actual transfer and success in terms of returns on the venture. However, difficulties in achieving cooperation from firms in our sample frame may be indicative of problems not uncovered in our eventual sample. This may particularly be the case in India. The sole unsuccessful venture was due to the failure of an adequate market to emerge rather than to technological problems. However, conclusions regarding the success of transfers may not be exactly replicated from the point of view of the technology recipient because several supplies firms kept back elements of the technology package.

The high degree of perceived success may well arise from the fact that each SME studied has a clear competitive advantage, although its nature varies enormously – from a niche product, through cheap and effective equipment, to experience and skills and specialist technology. Modes of international transfer also seem to be correctly matched to the specific skills and market positioning of the companies, though this is often influenced, or even determined by the host country's regulatory policies as well as the host-country partner through the technology agreement. It is notable that Singapore which has a completely open policy is host to three FDIs (half of all FDIs in the sample).

In many cases, the initiating force which began the process of transfer arose in the host country. This suggests that the market opportunity was largely identified by host-country nationals. Indeed many United Kingdom SMEs were passive until approached by host-country interests. This suggests that a high degree of entrepreneurial flair exists in the host countries which can be successfully combined with technological expertise in advanced countries.

However, the scope for certain type of technology transfer is changing. The case of Singapore illustrates the impact which increasing wages can have on 'offshore'-type investments. The opportunities in host countries are clearly evolving and British SMEs must become increasingly flexible in seeking opportunities for international technology transfer.

Appendix: Case Studies, Analytical Summaries

TECHNOLOGY SUPPLIER 1: SPECIALITY CHEMICALS MANUFACTURER IN SINGAPORE

General Description and Competition

Firm 1 was founded in 1934 and produces a range of speciality chemicals, especially adhesives and sealants. Its global sales were $50 million in 1987 (stable in real terms over the last five years) and it employs 993 people world-wide (390 in the United Kingdom and 47 in Singapore). Though it is now 100 per cent owned by a major MNC it can be regarded as functionally au-tonomous entity which is effectively managed by hired officers. 40 per cent of its output is sold to the parent company's network world-wide, while the remainder is bought by industrial customers from across the globe. As a con-sequence, 60 per cent of its output is exported from the United Kingdom.

The firm's market share varies dramatically across the product range, by market segment and around the globe. In the United Kingdom it is moder-ately strong and has about 15 per cent of the overall market. The market is competitive, both on the demand and supply sides. Most of its competitors are focused by product, but its own range is quite diverse; clearly the number of competitors varies by product. Three manufacturing plants (one large) are operated in the United Kingdom and the subcontracting is seldom employed.

R&D as a proportion of sales is only 2 per cent world-wide (higher in the United Kingdom) and varies with product. About 20 persons are devoted to this activity in the United Kingdom. Possibly five 'new' products were launched over the last two years (but there is a key problem of definition) and three of these were patented. However patents are not applied for in general, since there is an exposure problem with formulated materials.

In the plant most similar to the Singapore operation, batch and serial pro-duction is for an expected demand. The plant size is about average in UK terms, though it was not possible to estimate the size of the largest plant world-wide.

The Internationalisation Process: Motivation and Form of Overseas Involvement

The internationalisation process began in the 1950s with 100 per cent direct investments in countries such as Australia. Other ventures have since been made: the 1964 Singapore wholly-owned affiliate was 'empire-led' and was motivated by the country's participation in the Malaysian Federation; a dis-tributive capacity was acquired in Hong Kong in 1981; and there are a few joint ventures in Spain, Ireland and elsewhere. In general the company can be described as an 'active market-seeker' whose main motivations for establishing overseas ventures was to secure a foothold in these markets and increase imports from the home economy. Both Singapore and Hong Kong were also deemed to be valuable entrepôt bases.

Singapore Operations

The Singapore venture was established in 1964 at a time when the company was actively seeking new markets. The growth perspective was important and Singapore/Malaysia's growth potential was the main reason for the establishment. Historical links were important and other countries were not considered. The original plant established was a bit of a 'cast-off', though ideal for local conditions.

At the time of establishment exports to singapore were not appreciable, though there was a local agent (possibly also responsible for local sales). A full feasibility study was made by a dispatched officer and a wholly-owned affiliate established as intended. The Singapore subsidiary was intended as an agent for the group and outside involvement was not desired. There was no need to seek permission or help from either the home or recipient country. At the time foreign exchange (though the affiliate has been a net contributor for some time), capital goods (albeit a cast-off plant, followed by equipment as necessary) and technology were all supplied to the new venture which was begun from scratch. It should be noted that the technical support to the affiliate has been limited because of mature product lines – but this applies to the United Kingdom too. The Singapore operation is autonomous in most respects, although some United Kingdom testing facilities, etc. are offered.

Technology Transfer

An initial plant was transferred (this was smaller, older, but otherwise similar to United Kingdom plant) and since then there has been a transfer of process and product technology as warranted by regional requirements. This has involved the transfer of critical components and parts, technical assistance and limited technical training of Singapore employees. At present there is only one laboratory man in Singapore who occasionally comes for discussion/assistance to the United Kingdom. There is no special training programme, only on-the-job training.

Modifications were made to the original plant because of the smaller size of the Singapore/Asean market and the different mix of products required. The product range needed is narrow, although it is changing. For example, there was initially a great need for sealants in water tanks, etc. but there is now a greater need for products to aid in maintenance and repair. Singapore and the rest of Asean are going through the following product cycle – Infrastructure -> Development -> Maintenance – and this has had a direct impact on the product range needed. Apart from this, there has been no need to design or modify products specifically for the local market, although products sold in Singapore were generally launched 5–10 years ago. There is no policy of restricting the supply of more recent products: local compatibilities and cost-effectiveness determines the choice.

The affiliate has achieved mastery of the transferred technology, but given the narrow range of its operations has a limited technological capacity. It is nevertheless quite proficient in what is produced, e.g. it is more advanced than the United Kingdom in epoxy mortar materials.

There are no technical agreements with the Singapore subsidiary since it is policy not to create rigidities in the system (though some situations have warranted formalised agreements).

Post-implementation Relationships

The affiliate is normally entirely staffed by local Chinese, although the new Chief Executive is a New Zealander. Staffing in terms of local nationals is a general principle.

Since the affiliate was established, technological assistance has been granted as needed (e.g. for Singapore's new Rapid Transit System). This has taken the form of new product designs, process engineering, quality control and technical assistance.

Since the operation began, exports to Singapore have increased, but this probably reflects the growth of the country/region and the long time scale as much as anything else. Components exported to Singapore are priced using a transfer pricing system to ensure local incentives. This price system is not tax-effective. Essentially marginal cost plus transfer pricing is used, but this depends on local situation, production runs, etc. There is also a lower discretionary price based on various formulas, since the firm recognises the high expenses involved in sales and management. Goods are seldom imported from Singapore itself.

The Singapore operation is quite autonomous and makes its own plans which the parent company approves. Only in the plans for future investment does the parent company elaborate or alter plans to any extent. There is a monthly reporting system, but accuracy is not a forte! The parent company controls treasury functions.

Visits by parent company officers take place once a year, while the affiliate's officers come to the United Kingdom every six months or so. The affiliate is responsible for marketing, purchasing, wages, pricing and management recruitment, but little independent R&D is carried out.

Evaluation

The Singapore affiliate is very competitive for a number of reasons:

- Niche products which few multinationals can match, e.g. in specific adhesives/sealants required by the construction industry
- Commitment to local market and a willingness to adapt technology/formulations to local requirements
- Advanced proprietary knowledge which allows the production of new products to match new requirements
- Low costs because of high quality and low inventories
- Good, flexible management, technical back-up
- A long period of establishment, wealth of experience

- International prestige arising from long history
- Local operations of long standing which have reinforced links with local companies and authorities

Though there have been no technological advances in Singapore which could be transferred to the United Kingdom, the affiliate has found interesting uses for existing products which have been adapted elsewhere.

The Singapore affiliate surpassed all objectives, although there has been slow growth in the earliest and most recent periods. The main problems encountered by the affiliate has been the 1985–6 recession and the continous need to develop new products. Until recently the Singapore operations performed far better than United Kingdom operations (in sales, profitability, productivity, or market position), but the recession reversed the situation.

There have never been any political or legal problems in operating in Singapore and the firm expects to expand its operations there. In general there is no policy towards reinvestment of profits, but there may occur as market conditions warrant.

TECHNOLOGY SUPPLIER 2: AUTOMOTIVE CONSULTING COMPANY IN KOREA

General Description and Competition

Firm 2 was established in 1915 and is best regarded as a highly specialised consultancy company which conducts work related to the internal combustion engine (for cars, trucks, power generation equipment, etc.). Though a number of subsidiaries manufacture scientific equipment and the company receives some income from patents (via licences), most of its business is derived from design, R&D for specific client requirements. It currently employs 545 people, some of whom are dispatched abroad when necessary. In 1987 the firm's turnover was $27 million, although it must be mentioned that this is almost entirely value added given the nature of the business. This turnover is some 190 per cent up on 1982, though there has been a slight decrease since 1986. 'Exports' represent some 70 per cent of this turnover. The main destination for these exports are East Asia (especially Japan with 10 per cent of the total turnover), United States and Europe – the shares are roughly equal for these three areas.

The original founder was an inventor, but the firm was never 'family-owned' as such. There are no links with other companies, apart from the normal ones with clients. It remains a Plc today and is managed by hired officers.

It is not possible to compute a market share given the nature of the business; and also because its main 'competitors are the internal engineering departments of major manufacturing companies. The industry is concentrated in terms of other consultants, but is competitive if these internal departments are included. On the latter basis competition is increasing as internal departments seek outside work. There are a specific number of clients around the globe and the market can be said to be concentrated on the demand side.

275 out of 545 people are directly employed in R&D and all employees

are involved at some stage. But this is the nature of the business and the basis of the company's competitive advantage. There have been some innovations over the last few years, but these are not directly relevant to the main activities. Computer programs pertinent to the design and research activities are most important.

The Internationalisation Process: Motivation and Form of Overseas Involvement

Since the main clients are the motor industry, the company has been international since 1915! In Europe, clients include Peugeot, Volkswagen and many other major companies; in the United States, Ford is a major client; and in East Asia, the firm has had business deals with all of the major motor car manufacturers in Japan (from 1964 onwards). China was a major market during 1979–85 through a variety of contracts and consulting agreements, but is less so at present. Taiwan has risen as a market since 1982, as has Singapore which is a major manufacturing centre – a number of companies have received licensed technology. India, too, is a prominent market at times. South Korea, however, has perhaps the most prospects at the moment and can be regarded as the 'new Japan'. The firm has strong links with Hyundai, Kia, Daewoo and other major Korean manufacturers; these links have been established because there is the need to refine engine technology as these firms try and push even further into industrialised country markets (Hyundai is already manufacturing cars in Canada). Most of these companies are also trying to reduce their dependence on Japanese suppliers.

Motivation-wise the firm simply goes to where the clients are, and most of them are overseas! Clients and agreements are constantly sought.

Korean Operations

Korea became a major market for 'technology transfer' simply because of the country's growth prospect and many significant manufacturing companies, especially in the motor industry. The country's share of turnover varies considerably with contracts, but is significant. The company has a number of technology agreements with Korean firms. These are formulated through discussion with clients and are subject to an agreed programme/schedule. Usually there is discussion both in the United Kingdom and Korea.

Technology Transfer

There are agreements regarding the design of car engines with major Korean car manufacturers. One company also has had assistance in the design of power generation and highway equipment; Ssangyong is a regular customer; others are occasional. In nearly all cases plant design, process and product technology is involved; blueprints and special equipment (where relevant) are also transferred. Technical assistance is a part of this process.

One example of the training input is the design of a new engine for a particular Korean car company. (This company also had strong links with General Motors which has also transferred employees). Firm 2 despatched a number of employees to Kia during the design and implementation period. One man stayed in Korea for three months; others were sent for varying periods. Four Korean personnel also came to the United Kingdom of for a number of weeks (12 came from another Korean company in a similar agreement) and were involved in formal training at the firm's headquarters.

The net result of these agreements is that Korean companies now have more advanced engines, essentially geared to United States market standards. However the essential 'infrastructure' already existed for these advances. There was complete interaction with client firms during the design and implementation period.

Technology Agreements

Technology agreements were the core of the activity and essentially involved design, the transfer of know-how and other technical services. The agreements signed were standard and unaffected by any differences with clients or government pressures. The preparation of the design and implementation was subject to specific durations, but the contracts (e.g. for trouble shooting, etc.) are ongoing. The payment was in the form of a straight consultancy fee which was entirely remited to the United Kingdom. There are no restrictions placed on clients after the agreed work is done.

Evaluation and Post-implementation Relationships

Firm 2 believed that its competitive advantage was defined by its long-standing international experience in the field, international prestige, an ongoing research programmed and the willingness (necessity!) to adapt technology for clients' requirements. The size of the firm (difficult to gauge because of its nature) was not deemed important.

All agreements were successfully completed and there are plans to continue/expand involvement with Korean companies. The main problems encountered are: (1) though the Koreans are generally appreciative, they tend to photocopy everything – and it is necessary to ensure that details of core research and computer program for engine designs (the basis of the company's expertise and advantage) not lost; (2) it was discovered that good relationships with key individuals are paramount – if you miss your chance with just one man there will be no agreement; (3) there was the danger of creating competitors for *other clients*.

Some other points were made in terms of doing business in Korea:

- Koreans are very nationalistic and 'think differently' They need foreign advice, but find this difficult to accept – so sensitivity is needed in all dealings.
- The Japanese (sophisticated, polite) and Chinese (recognise technology gap, humble, amenable) are easier to deal with. The Koreans are blunt and brash.
- Firm 2 has some licensing agreements with a number of companies, but has to deal with (United States) PhDs! The society is very structured and hierarchical – if the right impression is not made on a single person, all may be lost. Try and impress everybody!

- Trust is essential. If a good job is done, Korean companies will maintain the relationship and give you priority over the competition.

TECHNOLOGY SUPPLIER: TEXTILE MACHINERY MANUFACTURER IN BRAZIL

General Description

This company began manufacturing woollen-carding machinery in 1947. It introduced cotton-carding machinery in 1962 and ended the production of woollen-carding machines in 1970. It employs 460 people and has a sales turnover of £26 million (1987). It is a family-owned company, managed jointly by family members and professional managers, which include the Managing Director.

Competition and Product

The firm has 15 per cent of the world market in new cotton-carding machines and the same share of the used second hand converted machines. The firm exports 98–99 per cent of its output and its major destinations are (1) F. East Asia (Taiwan, Hong Kong, PRC, Thailand, Indonesia), (2) the United States, (3) Pakistan. Its exports have grown over 400 per cent in the last five years (£8 million, £8 million, £11.5 million, £26 million, £40 million (1987)). The business is highly cynical and the world market is currently beginning to slump after the height of a boom.

The interviewee (Managing Director) described the market as 'a buyers' market'.

The plant is the largest in the world, producing 35 machines per week (over 45 weeks) 1575 per year in 1987, although 1000 is more usual. The plant produces 98 per cent of all United Kingdom output of the machines. The next largest plant is in Germany and produces between 20 and 25 per week. The current machine was launched in 1983.

The firm has a 'sister plant' in the United States established in 1965 which produces components for machines and spares, but also carries out sales. It is 100 per cent – owned. The only other foreign involvement is the 100 per cent – owned Brazilian factory which is currently going into production. It was established in 1970 as a sales plant and to refurbish old machines.

Motivation and Form of Involvement

The plant in Brazil was set up because a German competitor established production in Brazil and the United Kingdom firm could no longer import. The United Kingdom firm either had to also produce in Brazil or lose the market.

Brazil accounts for only 2 per cent of production, but the existence of the sales subsidiary, 18 years old, led them to manufacture. The firm assessed the market via the US company. The wholly-owned sales subsidiary thus added new production to its reconditioning business. No home or host assistance has so far been sought or offered. The financing is a mixture of foreign exchange, capital goods and technology from the United Kingdom plus reinvestment of funds in Brazil. The firm has 16 qualified engineers ('how you make the product') plus six textile technologists ('how you process cotton').

Technology Transfer Process

The main object of the transfer was the product technology embodied in the machine to be manufactured. Process technology was also involved to a lesser extent. The mechanism used were blueprints/designs, special equipment, the export of critical parts and components and technical assistance. 'Two or three' technical personnel was transferred to Brazil temporarily. No technology agreement as such was implemented because royalties are heavily taxed in Brazil. It is envisaged that two or three staff from Brazil will visit the head office in the United Kingdom.

The machine was altered only in detail to accommodate Brazilian motors and because the production plant in Brazil is to be less sophisticated/automated e.g. simple manual lathes are used in Brazil, rather than computer-controlled lathes. The minor modifications are necessary because of the need to adopt to local needs and the non-availability of imported inputs. The Brazilian plant is less vertically integrated than the United Kingdom to avoid buying the large machine tools which the United Kingdom plant has – more subcontracting access in Brazil. Labour costs are much lower in Brazil (there is no quantitative estimates as production has not yet begun) but the Brazilian plant will be 20 per cent of the United Kingdom in terms of employment, 15 per cent in physical size and 5 per cent of United Kingdom turnover.

The product, with minor modification as above, will be essentially the same as the United Kingdom, as the company is essentially a single-product operation. The United Kingdom company rates the Brazilian engineering staff very highly – they are 'competent, but few in number'.

Post-implementation Relationships

The firm does not employ United Kingdom personnel in Brazil. They are currently half-way through the agreement – 16 machines went to Brazil complete, the next 16 partially complete. Phase I of the project is 'putting metal round the machine', then a move to fuller manufacture. The first machines were sold in dollars, the next set in cruzeiros. Prices are still to be negotiated, but will account for tax differences.

The management of the process was essentially from United Kingdom. The Managing Director will spend 1 week every six months in Brazil and a small number of engineers will visit for longer. One or two officers from Brazil are expected to visit the United Kingdom.

The company in Brazil is responsible for its own marketing, purchasing, management recruitment, wage policy and prices, but will do no R&D.

Evaluation

There is only one local competitor in Brazil, German-owned. The British company has the advantage of (1) a simple machine; easier to make and operate and therefore cheaper and (2) its sells in local currency so has no foreign exchange problems.

The main problems are (1) an initial cash flow, (2) entry into the market 2 or 3 years behind its German competitor and (3) the Germany company has existing works and machine tools: the United Kingdom company has to sub-contract.

Production is likely to be more difficult in Brazil and the cost and selling price will be three times higher. The United Kingdom company does not feel it has been discriminated against, but finds it difficult to get local finance (its customers may, too) and finds it difficult to import second hand machines to renovate in Brazil (these machines are ideal for the Brazilian market).

The company expects to expand in Brazil and, for the next 10 years at least, to reinvest its profits in Brazil.

TECHNOLOGY SUPPLIER 4: SPECIALITY CHEMICALS MANUFACTURER IN SINGAPORE

General Description and Competition

Firm 4 can be effectively dated to 1969 in its present form. It existed prior to this date, but was bought up by the three entrepreneural founders as a vehicle for their plans. The global sales of the company are $131 million (1987), and have greatly increased over the last few years. However the 'true' growth rate is difficult to measure since much of the expansion has been through acquisitions. There are 860 employees in the United Kingdom and 220 over-seas. The company is a Plc which is run by hired officers (though some of the directors are owners) and does not have any 'network' links with other firms. The export ratio is low and reducing since the company relies heavily on FDI in Europe (France, Spain, Germany, etc.), Asia (Singapore, India, Hong Kong) and the Americas (the United States, Canada, Brazil, Mexico, etc.).

There are three core businesses and one emerging one: (i) metal finishing chemicals; (ii) chemicals for the aerospace industry; (iii) chemicals for food and beverages; and (iv) chemicals for printed circuit boards. There is fre-quent organic growth through geographic and industrial acquisition. The company is a market leader in most of its products in the United Kingdom, but not so in aerospace and printed circuit board chemicals. The printed circuit boards and food areas are regarded as competitive, while the other two are fairly concentrated by supplier and user. Sub-categories are more or less competi-tive, depending on technical content.

R&D expenditures are about 3–3.5 per cent of total sales. Between 10 and 14 per cent of personnel are involved in R&D – this varies by product group – and is highly decentralised. There is also localised development fine tuning in overseas subsidiaries e.g. in Singapore there are two people involved in such activities because of special customer requirements.

The International Process: Motivation and Form of Overseas Involvement

The firm had three overseas licensing agreements 'at inception' in 1969 in Spain, France and Belgium. Between 1969 and 1973 these were converted into FDIs with an 80 per cent stake, rising to 100 per cent in the 1980s. There was a strong acquisition programme at home and abroad to ensure entry into new lines of business after 1973: Food and chemicals were acquired in 1976, packaging companies in 1981, etc. The Singapore subsidiary was established as – 100 per cent – owned in 1977; the US affiliate in 1981; the German in 1982–3 – and further international establishments were made in Mexico, Italy, Brazil, Argentina, etc. in ensuing years. During 1984–7 as a move to enter the printed circuits board industry and this has resulted in new subsidiaries in the United States, as well as the United Kingdom.

The company is constantly on the look out for opportunities, both geographically and industrially and this attitude determines its internationalisation drive. In the Singapore case it was recognised that entry into Asean was essential, particularly because of the rapid growth and industrialisation of the region. Singapore was the ideal central location for Asean, especially because of the local infrastructure, incentives and proximity of customers. There is also a well developed distribution network established by firm 4 in the area. The use of local nationals is the norm; in Indonesia there is also the labour of the local Chinese.

Singapore Operations

The Singapore affiliate was established in 1977 for the reasons given above. No other country was considered in the area since it was clearly the ideal location and additionally was free of financial and political restrictions. At the time of involvement there were exports to the region (though less than 5 per cent of total turnover), especially to Singapore Airlines, and this provided a good central core around which the affiliate could be established. Since establishment, other countries in Asean and East Asia have been looked at: there is now a small affiliate in Hong Kong (a listening post for China) and potential targets for acquisition are being actively sought elsewhere.

Before the Singapore affiliate was established, there was a local agent. Someone was sent to assess the prospects, but did not need to do an extensive job since the country's prospects were clear; a wholly-owned subsidiary was established since this is preferred for reasons of control. There were no problems or government restrictions in this or other respects. No incentives were sought from the authorities as such, but of course many are available. For example there is significant training and exhibition support; aid for exports; aid for training; and funds for staff training (which can occur abroad). All these have been useful.

The company established was entirely new, and resources contributed included foreign exchange, capital goods and technology.

Technology Transfer

Firm 4 has a policy of continually transferring technology to its subsidiaries, depending on local conditions and absorptive capacity. As the Singapore subsidiary has evolved, more technology has been transferred. Initially the breadth of technology transfer had to be restricted because a well defined direction for growth had to be established and maintained. Initial technology transfer was in aerospace since this was the most rapidly-growing sector and the firm is a significant niche supplier. This process is now complete and the affiliate has access to the entire product range, data sheets, health and advisory sheets, etc. The parent company has advised on the most appropriate formulation. Technically experienced people have been seconded to determine that technology can now be feasibly released, bearing in mind that initially there were 3–4 people in the Singapore technical department – and 500–600 products. The way to transfer technology best is believed to be to start with a small tranche, backed up technically and expanded as necessary. The appropriate formulations will be automatically given. Of course the affiliate has to sign all the normal forms, etc. The process is very controlled.

In terms of the transfer of technology for aerospace chemicals, the know-how transferred included plant design, process technology and product technology. Blueprints and special equipment was transferred and technical assistance given. There are no 'critical components', but some items had to be exported from the United Kingdom in the early phase. There was no special modification or preparation for the know-how transferred.

A technical person was sent to Singapore for one year, followed by a more technically knowledgeable and sales-experienced person when the requirements were clear. In 1982 a technical manager was sent out permanently (he is the only expatriate). This process has since been repeated for metal finishing chemicals (from 1982) and printed circuit board chemicals (from 1987). People from the Singapore affiliate have also come to the United Kingdom for training/experience for a number of weeks at a time, as necessary. Technical persons have also been sent to Malaysia and Indonesia for six-monthly periods to support distributors. Allied with the stress on an indigenous work force, this is seen as the classic way of doing things: secure, though not swift.

The plant design has not been specially modified for local conditions, although small changes were made because of the availability of certain raw materials and climate (cheaper solvents can be used). The production systems are similar in the United Kingdom and Singapore, though they rely more on sub-contractors. There are no major time-lags in the use of technology in Singapore – the transfer depends on opportunity and timing. For example, technology for food and beverages chemicals has not been transferred, but that for printed circuit boards has.

Technology Agreements

There is no formalised system of agreements with wholly-owned ventures (joint ventures are different). There is a tendency to use standard agreements (with few alterations) which determine the number of parties, royalties, up-front technology fees, time limits, etc. Royalties are usually for 5 years. The subject matter of course varies with the specific technology and intent. In the case of Singapore, where such agreements have been entered into, there are no time limits or geographical restrictions (though S E Asia is the clear scope of the affiliate's market), and the usual royalties are paid. There has been no interference by the Singapore government.

Post-implementation Relationships

Only the technical manager is a United Kingdom expatriate (the M D is Australian, but clearly the right man for the task – Singaporeans with the experience are difficult to attract and retain); otherwise the group policy is to employ indigenous personnel. There is continous assistance from the parent company (as necessary) and to some extent this was programmed in advance (see the 'classic' approach mentioned above). This assistance relates to design, quality control, process engineering, etc. There are few imports from the parent company which prefers to service Singapore/Asean through FDI rather than exports. Where there are imports (e.g. of equipment) the pricing is as for other overseas customers – the company sells for profit.

The affiliate is very autonomous in its operations. Investment, finance, etc. is planned every year (rolled into the 5-year strategic plan) and discussed with the parent company. The parent formally approves, but seldom changes the plan. The affiliate is responsible for its own marketing, purchasing, etc.; and for a small share of the group's R&D.

Parent company officers visit Singapore twice a year for 10 days at a time. Distributors and major customers are visited at the same time. Officers from the affiliate also visit the parent frequently, but nothing formal is established.

Evaluation

The main competition to the Singapore affiliate is from other international competitors in Asean and East Asia. The level of competitive advantage varies across products and by origin of competitor.

Apart from the technology and expertise, the Singapore company's advantages are twofold: (i) it is run by locals which gives it 'kudos' by earning the respect of Asean governments and enables it to establish a more effective linkage with customers; (ii) the affiliate has a sophisticated, well defined regional distributor network run by 'bumiputras'. These differs from the opposition. US firms have distributors, but no local presence. 'Occasionally the seventh cavalry appears! 'The main competition is in aerospace-related chemicals.

The Japanese are a much greater threat, particularly in metal finishing. However they are resented which is to firm 4's benefit. A third advantage is that the group makes a point of autonomy: employees are trained and advance technology transmitted. The Japanese only do this on an 'absolute needs' basis which means that they are resented and viewed as the 'new imperialists'. Nevertheless, Japanese competition is regarded as very tough because of a different profit ethic. The Singapore affiliate also suffers from the 'British image' though the group's technology is as good as that of Japanese firms. Firm 4's niche ideology helps it fend off the Japanese who are volume-orientated. Competition is likely to get tougher and a 'war of attrition' is expected. However, the group has good friends in the region who are screening companies in the area for potential acquisition: size will help.

Overall the Singapore affiliate's performance has surpassed expectations, with regard to sales, productivity performance, etc. (though there has been no reverse flow of technology). There are intentions to expand further. The chief problems have been: (i) the 1985 economic crisis in Singapore; (ii) the inexperienced Singapore team's panic during this period; and (iii) difficulties in attracting and keeping good people (very volatile job market).

Much of the profits made in Singapore have been reinvested, but this really depends on opportunities.

TECHNOLOGY SUPPLIER 5: SPECIALIST RAIL TRAIN COMPONENTS MANUFACTURER IN KOREA

General Description and Competition

Firm 5 was established in 1938 and is a specialist manufacturer of resilient rail track components. In 1987 its turnover was $50 million and it employed 519 workers (mostly in the United Kingdom). These figures slightly understate the size of the company since there are a number of associate companies e.g. the Korean venture is unconsolidated. The company has 11 plants worldwide, but not all are involved in exports. The United Kingdom plant is the primary exporter and exports 50 per cent of its output. There are also some exports by its Korean and Australian companies. The main destination of exports are Sweden, Norway, Taiwan and Japan.

The company was originally owned by individuals, but since the mid-sixties has been owned by a holding company. It is functionally independent and has little involvement with other group companies. The management of the company is entirely by hired officers.

The industry is highly competitive from the 'supply' side with many firms able to supply similar products. However there is a degree of stability since ex-colonial territories tend to look to former metropole countries for supplies; thus French firms have advantages in former French territories; and similarly United Kingdom firms (as in this case) have an advantage in ex-British territories. The greatest competition is often in places such as Korea, but once a particular supplier is established the competition is severely reduced. This is because most countries have a single national railway, though the market is not quite so concentrated because of liberalisation measures (break-up Japan Railways for example) and the existence of major urban railway networks.

The firm's R&D is about 4 per cent of its sales, though the number of engineers/technicians devoted to R&D is highly variable. Five new products were launched during 1986–8 and all received patent protection. The company tends to subcontract the non-steel parts of its products, but could not give a figure by value. The company produces on a customer-order basis and in 1987 the output was 11 million units (of which 9 million were railway components). Its plant produces 100 per cent of all such output in the United Kingdom, but then it is a unique product. It suspects that its United Kingdom plant has the largest capacity for similar products world-wide.

The Internationalisation Process: Motivation and Form of Overseas Involvement

The nature of the industry means that the firm has had a number of overseas involvements for a long period. By the mix-sixties there were 100 per cent affiliates in Australia, South Africa and Argentina. In 1984 the Korean venture (50:50 joint venture) was established and in 1986 a 100 per cent affiliate was established in Indonesia.

The Korean Case

In all cases the local market was the primary reasons for establishing an affiliate. In the Korean case, the host government literally closed the border for the sale of rail components. Previous to this Korea was serviced by exports, but following the government's requirement that the product should be produced locally (and the fact that a particular product tends to get the entire railway market) the company decided to set up local production – or forgo the market. There was also the possibility so sales to the Seoul Metro. The United Kingdom company was approached by a Korean company already in the field and a joint venture was established. There was also a local manufacturing strategy to differentiate the product from its competitors. Prior to the manufacturing presence, a local agent was used – the agent is still represented as a director in the joint venture.

Before the decision to establish a joint venture was made, a feasibility study was conducted and a visit was made by the Commercial/Business Development director. A majority-owned venture was preferred because there was a preference for controlling the operation, particularly since little was known about the local partner. However the 50:50 ratio was imposed by Korean government requirements. Similarly a 7.5 per cent royalty rate would have been preferred, but 5 per cent had to be accepted. The total process of receiving host-government permission took about 3 months; no incentives were available because the product was classified as 'low technology'.

The Korean partner was a smaller company manufacturing springs, and in hindsight they were the right choice. They sent samples and discussions indicated the basis for cooperation. An element of protecting the United Kingdom company's interest was also involved since the prospective partners or others could potentially supply Korean railways. Fortunately the production of railtrack components was more difficult than the partner could have anticipated – hence their desire for a relationship. The United Kingdom company contributed cash, capital goods and technology to the relationship.

Technology Transfer

The know-how transferred to Korea included plant, process and product technology. Blueprints, special equipment and technical assistance were all part of the transfer mechanism. No special modifications were required for the transfer, though there is a policy of continuing (re)design. Local workers were trained by three persons from the United Kingdom company, despatched for a number of weeks. Two Koreans also received some training in the United Kingdom.

The plant output in Korea is about a quarter of the United Kingdom plant (3 million units), though the production process is roughly the same. The product mix is about the same. There is no time lag between in the transfer of technology – some is oldish technology, but this is also used in the United Kingdom. Indeed some new products have been offered to the Korean affiliate – but they do not wish to be guinea pigs!

The local partner has achieved complete mastery of the received technology. Their technological capacity is on par with the United Kingdom firm, but they are more expansion-minded and likely to diversify (using existing technology, sometimes through licensing).

Technology Agreements

The technology agreement concerned the transfer of patents, trademarks, know-how and technical services. Future assistance and a sharing of future developments were also included. The negotiations took place over three visits to Korea, a week and a and a half in total. Both British and Korean lawyers were consulted and the agreement was drawn in English and then translated into Korean. An application to the government was also drawn up and (apart from changes mentioned earlier) there was no problem with the authorisation procedure. The Korean negotiators were regarded as remarkably trusting, although there were a few minor sticking points (e.g. they only paid a small up-front sum).

The joint venture is indefinite, but the royalties payable (lump sum plus 5 per cent on sales) are limited by the duration of patents. There are no official geographical restrictions (not allowed), but exports have been limited. There are no obligations to import parts from the United Kingdom (imports have virtually ceased) and the Should be joint venture is free to introduce improvements (which are shared with the parent companies).

All employees of the joint venture are Koreans, but officers from the United Kingdom parent visit the company four times a year for a shareholders' meeting and technical/marketing support. Joint venture officers visit the United Kingdom twice a year for group conferences. There is considerable applications assistance and this is supplied at the request of the recipient. The joint venture is autonomous in day-to-day operations and is responsible for investment, sales, etc., though clearly the parent companies approve and elaborate.

Post-implementation Relationships and Evaluation

Firm 5 believed that its competitive advantage in Korea was owed mainly to the appropriateness of its technology (not too high-tech), its previous experience in similar projects and its international prestige. By moving in quickly it was able to establish a dominant position, thereby reducing the incentive for foreign competitors to try and break into the Korean market. With regard to local competitors the joint venture was able to market a proven product and win the approval of Korean Railways. Being a small company was valuable since, 'We are small enough to have a monopoly without causing embarrassment'. Previous international experience was also regarded as a plus factor,: 'We were not terrified and thus bogged down by negotiations, we could afford to take the risk and knew what we were doing.' The results of the venture surpassed all objectives and performance in Korea is as good as in the United Kingdom in terms of sales, profitability, etc. (relative to size).

The two main concerns of the United Kingdom firm were first, to ensure that no other foreign firm was able to participate in the Korean market and get approval from Korean National Railways and, secondly, to ensure that the joint venture was essentially confined to the Korean market. The firm has been successful in both respects.

The situation in Korea remains favourable and expansion will be considered should the opportunity arise.

TECHNOLOGY SUPPLIERS 6/7: GEARBOX MANUFACTURER IN KOREA AND INDIA

General Description and Competition

Firm 6 was established in the 1920s as a development company in vehicle transmissions and related products. Its main lines today are heavy duty transmissions (gearboxes) in military vehicles, rail vehicles, buses and marine transportation. The firm currently employs about 200 people on site and has an annual turnover of about $12.4 million. About 45 per cent of these sales are accounted for by direct exports; and there is a variable amount of 'indirect' exports via customers exporting vehicles and other equipment. The main destination countries are Korea, Sweden, the Netherlands, Kenya and India.

Originally an independent company, the firm was later taken by a United Kingdom group and, more recently, was acquired by an American multinational. It is likely to be sold in the near future and can be regarded as being functionally independent. It has its own board of directors and management and is a completely autonomous profit centre.

It is not possible to arrive at a market share, but the share would be small ('crumbs from the giant's table'), except for the fact that one needs to take into account 'niche-type' markets for the products. The industry is highly competitive on the supply side, but the number of customers (major companies) is very concentrated.

The firm regards itself as a 'development company' – though basic R&D only constitutes 5 per cent of sales, there is also a considerable amount of applied research for customers. This fact is reflected in a high proportion of engineers and scientists in the workforce. About one new product is launched every year as a result of non-funded research.

The firm operates one plant in the United Kingdom and also subcontracts about a third of its activities (mainly machine work). Only custom-order work is undertaken, resulting in an output of about 500 transmissions per year. This is less than 5 per cent of total transmissions produced in the United Kingdom, but most are for cars, whereas firm 6 supplies other types of manufacturers also. The firm argues that there are no similar plants in the United Kingdom (because of the product mix) and that its main competitors are from overseas, especially the United States and Germany. These tend to be larger producers.

The Internationalisation Process. Motivation and Form of Overseas Involvement

In the immediate post-war period firm 6 began to internationalise overseas through service exports on the back of other major suppliers. By the early 1980s there was an increasing reliance on direct exports because of declining markets at home. It was not possible to operate efficiently world-wide because of size, so the company evolved a policy of establishing four major bases for further expansion in Brazil, South Africa, India and Australia. These bases were used as a means of fanning out into four geographical areas: South America, Africa, South Asia and the Asia-Pacific respectively. In 1982 an approach was made by a Korean company (not a previous customer) and a licensing contract was signed in due course for the local production of transmissions; this was sufficiently successful to ensure a second contract in 1989. Another licence was granted to another Korean company in 1984 which was contacted by firm 6 after discussions with the British Embassy. There are also arrangements with an Indian company (previously a fellow member of company 6 and 7's former United Kingdom group) for the development of bus transmissions and a Brazilian company (an agent who has been given a licence to produce transmissions previously imported). The main motivation behind the internationalisation process has been the need to seek new markets, but other factors have clearly also played a role.

Korean Operations

The key reason for the initial product licence in Korea was the approach by the Korean partner. However, the growth perspective of Korean vehicle manufacturers and the capacity to work with Koreans were also factors. The Korean firm was also regarded as a good partner because of its position, experience, technological capacity and financial resources. ('A second licence will follow soon. They love to learn to trust each other; believe in growing together. They believe we are as hard as nails!') The Korean market represented above 5 per cent of firm 6's output in 1982 (no local agent, though), but this was not directly affected by the licensing decision.

The decision to enter the Korean market through a non-equity technology agreement was based on three main reasons: (1) financial and other resources (people) were used minimally ('we are bigger than we appear as a consequence'); (2) to ensure potential additional business; and (3) to enable firm 6 to use the additional funds to develop new products.

Indian Operations

The technology agreement in India was also due to an outside proposal, although in this case the Indian firm was a known quantity. At the time exports in India were low and there was no local agent. A person was despatched to India to study the proposal and make a feasibility study. The agreement can be regarded as a joint research venture for a new product (the venture was 50:50 at the research level), although in another respect firm 6 was acting as a consultant. An interesting part of the arrangement was that the new product would be manufactured by the local partner, but the technology would be owned by firm 6.

Technology Transfer to Korea

The licensing agreement with the Korean recipient included the transfer of product and process technology through all possible mechanisms. The only technology not transferred was that relating to products of other firms: ball bearings, filters, etc. Such items are bought by firm 6 and exported to the Korean licensee. Blueprints, etc. were used to transfer the technology, but these were not specially developed for Korea. Training was done by means of despatching United Kingdom employees to Korea and training local employees in the United Kingdom (eight over a few weeks – this was laid down in the contract; the Korean company wished to send more).

Efforts were made to choose equipment suitable to Korean conditions, though it is similar to that employed in the United Kingdom. Fortunately the technology used by firm 6 is not too sophisticated (unlike that of German firms). The technology itself is tried and tested, but still in use with the British Army! It lends itself to less sophisticated production methods, although the Koreans are increasingly using sophisticated computer-controlled methods Korean labour costs are escalating).

The plant in Korea is some – 2–4 times smaller than the United Kingdom plant, but then it is only producing one type of transmission. Modifications are made through close technical cooperation on the transmissions. The licensee wanted closer coupling of transmission and engine; United Kingdom engineers said this was impossible, but the licensee was able to achieve this in 3 months! The product mix is different between companies; the Korean company is a major, highly diversified conglomerate. On the other hand, it could not yet design a transmission. It has nevertheless assimilated the manufacturing technology and is constantly learning.

Technology Transfer to India

The Indian venture was a joint design product for bus transmissions; the technology transfer element consists of (a) the supply of expertise from the United Kingdom and (b) the retention of ownership of the new design with the United Kingdom company. Blueprints, special equipment and technical training programmes were all prepared for the agreement/design/product. There was little similarity with United Kingdom production or equipment since the development was specifically for Indian conditions. In general the technological expertise of the Indian partner was regarded as being very high.

Technology Agreement in Korea

The agreement related to patents, know-how, technical services and a certain amount of applications know-how. For example, help was also given in the design of vehicles. Prior to the agreement advice was sought from various sources, especially a qualified lawyer – there were four or five drafts in the end. The negotiation itself took between 1 year and 18 months and there were a number of difficulties. The main problem was that the previous MD had wanted $800 000 in a back account which the Koreans (with their view on trust) were not willing to accept. The agreement was stipulated for 10 years and will be renewed.

The agreement included an initial lump sum and a percentage of the invoice price (the United Kingdom firm can check the Korean firm's accounts). Only production for the Korean market (and export to firm 6) is allowed. Some proprietary parts need to be sourced from the United Kingdom firm (about 20 per cent of the value of the transmission − a profit is made as a 'middleman' for ball-bearings, etc.). The licensee is allowed to improve the technology of the United Kingdom firm has access to these improvements.

Technology Agreement in India

The main subject matter of the agreement related to the patent resulting from the joint development; this was retained by firm 6. There was little need to obtain specialist advice about the agreement because of previous experience and relations with the Indian firm. The agreement had to be registered with the Indian government who created no problems at all. There were no problems during negotiation and the eventual agreement was for 10 years.

A lump sum and a percentage of the royalties were stipulated in the contract and the recipient's accounts can be checked. Production is only allowed for the Indian market or for exports to the United Kingdom firm. Proprietary parts need to be imported from the United Kingdom.

Post-implementation Relationships and Evaluation

Firm 6 (7) argued that its competitive advantage against foreign competitors was mainly due to the appropriateness of its technology and flexibility of management:

> As a small company we can respond quickly. People in the firm are close to decision makers and the MD. We do not feel vulnerable. We do not feel we are giving away our lifeblood through these ventures. Even our unions are not worried in this respect, unlike our German and United States competitors which are afraid of job losses at home.

In addition it was argued that there were disadvantages of being small, because of the lack of resources. Hence it is not always possible to send engineers to recipients of technology. Former international experience and a world-wide outlook was also deemed as being important for the success of the United Kingdom firm's technology agreements. The Korean agreement surpassed all expectations; the Indian once met the objectives of firm 6.

After implementation assistance, new designs, etc. were rendered to both the Korean and Indian company. These were programmed in advance. In both cases, exports have increased from the United Kingdom: apart from other exports these ventures also ensure trade in spares and proprietary parts. The prices charged are as for other customers and a discount structure is operated.

There were few problems formed in Korea or India. The main one in Korea was cultural differences:

We are constantly being lectured about saying no, trust is important and our MD upset the Koreans considerably with his demand for large up-front sums of money; the Koreans do not readily admit to mistakes.

In both cases there was a considerable amount of technological feedback to the United Kingdom company. The Indian venture was developmental from its inception; in the Korean case much was learned (e.g. the close coupling of the engine and transmission) since problems and solutions often do not emerge until implementation.

In both Korea and India, expansion is planned or underway.

TECHNOLOGY SUPPLIER 8/9: MANUFACTURER OF NON-DESTRUCTIVE TESTING EQUIPMENT IN INDIA AND BRAZIL

General Description and Competition

Supplier 8 was established in 1946 with the original aim of producing a dictaphone system. Since 1968 the main product has been non-destructive testing equipment which represents two-thirds of sales. These instruments are not for 'quality control' (here defined as designing out problems), but rather for ensuring a low rejection rate during operations. These are also products for the dairy industry and some subcontracting for defence-related equipment. The firm employs 21 people and had a turnover (in 1988) of $1.25 which has been growing at some 5 per cent compound. 35 per cent of the firm's output is exported, and the main destination countries are Japan, Korea and Germany.

The company was originally part of a family-owned concern which was subsequently bought up by a holding company. The managing director of firm 8 was a member of the original family. He was unhappy with the holding company and bought out firm 8 which now belongs entirely to him. He manages the company himself.

Firm 8 is one of the top five firms in non-destructive testing equipment worldwide. It controls 60 per cent of the United Kingdom market and 15–20 per cent of the world market. Clearly a concentrated industry from the supply side, the demand end is 'competitive' (many customers), but in actual fact they have a lot of monopsonistic power – they are large, while firm 8 is small.

There are the equivalent of two people (10 per cent of the workforce) employed in R&D and the expenditure is about 5 per cent of sales. 11 new products were launched in 1987–8 (about five per year) including new and updated equipment. No patents were possible and these could be 'cracked' by the stronger customers in any case. On plant is operated in the United Kingdom and very little production is sub-constracted.

The Internationalisation Process: Motivation and Form of Overseas Involvement

Since growth in the United Kingdom tends to be slow (many United Kingdom firms are not interested), overseas customers have always been important and firm 8 has moved from market to market as countries have become 'saturated' (the equipment lasts some time). Up to the 1970s exporting was done by use of ad hoc agencies, but from the 1970s a specialist agency route was taken. The equipment requires specialist expertise (not 'catalogue material') and the agent also carries the financial burden. In the 1980s two licences were granted, one to a Brazilian firm, the other to an Indian one. The Brazilian firm was a former agent which reckoned that the market was now big enough for local production. The Indian firm was not previously known and the approached company 8 out of the blue. The licence was granted mainly to get a toehold into the Indian market which is dominated by a German competitor.

Indian and Brazilian Operations

At the time the approach was made by the Indian firm, sales to India were below 5 per cent of total exports, though there had been a few sales to companies such as Tata Iron and Steel, Bihar Steel, etc. (No agents were employed, but there were occasional middlemen.) As a result, the decision to proceed with the licence was strongly influenced by the need to establish a position in the Indian market. The local firm was considered ideal since it was well positioned in the local market and had both the technological and financial capacity. No feasibility study was conducted, but approaches were made to the Indian commercial attaché and others to ascertain the strength of the Indian firm and the difficulties, etc. in granting a licence. The licensing was preferred because firm 8 would risk nothing, the agreement was lucrative and there would be, nevertheless, a potential future entry into the Indian market. It was possible that the Indian firm was the wrong partner for this agreement (it was certainly not a specialist in this field; indeed it was a very diversified company in terms of product mix), but it was reckoned that the ultimate reasons for failure were more to do with the market.

In the Brazilian case, local production began because the scale of equipment sales exceeded a certain level. Firm 8 was dominant in Brazil to the extent of supplying German firms such as Volkswagen. The licence was granted because of the prospects of greater sales and earnings and further details were left to the local agent (itself a manufacturer).

Technology Transfer to India and Brazil

In both cases the transfer consisted of product technology and mechanisms included blueprints, technical assistance and export of 'critical' components. Essentially, completely assembled circuit boards were supplied from the United Kingdom. The local firms made a few changes for the local market, but this was mainly a matter of customisation rather than anything major. Training consisted of host country employees visiting the United Kingdom plant. In the Indian case, two people came for a fortnight ('about the right number, they were very able') – these then trained others. In both cases the mastery of the received technology was very high, but in the Indian case marketing expertise was probably lacking. The equipment supplied had been launched some 5-10 years previously, but was not obsolete (it was still supplied to United Kingdom firms).

Technology Agreements

The subject matter of the licensing agreements consisted of know-how, drawings and the right to manufacture. In the Indian case advice was obtained from the Indian Investment Centre on legislation regarding agreements. The agreements had to be registered with the governments in both Brazil and India, but no problems arose (apart from minor modifications) – only time was lost! The negotiations with the Indian firm had only one sticking point – they wanted rights to worldwide sales, but these were refused. The payment in the Indian case was based on an initial lump sum; the Brazilians also paid royalties. Geographically sales were restricted to the host countries and a few neighbouring ones. The equipment could be modified, subject to firm 8's approval.

In the Indian case, the agreement was signed in 1981 and production began in 1983–4. It lapsed in 1988, because a significant market did not emerge.

Evaluation

The Brazilian operation was successful, the Indian operation failed. Neither result had much to do with the size of the United Kingdom firm, but more to do with the experience of servicing the local market. The Indian company was new to the field and may not have had the appropriate marketing skills. Many sales are through existing networks and the Germans had an entrenched position. Finally, the Indian firm was overcommitted – it had also acquired licences for televisions and recording equipment and thus probably accorded these higher priority since they were easier to sell and brought quicker returns.

Firm 8 regarded its main technological advantage as a greater appropriateness of its technology to customers. Its products were (a) designed for specific customers; (b) updated continously; and (c) 'lower-tech'. 'Our German competitor employs 250 Ph.Ds. New products are constantly produced and these are expensive. Old products are not updated or promoted, though these are often more appropriate, especially in developing countries. Unfortunately this can sometimes be to our disadvantage. If we charge £30 000 and they charge £120 000, some customers cannot believe that our equipment can do the job!' A willingness to adapt technology and lower prices and costs were also quoted as advantages.

Finally, firm 8/9 did admit to having been discriminated against for being foreign-owned – in France and Germany! 'This can also work to our advantage. The Japanese prefer to work with us rather than the Americans.'

TECHNOLOGY SUPPLIER 10: AUTOMOTIVE COMPONENT SUPPLIER IN KOREA

General Description and Competition

The firm was founded about 70 years ago as a supplier to transport manufacturers. 50 per cent of its current output consists of metal car components (door hinges, handbrakes and a variety of 'pressings'). In addition the firm is a major supplier of truck and container hinges and other items. It is the largest company worldwide in container-door gear forging. Its present size is over 400 employees and in 1988 had a turnover in excess of $25 million. It has been growing recently at some 10 per cent per annum in terms of nominal turnover. About 17 per cent of its output is exported. The amount had previously been about 25 per cent, but Korean companies have taken its East Asian markets. The main destination countries of exports are Korea, China, Taiwan and Thailand. Taiwan and others are being lost to the company's own joint venture in Korea! ('They do not understand business methods and are undercutting us by 25–40 per cent. They maintain low profitability and pay marginal wages. Workers are treated as serfs and will rebel.')

The firm is family-owned, not part of a network and managed by hired managers.

The industry is highly competitive (many suppliers), but is faced with a highly concentrated picture in terms of its customers. In order to maintain a competitive advantage, the company has forged excellent links with leasing companies: 'We supply all automobile companies in the United Kingdom and most in Europe. We supply most truck companies and container companies. We know the bosses of container *leasing* companies, so though our components are 'low-tech' we get them to specify our product to the manufacturers.'

It was not possible to give an indication of market share because of the nature and variety of the products ('meaningless'). About 36 workers are involved in R&D but it was difficult to state how many 'new' products were launched in recent years. The answer would be none in one sense, but many in another sense because the company works very closely with its customers. The company operates only one plant (a new one is due) and tends not to subcontract work. Custom-order production is the mainstay of the company, but it is not possible to give the size of output in physical units because of the great variety of products.

The Internationalisation Process: Motivation and Form of Overseas Involvement

Apart form exporting the company tends not to operate overseas. It prefers not to grant licences for reasons of security. Its sole foreign direct investment (a joint venture) was forced upon it by Korean companies which began to copy its products. There were two main companies involved and one was chosen as a joint venture partner to pre-empt further inroads into its markets. This broadly did occur, but there were other problems – 'our partner is a rogue'!

Korean Operations

The reason for entry into Korea was to protect firm 10's markets in Korea (above 5 per cent of exports) and elsewhere in East Asia. Before the involvement, the firm did have an agent in Korea, but this was not chosen as a partner. The firm made a feasibility study and sent a team to Korea in order to do this. This worked closely with the Embassy, the Chamber of Commerce and a Korean Merchant Bank. The last appears to have been involved with both Hyundai and the eventual partner (a family business itself supplying Hyundai) and this choice of adviser is much regretted.

The initial preference was a majority-owned subsidiary to ensure control, but this was not permitted by Government regulations. Eventually a '50:50' joint venture was formed with the Korean firm having 50 per cent ownership, firm 10 having 45 per cent, and the final 5 per cent going to an 'American friend' – a company with which firm 10 had a good relationship. The main problem, as it transpired, was that the chair of the Board (the head of the Korean family) had the casting vote. The Korean partner was chosen because of its financial capacity and on the advice of the Merchant Bank. In hindsight, this was not a wise choice.

The Korean Government's permission had to be sought and this resulted in an eventual document of 3/8 inch thick! No grants were received, but it is possible that some assistance was receiving by the joint venture partner. Firm 10 contributed foreign exchange and technology to the venture.

Technology Transfer

Product technology was transferred through the use of blueprints and technical assistance. The latter involved the despatch of 10–12 people to Korea (including the press shop superintendent) for a month to train local workers. Three Koreans also came to the United Kingdom for a period. The Korean workers had a high technical competence which was essential to the transfer – this was entirely successful. Few modifications were made to the process or products since the same world markets were to be served and standards needed to be maintained. No changes were made because of local conditions, though clearly cheap labour gave an edge to the joint venture: 'Their treatment of workers is disgraceful. They are often beaten up and "heavy gangs" employed. We have no say in this, but believe the consequences will be dire.' All the products transferred were also currently being sold by the United Kingdom company.

Technology Agreement

The subject matter of the agreement included trademarks, know-how, technical services and access to sale outlets worldwide. As indicated earlier, advice had been sought from various parties, but this had not been adequate and – additionally – the present Chief Executive felt that his predecessor had been a little hasty, and that the agreement had been rushed. The agreement had to be approved by the Korean Government which created difficulties: (a) it insisted that the joint venture not be bound by a restrictive geographical clause and (b) that the joint venture need not use firm 10's agents in other countries. Both these demands had been complied with.

The agreement was for 7 years and this period ended in June 1989. The joint venture is being continued, however, because firm 10 feels that it still needs to maintain its presence (and retrieve some of its money). Payment was in the form of dividends which had been very low. There were no requirements to imports from the United Kingdom.

Post-implementation Relationships and Evaluation

Firm 10 characterised its competitive advantages in terms of its better organisation, international links and management. It also underlined the international prestige of its products. 'For decades this company has built up its
name as the international leader in container door hinges and other items.
We get leading companies, especially leading leasing companies and other
dealers, to specify our product to manufacturers.'

Though the technology transfer was successful, the venture did not meet
firm 10's objectives. The main problem was that profits could not be repatriated
(the preferred option) because dividends were kept low by the joint venture
whose Board was controlled by the Korean partner. Thus, though firm 10 had
a theoretical say on decisions to do with sales, investments, etc.; in actuality,
it was powerless in the face of the joint venture's expansion into its established
markets. Firm 10 would prefer a lower rate of expansion and a higher rate of
profits. This was particularly the view because though the joint venture plant
was about half the size of the United Kingdom one, the Korea joint venture
was growing much faster and in general was showing a superior performance.

It was felt that their small size did have some bearing on their problems in
Korea because of a lack of experience and clout. In deed the lack of clout
was also the case in the United Kingdom where the DTI was ignoring demands
that there should be greater reciprocity between Korea and the United Kingdom.
Another reason for 'failure' was given: the wrong time to go in – BP and
Shell also had problems – the situation (legislation, etc.) has since improved
in Korea. The company's main problems in Korea were deemed to be lack of
control, an unscruplous joint venture partner, and restrictive Government legislation.

TECHNOLOGY SUPPLIER 11: TURNKEY COMPANY PROVIDING CAR PAINT FINISHING PLANTS IN INDIA

General Description and Competition

Firm 11 was founded in 1934 and is involved in providing paint finishing
plants for the car industry. This is a complex task which provides customers
with 'a range of specialist skills and services designed to improve product
quality and system efficiency, control maintenance and establish paint finishing plants and ancillary equipment'. This is done through 'an integrated service of project management, maintenance management, operator training, systems
analysis, etc.'. It currently employs 90 people and has a turnover of $35
million (1988). It is not possible to give a growth rate because the size and
frequency of contracts (essentially of a turnkey nature) is very variable. 20
per cent of its turnover is generated abroad. The main foreign markets are at
present China and India.

The company is a subsidiary, but regards itself as being functionally independent, although there is some market-sharing (it does not operate in continental Europe or North America).

The industry is highly concentrated from both the supply and demand side.
The firm's main competitors are one firm each from Germany, Japan, Sweden,

France and Italy. The R&D is entirely carried out by the US subsidiary of its parent and one new product has been launched in the last two years. The firm operates no plant and subcontracts its work (85 per cent – i.e. all materials are subcontracted).

The Internationalisation Process: Motivation and Form of Overseas Involvement

Most activities and trade were initially in the United Kingdom, but enquiries from abroad increased exports (turnkey operations). Formerly business was 'automatic' (world leaders), but recently there has been greater competition (especially from the Germans). There is thus a greater tendency to seek orders internationally: 'As part of the turnkey process we leave subcontracting to local suppliers, but of course transfer the necessary technology/expertise. We supervise and expedite quality control and train the local firm as part of the agreement. As they get better, there are problems for us because we are no longer needed! Our main problem is in retaining our fundamental skills, but these are not so easy for others to learn.' China and India are two major overseas markets at the moment, but there have been projects elsewhere, including Brazil, Argentina the Soviet Union and Poland.

Indian Operations

India is currently a good market because of its growth potential. Previous agreements include one with TELCO. The current major agreement is with a company with which firm 11 has a long period of cooperation, stretching back some 10–12 years. No feasibility study was conducted (all this was left to the Indian firm), though a person was sent to India to conduct negotiations and reach a decision. The preferred and actual involvement was an agreement with a local firm without equity involvement. This decision was based on the fact that (a) the India company was an existing business with local knowledge and the technological capacity; (b) there would be less statutory involvement; and (c) personal history – the company was known and trusted. In hindsight, the recipient company was the correct one.

Technology Transfer

Process technology was transferred through blueprint designs and technical assistance. Training of recipient employees were done in both India and the United Kingdom. There was no need to modify the plant design or equipment for India conditions.

Technology Agreements

The subject matter of the agreement was know-how and technical services. The licencee provided advice on local legislation, but in the end the governments approval required alterations which neither the supplier or recipient agreed with (these had to do with the agreement period and definition of turnover). The negotiations lasted nine months and there were no difficulties.

The agreement period was 10 years and was not renewed because of the nature of the project (turnkey). Royalties at the rate of 5 per cent were charged and the geographical scope of the agreement covered the entire world except for the United Kingdom, United States, Europe and Japan. Prices charged were the same as elsewhere.

After the start of the operation new designs and related technical assistance were given.

Evaluation

Firm 11's competitive advantages were said to be better proprietary technology, previous experience in similar projects and international prestige.

The project entirely met objectives, but too soon! That is, the technology transfer was affected early so the Indian company did not have need of further services.

TECHNOLOGY SUPPLIER 12: RUBBER PARTS MANUFACTURER IN SINGAPORE

General Description

Firm 12 is a family-owned company which makes two distinct products (1) rubber car mats for cars and (2) baby feeding products. It began production in 1936 and has been family-owned and managed ever since. It employs 550 people and has a sales turnover of £25 million. It produces on two sites in the United Kingdom.

Competition and Products

This firm has 80 per cent of the British market in rubber car mats and 20 per cent of the baby feeding products market. It exports 50 per cent of its production, mainly to continental Europe and has won two Queen's Awards for Exporting (1966, 1971). Its current growth is good, but is mainly in the home market. Its plant for car mats is the biggest in Europe – in fact, it is a big as all the others combines.

Motivation and Form of Involvement

The firm has two distinct ventures in Singapore. The first was begun in 1973 and ended in 1985. It was a typical offshore plant, manufacturing products for re-export to Europe. The British firm was approached by the Singapore Economic Development Board acting as 'marriage brokers'. The United Kingdom firm entered a joint venture with two loss-making Singaporean firms, taking 50 per cent of the equity in return for technology, tooling, marketing and machinery. They were, however, looking generally for an offshore plant and examined Malaysia, Sri Lanka, Indonesia and Thailand. The main motivation was to reduce labour costs but these other countries were ruled out because of political instability and worries about corruption. Over the life of this venture, labour costs in Singapore overtook those in the United Kingdom, as did availability of labour. This was partly Singaporean Government policy in moving into areas considered more 'high-tech'. The plant was sold at a reasonable price and re-exporting to Europe was effectively ended.

The second venture is wholly-owned, was established in 1978 and serves local markets only. It can therefore be considered a market-seeking venture. The firm feels that a larger venture needs to have local ownership to spread risks but that a wholly-owned venture, is easier to manage (the first plant was one-fifth the size of the UKs the second is one-tenth the size of the British activity).

Technology Transfer Process

In both cases, there was a complete transfer of technology involving plant design technology, process and product technology. Blueprints, designs, drawings, special equipment from the United Kingdom and technical assistance were provided. The firm produces lots of patents and innovations and these too were made available (1 per cent of turnover is R&D expenditure). Formal training was provided in-house in both the United Kingdom and Singapore. Plant was modified in order to cope with heat and humidity in Singapore. The equipment was exactly as used in the United Kingdom except as modified by refrigeration and air conditioning requirements. The products were and are identical. There were no problems in achieving the transfer.

Post-implementation Relationships and Evaluation

The firm uses only one permanent British manager in its foreign operations (expatriates are too expensive), although technical assistants are sent from the United Kingdom as appropriate. Financial policies are controlled from the United Kingdom, although functions like marketing, wage policies and prices for local production are determined in Singapore.

The first Singapore operation was overcome by changing external factors which could not be controlled, notably changing relative wage costs and labour availability. In 1973, the decision was right and the firm operated a successful offshore plant but Singapore 'has grown up quickly' and the rubber sector was paralysed as policies shifted to 'high-tech' output. The wage rate increased very rapidly relative to the United Kingdom, the Singapore currency was tied to the dollar and the costs of being there multiplied. The decision to sell the plant was beneficial.

The second plant is successful at meeting local regional demand. Both plants met or exceeded expectations. There has been a 'reverse transfer' of technology from Singapore in that air conditioning and refrigeration have been added United Kingdom to the processer, thus increasing efficiency in the United Kingdom.

10 The Case of the United States

Benjamin Gomes-Casseres and Tomás Kohn

'To compete globally you have to be big', concluded the *Harvard Business Review* comment on Alfred Chandler's study on the dynmics of industrial capitalism (1990a and 1990b). Even before that study, the traditional view among researchers had been that small firms were disadvantaged in international competition, because of the fixed costs of learning about foreign environments, communicating at long distances, and negotiating with national governments. These costs 'constitute an important reason for expecting that foreign investment will be mainly an activity of large firms', argued Caves (1982) in his comprehensive review of the literature on the multinational enterprise. A number of empirical studies seemed to back up this conclusion. Horst (1972) found that after controlling for industry effects, the only factor significantly affecting the propensity of firms to invest abroad was their size. Vernon (1970a) found that technological advantages were important in firms' propensity to invest abroad, but that these advantages were often correlated with scale.

During the 1980s, however, new evidence and analyses appeared that began to modify this traditional picture. These new data suggested that small US firms were quite active abroad, and that they operated in precisely those high-technology industries formerly thought to be the preserve of large firms. Roughly *half* the firms in the Commerce Department's 1982 survey of US investment abroad employed fewer than 2000 people. Although these firms accounted for only 18 per cent of the number of US affiliates abroad and 2 per cent of the value of US foreign direct investment (FDI), their large numbers suggest that small firms were able to compete effectively abroad.[1]

The traditional models of international business do not explain adequately the apparent viability of small firms in foreign markets.[2] We address this problem in this paper by developing a conceptual framework and applying it to a data from a small group of US firms. Our framework builds on relevant parts of the traditional international business literature, and incorporates findings of the few researchers that have focused on limited aspects of how small firms compete abroad.[3] The results of our field research on this select group of firms are broadly consistent with the statistical analysis of a larger sample of firms in Kohn (1988).

10.1 CONCEPTUAL FRAMEWORK

Overcoming Disadvantages of Small Size

Two complementary sets of ideas were useful in building a conceptual framework of how small firms compete abroad. The first revolves around how firms use FDI to exploit firm-specific advantages. In the product cycle model, for example, firms invested abroad on the basis of strengths developed in their home markets (Vernon, 1966; Caves, 1971). The firm needs these advantages, so the argument goes, in order to compete against host-country firms that have better knowledge of the local environment. The transaction cost model of foreign investment (Buckley and Casson, 1976; Hennart, 1982) also assumes the existence of a firm-specific advantage, but focuses more on the governance structures involved in exploiting this advantage.

Small firms, too, it would seem, need a firm-specific competitive advantage in order to overcome the added costs of doing business abroad. But the types of advantages typically cited in the traditional literature – R&D, advertising, diversified organisations – were all typically positive correlated with scale, so that they would not be available to small firm. To account for the behaviour of small firms abroad, therefore, we focused on conditions that enabled small firms to overcome the disadvantages from their lack of scale. In other words, we expected to find small firms active in areas where there were *dis*economies of scale. In Penrose's words (1959, 1980: 222–3):

> The productive opportunities of small firms are . . . composed of those interstices left open by the large firms which the small firms see and believe they can take advantage of . . . [T]he nature of the interstices is determined by the kind of activity in which the larger firms specialize, leaving other opportunities open.

Previous studies of small firms investing abroad found patterns that seem consistent with this view (Hackett, 1977; Newbould *et al.*, 1978; and Buckley, *et al.*, 1983). In Hackett's words,

Multinational firms typically concentrate on expansion into those markets that offer the greatest profit potential and knowingly bypass smaller market segments. (1977, p. 11)

He found, as did Mascarenhas (1986), that small firms often went abroad in order to avoid head-on competition with larger domestic rivals. Mascarenhas (1986) and Namiki (1988) also found that 'follower' firms tended to be most successful internationally when they focused on specialty markets or products, where economies of scale were not critical. Sweeney (1970) and Vlachoutsikos (1989) also described how the small size of firms might be an advantage in entry negotiations with governments. Due to the 'low profile' of these firms, they might get concessions unavailable to larger firms. Finally, the often flexible and flat organisational structures of small firms, according to Vlachoutsikos (1989) and Hackett (1977), allowed them to respond more quickly and creatively than larger firms to opportunities abroad.

Creating Advantages Through International Activities

The second set of ideas we drew upon to understand the behaviour of small firms abroad revolved around the advantages that firms could gain from operating internationally. Broadly, these include economies of scale and scope (Porter, 1980), the creation of multiple options for future expansion (Kogut, 1983), the ability to cross-subsidise among country strategies (Hamel and Prahalad, 1985), and learning from foreign markets (Vernon, 1979; Ghoshal and Bartlett, 1988). While these authors agreed that firms that were successful abroad started out from a basic strength, they described how the firms' capabilities could be expanded further through international operations.

For our purpose, the critical question became to consider whether small firms might in some way be privileged in gaining advantages from their international operations. A number of findings from previous studies suggested that at least three features of small firms made them particularly effective in gaining advantages from the international operations. The first was that small firms were often most active in emerging industries, where first-mover advantages could be important. As Sweeney pointed out from personal experience taking his small firm into Europe:

If one or more of our larger competitors – or even those of our size – became established in Europe before we did, we might never be able to penetrate that market. (1970, p. 127)

The second characteristic of small firms that might help them draw advantages from international operations seemed to be the very importance to their survival of these international activities. Sweeney (1970), Hackett (1977), and Mascarenhas (1986) all argued that doing business abroad was often central to a small firm's strategy – or, at least, that it should be – if it is to be successful. In Sweeney's words, his firm's move into Europe required 'an absolute commitment' (1970, p. 128). Because of this, as well as the typically flat organisational structure of small firms mentioned above, small firms could be expected to be effective at acquiring competitive advantage from their international activities.

A Deep Niche Strategy

Combining these two sets of ideas, we expected that small firms investing abroad probably competed in niche markets that were of minor interest to large firms, but where experience and depth of capability were important. Because of their narrow bases of expertise, there firms would then probably find it easier to expand their business into new markets abroad than into new product markets at home. The move abroad, therefore, might be quite important to these firms, because of their narrow product bases. Once operating abroad, the firms would inevitably face new demands from buyers and gain opportunities to draw on resources in foreign production sites. This, in turn, might lead to a learning process that would further deepen the firms' capabilities in their niche. Because of the firms' dependence on leadership in their product niche they would not be able to afford to fall behind in any country, and so had to adapt to disparate country environments. This learning process would then be enhanced by the organisational structures of the firms. We use the term 'deep niche' to describe this strategy.

In applying this framework to the firms we studied, we focused on three inter-related sets of factors: (1) the nature of the firms' businesses; (2) the sources of their competitive advantages;[4] and (3) the role of international operations in building these advantages. The combined evidence tends to support the expectations outlined above.

10.2   EMPIRICAL FINDINGS

Data and Methods

Our research was part of a larger project on technology transfer by small firms from the United States, Canada, Europe, and Japan that was coordinated by Argentina's Centro de Estudios de Desarollo y Relaciones Economicas Internacionales (CEDREI, see White and Campos, 1986). The larger project focuses on technology transfers to six newly industrialising countries (NICs) and involves researchers from seven home and six host countries. The firms in this project were all in manufacturing and each employed fewer than 1000 people worldwide. Our research represents the United States' portion of this project.

The firms in our group were selected out of a group of 28 small US firms that CEDREI researchers found had transferred technology to the NICs through licensing, joint ventures, or wholly-owned subsidiaries. From this group we selected for detailed study 12 firms that had extensive operations in *both* developing and developed countries according to Dun and Bradstreet data. Our research was not restricted to these firms' operations in the NICs – we gathered data on their overall international positions and their 81 operations abroad.[5] Although 62 per cent of these affiliates were in developed countries, our selection procedure led to a group of firms with relatively fewer affiliates in these countries than in the Commerce Department data, as shown in Table 10.1.

On other dimensions the firms in our group are comparable to those in the Commerce Department data (Table 10.1). Our firms tended to be concentrated in industries with greater R&D intensity than those in the Commerce Department sample,[6] slightly more of them were in emerging industries, and on average they had more subsidiaries abroad. Kohn's (1988) analysis of the Commerce Department sample concluded that small firms investing abroad tended to concentrate in high-technology industries that supplied intermediate goods. That characterisation also fits the group of firms we studied. But we do not claim to have a representative sample; rather, our firms appeared to be extreme cases in the pattern observed in the broader data. As such, they can be expected to provide evidence that highlights key aspects of how small technology-based firms compete abroad.

We collected evidence on the firms in our group through semi-structured interviews at their US headquarters, usually with the chief executive officer responsible for international operations. Answers to several

Table 10.1 Characteristics of the sample: comparison with Commerce Department survey

	Department of Commerce[a]	Research sample[b]
A Average characteristics of parent firms' industries		
R&D expenditures as % of sales[c]	2.4	4.6*
Maturity index[d]	0.50	0.50
Growth index[e]	0.68	0.92**
Consumer intensity index[f]	0.16	0
B Parent firms' foreign investment behaviour		
Number of foreign subsidiaries per parent	2.1	5.0
Investments in developed countries as % of total	77	62*

	No. of affiliates (and %)	
C Main industries of parent firms		
Food and kindred products	71 (3)	0 –
Chemicals and allied products	17 (19)	32 (39)*
Primary and fabricated metals	333 (12)	24 (30)*
Non-electrical machinery	550 (20)	7 (9)*
Electric/onic equipment	315 (11)	9 (11)
Transportation equipment	69 (2)	0 –
Other manufacturing	874 (32)	9 (11)**
Total	2729 (100)	81 (100)

Notes:
* Statistically different from the Commerce Department number at the 85 per cent level.
** Statistically different from the Commerce Department number at the 95 per cent level.

[a] Bureau of Economic Analysis, special tabulation from 1982 Benchmark Survey of US Direct Investment Abroad. Data include affiliates of U.S. manufacturing firms with fewer than 2000 employees in the United States. See Commerce Department (1985, pp. 1–26), and Kohn (1988) for methodological details.
[b] There were 12 parent firms in our sample. These firms had a total of 82 affiliates, of which 60 were direct investments and 21 were licensees.
[c] The number for the Research Sample excludes two firms engaged almost exclusively in R&D contract work, and one firm on which no data were available.
[d] Measures an industry's position in its life cycle; one is mature, and zero is emerging, see Kohn (1988).
[e] Measures the dynamism of the industry; one is high growth, zero is low growth, see Kohn (1988).
[f] Measures the extent to which an industry sells its output to final consumers, as opposed to industrial customers; one is a predominantly consumer-good industry, zero is a predominantly producer-good industry, see Kohn (1988).

of our questions involved ranking the importance of a factor on a five-point scale; Tables 10.3 below provides averages of these rankings. In addition, we collected case descriptions of selected aspects of the firms' foreign operations, as reported in the text below. Finally, we used published data (10-K's, Dun and Bradstreet) where available. Because of confidentiality agreements with our interviewees, we have not been able to indentify the firms in this chapter by name. Some key features of the firms in our group are summarised in Table 10.2, together with the firms' scores on interview questions that we discuss below.

Limitations

We recognise that our study had a number of limitations. First, although we discuss conceptually some differences between large and small firms, we have no comparable data on the former. Strictly speaking, therefore, we do not have direct empirical evidence to attribute some of the patterns that we see to the effects of firm size. Instead we have compared the patterns we found with the existing picture of how large multinational enterprises compete abroad that has been developed in the traditional international business literature. We therefore feel confident that our conclusions about the distinctiveness of the patterns of small-firm behaviour will hold up under a more direct empirical comparison.

Second, the group of firms we studied is, as stated before, not representative of the population of small firms doing business abroad, and the small number of firms we studied does not allow rigorous statistical tests. The results, therefore, may not be generalisable to firms very different from those in our group. In particular, we expect that these results apply most directly to small firms in industrial sectors that rely on a technical expertise to compete abroad. And while we used numerical scores to build a picture of how the firms compete, we complemented these with interviews and case data to make sure the picture made sense logically.

Nature of the Businesses

The nature of the business of the firms in our group was consistent with our expectations above. First, the firms focused on market niches, and, in fact, tended to dominate these market segments. Second, they were often technological leaders within these segments, often pursuing first-mover strategies. Third, they were usually in producer industries, where economies of scale in marketing and distribution were not important.

Table 10.2 Characteristics of firms studied

Co.	Product	No. employees		No. of affiliates	Nature of the businesses		Sources of competitive advantage[a]		
		US	Abroad		Degree of competition[b]	Technological position[c]	International activities	First mover	Learning curve
	Chemicals and allied								
A	Micro-biocides	440	360	9	4	1	5	3	5
B	Specialty chemicals		460[d]	8	4	2	3	4	4
C	Anti-viral drugs	350	19	3	5	1	4	5	5
D	Anti-viral drugs	1500	800	5	4	1	4	4	4
E	Anti-viral drugs	133	92	7	3	3	5	5	2
	Fabricated metals								
F	Expansion joints	220	10	5	2	1	4	4	2
G	Aerosol valves	650	2050	19	2	1	5	4	5
	Non-elec. machinery								
H	Rolling mill parts	640	10	7	2	1	5	5	3
	Electric/onic equip.								
I	Electric connectors	175	665	3	4	2	4	4	4
J	Electronic filters	120	780	6	2	1	5	4	4
	Other manufacturing								
K	Measuring equipment	550	550	8	2	1	5	4	5
L	Infrared viewers	15	10	1	2	4	4	2	4

Notes:

[a] Interviewees were asked: How important are each of the following to maintain the firm's competitive advantage? Answers were scored from 1 (negligible) to 5 (vital); see also averages and answers to other related questions in Table 10.3.

[b] Interviewees were asked to rate the level of competition in their firms' product market. Answers were scored from 1 (firm is sole producer) to 5 (there are many producers).

[c] Interviewees were asked to rate the relative technological position of their firms. Answers were scored from 1 (firm is absolute leader) to 5 (firm is last follower).

[d] This is world employment; breakdown between US and abroad not available.

Market Dominance

While the firms in our group were small when compared to US multi-national enterprises, they were generally large relative to their direct competitors. They usually occupied dominant positions within their narrow market niches, typically having few direct competitors. On a scale of 1 (no competitor) to 5 (many competitors), six of the 12 firms classified the competitive environment in their industry as 2, and only one firm stated that it faced may competitors. Many of the firms in our group had major shares in their markets. Company *A*, for example, estimated that its US market share in different products ranged between 10 per cent and 100 per cent. Companies *K* and *B* estimated that they held approximately a 30 per cent share of the US market, while Companies *F*, *G*, and *H* each estimated that they held over of 40 per cent of the *world* market for their products. Company *H*'s dominance of the world market for a highly specialised bearing used in flat steel rolling mills provides an extreme, yet illustrative example. This company perfected the manufacturing process for this special bearing to the point where today it is the world's sole manufacturer of that type of bearing. Other researchers participating in the CEDREI project found similar patterns of market dominance by small firms originating in Canada (chapter 4 in this volume), the United Kingdom (chapter 9, in this volume), and Japan (chapter 8 in this volume).

To some extent, therefore, the firms in our group differed from the 'follower' firms in Mascarenhas' (1986) study. In that study, follower firms went abroad to avoid competing head-on with the market leaders. Our firms did not face that danger. Rather, they dominated the 'interstices' referred to by Penrose – those areas left open by larger companies. Their move abroad is more likely to have been the result of an aggressive effort to diversify geographically than a defensive strategy of fleeing from competition.

Technological Leadership

The firms were also often technological leaders within their industries. We asked our interviewees to rank their firms' relative technological position in the industry between 1 (absolute leader) and 5 (last follower) and also to classify their firm's industry as being in an emerging, growth, mature, or declining phase. Eight of the 12 firms reported that they were absolute leaders and only one reported that it was a follower; the average score for this question was 1.6. Eight of the 12 operated in either emerging or growth industries. Of the four firms in mature industries (none was in a declining industry) three were absolute technological leaders and the fourth ranked its technological leadership as 2. In mature and stable industries, therefore, the firms carved out strong leadership positions. Even in the more fluid environments of emerging and growing industries, all but one of the firms were industry leaders.

A number of the firms found from experience that becoming a technological leader in a specialised business was the only way to survive. Company *K*, for example, entered the testing equipment business in the late 1940s, when larger firms were already well established. After struggling for years to survive in the face of competition from these incumbents, it decided to focus on specialised engineering. It expanded its customer service network in the world's main markets for testing equipment, and developed further its capability to design applications-specific fixtures and adapters. The company now has almost one-third of the US market, it has manufacturing facilities in the United States and England, and sales and service offices in 17 countries. After 1981, its sales and net income more than doubled to, respectively, over $100 million and $2.4 million dollars. The company continues to deepen its capabilities through investments in technology – it spends over 7 per cent of sales on R&D. As a result, it poineered the use of digital and other advanced measuring and testing instruments in its field.

This pattern of concentration in growth markets and technological specialisation in mature markets is consistent with some of Vernon's (1970) hypotheses about economies of scale in corporate organisation. Vermon speculated that the role of small firms in R&D would be greatest in intermediate stages of the product cycle – the 'emerging' and 'growth' stages in our survey – and that in the later stages they would play a role as specialty producers and distributors. It is also consistent with the finding of previous researchers that small firms in the domestic market tend to concentrate on selling 'highly specialised products in profitable market niches' (Smith and Fleck, 1987, p. 61; see also Birley, 1982).

Focus on Producer Goods

A corollary to the specialty role of the small firms was that they usually sold producer goods to a limited group of industrial buyers. All the firms in our group sold such goods. Similarly, 84 per cent of the small firms in the US Commerce Department survey were in predominantly producer-goods industries (Table 10.1). One manufacturer of aerosol valves, for example, reported that 80 per cent of its sales were to 20 per cent of its customers. Furthermore, many of its customers were themselves multinational firms buying similar types of valves in several countries. The valve producer, therefore, like other specialty suppliers in our group, did not need to invest in extensive distribution networks or advertising. Rather, its sales strategy consisted of maintaining a leadership position in technology and cost, and cultivating relationships with a handful of multinational buyers.

This pattern of concentration on producer goods industries seems to be quite common among small firms competing abroad. Kohn (1988, p. 55) measured the 'consumer intensity' of an industry according to the share of its output that is sold to final consumers. Using aggregate data from the US Census of Manufacturers and the Commerce Department's 1982 Benchmark Survey, Kohn found that 35 per cent of large firms investing abroad were predominantly in consumer-goods industries, while only 15 per cent of small firms investing abroad were in these industries. In the domestic market, there was no difference in consumer intensity between large and small firms.

There may be three main reasons for this pattern. First, consumer goods are more likely than producer goods to require tailoring to host-country tastes. Such adaptation may entail large fixed costs that would deter small firms more than they would large firms (Kohn, 1988). Second, consumer goods would require investments in distribution networks and advertising, which also tend to be scale-intensive, fixed-cost items. As discussed below, the firms in our group rated distribution channels as their least important competitive tool. Third, the alternative for a firm choosing not to invest in these methods of differentiating product might be to pursue a low-cost strategy (Porter, 1980). But, that, in turn, requires mass-production, which would again favour large over small firms. As could be expected, Namiki (1988) found that such low-cost strategies were less likely to yield successful results for small firms than were differentiation strategies.

Sources of Competitive Advantage

The small firms' choice of markets and strategic posture seem to have protected them from competition through two types of entry barriers – one deterring entry by large firms, the other, entry by small firms. Large firms might decline to compete directly with them, preferring instead to focus on larger markets where their economies of scale and scope provide significant advantages (Hackett, 1977). In single-product, specialty, producer-goods industries such economies tended to be less important than in multi-product, mass-consumption sectors. At the same time, potential entry by other small firms was deterred by the substantial investments and experience of the incumbents. They dominated their niches and continuously tried to deepen their capabilities and leadership position. Within their niches, therefore, they exploited those economies of scale and learning that were available.

This strategic profile is consistent with our interviewees' estimate of the sources of their firms' competitive advantage. We asked the executives to rank the importance of various types of competitive advantage on a scale of 5 (essential) to 1 (not important). The results, shown in Table 10.3A, suggest that some of these sources were important to most of the respondents, while the importance of others varied by industry.

Almost without exception, the firms ranked their international activities as a source of advantage, followed by first-mover and learning-curve advantages. The importance of the last two factors is further evident in the interviewees' estimates of how potential competitors might acquire the expertise to enter the industry (Table 10.3B). On this question, learning by doing and hiring away personnel ranked highest, compared to low rankings for mechanisms that depend less on the accumulated experience of the firm, such as licensing and purchasing specialised machinery.

The responses to our question about competitive advantages were also instructive for what the managers thought was least important to their firms. Several of the business characteristics important to larger multinationals, such as distribution channels and, to a lesser extent, brandnames, ended up low on our list of responses. This is no doubt partly a reflection of the fact that there were no consumer-good industries in our study, which probably stemmed from the high economies of scale and scope in these sectors, as discussed above. Patents and trade secrets were also less important for these firms than the literature on multinational enterprises suggests (Bertin and Wyatt, 1988). But, as could be expected (Levin, *et al.*, 1984), patents tended to be relatively more important in chemicals and pharmaceuticals, where they ranked first among the seven factors we asked about.

Advantages of International Networks

Several cases illustrated how international activities could be a source of competitive advantage for small firms, as would be expected in the

Table 10.3   Sources of competitive advantage and learning

	Drugs and chemicals (N = 5)		Other industries (N = 7)	
	Score	Rank	Score	Rank
A Sources of competitive advantage[a]				
International activities	4.2[d]	2	4.6	1
First-mover advantages	4.2	2	3.9	3
Learning-curve effects	4.0	4	3.9	3
Patents	4.4	1	2.3	7
Trade secrets	3.8	5	2.9	5
Brandnames[b]	3.0	6	4.0	2
Distribution channels	2.8	7	2.7	6
B How competitors acquire technology[c]				
Learning by doing	4.0	1	2.6	3
Reverse engineering	3.6	2	2.7	2
Hiring away people	3.4	3	2.9	1
Acquiring licenses	3.0	4	2.2	4
Independent R&D	2.8	5	1.8	6
Buying special machinery	1.4	6	1.9	5

Notes:

[a] Interviewees were asked: How important are each of the following to maintain the firm's competitive advantage? Answers were scored from 1 (negligible) to 5 (vital). Individual scores for some categories are shown in Table 10.2.

[b] Respondents often interpreted brandnames as representing reputation, not image developed through advertising or promotional activities.

[c] Interviewees were asked: How feasible and/or common is it for firm to gain the needed technology to enter the business through each of the following means? Answers were scored from 1 (extremely uncommon/infeasible) to 5 (very common/feasible).

[d] The confidence intervals for the differences between any two scores in a column depend, of course, on the standard deviations (SDs) of each of the two scores. The SDs of the scores above ranged from 0.5 to 1.8, with a mean of 1.2. Based on this mean SD, two scores above that differ by more than 1.9 points can be considered to be statistically different at the 85 per cent level; thsoe differing by more than 1.2 points, at the 75 per cent level. (Because of the small samples, none of the differences are significant at higher levels.)

For example, in the column for Other industries, the score on International activities (4.6) is higher than that for Trade secrets (2.9) at the 75 per cent level, but not at the 85 per cent level. (The difference between 4.6 and 2.9 is 1.7, which is greater than 1.2 (the 75 per cent interval), but less than 1.9 (the 85 per cent interval).)

'deep niche' strategy we described above. Company *A*, which produced microbiocides, found that a presence in foreign markets was critical to selling there because its product required host-government approval. As a result, the firm set up manufacturing and sales operation in foreign countries, facilitating its international sales and spreading its development costs over several markets.

Company *B*, a specialty chemicals producer, benefited from the different customer needs in its foreign markets. In each location its plants worked to solve local problems and then communicated their solutions to headquarters. That gave the firm information that could be used to solve customer demands elsewhere. For example, Company *B* developed a product in France that was ideally suited to some of its Korean customers; later, this product became the company's biggest export from the US to Korea.

The case of Company *I*, an electrical components manufacturer, illustrates how responsive a small firm can be to foreign demands. The company's sales respresentative in France received an order from a local customer and relayed it immediately to the manufacturing subsidiary in the United Kingdom. The latter lacked the capability to make the parts, but accepted the order anyway, well aware that the necessary capability existed elsewhere in the organisation. Details of the customer's needs were then transmitted by facsimile to the company's design department in the United States. Using computer-aided design (CAD) methods, the US lab prepared production specifications that were transmitted by phone to Company *I*'s manufacturing plant in El Paso, Texas. This plant then coordinated with its 'twin' unit in Juarez, Mexico to manufacture the parts. From Juarez the finished parts were shipped to El Paso, and from there to the French customer's client in Venezuela. The whole process, from initial order to delivery, took only 11 days! While we do not have a direct comparison with a large firm in this business, we would expect that a large firm with an extensive bureaucracy could not match this response time.

Such networks of international operations constituted barriers to entry by other small firms. Furthermore, the learning-curve advantages that the firms exploited implied that follower firms were constantly playing catch-up with the first movers.

Company *G* illustrates how first-mover and learning-curve advantages can be exploited by small firms. Having invented the aerosol valve in 1948, the company quickly established footholds in potential markets in Europe, Latin America, and the Far East. To do so, the company licensed its technology to firms in several countries. The licences, however, were for relatively short periods and were soon bought back by Company *G*, which then started its own manufacturing operations. In this way, the company was able to prevent its ex-licencees from encroaching on its leadership position. As a result of the accumulated manufacturing experience of the company, its initial technological advantage in product design came to be augmented by a low-cost position in high-speed assembly of the product.

10.3   CONCLUSIONS AND IMPLICATIONS

Our research provided an opportunity to re-examine some of the traditional assumptions in the international business literature. The emphasis in this literature on large firms can surely be justified by the fact that their subsidiaries account for the bulk of US investments abroad. Those interested in the balance of payments, employment, or other impacts of FDI, whether on home or host countries, should thus not be led astray by ignoring the foreign activities of small firms. The impact of the small firms' activities is relatively minor in these respects. But students of the process of foreign investment and of variants of international strategy would do well to examine the experience of small firms abroad. These experiences can be used to test hypotheses about the effect of scale on foreign operations. But, perhaps more importantly, they illustrate a type of international competition that is relatively uncommon with large firms.

In this type of competition, patents, trade secrets, trademarks, and advantages of scale and scope – the typical strengths of multinational firms – are less important than capabilities derived from experience and international learning. Also, the depth of a firm's capabilities in its product niche appears to be more important in the type of competition we studied than the scope of the firm across various markets. Based on this observation, we suspect that even large multinational firms might benefit from focusing and deepening their capabilities.

Of course, one implication of this finding is that small firms need not feel themselves shut out from international markets. Venturing abroad can be an attractive option for some of these firms. But, based on the limited group of firms we examined, it is an attractive option only for certain types of firms in certain types of industries. The industry should be one where large firms are unlikely to be serious competitors; it should be one where product requirements are not likely to differ significantly from one host country to the next; product quality and differentiation should be more important than low costs; and extensive distribution networks should not be the norm in the industry. Usually, this will imply a producer-good industry, such as those we examined, but one cannot rule out selected consumer-good sectors having these characteristics.

Given an appropriate industry, our study suggests that the option of international expansion would be most attractive to firms that occupy a leadership position within their niche. These are the firms that can afford to go abroad in an effort to establish first-mover advantages. Furthermore, the firm should be structured so as to maximise the learning opportunities available abroad. The international network of a small firm can become one of its major assets, much as it is for large global firms. But, for the small firm, a few investments abroad already constitute a substantial commitment and would offer significant learning opportunities.

Lest we paint a picture that suggests that small technology-based firms are invincible international competitors, we must point out some of their limitations. Managers of these firms should be conscious of these, just as much as they should be of the hidden advantages they have. The ability of small firms to compete abroad is limited precisely by the features that give them strength: the narrow nature of their business and their depth of experience in their niches. These features make it hard for the firms to grow faster than their narrow markets or to diversify into other products. Their expertise is often so specific to their clients and products that if may not be transferrable to other businesses. Still, having pursued vigorously a strategy of geographic, not product, diversification, a firm may find opportunities in its niche exhausted and those outside it unreachable.

The firms in our group typically did not yet face this dilemma. Their markets, although narrow and sometimes quite mature, were often being transformed or expanded by some event or another, creating new opportunities for growth. Drawing on their experience and dominating worldwide presence in their industries, these firms were often in ideal positions to take advantage of new trends. The competitive advantages developed by the firms, therefore, not only allowed them to venture abroad, but also to adapt and evolve with changes in the international economy.

Notes

1. The Commerce Department data we used was a special tabulation of the 1982 *Benchmark Survey* that breaks down FDI patterns by the size of the parent firm (see Kohn, 1988).

2. The literature on entrepreneurship has even less to say about the international activities of small firms. The otherwise comprehensive review of the field in Kent, Sexton and Vesper's *Encyclopedia of Entrepreneurship* (1982) contains no mention of entrepreneurial behaviour that crosses national borders. Similarly, not one of the 23 teaching cases in Stevenson, Roberts and Grousbeck's *New Business Ventures and the Entrepreneur* (1985) describes a firm doing business abroad.

3. In particular, we draw on findings of Hackett (1977), Mascarenhas (1986), and Namiki (1988), All of which used aggregate data to address a broad range of questions, and Sweeney (1970) who used the authors' personal experiences to derive guidelines for small businesses competing abroad. These studies differed substantially form ours. Mascarenhas, for example, studied strategies of both large and small 'followers' firms; we confined our study to small firms, whether followers or leaders. The domain of Hackett's research is more closely related to ours, but he offered no case or statistical evidence to support his arguments, and focused more than we do on 'how to' advice to managers. The latter is also true for Sweeney's and Vlachoutsikos' studies. In addition, Vlachoutsikos focuses exclusively on opportunities in the Soviet Union, and Sweeney describes mostly the entry of his firm into the European market. Namiki takes a broader view, but concentrates on export strategies.

4. The term 'competitive advantage' is used below because that was the precise phrasing used in the questionnaire administered to the firms. But since neither we nor the interviewees conducted a full industry analysis in order to determine the sources of competitive advantage in a technical sense (Porter, 1980, 1985), the term as used here should be interpreted somewhat more loosely as the 'strength' or 'distinctive competence' of a firm (Andrews, 1971). That was the interpretation used by interviewees in answering the questionnaire.

5. 21 of these foreign ventures were licensing arrangements, and 60 were direct investments. In this chapter, we refer to both of these as 'affiliates' of the US firms, but only the direct investments are called 'subsidiaries.'

6. The average R&D intensity of the industries in our sample (4.6 per cent) is statistically different from the average of the Department of Commerce sample (2.4 per cent) at the 85 per cent confidence level (Table 10.1). The Department of Commerce number is, in turn, higher than the R&D intensity of comparably-sized firms that did *not* invest abroad (1.5 per cent), see Kohn (1988, p. 51). In other words, small firms investing abroad are generally more technology-based that domestic firms of the same size, and those in our sample are even more so than the average small firm investing abroad.

Part III

Technology Recipients

11 The Case of Argentina

Eduardo White and Jaime Campos

11.1 THE SHARE OF SMALL SUPPLIERS IN THE TRANSFER OF TECHNOLOGY TO ARGENTINA

The research conducted during the first phase of this program revealed that the contribution of smaller firms of industrialised countries in the transfer of technology to Argentina was concentrated in two industrial sectors: metalworking and chemicals. An analysis of the overall quantitative evidence reflected in the Government Register of Technology Contracts and other sources of information on foreign investment[1] showed the presence of 128 firms with less than 500 employees in their respective home countries,[2] which appeared to have transferred technology for these two sectors in the late seventies and early eighties, via technology agreements or direct foreign investments (see Table 11.1 and 11.2). The share of SMEs was 19.4 per cent in the case of technology agreements and 8.1 per cent in the case of direct investments.

Although an exploration of other industrial sectors would have certainly revealed foreign SMEs' activity, there is no doubt that metalworking and chemicals account for a large share of the phenomenon. In fact, the recent evidence collected in various countries of origin, including Japan, the United States, France, the United Kingdom, Italy and Canada suggest that the grouping of primary and fabricated metals, non – electrical machinery and electric and electronic equipment accounts for between 40 and 60 per cent of the overseas operations of SMEs in the manufacturing sectors, and that chemicals take between 8 and 30 per cent.[3] On the other hand, these two sectors concentrate the bulk of the technology imported to Argentina (from companies of all sizes) via technology agreements and direct foreign investments: the former accounted for 33 per cent of the total number of technology agreements registered by the government in the period 1978–7, and about 40 per cent of the value of FDIs accumulated in the last three decades; the latter accounted for 26 per cent of the technology agreements and more than 30 per cent of the FDIs in the same periods.

In terms of the national origins of the smaller suppliers, Table 11.2

299

300

Table 11.1 Argentina: foreign firms with direct investments, 1983, and technology agreements, 1977–83, chemical and metalworking industries, classified by sizes at home and forms of involvement

Forms of involvement / Size of foreign firms (No. of employees)	Direct investment		Technology agreements	
	%	Absolute figures	%	Absolute figures
Small (up to 250)	4.3	(9)	12.1	(69)
Medium (251–500)	3.8	(8)	7.3	(42)
Subtotal SMEs	8.1	(17)	19.4	(111)
Medium to large (501–1000)	2.8	(6)	5.2	(30)
Large	89.1	(188)	75.4	(432)
of which: included in the Fortune Lists	72.0	(152)	37.0	(212)
Total firms with identified size	100.0	(211)	100.0	(573)
Size not identified		(32)		(244)
Total no. of firms		(243)		(817)
Memo item: SMEs which were found to be dependent of larger firms		(2)		(42)

Source: INTI–CEDREI data bank.

Table 11.2 No. of foreign firms with technology contracts registered in the chemical and metalworking sectors, classified by size of suppliers and country of origin, August 1977–December 1983

Country of origin	SMEs Small up to 250 %	Abs. Fig.	SMEs Medium 251–500 %	Abs. Fig.	Subtotal %	Abs. Fig.	Medium to large 500–1000 %	Abs. Fig.	Large firms %	Abs. fig.	of which in fortune %	Abs. fig.	Total firms with identified size %	Abs. fig.	Memo item: Firms with size not identified Abs. fig.	Total no. firms Abs. fig.
United States	6.5	(16)	4.9	(12)	11.4	(28)	5.7	(14)	82.9	(203)	49.8	(122)	100	(245)	(93)	(338)
Germany (FDR)	12.4	(13)	15.2	(16)	27.6	(29)	6.7	(7)	65.7	(69)	22.9	(24)	100	(105)	(41)	(146)
France	7.9	(5)	11.1	(7)	19.0	(12)	3.2	(2)	77.8	(49)	36.5	(23)	100	(63)	(22)	(85)
Italy	41.2	(21)	7.8	(4)	49.0	(25)	2.0	(1)	49.0	(25)	3.9	(2)	100	(51)	(11)	(62)
United Kingdom	19.3	(6)	6.5	(2)	25.8	(8)	3.2	(1)	71.0	(22)	58.1	(18)	100	(30)	(20)	(51)
Japan	–	(–)	3.0	(1)	3.0	(1)	6.1	(2)	90.9	(30)	21.2	(7)	100	(33)	–	(33)
Others[a]	17.8	(8)	–	(–)	17.8	(8)	6.7	(3)	75.6	(34)	35.5	(16)	100	(16)	(57)	(102)
Total %	12.1		7.3		19.4		5.2		75.4		37.0		100			
(Absolute figures)		(69)		(42)		(111)		(30)		(432)		(212)		(573)	(244)	(817)

Note:

[a] Includes Switzerland, Netherlands, Sweden and Canada.

Source: INTI–CEDREI data bank.

reveals that the United States, Germany, Italy and France account for 84 per cent of the SMEs that have transferred technology through contractual agreements. Yet only in the case of Italy, and to a lesser extent of Germany, do SMEs seem to have a protagonistic participation. In fact, Italian SMEs account for nearly 50 per cent of all firms of this country (while the number of Italian firms of all sizes represents just 9 per cent of the total number of technology suppliers to Argentina) and German SMEs represent nearly 28 per cent of the transfers from this origin.

On the other hand, the relative significance of SMEs as direct foreign investors is, as above noted, much weaker. Only 17 of the firms in the two sectors whose size at home could be identified were small or medium-sized. Probably the best explanation of this contrast lies in the gradual loss of attractiveness of Argentina as a location for direct foreign investments, a noticeable phenomenon since the late 60's, aggravated during the first half of the following decade and persisting until the present time, particularly with regard to the manufacturing sector.[4] Thus the process of internationalisation of smaller firms of developed countries, which accelerated during the last two decades (as shown by the experience of a number of recipient developing countries, including Latin American countries such as Brazil and Mexico) was not represented in Argentina in terms of FDIs. This circumstance, however, has not prevented the participation of SMEs in the transfer of technology through other channels, and for reasons different to those that usually trigger decisions to locate capital abroad.

An interesting pattern of the technology transfer to Argentina, as revealed by the data on technology agreements, is that the size of the recipient companies tends to match that of their respective suppliers. Table 11.3 (based on the total number of agreements for the metalworking and chemical industries registered in 1977–83) shows, in effect, that 71 per cent of the agreement with smaller suppliers had non-large Argentine companies as recipients. The percentage of agreements with larger local recipients increased for the larger foreign suppliers.

11.2 THE SAMPLE

A sample of 20 Argentine firms that have received technology from SMEs of developed countries were interviewed during the first semester of 1988. The composition of the sample reflects both the general patterns of the context above described, and the logical incidence of

Table 11.3 Technology agreements in the metalworking and chemical sector, 1977–83, classified by size of supplier and recipient companies, %

Size of supplier	Recipient is a large firm (1000 employees)		Total
	%	Abs. fig.	
SMEs (1000 employees)	29	41	140
large firms	53	347	652
Fortune ranking	54	211	388
N.A.	47	86	184
Total	49	474	976

uncontrollable factors during the process of selection of cases. The Appendix to this chapter (p. 339) describes the process followed for the selection of the sample.

Tables 11.4 and 11.5 present the main features of the sample. Italy appears as the main country of origin, with half the number of cases, followed by Germany, the United States and France. The metalworking sector accounts for 15 for the 20 cases, a circumstance which in part reflects the higher number of German agreements registered in the sector as compared to the chemical industry, and also the finding of more interesting cases at the micro-level.

Finally, non-equity arrangements, and in particular technology agreements, are the main channel of technology transfer.

11.3 THE RECIPIENT COMPANIES AND THEIR MARKETS

The local companies involved in experiences of technology transfer with SMEs of developed countries are, except for one case, producers of capital or intermediate goods. Table 11.5 shows that six companies manufacture industrial machinery and equipment; nine and producers of parts, components or intermediate goods for other industries; three manufacture equipment for electronic transmission, distribution or control; and only one operates in a consumer-goods sector.

In terms of Argentine standards, 75 per cent of the local recipients are 'typical' SMEs. Almost half of the sample firms have less than 50 employees, and only three companies can be classified as large, having more than 500 employees. As Table 11.6 reveals, the larger companies are those with a higher diversification of product lines. Nine companies

Table 11.4 Countries of origin and forms of technology transfer

Relationship between local firm and SME	Non-equity forms		Equity participation of SME			
SMEs home country	Technology contract	Informal agreements	Minority	50:50	Majority	Total
USA	3	–	–	–	–	3
Germany	4	–	–	1	–	5
Italy	7	2	1	–	–	10
France	1	–	–	–	1	2
Total	15	2	1	1	1	20

Table 11.5 Sectoral distribution of sample cases

I Industrial machinery and equipment

ISIC	No. of cases	Products
3823	2	Milling machines Surface treatment machinery
3824	3	Plastic industry machinery and equipment Construction machinery and equipment Packing machinery
3825	1	Computers and equipment for banks; personal and multiuser computers
3829	1	Industrial furnaces; furnace plants.
Total	7	

II Industrial parts, components and intermediate goods

ISIC	No. of cases	Products
3513	1	Chemical auxiliaries for textile and leather industries, additives for hair and skin products; PVC additives or stabilizers
3523	1	Essences for perfumery and flavors for food
3560	1	Plastic containers reinforced with glass fibre
3813	1	Ironwork for aluminium window and door frames; coins
3829	2	Valves; spare parts for cement industry machinery; mining machinery, earthmoving equipment; railroad equipment
3839	1	Lighting devices
3843	2	Drivers' seats for agricultural machinery and buses and trucks; parts for tractors; autoparts; other metalworking products; water measuring equipment
Total	9	

continued on p. 306

Table 11.5   continued

III Electric transmission, distribution and control equipment		
ISIC	*No. of cases*	*Products*
3831	3	Medium voltage electric cabinets, cabinet components or high voltage operation devices (switches) Low, medium and high voltage switches; electric cabinets; resistor units for household appliances, electronics and electric engineering
Total	3	

IV Consumer goods		
ISIC	*No. of cases*	*Products*
3559	1	Sport shoes, soles and sportwear
Total	1	

are specialised in a single line of production, although in most cases they are able to differentiate it in goods with various specifications and different applications and markets.

The majority of the recipients are 100 per cent locally owned; only six of the firms have a foreign share in their capital. Most of the locally-owned firms were established by families or individuals, very frequently engineers, technicians or workers with previous manufacturing experience; only a few are controlled by relatively large domestic groups. On the other hand, in only one of the six firms with a foreign partner does this hold a majority share; another case is a 50'50 joint venture, and the rest are equity-controlled by local investors. The foreign partner is the technology supplier in four of the six cases. In the other two cases, the local firms had a foreign partner before the technology transfer from the SME (one is a transnational corporation and the other-another SME of the same national origin).

Most of the sample firms have more than 20 years of existence. They were established in the 40s, 50s and 60s, three decades of continous growth of the Argentine industry, which at those times was the most developed and diversified in Latin America. The very few cases of companies created since the mid-1970s reflect the stagnant and erratic

Table 11.6 Sizes of local companies, product diversification and ownership

No. of employees of local firm	*Product lines*			*Ownership of capital*				*Total*
				Local (100%)	*Foreign share*			
	1	*2*	*3 or more*		*Minority*	*50%*	*Majority*	
1–25	4	1	1	5	1	–	–	6
26–50	1	1	1	2	–	–	1	3
51–100	3	1	2	4	1	1	–	6
101–500	1	1	–	2	–	–	–	2
More than 500	–	–	3	2	1	–	–	3
Total	9	4	7	15	3	1	1	20

evolution of the Argentine manufacturing sector in the last 10 or 15 years (see Figure 11.1). Between 1975 and 1982, the gross manufacturing product declined 23 per cent to a level lower than that of the late 1960s; many establishments disappeared, including hundreds of SMEs. The crisis was worst in certain sectors such as the capital-goods industry, which was particularly affected by the economic policies implemented in the late 70s, and where smaller firms had an important participation.

Except for the few cases in which the creation of the local enterprises was based on the transfer of the SMEs' technology, most recipients had a relatively long manufacturing experience before embarking in technology arrangements with the small suppliers; 14 of them had been operating since at least a decade before. But in most cases was the technology transfer from the SME was the first and only at the time of interviewing. Only three firms intended to have two or more additional experiences with other foreign sources, revealing the existence of some systematic strategy regarding foreign acquisition of technology (see Table 11.7). They were among the largest in the sample.

Most of the local firms were leaders in relatively small market niches. At least nine of the 20 companies had a share of 40 per cent or more in their respective market segments. More than half of the relevant markets were highly concentrated, with few competitors. From the demand side, the sample is evenly divided between concentrated and competitive markets. Not surprisingly, a few large clients provided the main market for the manufacturers of industrial parts and components and electrical transmission equipment; public sector agencies were the strongest clients for five or six of the firms. On the other hand, most manufacturers of machinery and intermediates sold their specialised products to a variety of firms operating in general in competitive markets such as the elaboration of plastic products, food, chemical specialities, metalworking goods and civil construction. Most sample firms had therefore to compete in narrow segments provided in general by other industries, a fact that made them extremely dependent on the evolution of the domestic economy.

With only three exceptions, the cases of technology transfer included in the sample were initiated during the last 15 years, which were a period of economic recession. 12 agreements were started in 1975–81, probably the worst years of the period.[5] Both public and private investments in capital and intermediate goods slowed down dramatically; the markets shrank and many buyers closed their plants. Some of the sample firms are in effect survivors in their own reduced segments. They have increased their market shares, but without compensating

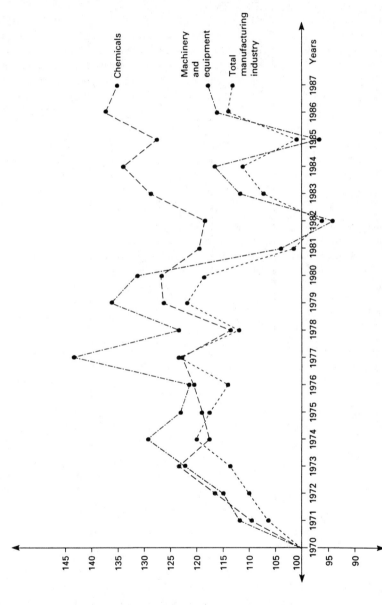

Figure 11.1 Argentina: evolution of gross manufacturing product, 1970–87, total manufacturing industry, chemicals, machinery and equipment; Index 1970 = 100

Table 11.7 Age and experience of recipient companies

Data of creation (periods)	Time of existence before technology transfer					Previous cases of technology transfer			
	Less than 1 year	1–5 years	6–10 years	11–20 years	More than 20 years	None	1	2 or more	Total
1940–9	–	–	–	–	3	3	–	–	3
1950–9	1	–	–	1	2	2	1	1	4
1960–5	–	1	–	5	–	3	1	2	6
1966–9	–	–	–	3	–	2	1	–	3
1970–5	–	–	1	–	–	1	–	–	1
1976–9	2	–	–	–	–	2	–	–	2
1980	–	–	1	–	–	–	1	–	1
Total	3	1	2	9	5	13	4	3	20

for the decay in the orders for their products, which in the late seventies and early eighties had to compete with imports liberalised by the government.

11.4 REASONS FOR TECHNOLOGY TRANSFER

It is in this context that most sample firms made their decisions to import technology. The typical scenario is one of a firm that, after a relatively long period of manufacturing and competing in the local market with a relatively narrow line of products, views an opportunity for diversification by introducing a product innovation. Very often the diversification strategy is explained by the need to compensate for the sluggish growth of sales.

There are, however, four cases in which the technology transfer experience had a 'fundamental' significance on the local enterprises, in the sense that the foreign SME was the basis for the creation of the recipient firms. In three of these cases, the SMEs were brought to Argentina by experienced engineers who left the enterprises where they were working (and where they had the opportunity to identify the supplier) to start their own business (two cases) or, as in one case, needed external finance and technical support for setting up a modern undertaking. In another case, a promotional regime for the introduction of new technologies in the computer industry prompted a distributor of imported equipment to initiate local production with the collaboration of the foreign supplier.

In most other cases, the triggering factor was the need of an established enterprise to innovate in their product mix. None of these firms tried to develop the target products by their own efforts, despite the fact that they had revealed sufficient engineering and manufacturing capacity to copy and adapt technology in their respective sectors (in a few cases, the firms had in-house departments dedicated to development activities). The sample firms were questioned about the reasons for importing technology, rather than trying to find a solution by themselves. The following seem to be the main factors.

First, in most cases the object of the technology transfer was a specific design that the recipients had identified in the international market. The technology had thus already been developed by someone else and the possibility of transplanting it from one of its foreign sources appeared as a relatively simpler step. In several cases, the technology was going to be introduced for the first time in the local market shortly after its international appearance. Thus, the local firms needed the external support for both technical and marketing reasons. For example, a local manufacturer of construction machinery had to incorporate a new type of equipment that would complete its already diversified product line, which had been developed internally. The development of the new design, however, would have involved technical complexities for which the firm was not prepared. In fact, production started with a high dependence on parts and components imported from the small Italian firm that pioneered the innovation, and were gradually reduced as local subcontractors developed with the assistance of the foreign supplier. In another case, the client's requirements included the construction of a prototype and a number of technical trials in special laboratories which were not easily available in Argentina at the time of the technology transfer; thus the local company decided to look for a foreign supplier.

Second, local recipients were no technological innovators. They needed the new technology to increase their competitive strengths but the domestic markets for the innovations were relatively small, uncertain and probably unstable. The turnover expected did not justify investments in local development, particularly when the rate of renewal of designs in the product line was relatively high. Moreover, in various cases the link with the technology supplier was perceived as a long-term affiliation to a continous flow of innovations in the international market. This was particularly the case in sectors with certain rhythm of change in product designs.

Third, the technology import was in some cases a reaction to a sudden opportunity or challenge in the local market. In a few cases, the local firms were importing the product from the SME. The fear of protectionist barriers triggered by balance of payment problems prompted the substitution of imports by local production. For example, a former manufacturer of food packing machines which after the import liberalisation measures of the late seventies closed production and dedicated itself to representing foreign producers, decided to return to manufacturing activities when new trade barriers were established, a few years later; one of the small companies represented was prepared to license its technology in order to assure its presence in the Argentine market.

In other cases, an opportunity was suddenly provided by public tenders of state agencies, for local suppliers of certain goods. For example, a big manufacturer of autoparts had to contact a small Italian firm in order to participate in a public bid for water measurement devices opened by the water supply Agency, a field in which it had no experience. In a number of cases, the decision to license abroad was a reaction to similar moves by local competitors.

Finally, in a couple of cases the local firms had no alternative but to follow the indications of larger customers which were interested in certain designs with specific characteristics, which were already available abroad. For example, one of the main electricity supply companies introduced an important change in transmission systems, which involved the utilisation of new equipment with stringent security standards, for which the local company and its competitors did not offer sufficient previous experience. Also typical of this situation was the case of a licensing contract with an Italian specialist of ironworks for aluminium frames, that was introduced to the local company by its main customer, a big manufacturer of aluminium products which had to develop new capacities in its subcontractors.

Behind the various specific circumstances and motivations for the decisions to import technology, there seem to be two broad strategies or attitudes in the local recipients. On the one hand, there are firms with a systematic growth strategy, based on the gradual introduction and mastery of successive innovations of increasing complexity. Some of these firms had already developed a number of product designs internally; for a few of them, licensing was an alternative that they had already experimented with; for others, the experience with the small supplier was a first step in a more sophisticated strategy of technological innovation. Several of these firms were usual visitors to international fairs and exhibitions and were permanently updated with respect to new developments.

On the other hand, several local firms reveal a more opportunistic strategy *vis à vis* the role of technology transfer. Very often they have simply reacted to an external impulse, either in terms of an unexpected opportunity – such as a government incentive or a public tender by a state agency – or by way of a change in the market conditions, such as protectionist barriers to previous imports, or demands by local customers.

11.5 CHOICE OF A SMALL SUPPLIER

Except for one case, the initiative to undertake the technology transfer came from the recipient side. The exception was a joint venture established by a German company with a local firm that was copying its seats for tractors and other vehicles.

Table 11.8 Countries of origin and sizes of technology suppliers at the moment of the technology transfer

SMEs home country \ SMEs no. of full time employees	0–100	101–200	201–400	401–600	more than 601	Total
United States	1	–	2	–	–	3
Germany	1	1	–	2	1	5
Italy	4	2	4	–	–	10
France	–	–	2	–	–	2
Total	6	3	8	2	1	20

The outcome was, in all cases, an arrangement between a new or already operating local enterprise, and a small firm of a developed country. Table 11.8 present the sizes of the technology suppliers in their respective countries of origin, at the time of the transfer to the local companies. In 12 cases, the foreign SMEs were substantially larger than the recipients; there were five cases in which the local firm was larger, and three of similar sizes (considering a variance of up to 50 per cent or more in the number of employees).

Most technology suppliers were, as their Argentine recipients, competing in narrow segments of the metalworking and chemical industries. Some were highly visible internationally. At least 12 of the 20 SMEs were leaders in their respective markets; a few were small oligopolists, one of the few world-wide specialists in certain products. Half the sample SMEs had subsidiaries abroad or licensed their technologies to foreign enterprises.

The international reputation of the SME was sufficiently strong to convince three recipients that there was no need to shop around for alternative sources. In one of these cases, the Argentine company had to wait until a local competitor finished its licensing contract with a leading manufacturer of shock absorbers for couplings of railroad wagons, in order to obtain the same technology.

The choice of the SME was determined for other reasons in six cases, four in which the recipients were already importing and commercialising the same products from the same SME; one in which the supplier was indicated by the client, and another one in which the founder of the local firm knew already the SME from his past experience in another company.

In most cases, however, the Argentine companies decided to explore different alternatives in the international market. Various firms directed their efforts towards certain countries for considerations other than technological. The Italian origin of a number of local entrepreneurs, or the need for easier personal contacts influenced the search of contacts in that country. This circumstance may have had an indirect incidence on the size of the suppliers selected, given the high participation of smaller companies in the Italian mechanical engineering sector, where several sample cases come from.[6] The same influence of cultural factors could be observed in two of the cases of technology transfer from Germany.

The selection of small or medium-sized suppliers was an obvious outcome in several sectors where, as already mentioned, relatively small companies predominate and even enjoy oligopolistic positions in certain market segments. In several cases, the recipients had few options among the leading companies, none of them being large. This was the case of technologies for various types of industrial machinery and equipment. Yet the sizes of SMEs in developed countries tend to be relatively large from the viewpoint of the recipients. In fact, some of these oriented their choices towards the smallest segments within certain criteria of international competitiveness. For example, an Argentine producer of construction machinery viewed the Italian alternatives as more appropriate than the German and the English ones, which were of better quality but more expensive and less versatile, a couple of traits that the recipient felt were also reflected in the relatively larger size and lower flexibility of their respective structures.

For the same reasons, Argentine firms and/or their proposals or markets could be perceived as too small by developed countries' firms. In at least two cases, a willing supplier was found only among second-line firms, after many failed attempts with other small firms.

On the other hand, six of the small suppliers in the sample were found in sectors where major TNCs predominate. In one case, the technology for street lightening of a French SME was, at the time of transfer, very competitive with those of General Electric and Siemens, the industry leader (the SME was taken over later by GE). In another case, a small manufacturer of electrical equipment was an important supplier of Siemens in Germany. In the three other cases, the local companies went direct to the smallest suppliers, assuming that there was no point in trying to obtain the technology from major TNCs, either because they were already operating in the Argentine market, or because larger companies would impose higher costs or more restrictive conditions. For a small domestic producer of fine chemical specialities.

the larger firms in the industry such as Hoestch or Ciba-Geigy wouldn't bother to talk about a licensing contract; big TNCs only operate through subsidiaries or take over local firms; they wouldn't accept royalties or any other payment for a transfer of their technologies.

11.6   FORMS OF TECHNOLOGY TRANSFER

Initiative and Contact

The linking of small enterprises of developed countries with potential recipients of developing countries seems to face much more serious transaction costs than in the case of arrangements with and between larger firms, particularly if the suppliers are transnational corporations. Both smaller potential suppliers of technology and their potential recipients suffer a number of reciprocal communication difficulties; the former are in general less visible internationally, and they are seldom prepared to afford the risks and to undertake the special efforts involved by technology export programmes; the latter are not always endowed with the economic and technical resources needed to screen, identify and mobilise foreign enterprises willing to invest in their usually modest projects and markets.

As we saw in section 11.8, only four of the 20 couples of local firms and SMEs knew each other before embarking upon the technology transfer experience. In those few cases, a commercial relationship had been established years before, the local firm importing and commercialising the future technology supplier's products. Thus in most sample cases a special effort had to be made by one of the two partners, first to detect and second, to convince the other to participate in the arrangement.

In only one case was the effort made by the technology supplier. The owner was visiting Argentina and casually found a tractor with an older, cheap copy of the seats originally developed by his firm. He contacted the copier through the local German Chamber and convinced him to form a joint venture to manufacture the new designs.

In the remaining cases, the local firm took the initiative. For some of the enterprises with more experience and technical capacity, the process of identification of the supplier was relatively easy. A local manufacturer of chemical specialties had a vast knowledge of the international market and personal contacts with a number of European firms; similarly, an engineer which established its own enterprise with the technology imported from the SME had met this firm during his previous work in a larger company in Argentina. Other local firms were helped by clients which were familiar with the international market of certain goods. Chance and very informal actions were at the origin of a very successful case, whereby a small manufacturer of shoes was convinced by a friend to visit a company he had found in Italy. The resulting agreement for the transfer of a new technique for the fabrication of rubber soles provided the basis for the subsequent evolution and impressive growth of the Argentine company.

But, in general, the searchers for potential technology suppliers used three systems to detect and contact their future cooperators: meetings at international trade fairs and exhibitions, correspondence, and direct visits to companies and their plants. For several manufacturers of special machinery and equipment, appearing at the main sectoral fairs taking place periodically in industrialised countries was almost an imperative. A few cases were born from personal encounters at such events. Other local companies wrote letters exploring possibilities of cooperation to a number of potential suppliers whose data were obtained from business reviews and technical cathalogues, official trade representations and other public information sources. The most frequent method, however, was a visit to the companies' plants. Several recipients inspected various possibilities and alternatives before taking a final decision.

Organisation

As we already know, the origin of the initiative for the technology transfer has a direct incidence on the organisational form adopted for the transfer. In our previous study on Brazil and Argentina, we found that when the initiative comes from the supplier, the outcome tends to be an equity joint venture, with high chances that it will be controlled by the foreign firm; in contrast, when the move is made by the recipient, the usual form is a licensing contract or a locally-controlled joint venture.[7]

This pattern is clearly confirmed in our present sample. The only case of foreign initiative gave rise to a 50/50 joint venture under technical control by the SME. Of the three other equity joint ventures, the two cases of local majority were the result of local proposals.

The remaining case is the only one in which the majority control is in the SME's hands, and was originated in a local initiative. But contrary to the other situations, there was no domestic enterprise established before the transfer. Not only the technology, but also the organisational and capital resources of the foreign supplier were needed to carry out the project.

Table 11.9   Items of technology agreements and relationships with suppliers

Items Relationship with suppliers	A Know-how only	B Know-how and patents or trademarks	C Know-how and technical assistance	D Know-how, technical assistance and trademark
Arm's length (17 agreements)[a]	4	2	6	5
Joint ventures (3 agreements)	–	–	1	2
Total (20 agreements)	4	2	7	7

Note:
[a] Two agreements were not drawn up in formal contracts.

On the other hand, the 16 cases of arms-length technology agreements were all initiated by the recipients.

It is interesting to note that in the few cases of equity joint ventures, the foreign participation was not always a deliberate requirement of the SME. In one case, the local firm persuaded the foreign supplier to take at least a minority share of the capital, as a means to assure its deeper engagement in the project; in another, the transfer was initiated as a technology agreement, but years afterwards, when for several reasons it was difficult to remit the royalty payments, these had to be capitalised. Another relevant observation as to the reasons for equity participation is that the four cases belong to the category in which the scope of technology transfer was larger and more complex, and required an active involvement of the supplier.

Technology Agreements

The prevailing mode of technology transfer in the sample is therefore a contractual agreement. Table 11.9 presents the sample technology contracts classified by the relationship existing with the supplier and the contents of the transfer. It shows that all the joint ventures were accompanied by technology agreements, and two of the arms-length agreements were not formalised into written contracts.

Second, know-how always appears as the main object of the transfer.

In fact, the transmission of product technology and engineering was present in all cases; these know-hows were in less than half of the cases protected by patents or trademarks, and in a few cases were the only item of the agreement, suggesting that the main need of the recipient was to acquire a specific design. In several cases, however, the transfer of know-how was complemented by technical assistance during the life of the contract (see p. 318). Second, despite the limited number of observations, Table 11.9 suggests that the contents of the agreements tend to become more complex with the increase in the involvement of the supplier in the structure of the recipient.

Table 11.10 presents the duration and forms of payment of the agreements classified by their different contents.

Regarding the time period of the agreements, the main observation is that most contracts contain the minimum term of 5 years, which is generally considered as reasonable for the transfer of know-how in industries such as capital goods. In fact, for several enterprises the link with the supplier was viewed as a long-term relationship involving not only the transfer of the original designs but also the supply of improvements and new developments in the product line. Three of the four cases of equity joint venture maintained their agreements for more than 10 years, and in another six cases the agreements were renewed at termination. On the other hand, among the cases in which the agreements lasted for 5 years or less, there are two cases in which the supplier closed its operations or changed its line of business, and one case in which the local production of the goods concerned didn't take off.

With respect to payments, royalties on sales were the most common form of remuneration, but lump sums are frequently stipulated as an initial payment for the disclosure of know-how. In six cases, the payment was included in the price of the parts and components imported from the supplier, revealing that SMEs are also familiar with the transfer pricing techniques. The two cases of informal agreements used this system.

Finally, Table 11.11 shows that 75 per cent of the agreements included territorial restrictions as to the use of the technology. In most cases, the recipients were not free to export the products concerned: exports were allowed to a specific list of countries, generally in South America. Thus many suppliers wished to avoid the recipient's competition in other markets where the former were already present with their own exports. There were, however, five cases in which the recipients were able to exploit the international market without limitations. It seems that territorial limitations are related both to the presence of

Table 11.10 Duration and forms of payment of technology agreements

| | Duration (years) | | | Form of payment | | | | | |
Items	Up to 5	6–10	More than 10	Royalties	Lump sums	Included and in imports	Royalties and lump sums	Royalties included in imports	Total
A	3	—	1	1	—	1	1	1	4
B	1	—	1	—	—	—	2	—	2
C	2	3	2	1	1	2	2	1	7
D	1	3	3	3	—	—	3	1	7
Total	7	6	7	5	1	3	8	3	20

Note: For codes in items, see Table 11.5.

Table 11.11 Restrictive conditions of technology agreements

Items	Geographical limitations			Tied imports		Restriction to technology modification		Total
	Local market	Specific markets	No limits	Yes	No	Yes	No	
A	2	2	–	3	1	1	3	4
B	–	1	1	–	2	1	1	2
C	–	4	3	3	4	2	5	7
D	1	5	1	3	4	4	3	7
Total	3	12	5	9	11	8	12	20

Note: For codes on items, see Table 11.5.

patents or trademarks, or with the equity participation of the supplier.

Tied imports, or the obligation of the recipient to import parts, components or inputs from the supplier, were stipulated in nine of the 20 cases, including three of the equity joint ventures. In fact, as mentioned above, technology was explicitly paid through the invoice of goods imported from the supplier. Some limitations on the freedom of the recipient to introduce modifications in the technology were found in eight cases; most of them included patents or trademarks in the object of the transfer.

In conclusion, it seems that the modalities and conditions of technology contracts with smaller suppliers do not necesarily differ from the general patterns of technology transfer based on the experience with transnational corporations. There are certain aspects in which the terms of agreement could be more favourable, though, such as the less frequent use of intellectual property rights and transfer pricing mechanisms, as well as the lower insistance on ownership participation as a condition for the transfer of technology. Yet the main potential benefits seem to be related not to the contractual modalities, but to the inner conditions and characteristics of the technology that is transferred itself.

11.7 CONTENT AND SCOPE OF THE TECHNOLOGY TRANSFER PROCESS

Content

The know-hows received by the Argentine firms included: (i) product technology, (ii) process technology, and (iii) plant design technology. All cases studied involved the transfer of the first type of know-hows, while 17 had to do with process technology, as well, and only two with plant design technology. These know-hows were transferred in a package or separately. Plant design technology, for example, was transferred together with process as well as product technology. Process technology, on the other hand, was transferred in all cases together with product technology, while the latter was transferred independently from any other form in only four cases.

The pattern of technology transfer that emerges from the sample can be better understood by classifying the cases under three groupings: those in which product technology was the only or the main asset transferred by the SMEs, those in which product as well as process technology were important, and the few in which plant, process and product technology were all involved.

In nine cases SMEs transferred only product know-hows, or product as well as 'supporting' process technology. Local firms received drawings and specifications related to the product, as well as – in some cases – assistance regarding the use of auxiliary devices to manufacture certain parts or components of the product. But clearly product know-hows were the main interest of the recipient firm; process technologies were not crucial for undertaking manufacture.

The different scope of technology transfers reflects to a great extent the sectoral distribution of the sample. Not surprisingly, the nine cases in which product technology was the single or the main content belong to metalworking firms; as we have seen, the interest of these companies was focused on the acquisition of new designs.

The other nine cases involved the transfer of product as well as process technology. Both know-hows were considered important by the recipients (in fact, for three of them production techniques were the main interest of the transfer). The four chemical firms in the sample were all in this situation.

Finally, the sample includes two cases whereby the SME supplied a complete package of know-hows. For example, a leading US small firm agreed to transfer plant, product and process technology for the establishment of a new company dedicated to the manufacture of special-purpose machines. The transfer was made in the two cases under a simple technology agreement, and not through an equity investment, which would seem better to represent the cases of higher involvement of the supplier. Yet as we have found in our earlier work[8] many SMEs are both willing and prepared to provide a complete set of technologies without insisting on their equity participation in the project. But of course, licensing agreements are in general more adapted to the transfer of specific items of technology, and the fact that such agreements predominate in the sample may have determined the low frequency of cases of more comprehensive transfer.

Another relevant fact is that, as we have noted, most cases derived from local proposals of existing enterprises that were interested in introducing one or two additional designs to their product lines. The transfer was thus limited mainly to products and, to a lesser degree, to process technologies.

At the same time, the relatively modest volume of the potential markets for the technology transfer – given the limited size of the Argentine economy and its low rate of growth at the moment of making the arrangements – may have discouraged a larger involvement of the small suppliers, for whom the transmission of product technology, particularly if it does not involve the mobilisation of human resources to the recipient country, entails a relatively low cost and easy operation. In fact, while process technology transfer usually is more intensive in the use of technical personnel, product know-hows can be transferred basically through technical documentation, at least when the recipient has some productive experience. For smaller suppliers, which almost by definition have no excess human resources, the possibility of minimising their use when transferring technology abroad may be an important aspect.

Finally, another factor that may have had influence on the higher frequency of product v. process technology in the sample cases may have to do with certain characteristics of the demand for technology in the Argentine industrial sector. In fact, the import substitution policies followed by Argentina for many decades have given rise to a relatively low sensitiveness in many manufacturing firms *vis à vis* the possibilities of reducing production costs by introducing changes in manufacturing processes.[9]

Items of Technology

The recipients were asked about the instruments used by the SMEs to transfer the relevant know-hows, such as blueprints, designs and drawings, technical assistance, special equipment and the supply of critical components. Drawings and technical assistance were mechanisms frequently used, while the transfer of special equipment and of critical components were as a whole less relevant.

Drawings and blueprints accounted for most of the product technology transferred by the SMEs, and were present in all the sample cases. Although most recipient firms declared that they were reasonably satisfied with the quality and clarity of the documents transmitted and their technical specifications, several indicated that some problems of interpretation had to be solved with the assistance of the supplier's technicians. The impression was that for many recipients the drawings and specifications received by them were a critical aspect of the transfer, which was insufficiently dealt with by the small suppliers. For example, not all the technical details needed were included and in several cases the 'formalization' of the know-hows was not complete. Several local companies shared the perception that their suppliers were probably less prepared than larger companies for this task, reflecting several weaknesses in this respect:

(a) For some SMEs the technology transfer was the only one or the first experience of this kind at the international level.

(b) Other SMEs, not having at home any internal organisation dedicated to licensing out their technologies, faced difficulties in updating the drawings and preparing the technical specifications.

(c) Several suppliers were specialised in the assembly of parts or components of mechanical goods. Assembly skills are among the more difficult to transfer through written specifications.[10]

In fact, four firms in the sample reported serious difficulties in the comprehension and utilisation of the technical documentation transmitted by the suppliers. For example, in one case the diagrams were not only incomplete but were based on components which were standard in the country of origin but not available in Argentina. The recipient had to re-design by itself all the specifications in order to adapt the construction to the local market possibilities.

As to the second most important item in the technology transfer, technical assistance, the sample firms were questioned about the various possible modalities for its supply, such as engineering and technical information and advice given periodically by SMEs' technicians at headquarters or in the recipient country: the organisation of formal or on-the-job training programmes, and the simple provision of long-distance information or documentation on request, on a case-by-case basis.

The sample offered two distinct situations in this respect. In a group of 12 cases, the SMEs didn't have to mobilise their human resources to assist the recipients *in situ*, nor organise any kind of training programme. Yet in all these cases, the local technicians had the opportunity to visit the SME plant in order to become familiar with the production problems or to discuss technical questions. The local engineers and technicians that went to the country of origin of the technology seems to have played a critical role, very often guiding and helping the supplier's personnel as to specific types of technical assistance that were desired. In some of these cases, the SMEs' technicians would simply react passively to the requests and suggestions of the recipients.

The case of an Argentine firm which produced industrial furnaces illustrates this situation. The top engineer of the firm visited regularly the SME plant and selected those designs that were considered most attractive for the Argentine market. It is interesting to note that no technician from the SME ever came to Argentina to get acquainted with the country's demand requirements and manufacturing facilities.

There is another, less numerous group of cases in which the SME played a more active role. The technicians travelled and stayed for some time in the recipient country, and continued to provide technical advice after the initial stage. In a couple of cases, special training programmes were carried out.

This second situation corresponds to the case of a local firm which undertook a licensing contract with an Italian company through which it received product and process know-hows to manufacture plastic containers reinforced with glass fibre. The agreement included the training of 10 employees and six technicians in the Brazilian subsidiary of the SME. In addition, the SME has provided continously technical advice on diverse aspects of interest for the recipient.

Finally, the technology was partially 'embodied' in capital goods (special equipment) in three cases, and in critical parts and components in eight cases, the goods being always imported from the SME. The significance of these supplies was specially important during the first phase of the technology transfer, and in various cases they made an explicit or implicit contribution in terms of the value of the know-hows transferred; but in most instances such significance was gradually lost as the recipients managed to substitute the imports by local production, either directly or through subcontracting.

11.8 ADAPTIVE EFFORTS

This section of the study deals with the issue of technological adaptation, i.e. to what extent, for what reasons, and how, efforts to adapt the original technology to local conditions were made. The analysis takes into account two separate objects of the adaptative activities: products and production processes.

Product Adaptations

Product know-hows were in some cases imported and assimilated by the local firm without any significant effort in changing the original designs, while in other cases it was necessary to carry out certain adaptations.

The first type can be illustrated by the case of a producer of spare parts for the cement industry machinery, mining machinery, earthmoving equipment, etc. who decided to import know-hows to manufacture shock absorbers for railroad wagons. This product was produced following the exact specifications (not only in terms of materials and components but also in all the external appearance) provided by a small US supplier (one of the few world specialists in these products), since only in this way could the recipient fulfil the technical conditions set up by the main clients, the National Railways Company and a few other large public firms.

In another case, the reason for not modifying the technology imported from a small German supplier for the manufacture of valves used in large ships was the need to satisfy the requirements of the cosmetic client, a shipyard who had to provide after-sales services for its own clients in Europe, where the ships were exported – and where such services had to be directly rendered by the technology supplier.

In several cases, however, the recipients were not obliged by their clients to import and manufacture specific designs, but they did not introduce changes in the technology, expect for some modifications which were not viewed as significant.

Sometimes, minor adaptations were made in order to respond to the characteristics of the local demand, the inputs available locally or the manufacturing process used by the local firms. For example, the design of a new equipment for the construction industry was modified in order to make it more solid and resistant for highly cost-sensitive users who were not eager to replace the machinery very often, at least not as frequently as the costumers in the country of origin.

Similarly, a local producer of auxiliary substances for the textile and leather industries explained that small changes were introduced in the chemical composition of the good for which it received the SME technology, since some basic inputs of the original formula were not available in the Argentine market and it was very costly and cumbersome to import them. Yet the interviewee did not consider such changes as major adaptations.

Finally, the sample included some cases in which the original product designs had to be somewhat modified in order to produce the respective goods with different equipment. This occurred with a local manufacturer of lighting devices, which indicated that small designs changes had to be introduced in the imported know-hows so as to manufacturer them with the multipurpose equipment available in the Argentine plant, while in France, the basic format of the same types of apparatus was obtained through the operation of a single specialised press.

The finding that in most cases product adaptations were not significant implies that recipient firms made a good selection of the imported know-hows. It is possible that without their prior manufacturing experience and, in some cases, broad knowledge of the international market of know-hows, the need for adaptation would have been higher.

On the other hand, the analysis reveals that the issue of adaptation involved little effort on the part of the suppliers, in terms of the selection or adaptation of the designs to fit the local market conditions. This is explained, as we have noted, by the protagonistic role of recipients in most cases of technology transfer. In fact, in the only case in which the initiative was taken by the supplier, this had a policy whereby the designs produced in Argentina were simpler than the ones being marketed in the country of origin, and the decisions as to the type and the timing of introduction of new products were made in consultation with the local partner.

Production Process Adaptations

As we have seen, most recipient firms had been operating in the local market for some time before embarking upon their respective experiences of technology acquisition from SMEs of developed countries. The question thus arises as to what extent they had to change their production processes in order to adapt them to the manufacturing of the products for which the know-hows were imported from the SME.

In nine cases, the recipient firms indicated that no changes, or only small modifications such as the introduction of new auxiliary devices for the fabrication of certain parts or components, were introduced in their manufacturing processes. In another eight cases, the modifications were relatively more significant, involving for example the incorporation of new equipment to perform a specific manufacturing activity. But cases of major adaptations were not found. In no case did the recipients have to undertake in-depth restructuring, nor were they obliged to introduce sophisticated equipment such as electronically-controlled machines.

This outcome seems to be more related to the characteristics of the local enterprises than with those of small suppliers. In fact, we have already noticed that for most recipient firms the main objective was to diversify their product lines, while minimising the need to make new costly investments, which were not seen as justified given the weak growth potential of the domestic market. But in connection with this, from the interviews at some local firms it was possible to gather that one of the factors that oriented the search of technology towards smaller suppliers was in fact the objective of avoiding the possibility of having to introduce significant modifications in their own production process, probably assuming that negotiations with larger enterprises would have involved such investments. In fact, most small suppliers did not seem to be particularly concerned with the manufacturing techniques of their Argentine clients, as reflected in their lack of interest in visiting the local plants where their designs were manufactured.

Of course, the relatively low significance of the adaptive efforts carried out in the sample firms could be also explained by the possibility that the process-know hows utilised in the home countries' plants were not very different to those that were being used in Argentina by the local enterprises, or in other words, that the know-hows were *a priori* adapted to the domestic conditions.

Yet, given the huge factor costs differentials between the industrialised countries of origin of the technology and Argentina, as well as the distance in terms of the relative size and sophistication of the respective markets, the above hypothesis does not seem realistic. In fact, all the recipient companies recognised that there were important differences in the level of specialisation, equipment used, etc.; in short, the respective productive organisation structures were seen as different. Section 11.9 explores this aspect in order to find some relationships between the technological differences and prevailing modes of production of suppliers and recipients, and the findings about adaptive efforts already explored.

11.9 MODES OF PRODUCTION, OUTPUT DIFFERENTIALS AND APPROPRIATENESS OF TECHNOLOGY

Local firms were asked about their respective 'average' production levels, relative to those of the suppliers. Given that in most cases the relevant technology had been transferred through licensing agreements to local enterprises that could be manufacturing other products as well, the survey was conducted only on 17 cases where both the supplier and the recipient had a 'similar' output mix.

In 13 of these cases, the recipients stated that the output of the respective suppliers was at least ten times larger (in the remaining four cases, the difference was between five and nine times). Yet 11 of the companies stated that, despite such huge scale differentials, they employed mainly production technologies similar to those used by their suppliers.

In order to understand this finding, the recipient firms were classified according to the production organisation prevailing in their respective

Table 11.12   Modes of production and use of different technology

Mode of production / Use of different technology than SME	Custom-order production	Batch production	Total
No	7	4	11
Yes	1	5	6
Total	8	9	17

plants. Table 11.12 shows that the plants were organised for either 'custom-order' or 'batch' production, and that there were no cases of 'serial' production.[11]

Table 11.12 shows a certain relationship between production modes and propensity to introduce changes. Such propensity is higher among producers in 'batches'. In fact, we have the impression that in the cases of custom-order production, the low absolute output volume and the varied output mix, characteristics of this mode of production that are present in the plants of both suppliers and recipients, limit the scope of possible modifications. In effect, the firms interviewed emphasised that the main features of the production process were similar to those in the industrialised country's plant, despite some differences such as in the relative intensity of subcontracting.

On the other hand, in the case of small batch production, the much larger level of output than in the recipient's country plants led to the use of different equipment in order to take advantage of economies of scale.

These results can be compared with those of a survey conducted by the Argentine government, whereby firms operating in industries organised for serial production were asked to qualify their current outputs with what they considered as the optimal international scale in their respective industries.[12] According to the companies' estimates, the optimal scale was never more than six times larger, that is, the differences appeared to be much less significant than in our sample.[13] In addition, studies on serial production industries in Latin America suggest that technology imports to these industries may give rise to significant adaptive efforts in the recipient plant.[14]

Of course, the existence of adaptative efforts should not be always taken as evidence of effective adaptation of the technology to the local conditions; but for the present discussion it seems relevant to argue that it is the prevailing mode of production – be it serial, small batch or custom-order – and not the relative output differential, that is the key determinant of the need to carry out adaptations in order to reduce the gap between production technologies used by the supplier and the recipient. The hypothesis suggested is, then, that when serial production predominates in a given industry, the need to adapt the technology is higher than in industries characterised by batch or custom-order production.

There is also a strong relationship between the prevailing modes of production in different industries and the relative participation of firms of different sizes. In fact, SMEs tend to be relatively more important in custom-order and batch-production industries than in industries where serial production predominates. Given that, as we have argued, the first two industries involve less costs of adaptation – because the technologies are probably more flexible to volume of production reductions – developing countries should be interested in importing technology related to these industries, and at the same time take into account that such technologies are to a great extent controlled by the smaller companies of industrialised countries.

11.10 IMPACT OF THE TRANSFER

This final section of the chapter deals with some aspects of the impact of the technology transfer on the performance and evolution of the recipient enterprises. For this purpose, the sample firms were asked about their own evaluation of their experiences with the respective SMEs; in addition, the effects of the transfers on a number of aspects, including technological development, competitive position and export performance of the local companies were explored.

In terms of the overall assessment of the experience, 10 recipients considered it 'highly satisfactory', five 'satisfactory', and five, 'unsatisfactory' (the last category includes one case in which the technology was of little use because the project for which it was intended did not take off well). Most local enterprises thus had a positive evaluation of their relationships with the suppliers.

According to their judgement, and except for one case in which the technology transfer process had only just been initiated, the technology was already assimilated. For 10 firms this meant that they had the capacity to design new products with the same basic technology. In general, this reply reflected the familiarity of the local firms with the technology imported, or their ability to copy and adapt technology, rather than to undertake a systematic development programme aimed at introducing real innovations, which as we have seen were not the forte of any of the recipients. Six firms recognised that they were able to introduce minor adjustments on the suppliers' designs. In sum, the technology transfer was not a factor for any major modification in the technological development capacity of the firms. Yet, as we have seen, for some of them the transfer had some learning effects in terms of adaptation efforts; for many it was a first experience in the international negotiation of technology; and for a few it implied a first departure away from reliance on the mere copy of existing designs, and into the developments taking place in the international frontier.

The economic impact of the technology transfer can be measured in terms of the percentage of the sales represented by the products concerned. Apart from the two cases of foreign-controlled joint ventures, in which the imported technology accounts for 100 per cent of the local operations, there are eight cases in which the know-hows object of the transfer had a share of more than 20 per cent of the sales, and five in which they accounted for more than 50 per cent. In several cases, the commercial significance of the technology had decreased over the years or was very variable because of the volatile nature of the local markets.

For most local enterprises, the transfers had an important initial effect, in terms of the increased competitive capacity achieved with the new technology. 15 of the firms reported that on that basis, they had been able to secure a leading position, at least temporarily, in their respective market segments, as local pioneers in the introduction of new products, or as consequence of their enhanced prestige *vis à vis* important local customers. In a few cases, the technology transfer also allowed the firm to start or increase export operations.

Perhaps more importantly, in some cases the technology transfer played an important role in the subsequent growth performance of the recipient. Sometimes this effect was indirect, as illustrated by the case of the tiny shoemaker which in the early 1960s and almost casually, got involved with a small Italian firm which provided the technology to manufacture rubber soles. For several years, this technology was the main source of accumulation and growth for the local firm, but more importantly, the Italian company, which was an important supplier of Adidas, put the Argentine company in contact with this international group, who gave to it the whole manufacturing and marketing responsibilities for the local market. The local firm is now the leading company in its sector, has diversified into other markets and is one of the 100 largest private firms of Argentina.

This case is rather an exception in the sample, for as we know, most sample firms had to cope in recent years with negative conditions for growth in the local market. In fact, only five of the recipients reported a positive evolution in their businesses, and 10 declared that they were undergoing bad times for a long period; their working forces had been reduced dramatically in several cases.

Nevertheless, there are several cases in the sample which illustrate, in less dramatic but more direct fashion, the dynamic potential of the technology transfer from smaller firms. In fact, the sample cases were for some of the local recipients a critical factor to compensate for the otherwise discouraging evolution of the local market, and as already mentioned, also a springboard towards a gradually more sophisticated and diversified strategy of incorporation of technology.

Most local recipients produced for the domestic market. In this sense, the sample cases were no exception to the general pattern of the low export propensity of the Argentine industrial sector. Only five of the sample firms had regular export programs, and seven had exported only sporadically; but in no less than four cases foreign markets accounted for more than 25 per cent of total sales.

The products for which the technology was transferred were among those sold abroad in most of the firms with export programmes or experience. In at least four cases, such goods were the main or the only ones exported, in most cases, to the Latin American market.

Although at present of little significance, there seem to be some trends at work in the Argentine case indicating a larger potential in the role of SMEs' technology as a factor in the promotion of exports. In fact, Argentina entered into a couple of very important bilateral cooperation agreements, one with Brazil and the other with Italy. The first opened an important reciprocal market for the exchange of capital goods, in which many local firms, including companies of the size and characteristics of those included in the sample, are participating. The second, started in 1988, provides for significant financial assistance for the mobilisation of investments in Argentina, with emphasis on the participation of smaller firms of both countries, either through joint ventures or through technology agreements. These two programmes open up a number of possibilities for the combination of technologies of Italian SMEs with the expanded market potential provided by the agreement with Brazil. In fact, a case in our sample, a manufacturer of machine tools that has a technology agreement with an Italian small firm and exports 90 per cent of its production, most of it to Brazil, is a clear example of this new perspective for the immediate future.

11.11   PROBLEMS OF THE RELATIONSHIP

Together with the various actual and potential positive impacts of the transfer of technology experiences, the survey allowed us to detect a number of drawbacks and limitations in the relationship with the smaller suppliers, some of which have been already pointed out. In fact, nine of the recipient companies reported experiencing one or more of the following problems.

Changes in the Structure and Organisation of the Suppliers

Small firms are a highly dynamic reality, and significant changes can take place in very short periods of time, particularly in those areas of faster growth or more intensive competition. A few relatively small companies became relatively big and internationalised in a few years. In at least two cases, the suppliers were taken over by larger enterprises after their involvement with the recipient firm. In one of these cases, the technology transfer was discontinued. In another case, the foreign minority partner, a small German company, was bought by a larger group of the same origin, a fact that disturbed the relationship with the technology supplier, (another small firm) because the new partner of the local firm had taken over other firms in Germany that were competing directly in the same product line. There were also a couple of cases in which the small firms gave up their activities in the field in which the technology was transferred (as larger companies entered the market), or had to close operations as a consequence of the severe competition in the country of origin.

Insufficient Technology Transfer

As already noted (see in particular Section 11.7 above) in several cases the recipients complained about more or less serious problems with the scope and quality of the technical information provided by the SMEs. While in most cases and in some of the problematic ones the recipients praised the 'flexibility' and 'speed' of their suppliers, about eight local firms mentioned the 'incompleteness of technical information', (three cases), the 'uselessness' of the information, (one case), and the 'lack of experience' of the supplier, (four cases), as the main problems. In a few cases, however, the local executives acknowledged that the small firm had managed to improve its transfer capacity over the years.

Commercial Problems

Only a few recipients reported some problems in their experience of negotiation of technology contracts with their suppliers. Either because of their lack of international experience or their ignorance of the local situation, some suppliers didn't show the same flexibility at the moment of negotiating the terms of the agreement that they offered for the transmission of their know-hows. A German firm, for example, presented a very complex contract written in German, whose elucidation and discussion delayed the deal. Another problem was the lack of patience of some SMEs with the difficulties for the payment of royalties caused by the Argentine Government. In one case, the supplier reacted by restraining the flow of know-how and technical assistance.

11.12 SUMMARY AND CONCLUSIONS

Despite its poor economic performance of the last 20 years, Argentina has hosted a number of technology transfer projects with the participation of SMEs of several industrialised countries. Few of these inflows, however, were channelled through DFIs, a *rara avis* in the industrial sector of Argentina during the last two decades. The largest shares of the SMEs' technology was transferred through technology agreements with local enterprises.

The metalworking sector, and in particular the branches dedicated to the production of capital goods and machinery, as well as certain segments of the chemical industry, attracted the largest flows of technology from SMEs. It is in these two broad sectors that a sample of 20 Argentine firms was identified and subjected to case studies on their experiences with smaller suppliers from developed countries (with Italy as the main origin).

Most recipient companies were in the small-to-medium-size ranges and had been operating in the local market for at least one or two decades before the contact with the small foreign firms, which in most cases were for the former the first experience in importing technology in a formal way. In a few cases, the technology imports were the basis for the establishment of a new enterprise in the local market.

Several firms established prior to the technology transfer case were leaders in highly concentrated niches of unstable and, in most cases, slow-growing markets given the stagnant general economic conditions of the country. Some depended on a few important buyers, including the public sector.

For many of the sample firms the decision to import technology was prompted by the need to find new alternatives to fight poor demand conditions. The imported technologies offered a possibility of diversifying their product mix. Thus in most cases they were interested in introducing new designs via licensing agreements with competitive suppliers of technology. Sometimes they were stimulated by pressures from their main customers to improve their products with foreign assistance, but in several cases, they perceived the need to start a new relationship with a permanent source of technological innovation. Because of the specificity or complexity of the products envisaged, the market value assigned to the use of the name of the foreign supplier, the urgency with which they needed the innovations, or the smallness of the prospective market, none of them analysed the possibility of the technologies themselves developing instead of importing them. Yet while for some local companies the technology import was part of a more or less systematic competitive strategy, for others the move was clearly opportunistic, a reaction to a sudden change or challenge in the local market.

The Argentine companies acquired technology from firms which were in general bigger than them, but not beyond the SME category in their respective countries of origin. Several were leaders in their markets. A few couples were already connected by previous commercial links or personal contacts; in most cases, however, the local companies had to explore the international market and approach several alternatives in order to detect and persuade an adequate and willing supplier. The identification process was facilitated in several cases because the SMEs were one of the few world specialists in certain products; but these small oligopolists were not always willing to share their technology with unknown firms coming from a distant market and offering small profits; thus in some cases the Argentine companies had to accept second-line alternatives. Although in several cases the smallness of the supplier was a natural consequence of the market structures, there were some in which the local companies could have tried to licence the technology from transnational corporations. Yet the Argentine firms were convinced that it would have been impossible or extremely costly to make an arrangement with such companies.

In all but one of the cases the initiative was taken by the local enterprise, a fact that helps to explain the predominance of non-equity-controlled forms of technology transfer. In three of the four cases of DFI by the small supplier, such involvement was deliberately encouraged by the local enterprise.

The use of licensing contracts is also explained by the nature of the technologies sought by the Argentine firms, which in most cases consisted of product know-hows with their designs and specifications, while the transfer of production technology was much less significant. In fact, few suppliers appear to have been engaged in complex processes and packages of technology transfer. In most cases, the transfer seems to have involved more effort from the recipients, through an active participation of their engineers and technicians in the selection and assimilation of the know-hows.

The technology agreements didn't differ significantly from the practice with large enterprises. The contract periods were probably excessive in terms of the assimilation needs, but several recipients viewed them as a long-term link for the transfer of additional know-hows and improvements. Several cases included geographical limitations and tied imports, although this last clause was not reflected in a active, permanent strategy of the supplier to use the recipient as an export outlet.

Regarding imported product and process know-hows, the cases revealed that they were not subject to significant modifications.

Not even the very large output differentials between suppliers and recipients were a factor to introduce significant modifications in the production processes, particularly among the plants that were organised for custom-order production, and to a lesser extent, also in the case of batch production. Given that in industries using serial production technology the scale differentials seem to be much smaller and significant adaptation efforts can still be detected, we conclude that the mode of production, rather than the scale differentials, is a key variable for the need to undertake adaptive efforts, and that therefore, there is a clear point for developing countries to stimulate imports of technology for industries in which custom-order or batch production predominate, and where lower costs of adaptation are involved. At the same time, these imports, which have not received much attention in the industrial development experience of Argentina and other developing countries, are those in which smaller firms are significant potential suppliers.

The Argentine study allowed us to detect a number of advantages and some problems with small firms as technology suppliers. The contribution of these firms was viewed as satisfactory in most cases, in terms of the appropriateness of the know-hows, the flexibility and cost of its transfer, and the improvement of the competitive conditions in the local market or, in a few cases, in the export market. For some recipients, there was a clear positive impact on the firms as a whole and their subsequent evolution and growth.

At the same time, there were several elements of fragility in the small suppliers. A few disappeared or were taken over by larger companies, thus changing the basis for the relationship between firms of similar sizes and styles; and several revealed the lack of sufficient capacity to transfer their know-hows in a systematic way, a limitation which gave rise to the active participation of the recipients in the transfer experience.

Appendix: Note on the Selection of the Sample

The sample was selected in the following way. The main data base was the list of 1378 technology agreements registered at the National Register of Technology during 1978–83 whose recipient companies operated in the metalworking and chemical sectors.

First, the size of the technology suppliers was identified through various sources, leading to the identification of 140 agreements in such sectors, with 125 SMEs (defined for this purpose as firms with less than 1000 employees) from four countries of origin (that were given priority in the case of Argentina): Italy, the Federal Republic of Germany, the United States and France.

Secondly, the contents of the contracts were examined, in order to identify and select only those that included the supply of know-how, with or without other services or rights. 103 of the 140 agreements involving 96 SMEs were identified.

Thirdly, 50 suppliers were eliminated, on the grounds that the local recipients were very large firms, which led us to assume that the transfer had a marginal significance for them.

Fourthly, for the 46 remaining firms, the summaries of the agreements were examined and the following were eliminated: (a) those in which the payment was a lump sum, usually for specific, short-term technical services; (b) those whose content led us to suspect that the technology transfer was not significant (for example, 'technology' for the formulation of medicines, whose purpose is usually to formalise imports of raw materials); (c) those with recipients located far from the Buenos Aires area. As a result of this process a sample of 24 cases was identified.

Finally, eight of the 24 had to be eliminated because either phone contact revealed that the cases were not actually interesting (in a few cases the transfer had not taken place) or the recipient companies refused to be interviewed. 16 recipient companies were thus identified and ready for the interviews. To this group, four additional cases were added, identified with the help of binational chambers in Buenos Aires and the Secretary of Industry and Commerce.

Notes

1. See E. Basualdo, *La estructura de propiedad del capital extranjero en la Argentina* (Buenos Aires: CET, 1984).
2. The identification of sizes of the foreign firms that appeared listed in the formation sources had to be made through special data services in each of the countries of origin. A first screening was made in CEDREI using business directories such as Standard Poor Corporation, Dun & Bradstreet,

Kompass. Secondly, the research collaborators in the participating industrialised countries revised our lists, and provided additional information as to the degree of independence of the small suppliers that were identified.

3. See CEDREI, *Alternative technology sources for developing countries: The role of small and medium-sized enterprises from industrialised countries* 1986, Table 2, p. 20.

4. Between 1963 and 1972, the value of DFI amounted to about US$200 million, almost three times less than in the previous 5-year period. During the turbulent 1973–75 period, DFI flows virtually disappeared, and in the 1976–83 period of the military regime DFI was concentrated in the service sector. Manufacturing attracted less than half of the value of investments (traditionally its share was (90 per cent or more) and only 29 new establishments, while a number of disinvestments and closures of foreign plants took place.

5. It must be taken into account that the main source for identifying cases was the National Register of Technology Transfer, which was started in the early 1970s under increasingly restrictive legislation; in 1977 it was drastically liberalised, a fact that, together with the low cost of foreign exchange derived from the economic policies applied during 1978–82, explains the general propensity of Argentine companies to pay for technology imports, despite the economic situation. In fact, during 1977–83 the payments abroad for technology contracts amounted to at least US$1.7 billion, increasing by more than 1000 times between the two years, and accounting for about 3.3 per cent of a gross industrial product, which as we have seen had decreased by about 20 per cent in the same period. See INTI – SECYT, *Contratos de importación de tecnología 1977–83* (Buenos Aires, 1985).

6. By 1981, establishments with less than 500 employees accounted for 90 per cent of employment in the metallic products sector and 81 per cent in the case of non-electric machinery. See CEPAL, *El proceso de desarrollo de la pequeña y mediana empresa. y su papel en el sistema industrial: el case de Italia* (United Nations (ECLA), 1988).

7. See CEDREI, *Alternative technology sources* (1988), pp. 127–9.

8. See CEDREI, *Alternative technology sources* (1986).

9. See on this J. Katz, 'Cambio Technológico en la Industria Metalmecànica Latinoamericana', *Revista de la CEPAL*, (19 April 1983), pp. 122–3.

10. Assembly usually entails a series of small transformations in the different parts and components to ensure that all problems that might appear are solved; only people with wide experience in this operation can efficiently handle this job.

11. Plants that operate at the 'customer's request' produce small quantities of usually a variety of products in a discontinous way. Specifications vary for each product and require a significant participation of qualified personnel. Plants that produce in 'batches' manufacture limited quantities of certain goods. Production is usually organised around 'shops' that carry out special transformation activities. They tend to use more multipurpose equipment than those plants in which 'serial' or continous production prevail.

12. See Secretary of Industry, *Productivity Survey*, cited in W. Bank, *Argen-*

tina Industrial Sector Study (April 1988), p. 100.

13. In fact, if the sample firms had compared their outputs not with that of their suppliers but with their respective 'optimal scale', the differentials probably would have been even larger in our case study.

14. For example, a study on the metalworking industry found several cases in which significant efforts were performed in order to 'scale down' the production process and reduce the level of automation of the imported technology. See Katz, 'Cambio Technológico' (1983).

12 The Case of Brazil

Afonso Fleury

12.1 INTRODUCTION

The inflow of foreign capital to Brazil, especially in manufacturing industry, began initially at the end of the First World War. These investment flows intensified during the 1950s and there was a further expansion in the 1968–73 period. The participation indices of multinational companies (MNCs) in the Brazilian economy vary according to both the data base and sample adopted and the definition of different forms of foreign investment, but their presence is preponderant in the durable consumer goods sector and in the capital goods sector. They also dominate the pharmaceuticals, rubber, textiles, cosmetics and petrochemicals industries and others; and share the leadership, with a few large Brazilian firms, in the non-durable consumer goods sector.

Table 12.1 is illustrative of the considerable role of MNCs in Brazil's economy. 56 of Brazil's 100 largest firms were in the manufacturing sector in 1987 and, of these, the majority (31) were foreign-owned. Foreign presence was particularly prominent among the 50 largest Brazilian firms.

As for smaller MNCs, that is foreign SMEs operating in the country, there is no information to differentiate them from the rest. At first sight, this might suggest that the involvement of foreign SMEs is recent and still of little significance, a question pursued further below.

Table 12.1 Brazil: status of multinational manufacturing companies, 1987

Rank of firms	Manufacturing firms		
	Brazilian	*Foreign-owned*	*Triad*
50 target firms	5	19	24
Firms ranked 51–100	20	12	32
Total	25	31	56

Table 12.2   Brazil: foreign firms, classified by type of investment and sector of activity

Sector	Subsidiaries		Financial participation in local firms	
	No. of cases	*(per cent)*	*No. of cases*	*(per cent)*
Agriculture, cattle, food	265	7.1	95	5.2
Mining, metal, petrochemical	503	13.5	154	8.7
Mechanical, electrical electronics	1176	31.5	645	36.3
Chemical, pharmaccutical	682	18.3	246	13.9
Textile, footwear	88	2.4	58	3.3
Banks, insurance	462	12.4	200	11.3
Commerce, services	551	14.8	379	21.3
Total	3727	100	1777	100

Source: *Interinvest Guide* (1978); Rattner (1985).

12.2   METHODOLOGY AND OVERVIEW

Foreign firms operate in all economic sectors and Table 12.2 shows the number of firms of foreign origin in Brazil, according to the classification of the Interinvest Guide on foreign investors.

The figures in Table 12.2 reveal the preference of foreign firms to set up subsidiaries with direct control, as opposed to the alternative of financial participation in locally controlled firms. The *Interinvest Guide* also shows that the majority of investments are by firms from Europe (47 per cent), followed by North America (39 per cent) and finally by Asia (14 per cent). It is also clear that the mechanical electrical/electronics, chemical and pharmaceutical sectors are the most attractive manufacturing industries for foreign investment in Brazil. These are the sectors which have been selected for examination in this study. Furthermore, the countries of origin of the SMEs to be studied in Brazil were Germany, France, Italy and the United Kingdom in Europe; the United States and Canada in North America; and Japan in Asia.

Turning to a more detailed analysis of the presence of firms from these countries in Brazilian manufacturing activity (Table 12.3), there is evidence of the significance of the above selected factors as a focus of interest for the establishment of foreign investments in Brazil.

Table 12.3 shows a strong US presence and significant Japanese participation, even in 1978. The mechanical and electrical/electronics

Table 12.3 Number of firms[1] from selected home countries, by industry

	Germany[2]		France		Italy		UK		Canada		USA		Japan		Total	
	Subs.	FP[2]	Subs.	FP	Subs.	FP	Subs.	FP	Subs.	FP	Subs.	FP	Subs.	FP	Subs.	FP
Mechanical, elecrical/eletronics																
	335	220	127	70	99	48	74	36	10	5	640	324	161	92	1446	795
Chemicals, pharmaceuticals																
	183	52	90	26	44	13	46	19	5	3	371	156	50	36	789	305
	193	89	143	51	81	41	114	37	63	14	372	120	180	89	1146	441
Other manufacturing services																
	163	121	272	96	152	86	205	76	54	16	394	275	291	105	1531	775
Total																
	874	482	632	243	376	188	439	168	132	38	1777	875	682	322	4912	2316
	1356		875		564		607		170		2652		1004		7226	

Notes:
1. Firms belonging to the financial sector have been excluded.
2. Sub.: Subsidiaries of foreign firms;
   FP: Firms from specified countries with financial participation in locally controlled firms.

Source: Interinvest Guide (1978).

Table 12.4 Description of the sample, by countries of origin of SME and types of relationship with Brazilian firms

Origin and country	Types of relationship	Subs.	JV^1	LIC^2	Total	
Europe	Germany	3	0	2	5	
	France	2	0	0	2	12
	Italy	3	0	0	3	
	UK	1	0	1	2	
North America	USA	1	0	4	5	6
	Canada	0	0	0	1	
Asia	Japan	1	1	0	2	2
	Total	12	1	7	20	20

Notes:
1. JV: Joint Venture (the sole case of a foreign minority share joint venture was added to the licensing agreements for the purpose of the analysis).
2. LIC: Licensing agreement.

sectors are those preferred by American and German firms. Investments originating in France, Italy, the United Kingdom and Japan tend to be orientated towards the service sector, but they also show a significant participation in the manufacturing sectors selected for this study.

After an interchange of information with CEDREI a list of possible cases of transfer was drawn up and, after further investigation and contact, cases became available for analysis following a series of interviews. Table 12.4 classifies the cases according to the countries of origin and type of investment. These include instances of direct investments (establishment of subsidiaries or joint ventures) and licensing agreements between foreign SMEs and Brazilian firms of all sizes.

The sample includes 12 subsidiaries of foreign SMEs, seven licensing agreements of Brazilian firms with foreign SMEs and one joint venture with minority participation by a Japanese SME. 12 cases correspond to European SMEs, six to North American firms and two to Japanese firms. Comparing this information with the data presented at the beginning of this chapter, the composition of the sample is consistent with the pattern of investments of foreign firms in Brazilian industry, as will be described in what follows.

Characteristics of the Sample

The size distribution of Brazilian firms in our sample (Table 12.5) indicates a clear tendency towards the setting up of small subsidiaries once FDI is involved. Almost 60 per cent of the subsidiaries have less than 50 employees and 92 per cent have 100 employees or less. In fact, only one of the 12 subsidiaries has more than 100 employees, and can be considered as medium-sized. As regards licensing agreements the pattern is different: the number of medium- or large-sized Brazilian firms obtaining technology from foreign SMEs is greater (of course, like is not being compared with like in Table 12.5).

In terms of industries of investment/technology transfer there is a concentration in the mechanical sector which is a characteristic of Brazilian manufacturing structure and of the region in which the interviews were conducted (Table 12.6). The case in the pharmaceutical sector is related to the involvement of a Brazilian pharmaceutical firm that is diversifying its production into the biotechnology area. In as much as SMEs in general seek to operate in specific market niches, we tried to obtain a better characterisation of the relative size of the

Table 12.5   Size of Brazilian firms included in the case studies

Size 1/type	Subs.	JV	LIC	Total
0–50	7	0	0	7
51–100	4	0	1	5
101–500	1	1	3	5
Total	12	1	7	20

Note:
1. Total number of employees.

Table 12.6   Manufacturing sector of Brazilian firms included in the case studies

Sector of involvement/type	Subs.	JV	LIC	Total
Mechanical	10	0	4	14
Chemical	2	1	0	3
Electronics	0	0	2	2
Pharmaceutical	0	0	1	1
Total	12	1	7	20

Table 12.7 Relative position of subsidiaries in their respective sub-sectors

Sub-sector	Country of origin	Relative position in ranking
Metalworking	Germany	12th
Machinery	Germany	7th (of 20)
Metal industry	Italy	36th
Equipment	Italy	50th (of 100)
Other	(Canada	77th (of 110)
Mechanical	(Japan	106th (of 110)
Equipment	Italy	108th (of 110)
Textiles	UK	22nd
Rubber	France	n.a.
Chemical	US	78th
products	France	93rd

n.a.: Data not available.

Source: *Balanco Anual, Gazeta Mercantil* (1988).

subsidiaries, comparing available sales data (net sales) with the information referring to other firms of the same subsector. The results are presented in Table 12.7.

Some caution is necessary in analysing Table 12.7. In the first place, it was produced from a ranking produced by a specialised publication. As the filling of the data was left to the initiative of the firms, some subsidiaries that should have been included in the ranking are not quoted. In these cases interpolation was necessary in order to give an approximate idea of the relative position of the subsidiary. Three subsidiaries received this treatment.

The Brazilian recipient firms concluding licensing agreements with foreign SMEs are described in Table 12.8.

Both big Brazilian firms, leaders in their specific sub-sectors, of activity, and small firms are represented in Table 12.8; foreign technology can therefore be of value to all sizes and types of recipient firms.

12.3 THE DYNAMICS OF SME INVOLVEMENT IN BRAZIL

According to Cruz (1985, p. 42).

The Development Plan for 1957–61 brought an acceleration [by the State] principally made in the energy, transport, steel and petroleum

Table 12.8   Relative position of firms with licensing agreements with SMEs in their respective sub-sectors

Sub-sector	Position in the ranking
Metalworking machinery	2nd
Industrial furnaces	1st
Metallurgical equipment	46th (of 110)
Electronic equipment[1]	41st
Chemical/ plastics	42nd (of 70)
Pharmaceutical/ Veterinary[2]	34th

Notes:
1. Has two licence agreements with SMEs.
2. Has four licence agreementss with SMEs in the biotechnology area.

Source: *Balanco Anual, Gazeta Mercantil* (1988).

refining sectors; as well as the widening of the manufacturing sector, notably in the capital goods and the automatic industries. Several large firms of foreign capital were established during this period as a response to the series of incentives adopted.

In addition this period is also important from the point of view of foreign SMEs: two of the sample firms with licensing agreements and one that has a subsidiary had, in the 1950s, established sales offices in the country (Table 12.9). These were used both for marketing and the provision of technical assistance.

During the 1960s these incentives and transfers continued, and more than five out of the 12 SMEs from the sample had established offices in Brazil. However, it was only really during the 1970s that the greatest number of subsidiaries was established in the country, as shown in Table 12.9.

The isolated case of licensing observed before the 1970s in Table 12.9 is related to a SME that had set up a sales office during the 1950s and that, during the 1960s, concluded a licensing agreement

Table 12.9   Period of establishment of subsidiary or conclusion of licensing agreement

Type of involvement	Before 1970	1970–9	1980–7	*Total*
Subs.	–	10	2	12
JV	–	1	–	1
LIC	1	5	1	7
Total	1	16	3	20

with a large Brazilian firm. The intensification of foreign investment flows observed in Brazil during the period 1970–9 can be related to the political and economic characteristics of the period. In fact the 1970s marked a period of strong growth in industrial activity, together with relative political stability. The first half of that decade was the most favourable from the point of view of economic growth. Nine out of 12 subsidiaries in the sample started their productive activities between 1970 and 1976.

It is important to observe that during the period a group of protective measures were implemented for Brazilian industry, basically restricting imports. These measures were intended to strengthen the balance of trade and, simultaneously, to create conditions encouraging the investment in technological capacity by national firms. Given these policies, some SMEs that operated through sales offices decided to start productive activities in Brazil. The growing sensitivity of Brazilian government authorities regarding the technology problem was shown in other respects, e.g. with the creation of Programmes in Strategic Areas such as Information technology and Energy. One consequence of this was the tendency towards technology imports and this explains why five out of seven cases of licensing agreements in the sample were concluded between 1970 and 1979.

The period of expansion of industrial activity that occurred between 1970 and 1979 was followed by a period of deep recession in the 1980s and, given these conditions, foreign investment was significantly reduced and SME entry practically halted. Only the establishment of two subsidiaries can be observed in our sample, in very different conditions. These two firms started producing locally, sharing the productive facilities of other firms of the same origin (not necessarily SMEs) that already operated in Brazil. This strategy reduced investment risk. It is also significant that these cases occurred in sectors related to two areas considered as strategic by the Brazilian government. In total there were five 'strategic areas': information technology, fine chemicals, precision mechanics, new materials and biotechnology.

The only case of licensing observed after 1980, as shown in Table 12.9, refers to the area of biotechnology. It is interesting to make a few comments on this last case, in as much as it characterises a very peculiar area for the transfer of technology through foreign SMEs. The Brazilian firm involved operates in the pharmaceutical branch and, in its diversification process, is investing in the biotechnology sector. In fact, it has four technology agreements with foreign SMEs among which one was selected to illustrate the case. Another three Brazilian groups with the same strategy were identified, which means a total of nearly 20 technology transfer agreements between Brazilian firms and foreign SMEs in the biotechnology area.

The biotechnology sector shows characteristics that are especially relevant for this research subject. It is known that the development of the biotechnology area has been based on new firms in the industrialised countries. What can be observed now is a process of 'natural selection', which works through takeovers, restructuring and consolidation of the sector. In fact, in the United States alone there are perhaps 800 SMEs in that field and it is expected that, when restructuring occurs, not more than 50 will survive. The firms thus threatened show a greater disposition to transfer technology to other firms. This willingness can be extremely valuable for firms of countries with less technological capacity.

These characteristics seem not to exist in the areas of information technology. In the first place, this is because the early phase of microelectronics-based technologies seems to have finished; in the second place, there is now a clear predominance of large MNCs in the field. Given this, the presence of foreign SMEs in information technology in Brazil is of little significance and the potential for their contribution is very reduced.

In brief, it seems evident that the involvement of foreign SMEs is interrelated with the main cycles of the Brazilian economy.

The Establishment of Subsidiaries: SMEs' Reasons and Strategies

In all cases examined the decision to establish subsidiaries in Brazil was taken after earlier SME exports to the country. As illustrated by Table 12.10, the export process was carried out through local agents or sales offices established by the foreign firm.

Table 12.10 Brazil: antecedents of establishment of subsidiaries

Export pattern to Brazil	No.
• The SME exported through a local agent	7
• The SME installed a sales office	5
• The SME did not export to Brazil	0
Total	12

Table 12.11 Motivations for the establishment of subsidiaries

Motivation factors	No.
Growth + protective measures + government incentives	3
Growth + protective measures + re-export	3
Growth + presence of other firms of same origin	3
Growth + protect image	2
Growth + reduce costs	1
Total	12

The decision to establish a productive unit in the country was justified in many ways, depending on the SME. Nevertheless, there is a common factor: the political expansion of the firm in relation to Brazilian economic growth. In fact, a significant number of firms were established in the country during the 1970s, a period of considerable economic growth. Other reasons given are shown in Table 12.11. The first group of factors relate to the introduction of protective mechanisms which hampered the exports to Brazil, coupled with the existence of fiscal incentives for the establishment of firms or subsidiaries in priority sectors. For example, one of the sectors which benefited was that for machines for the ceramic industry; this led to the establishment of two subsidiaries by SMEs at the beginning of the 1970s.

A second group of factors are associated with the above-mentioned protectionist measures: the subsidiaries established in Brazil could be a productive structure for re-exporting. The principal target for re-exporting is South America, but in one case a firm referred to the intent (not fulfilled) to cover the entire American continent, including the United States and Canada.

The presence of other firms of the same origin (not necessarily customers) related to another group of motivations. In one area a firm was a supplier to a large French MNC. A second firm was an international supplier of equipment for manufacturing electric cables and the diversification of the activities of an Italian TNC in Brazil justified the installation of a subsidiary in the country. A third firm was invited by a financial group from Italy that had business in the country. Two subsidiaries were established because of the problem that European SMEs were facing in maintaining quality standards in the technical assistance associated with the machines they exported to Brazil. These two firms worked with Brazilian firms that supplied the technical assistance. In as much as these Brazilian firms failed to keep the quality standards established by the SME, risking the latter's reputation, and since the growth political of the Brazilian domestic market was deemed sufficient, these SMEs decided to establish their own manufacturing facilities. There was just one subsidiary, from the chemical sector, that justified its establishment in terms of cost. The firm concluded that the elimination of transport costs and the cheaper labour would place it at a stronger competitive position in the Brazilian market.

The Process of Establishment of Subsidiaries

The entry and permanence of subsidiaries of SMEs in Brazil seems to be related to specific capabilities. In terms of technological capacity, out of the 12 SMEs that established subsidiaries, five are international leading firms in specific market segments, and seven are followers (Table 12.12). Of the seven follower firms, five declared that they had no specific advantages in terms of technology. These were firms operating in the mechanical sector which had established a presence in Brazil with products orientated towards well-defined market niches in a strategy that can be called 'opportunistic'. Therefore, as they had products with 'very simple technology', as stated by the interviewees, they faced local competition as Brazilian firms copied their products. On the other hand, the speciality of the two subsidiaries that operated in the chemical sector is, notwithstanding their follower status, the capacity to pro-

Table 12.12   Relative international position of SMEs in specific segments

Segment	Segment leader	Followers in segment	
		Without specific advantages	*Small-scale economies*
Mechanical	5	5	0
Chemical	0	0	2
Total	5	5	2

Table 12.13 Market structure, supply

	Market		
Sector	Concentrated	Competitive	Total
Mechanical	10	0	10
Chemical	0	2	2
Total	10	2	12

Table 12.14 Market structure, demand

	Market		
Sector	Concentrated	Competitive	Total
Mechanical	3	7	10
Chemical	0	2	2
Total	3	9	12

duce efficiently at a small scale, which assures them a comparative advantage in the Brazilian market.

As regards the five subsidiaries of internationally leading SMEs, they have enjoyed, from the start, a very strong competitive position that could not be threatened, in technological terms, by Brazilian firms. These subsidiaries dominate their market segments and their main competitive advantage is quality and trademarks. For the kind of product they manufacture, price is a factor of less importance.

The logic of strategies adopted by SMEs can also be analysed in terms of the type of market in which the subsidiaries operate. As shown in Tables 12.13 and 12.14, all metalworking firms are in concentrated markets from the supply side (that is, a few producers) and seven admit that their market is competitive from the demand side (there are a greater number of consumers). The three firms that faced concentrated markets are firms that came to the country in terms of the relations that they maintained with large TNCs in their countries of origin. The subsidiaries in the chemical sector are located in a fairly competitive market, both from the supply and demand sides.

The strategic capabilities of the subsidiaries in the chemical sector lie in process technology, whereas the capabilities of the mechanical sector subsidiaries are related to product technology. Among these firms, those that have not updated their product lines have increasingly faced competition from Brazilian firms with similar products.

Technology Transfer Agreements

As mentioned before, eight technology transfer cases were examined, of which seven were licensing agreements and one a joint venture with participation by the foreign SME.[1] To analyse the technology transfer from SMEs of developed countries through licensing agreements, recipient firms were classified according to the technology strategies involved in these processes. Three types of licensing were identified:

- *Strategic licensing*: the Brazilian firm seeks a foreign supplier of technology as a result of market evolution and its technology upgrade polices
- *Compulsory licensing*: the Brazilian firm is obliged, because of certain circumstances, to look for a licence from a foreign firm which is only incidentally an SME
- *Defensive licensing*: the SME takes the initiative for establishing a licensing scheme with a Brazilian firm.

Of the eight cases of technology agreements examined, the breakdown in terms of type of licensing are given in Table 12.15, 12.16 and 12.17.

Compulsory licensing is associated, in general, with the investment programmes of the Brazilian government, both directly or through state enterprise. For example, for manufacturing specific equipment, such

Table 12.15   Different types of licensing found in the sample

Type of licensing	No. of cases
Strategic	5
Compulsory	1
Defensive	2

Table 12.16   Types of licensing, by industrial sectors of agreements

Type of licensing	Mechanical	Chemical	Electrical	Pharmaceutical
Strategic	1	1	2	1
Compulsory	1	–	–	–
Defensive	2	–	–	–

Table 12.17 Size of local firms involved in technology transfer agreements

Type of licensing	Size of local firm		
	$n < 100$	$100 < n < 500$	$n < 500$
Strategic	1	3	1
Compulsory	–	–	1
Defensive	–	–	2

as steel plants, or in order to finance or tax exemptions for technology development, the government requires the association of a Brazilian firm with a reputed foreign firm. This was the case with one of the interviewed firms which, in order to qualify as a supplier of equipment for Brazilian nuclear plants, had to seek technology from a German SME.

As regards defensive licensing, this does not seem to be very frequent, though we have found two cases in our sample. These correspond to SMEs that established sales facilities in Brazil during the 1950s and the 1960s and further invested to organise an agency or to train sales and technical assistance staff. The subsidiaries sub-contracted local firms to manufacture the products (or parts) which were then sold in the local market. In both cases the SMEs divested from Brazil, but in order not to abandon the market completely, they concluded a licensing agreement with the firms that manufactured its products. From the point of view of each Brazilian firm, these are not strategic products, but can be manufactured as long as they are demanded or there is a productive capacity available. This type of licensing seems to be part of a strategy of retreat by SMEs from Brazil. This will be reconsidered later.

Motives for Licensing

The diversification of product lines is the most important factor that explains the Brazilian firms' decision to undertake licensing agreements with foreign SMEs. Table 12.18 reveals that this is the case for seven out of the eight firms interviewed. In six out of the seven cases, licensing is related to a faster, less risky and less expensive entry into new markets. In only one case was the licensing of a new product orientated towards a specific customer, that is there was a product diversification for the same market. Only one Brazilian firm saw licensing

Table 12.18   Licensing motives

Sector	Diversification for new markets	Customer-oriented diversification	Introduction of changes in the product process
Mechanical	2	1	1
Chemicals	1	–	–
Electronics	2	–	–
Pharmaceuticals	1	–	–
Total	6	1	1

as a means to increase the efficiency of its productive process and therefore its competitive capacity.

This picture can be generalised: licensing is more related to a diversification strategy than to an increase in efficiency. A very unstable local market demand, the value placed on foreign trademarks and the relatively low technological capacity of Brazilian firms makes licensing useful as a strategy. In face, in only one of the eight cases studied, was licensing the first experience in terms of technology transfer. The rest of the Brazilian firms had not only had previous experience in licensing but also in joint ventures. One of the firms that was interviewed had almost 70 licence agreements at the time of the interview.

The setting up of licensing agreements with SMEs in six cases was preceded by other business relations. As shown in Table 12.19, in three cases the licensee imported and distributed products for the SME before the agreement. Similarly, two firms had earlier produced machinery and equipment as sub-contractors for the SME. There was also a case in which the agreement between the firms was arranged by a financial group with which both the licensee and the licensor had business relations.

In only two cases was there an absence of a previous relationship, but the selection process in these instances was not long or expensive. The technology required was sophisticated and there were few alternatives. The selection of the appropriate SME was possible because of recommendation by a customer, in one case, and because of personal contacts in the second.

The fact that the licensor is a SME seems, in principle, to make no difference, or is of small relevance during the selection process. This point will be further examined in the next section.

Table 12.19 Previous relations between SME and Brazilian licensees

Previous relationships		No.		Total
Had previous relationships	} The licensee was a sub-contractor	2	)	
	} The licensee distributed the SMEs products	3	)	**6**
	} Both companies had relations with a third firm	1	)	
No previous previous relationships		2		**2**

Table 12.20 Type of technology transferred by the SME

Type of technology sector	Product technology	Product and process technology	Product, process and plant technology	Total
Metal	4	5	1	10
Chemical	0	1	1	2
Total	4	6	2	12

12.4 THE TECHNOLOGY TRANSFER PROCESS

Type of Technology Transferred to Subsidiaries

Table 12.20 shows the type of technology transferred by the 12 SMEs to their Brazilian subsidiaries. Four firms only transferred product technology and these cases correspond to SMEs that had already invested in productive plants (two cases) or only operated as assembly plants, sub-contracting the greater part of the production process (two cases). The most usual case was the transfer of both product and process technology, in which the SME makes decisions that directly affect the setting up and operation of the productive process of the Brazilian factory.

Only in two cases did we find the transfer of product, process and plant technology. One of the firms operates in the chemical sector, which usually requires the transfer of such a 'package'. The second case was that of a French firm in the metalworking sector that besides transferring product and process technology tried to modify the local firm's plant design according to the pattern of its main plant at home.

Table 12.21   Human resources deployed in establishing Brazilian subsidiaries

Basic composition of human resources	No.
SMEs founder set up a subsidiary	2
SMEs technicians were sent as directors	5
SMEs technicians helped in setting-up	4
Brazilian technicians sent to SME	1

Human Resources in the Technology Transfer to Subsidiary

The critical moment in the process of setting up a subsidiary is the start up of operations. It is in this period when the local technological training assumes the greatest relevance. Table 12.21 shows SME strategies in terms of human resources devoted to the setting up of subsidiaries in Brazil.

We found two cases in which the founders of the SME themselves (a German and an Italian) came to Brazil to coordinate the setting up of the subsidiary. In both cases, this happened during a period in which the SMEs were passing through administrative reorganisation in their countries of origin. In nine cases, technicians from the SME were sent to Brazil. In five of these cases these technicians occupied permanent important posts in the Brazilian subsidiary. In the other four cases, SME technicians were sent to Brazil only for the start up of the subsidiary. The average stay of these technicians was two years. The only case in which there was a less intensive support from the SME is one in which Brazilian technicians were sent to the SME to arrange for technology transfer. This last case is important because it also illustrates the dynamics of the setting up of subsidiaries in Brazil. A gradual strategy was adopted by all SMEs which conducted business in the country for at least six years before investing in production. This implies that, at the time of the setting up of the productive system, in most cases, there already existed a pool of relatively qualified human resources.

The role of local technicians in the technology transfer process is related to the quality of the technology transferred to the subsidiary. An analysis of Table 12.22 must be made bearing in mind that there is a constant technology flow in terms of the product's life cycle and the technology transfer strategy adopted by the SME. The first four cases relate to subsidiaries that try to maintain their competitiveness through product and process updating. The next four cases are related to subsidiaries in which the SME shared little interest in investing in

Table 12.22   Role of local technicians in the technology flow

Subsidiary's evaluation	No.
Very significant	4
Significant	4
Relatively significant	4
Not very significant	0
Total	12

Table 12.23   Human resources' flow intensity in the technology transfer process

Frequency of interaction	No.
Send and receive technicians systematically	4
Send technicians under request	2
Send and/or receive technicians infrequently	6
Total	12

local technological capacity, though their products are still competitive. The four cases in which the role of local human resources was 'relatively significant' are related to subsidiaries that produced goods that are either becoming obsolete or being substituted by the SME, but still have an important market in the Brazil. In these cases the technology flow between the home firm and subsidiaries is scarce and technology transfer is not very intense.

Another way of studying the significance of human resources in the technology transfer process is given in Table 12.23. Four firms invested systematically in the technology transfer, sending technicians to the home firm for updating and training. These cases were two subsidiaries from the chemical sector and two in the high technology metalworking sector. Two German subsidiaries from the metalworking machinery sector sent technicians to the home firm only in cases in which there are orders for more sophisticated machinery. In these cases, the subsidiary's technicians travelled in order to help in designing the machine in the SME and then returned to Brazil to help in its construction. It is significant, however, that six firms (50 per cent of the subsidiaries) rarely sent their technicians to the SME or received technicians from the SME for training or updating the local group. One of the subsidiaries was in a critical situation because it could not achieve its strategic goal of penetrating the US market from Brazil. Consequently,

Table 12.24 Mechanisms used in the transfer of technology, mechanisms, special equipment

Industry	Blueprints [1]	no. of firms employing mechanism	Critical components
Mechanical (10 firms)	10	1	9
Chemical (2 firms)	2	0	1
Total	12	1	10

Note:
1. Design, drawing and basic product process manuals.

the Japanese parent is divesting and abandoning this subsidiary. Two firms report that they have already completed their technology transfer cycle for the product lines that they intended to produce in Brazil: technology transfer from the home firm is sporadic and these subsidiaries work exclusively with the blueprints of the traditional products.

Finally, in three cases (all Italian, metalworking firms) it was argued that technology transfer was seldom received because 'the products are very simple'.

Other Technology Transfer Mechanisms in Subsidiaries

Table 12.24 summarises the different types of mechanisms used for the transfer of technology between the home firm and the subsidiary. Blueprints were used in all cases, although for firms operating in the chemical sector 'blue prints' refer to the formula of their products. On the other hand, the virtual non-existence of specific equipment for production and quality control in the subsidiaries is remarkable. Two of these firms use the home firm's laboratory for quality control of their products, which suggests a very low degree of local independence.

Associated with this characteristic is the importance of critical parts for the products, which was evidenced in 90 per cent of the metalworking firms of the sample. This reveals that the most complex technological components are still produced in the home firms or are purchased by firms in their home markets and set to Brazil. This maintains a continuing technological gap between both the home firm and the subsidiaries the industrial structures of both countries.[2]

In the chemical sector, the technological secret lies in the formulae which, as already seen, are developed in the countries of origin. Thus,

Table 12.25 Types of technology transferred through licensing

Sector	Type of technology product			
	Product technology	Product and process	Product, process and plant	Total
Mechanical	2	2	0	4
Chemical/Pharmaceutical	0	1	1	2
Electronic	0	2	0	2
Total	2	5	1	8

blueprints are the main technology transfer mechanisms. Subsidiaries receive inputs, considered as essential, from the home firm.

Technology Transfer Through Licensing

The transfer of technology is mainly in terms of products and process technology (Table 12.25). It is also clear that the transfer of technology is usually through 'packages' of product and process technology. This is often revealed by the licensor's concern about the product's quality which is partly dependent on the licensee's technological capacity. Thus, though formally only a transfer of product technology is envisaged, both parties are interested in making the productive process as reliable as possible. It must be remembered that most licensing is related to Brazilian companies' product range diversification strategies and, though the technological base might not be very different, recipient firms do not always have enough resources for reverse-engineering or the necessary training in process technology; therefore, the licensor may transfer its own process know-how. We found only two cases in which nothing more than product technology was transferred. These cases relate to foreign SMEs that adopt defensive strategies, as described earlier. Finally, there was one case of product, process and plant technology transfer. This case refers to a Japanese SME, from the plastic sector, that has developed a 'modular' productive system and therefore all facilities, process and product technologies are exactly equal to those used by the Japanese firm.

Table 12.26   Participation of human resources in the technology transfer

| | Type of transfer | | | | |
| | Continuous | | Concentrated | | Total |
Participation	No. of cases	Average time	No. of cases	Average time	no. of cases
Local technicians sent to SME	5	48 days[1]	3	45 days[1]	8
SMEs technicians sent to Brazil	2	30 days[1]	2	15 days[1]	4

Note:
1. Man days per year.

Human Resources in Technology Transfer Through Licensing

All recipient firms considered the participation of local technicians in the technology transfer as very significant and Table 12.26 presents the efforts made by both parties, the license and the licensor, in the technology transfer.

The technology transfer process was classified into two categories: 'continuous' and 'concentrated'. The latter category includes firms that at the beginning of the agreement made a concentrated effort to transfer the technology and then continued interacting very sporadically with the recipient. The transfer process is considered when the interaction between the parties is distributed in time and a permanent process of information exchange occurs through human resource flows between licensors and license.

In three cases the transfer process was concentrated: the Brazilian firm invested an average of 45 man days in the initial transfer effort. In only two of these cases was there reciprocity form the SME. In both instances one technician was sent to Brazil for 15 days. Five Brazilian firms maintained a more stable link with the foreign SMEs, sending technicians continuously to the supplier's plant. The average stay in the SME was 48 man day per year. Only two suppliers systematically sent technicians to control and update the recipient, the average stay being 30 man days per year.

Two other remarks can be made from our analysis: first the transfer effort is mainly conducted by the Brazilian recipient: and secondly, some SMEs licence their technology without even sending their technicians to the recipient firm! In four cases (50 per cent of the total

Table 12.27   Licensing technology transfer mechanisms

Sector	Blue-prints	Mechanisms, special equipment (no. of cases)	Critical components
Mechanical (4 firms)	4	0	1
Chem./Pharm. (2 firms)	2	0	1
Electronics (2 firms)	2	0	0
Total	8	0	2

sample) the SME had not sent technicians to the Brazilian firm.

Other Technology Transfer Mechanisms Used in Licensing

Table 12.27 shows that blueprints (manual and formulae) are universally used to transfer know-how in the technology transfer process. There were no cases of transfer of special equipment and in only two out of eight cases was there the transfer of critical parts. These two cases refer to very advanced technology products, for which there was no production capability in Brazil.

Direct Investment versus Licensing as Technology Transfer Mechanisms

Table 12.28 shows that SMEs involved in licensing received better evaluations than direct investors. The only point in which investors are regarded as being better is 'in the ability to meet the changing technological requirements of the subsidiary', which is an expected result. However, it is surprising that licensing SMEs receive a better evaluation in the 'readiness' and 'willingness' items. On the other hand, licensing SMEs are also those that receive the harshest criticisms. This criticism is made, in general, by large recipient firms that have several licence agreements and consider that SMEs have less capacity to transfer technology than large foreign firms. Buth that values obtained by the investors are in general lower, which suggest that these firms make less effort in structuring the technology transfer process.

Table 12.28   Recipient firms' evaluation of SMEs' capacity to transfer technology

Opinion	*Good* (per cent)	Subsidiary *Regular* (per cent)	*Poor* (per cent)	*Good* (per cent)	Licensee *Regular* (per cent)	*Poor* (per cent)
1 Experience in tech. transfer	50	50	0	57	29	14
2 Readiness/expedience of tech. transfer	63	37	0	71	29	0
3 Willingness to transfer secret know-how	37	63	0	57	29	14
4 Training capacity	50	50	0	57	29	14
5 Training capacity relationship	78	25	0	86	14	0
6 Capacity to update know-how	75	25	0	86	0	14
7 Ability to meet local firm's requirements	88	12	0	72	14	14
Total	64	36	0	71	20	9

12.5 TECHNOLOGICAL BEHAVIOUR OF THE SUBSIDIARIES

In order to analyse the strategies and technological behaviour of subsidiaries it is necessary to understand a number of sequential and interdependent decisions. These are:

- Original product and market strategy
- Product design adaptations
- Product updating strategy
- Production scale selection
- Engineering training.

Original Product and Market Strategy

The initial strategy adopted by the SMEs regarding the setting up of productive facilities in Brazil was to explore specific Brazilian market niches. As mentioned earlier, prior to investing in productive activities, SMEs had already studied the Brazilian economic and political environment so that the setting up of a plant rose from a clear choice of product and market. In all cases the products were already distributed in Brazil through local agents or sales offices. The selection of

Table 12.29 Diversification of product lines of the subsidiary relative to home firms

	More diversified in SME	Same	More diversified in Brazil
Mechanical	7	2	1[1]
Chemical	2	0	0
Total	9	2	1

Note:
1. This subsidiary produces more 'custom orders' and considers that in Brazil it can service more diversified markets than in the country of origin.

Table 12.30 Factors that determine product design changes

Factors	% of firms
Type of demand	50
Inputs	70
Labour force	30
Equipment	10

these products was made from the existing range of products in the home firm. Not unexpectedly, the diversification of product lines in Brazil, in the majority of the cases, was lower than that of the home firm (Table 12.29). In no case has a subsidiary introduced products developed specifically for Brazilian market conditions.

Product Design Adaptations

Product design modifications were made most frequently because of different inputs compared to the home economy (Table 12.30). From the qualitative point of view, all the firms in the sample had problems with the type of inputs available. In some cases these inputs did not exist in the Brazilian market or, if they existed, they did not always have the same specifications as those originally determined by the SME in its country of origin. It was also observed that the changes in product design were often related to the market strategy of the subsidiaries and, more specifically, to the exporting activity. Therefore, when the subsidiary was more orientated towards the local market, there were less restrictions for product design changes than when it was orientated towards the external market,[3] mainly because of quality standards set by the home firm. The import of critical components from the home firms (observed in Table 12.24) was a means by which the firm minimised the impact of local supply conditions on the product design in Brazil. From the quantitative point of view it was occasionally the case that the import could not be purchased in volumes appropriate for a small or medium firm. This issue is related to the high concentration levels found in some sectors producing basic inputs, as for example, steel. Under these circumstances, the subsidiaries tended to modify product designs using other inputs.

The nature of the local demand was also related to the diversification process. For example, the small scale of Brazilian consumer market leads to important changes in the product mix of chemical firms and in the scale of production and product diversification in the mechanical industry.

Product Updating Strategy

It was frequently found that subsidiaries, after entering into market niches as almost exclusive producers, soon started facing competition from Brazilian firms that copied their products. To some extent there was a lack of responsiveness to this situation. For example, when asked about the updating of locally manufactured products in relation to products manufactured in the home country, only three out of 12 firms stated that their products were similar to those produced by the parent firm. In other words, nine subsidiaries manufacture products that are not manufactured at present by the home firms and are of an older vintage – and, therefore, there has been no upgrading in response to local competition. There is, in consequence, a certain stability of product lines and a lack of a more systematic process of introduction of innovations and new products.

Selection of the Scale of Production

An analysis of the relative scale of production of the home and subsidiary plants is revealing (Table 12.31). All subsidiary plants were smaller and in 50 per cent of cases the Brazilian plant was 10 per cent of the scale of the home plant or less. This difference between plant sizes raises doubts as to the effectiveness of technology transfer. In addition, there are other factors that make this situation even more critical. The first factor is related to the market structure prevailing in the country, which may force the subsidiary to increase vertical inte-

Table 12.31 Relationship between volume of production of the subsidiary and the parent

Sector	Relation	More than 10 times smaller	Between 4 and 9 times smaller	Between 2 and 4 times smaller	Similar
Mechanical		6	3	1[1]	0
Chemical		1	1	0	0
Total		7	4	1	0

Note:
1. No information for one subsidiary.

Table 12.32 Degree of vertical integration of the subsidiary in relation to the SME

Sector	More vertically integrated than SME	Similar	Less vertically integrated than SME	Total
Mechanical	6	2	1	9[1]
Chemical	0	0	2	2
Total	6	2	3	11

Note:
1. No information for one subsidiary.

gration, manufacturing components and/or intermediate products which are usually purchased in the home country market (Table 12.32).

Another factor makes the product process more complex: local suppliers. As seen earlier, there are problems for the purchase of small volumes from these suppliers. Moreover, even when it is possible to purchase the desired amount, there are problems related to quality and terms of delivery (Table 12.33). Consequently, local productive process characteristics are quite different from home SMEs which, to some extent, is an obstacle for technological transfer.

The emerging hypothesis is that SMEs' subsidiaries manufacture locally-adapted products, with craftsmanship-based production systems. Process technology transfer refers to some specific production process operations, but not to the productive process structure as a whole. This picture raises doubts as to the effectiveness of the technology transfer process from foreign SMEs, at least in the way implemented in Brazil.

Table 12.33　Problems of subsidiaries related to suppliers

	Problems with suppliers		
Sector	Yes	No	Total
Mechanical	6	1	7[1]
Chemical	2	0	2
Total	8	1	9

Note:
1. Three subsidiaries gave no response.

Table 12.34　Subsidiaries' evaluation as to mastery of technology

	Technology is mastered	Technology is not mastered	Technology is being mastered	Total
Mechanical	6	3	1	10
Chemical	2	0	0	2
Total	8	3	1	12

Local Technological Capacity

The picture described above converges with the issue of 'technological mastery', that is, local technological capacity. When asked about the mastery of the technology transferred by the SME, the interviewed firms supplied the answers given in Table 12.34.

For a better understanding of these responses, it is necessary to reconsider the earlier analysis. We have observed that SME subsidiaries are very conservative regarding product lines, having introduced only a few innovations. In several cases, there is a gap between products manufactured in Brazil and those manufactured in the home firms. On the other hand, regarding the productive process, there is a craftsmanship-based pattern, hardly formalised, and labour-intensive. In this context, the answers in Table 12.34 suggest that mastery of the technology means the capacity to continue manufacturing the present product line with the present productive process. In other words, if the flow of information with the home firm were suspended, the subsidiary has autonomy to continue operating, within the restrictions mentioned above. This means that there was an early flow of technology from the SME to the subsidiary, the intensity of which decreased over time. It also means that local technological capacity was created, although limited

Table 12.35 Number of employees involved in technological matters per firm

| Sector | No. of Employees involved | | | Total |
	1–5	5–10	More than 10	
Mechanical	9	1	0	10
Chemical	2	0	0	2
Total	11	1	0	12

in scope. Two of the subsidiaries mentioned that they had the capacity to product new products based on the technology transferred by the SME, and they had already done so. These two cases, notwithstanding, the number of employees involved in each firm with technological matters was small, revealing a limited capacity of autonomous technological production (Table 12.35). The lack of a fundamental technological capacity is also shown by the fact that no firm calculated R&D activities and the number of employees mentioned in Table 12.34 includes technicians and engineers who were partly or wholly devoted to engineering activities.

12.6 LICENSING AGREEMENTS AND LICENSEE'S STRATEGY

Regarding licensees, it is not possible, within the framework of this study, to discuss their technological strategies as a whole. The focus of this study was orientated towards a segment of the technological path of these firms, which represents the period in which the technology transfer from the selected SME took place. As already observed, all licensees included in the sample had already participated in formal technology transfer processes, both through joint ventures and through other licensing agreements before the specific agreements around which the interviews were conducted. Moreover, with the exception of one firm, the recipients considered that they had a greater diversification than the foreign SMEs. Nevertheless, although the licensing agreement with the SME was just one part of the technological strategy of the Brazilian licensee, there is some information that allows us to understand more clearly the use that these Brazilian firms make of the technology transfer process.

The first important issue is that the significance of licensing is greater for smaller and medium-sized Brazilian firms than for larger firms. The latter were involved with foreign SMEs within the compulsory and defensive strategies defined above. Given these conditions, the licensed products were not of priority in the market strategy of these firms, and regarding their investing alternatives, only a small effort was put into mastering the technology transferred. These larger firms were included in the technology transfer process in a 'concentrated' way, as discussed earlier. Little effort was placed in encouraging a continuous cycle of transfer. In the case of small-and medium-sized Brazilian firms, the licensing issue assumes a different form, turning into a key element in the technological strategy of these five firms. This point is reflected in the considerable efforts toward interaction with the licensing SMEs: these firms adopted 'continuous' technology transfer processes, which represented a great investment for firms of this size. This investment is justified as long as the sale of the products manufactured under the licence contributes to the economic and financial development of the recipient. In three out of five such cases interviewed, the technology is already mastered and these firms not only consider themselves able to lead new products from the same technology, but also to transfer this technology to other firms. The other two are undergoing an assimilation process, but expected this to be completed in the near future. In addition, in contradistinction to the SME subsidiaries discussed above, the products involved in the technology transfer are presently being manufactured by the foreign SME.

The number of employees devoted to technological activities is relatively larger for small- and medium-sized firms as compared to SME subsidiaries. Larger Brazilian firms came out even better in this comparison (Table 12.36). It can thus, be hypothesised that the intensity of the technology flow between foreign SMEs and Brazilian firms is larger in the case of licensing than in the case of subsidiaries.

Table 12.36 Number of employees involved in the technology issued by firms

No. of employees	0–5	5–10	10–25	25–50	more than 50
No. of firms	1[1]	3	1	1	1[2]

Notes:
1. Four technicians and engineers.
2. 120 technicians and engineers.

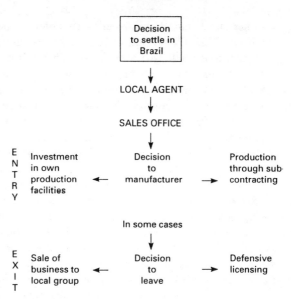

Figure 12.1   SME investment cycles in Brazil

12.7   SME CONTRIBUTION TO TECHNOLOGY DEVELOPMENT IN BRAZIL

The cases analysed above permit us to identify a sequence of stages that characterise the investment cycle of SMEs in Brazil. The entry process is initiated through the selection of a local agent to represent the SMEs' interests or even through the creation of a sales office. In some cases, this second option follows the former. In this phase, the products manufactured by the SME are imported and the locally-installed structure distributes the products and provides technical assistance. There is investment in salespeople and technicians. In this period, where appropriate, the SME gathers information related to the decision to set up a local plant: demand structure, competition characteristics, inputs and labour force issues, finance possibilities, in all the context of political, economic and social factoring, not especially the country's growth potential.

The decision to produce locally is finally triggered by a group of factors involving local macroeconomic conditions, a SME's international market strategy and various local conditions. In relation to this last matter, a critical decision seems related to subcontracting, which in practice was either 0 per cent or 100 per cent. That is, there were SMEs that invested in their own productive facilities, with different vertical integration levels, and there were SMEs that decided to sub-contract local firms to manufacture the products under the SMEs super-vision, and under the SMEs trademark. Following the decision to produce locally, there is a certain stabilisation of product lines and an upsurge of competition from local firms, a great number of which are created by former employees from subsidiaries (spin-offs). This fact was most evident in the case of follower firms in the metalworking sector. The upsurge of local competition, in some cases induced an 'exit' by the SME, although other factors were frequently involved. The exit of four SMEs can be explored. Three of them concluded that local demand for the type of product they manufactured was being saturated. Two abandoned the country and established a licensing agreement with a firm which was formerly subcontracted to manufacture their products (defensive licensing); and the third reduced its structure to a mini-mum, and started subcontracting. In the fourth case, a subsidiary was sold to a local group, because of restructuring in the parent company.

As regards two subsidiaries interviewed, there is a common pattern. In general, investments have been reduced due to political, economic and social uncertainties in Brazil. Some subsidiaries viewed the pol-itical and social environment (in the late 1950s) as threatening, while others underlined the lack of clear rules for foreign capital as the main obstacle to their activities. As these macroconditions became more appropriate, subsidiaries tend to adopt diversification strategies, using the present productive base to product new products for new markets, with the same basic technology. The priority was the local market, with only one subsidiary having the intention of participating in foreign markets in the near future.

The Dynamics of Licensing Agreements

The case studies reveal that the role of licensing SMEs, in contrast to those that set up subsidiaries, is generally passive. This attitude is such that Brazilian firms frequently alter their technology transfer strategies, give up interaction with SMEs, and seek licensing with larger foreign firms. Local firms observed that SMEs had a lack of information and knowledge on Brazilian and international markets; they lacked interest in obtaining such information; and often they allocated only a few resources to the relationship with Brazilian companies. Under these conditions, the initiative for the technology transfer basically depends on the Brazilian firm. So long as the latter identify and explore the potential of this process, the results can be quite positive. The licensees' evaluation of SMEs discussed earlier supports this point, especially when the recipient is a small- or medium-sized firm in the area of new technologies.

12.8 FINAL REMARKS

In the Brazilian industrial development process policies and programmes are rarely orientated toward SMEs. Thus all foreign SME involvement both through direct investment or licensing agreements were induced by the (Brazilian and foreign) manufacturing sector itself.

In the case of subsidiaries, the technology transfer of specific products and critical parts for the productive process gave rise not only to local production but to some spin-offs. This transfer process, limited in scope and time, increasingly requires a renewal which (in the late 1980s) was being postponed by a number of factors, both external and internal to the firm. The flexibility and mobility of SMEs makes it difficult to forecast the future duration of subsidiaries. Licensing agreements, intrinsically limited in scope and time, are an interesting alternative for the development of local technological capacities. It is possible to elaborate policy measures and programmes that can best exploit the technological reservoirs that foreign SMEs possess. It is not possible to go into great detail, but for example, the technology transfer process could be optimised in Brazil by encouraging (a) licensing from SMEs in high-technology sectors, (the effectiveness of the transfer being greater when the recipient is also a SME), and (b) direct investment by SMEs in less technologically advanced sectors where local capacity does not exist, but which would be stimulated by the presence of a foreign company 'leading the way'.

Notes

1. For the purpose of simplification, we shall treat the eight cases as if they all were licensing agreements.
2. At the same time, the importance of critical components for the home firm is a mechanism that results in the payment of royalties or fees to the SME, and can even conceal overpricing.
3. It is necessary to mention that five subsidiaries do not export, three export 2 per cent or less and the other two export.

13 The Case of India

Ashok V. Desai

13.1 INTRODUCTION

This chapter reviews and analyses the results of a survey of 24 cases of technology imports into India, the agreements for which were approved by the Government of India between 1980 and 1985. The survey was carried out as a part of an international project on technology transfer by small and medium enterprises organised by the Centro de Estudios de Desarrollo y Relaciones Economicas Internationales (CEDREI) of Argentina.

The sample of the present survey differs slightly from the Indian sample incorporated into the CEDREI project. The present sample went through three filters. First, we started with a list of technology import agreements compiled by the India Investment Centre. From this list, our colleagues doing surveys in the industrial countries chose cases in which the technology supplier could be traced. Based on their selection, we contacted the corresponding technology importers, and interviewed as many as possible, excluding only those that could not be traced, or were not prepared to give information or were in inconvenient locations. We interviewed about 40 per cent of the firms that were on the lists.

The CEDREI sample went through a fourth filter: it excluded the cases where the technology supplier was not an SME or where the technology involved was not industrial. The reason was that the CEDREI project aimed to 'bring up, explore or formulate hypotheses about the distinct effects, or circumstances, or other characteristics, of technology transfers conducted by smaller firms'. In the India survey, however, we found ourselves handicapped in following this objective. For we found that a significant proportion of Indian firms had either a vague or an inaccurate impression of the size of the technology supplier (and by and large tended to err on the higher side in reporting their size). And they were equally vague about whether the fact that the technology supplier was an SME had a favourable or an unfavourable effect: 11 of the 24 firms though it had a good effect (and one of them was

374

actually collaborating with a large firm), three thought it had a bad effect, five were neutral and five did not know.

It is, of course, possible that SMEs have specific effects as technology suppliers irrespective of the level of knowledge about them amongst the buyers of technology from them. If that knowledge was poor, however, information or opinions obtained from the buyers could not be used to test hypotheses about the effects of SMEs. Hence we inserted into our data, which otherwise consist entirely of information given by Indian firms, data on the actual employment by SMEs, and explored whether their size was associated with the rest of our variables. For the rest, we decided to leave those hypotheses to be tested against the total data obtained by CEDREI, and to concentrate on the characteristics of the Indian firms and their consequences. For this purpose, it made no difference whether the technology supplier was an SME or not, so we retained the cases where it was not.

Our sample is not representative of the population of technology imports in a number of respects. Large government firms are not represented in our sample at all, and large private firms are underrepresented. Engineering firms are overrepresented, and chemical and almost all other kinds of firms underrepresented. US, German and Japanese technology suppliers are underrepresented, and British and Canadian are overrepresented (thanks largely to our able colleagues in those countries).

In view of the small size and unrepresentativeness of the sample, we confined ourselves to simple tabulations to draw conclusions; we avoided regressions because the precision of their results would have been spurious and misleading. The credibility that the sample may have is due to the way its results fit into the picture of industrial growth in India that has begun to emerge from the studies made in the 1980s.

We begin by describing the industrial structure in terms of the major types of firms in section 13.2, and the changes in it over the last three decades in section 13.3. Section 13.4 traces the emergence of domestic sources of initial technology (i.e. technology required by new firms), and its effect on technology imports. In section 13.5, we describe inter-firm differences in access to foreign technology and in skills of adaptation to policy. In section 13.6, we group the firms on the basis of their management and on the technological distance between their previous specialisation and the current import of technology, and explore the effects of these two variables on technology transfer. Section 13.7 turns to the effects of trade policy. In section 13.8 we investigate the influence of the size of the technology supplier on technology transfer. In section 13.9 we conclude by summarising the arguments.

13.2   GROUPS AND SEQUENCES

To understand changes in the industrial structure it is necessary to start with a conceptual classification of firms. Unfortunately, empirical classifications never match conceptual schema, and one has to make do with approximations. Let us first begin with a conceptual grouping of firms, and then see what the known facts imply in terms of that classification.

The commonest type of firm in India – as in many other developing countries – is what we would call a *personal firm*. It would normally have a central person, a majority owner. Most of the firms of this type are started by a single man. As he grows older he would take in his sons, turning it into a patriarchal firm. When he dies his sons may carry it on, turning it into a partnership (although one brother – usually the eldest – would normally dominate; and the firm may be divided up by the brothers, if the father has not done so in his lifetime and given each son his own fiefdom). A variant that has become more common in recent times is a firm started by a group of unrelated friends, particularly men who have studied or worked together. But as they grow older, their families will begin to react upon the firm, which will tend to be dominated by a single man or will split. The essential feature of this type of firm is dominance by a man or men, often male members of a family. And the reason to distinguish this type of firm lies in its vulnerability to the life cycle of the dominant man or men – the loss of leadership as they age, the crises that arise at the times of their sickness or death, the difficulties of attracting and retaining professionals in a firm where some men wield power because of their kinship or friendship. Personal firms are often proprietorships or partnerships, formal or informal. But in recent years the income tax authorities have been increasingly tough with such traditional forms of organisation, so many growing personal firms adopt the legal form of a *private limited company*. This is in all essential features a partnership, except that the liability of the partners is limited to the capital they have paid into the firm. Legally, a private limited company has an obligation to keep accounts in a certain form and to get them audited. The government insists that (except in the case of outright purchase of blueprints) payments for technology imports must be spread out over a period of time. A personal firm, when it imports technology, would have to convince the technology supplier that it was stable enough to make payments over such a period. So it will normally have been incorporated, so that a few years' audited accounts can be shown to the technology supplier. If he invests in it, it will almost certainly have been incorporated.

The personal firm may be contracted with the *affiliate* of a conglomerate group; although most conglomerates have grown out of personal firms and there is a continum of variation between them. The affiliate would normally be a large firm; if it is small, its management would have been built up by people who have worked in large firms. Thus there would be a more or less professional management, and administration would be subject to some rules – a precondition for a professional to feel at home. Almost all conglomerates are headed by a patriarch and are often dominated by his family; but the size of the conglomerates ensures that family members are spread rather thin. The management has to be in the hands of a professional bureaucracy. This corps of professionals harbours the potential for technology absorption and innovation, although the potential of course varies considerably according to the quality and cohension of the management. Affiliates, once they grow beyond a certain size, will issue shares to the public and become *public limited companies* – although all conglomerates include a sprinkling of private limited companies. We have a number of such affiliates in our sample: for instance, Garlick Engineering of the Empire Group, Tractors India of the Larsen and Toubro Group, Sunco Machines of the TVS Group, and BPL Systems and Projects of the BPL Group. Garlick, L&T and BPL started under foreign ownership, but were under Indian control by the 1960s.

Subsidiaries of foreign firms were once easy to define and distinguish, but their definition had become rather hazy since the Foreign Exchange Regulation Act (FERA) of 1973, under which many foreign firms reduced their shareholding to 40 per cent or below in order to escape the industrial licensing restrictions levied on companies in which the foreign share exceeded 40 per cent. Now the shareholding tells one nothing about control; a company in which a foreign investor has 40 per cent equity may be a subsidiary, or a joint venture, or an affiliate of an Indian group, or a personal firm. However, the ownership of a subsidiary will be controlled by the foreign company by dispersing the ownership of the shares it does not own in such a way that its control is not threatened; and its management will be controlled by the appointment of directors and the managing director from amongst its professional employees (some of whom may be foreigners). Most subsidiaries which diluted the shareholding of their parent companies to 40 per cent after FERA did so by issuing shares to the public; they have thus become public limited companies, even if they were not before. In our sample, Ashok Leyland was a subsidiary of Leyland Motors of Britain which was then bought by the Hindujas, an Indian business house located in London. Western Thompson India is a subsidiary of Western Thompson of Britain. Both are public limited companies. All the four private limited companies with foreign investment – Fairbanks Morse (India), Eimco Elecon, Eastern Electrolyser Corporation, and FRC Composites India – are more or less personal firms in which foreign technology suppliers have taken a minority share.

Large public enterprises are distinguished from small ones by their political and economic clout. There are only a few of them; for instance, Steel Authority of India Limited (SAIL), Bharat Heavy Electricals Limited (BHEL), Oil and Natural Gas Commission (ONGC), and Indian Drugs and Pharmaceuticals Limited (IDPL). Being big and strategic, they are under close control of the central Government. They are well protected from competition from abroad as well as at home, and can freely run at a loss. Their applications for technology imports generally take a special fast track. None of them figures in our sample.

Small public enterprises may belong to either the central government or the state governments. Their losses, too, are borne by the governments that own them. But the state governments cannot and the central government usually would not manipulate trade restrictions and industrial licensing to insulate them entirely from competition; and they would not be allowed to grow irrespective of their economic performance. We have two in our sample: Bharat Process and Mechanical Engineers is an old and decrepit British firm taken over by the central Government to prevent its closure, and Meltron is an electronics subsidiary of the Maharashtra government.

13.3   CHANGES IN INDUSTRIAL STRUCTURE

The industrial structure in India has undergone two major changes in the last three decades. The first is the expansion of the public sector, which virtually did not exist in the 1950s and which now produces above 40 per cent of the industrial output with 60 per cent of the industrial capital. In terms of our grouping, both large and small public enterprises have gained. The growth of large enterprises is well documented, and they have a monopoly of or dominant positions in a number of industries, notably minerals, metals, oil, fertilisers and cars. Much less is known about the small ones; for state government enterprises, even the numbers are not precisely known, let alone the industries they are in and their market shares. Our general impression (based on electronics, pharmaceuticals and vehicles, three industries in which networks of state government enterprises were sought to be built up) is that their market shares are small and have been falling with the liberalisation in the 1980s.

The second major change is the gains made by small private firms at the expense of the big ones – in terms of our grouping, by personal firms at the expense of affiliates and subsidiaries. This shift is more controversial, but the evidence in its favour has been accumulating. In a wide range of industries, a large number of small firms emerged between 1963–4 and 1978–9, and concentration ratios fell with their emergence (Desai, 1985a). The evidence for all industry has been reviewed by Little, Majumdar and Page (1987) and Desai and Taneja (1989). The ambiguity arises from the fact that the share of unregistered firms in industrial output (i.e. of firms with fewer than 50 workers with power and fewer than 100 workers without power) shows no rise according to national accounts. The output estimates for these firms are very approximate and conservative, and may conceal a rise in their share. But more likely, it is the somewhat larger small firms – employing 50–500 workers – that have gained. Their capital – output ratios have been consistently lower than those of both smaller and larger firms, and their profitability (calculated as the difference between their value added and wages, divided by invested capital) higher. Let us say that it is the larger amongst the small firms that have grown faster than the rest.

The most important general reason for their faster growth is lower wages. Productivity does rise with size, but not as much as wages; consequently, wages costs per unit are higher in larger firms. This applies to both private and public sector firms. But the large public enterprises are well protected from competition, whereas larger private firms are not; so the latter – both affiliates and subsidiaries – have been losing ground. There are two other reasons, which, however, apply only to certain industries. One is official favours for small firms – notably exemptions from or rebates on excise taxes, which were important particularly in the textile industry. (But they were not the only form of discrimination against large textile firms see Lall, 1987 for the formidable batter of instruments used.) The other is higher capital – output ratios, and implicitly, poorer capital utilisation in larger firms. This is more a disease of public enterprises – and the biggest and most capital-intensive of them are in industries like metals and chemicals where they do not compete with small firms.

The wide wage differentials are attributed to trade union pressure, but with so many workers earning much lower wages outside indus- try, trade union pressure by itself would not have pushed up wages in large firms without active support from the government. The support has been given in two forms. One is the official adjudication machin- ery. The other is laws against closure and against dismissal of workers.

The adjudication machinery has consistently pushed up wages in large firms on the grounds of their 'ability to pay'. This was well described by Markensten (1972). In the 1970s and 1980s, as large firms began to succumb to the competition of small firms, the adjudication machinery became less effective in forcing them to raise wages. Its pressure was replaced in a few areas by new, militant trade unions. Despite them, however, the wage differentials have not widened in the last 15 years. But they have persisted undiminished. Although small firms are also subject to trade union pressure in the older industrial cities, trade unions cannot penetrate them effectively because of the threat of closure. Small firms are less capital-intensive, and are often only a small part of the total business of their owners. Some state governments have passed laws against the closure of firms, and pro- vided for the takeover without compensation of firms that close down. Quite a few sick large firms do not close down because of these laws, but the laws are ineffective against small firms because the state govern- ments cannot afford to take over hordes of them.

Small firms have grown not simply by competing against large firms but also by working for them. The wage differentials make it cheaper for large firms to buy components – and often fully finished goods – from small firms. This process of vertical disintegration has been docu- mented for Swedish firms in India by Jansson (1982). It did not occur in all industries. In pharmaceuticals, for instance, large firms were forced to go into bulk drug manufacture and hence into vertical integration (and also to sell half of their bulk drug output to small formulators) by government orders. In chemical industries, the scope for vertical disintegration was limited. But in engineering, the growth of small firms fed upon vertical disintegration in large firms, which were their most important customers (Desai and Taneja, 1989).

Let us now see how far the results of the present survey conform to the picture of dynamic competition we have painted. As we said earlier, our classification cannot be applied directly and unequivocally to firms. The difference between a personal firm and an affiliate of a conglom- erate is one of degree rather than of kind: family firms, as they multi- ply, turn into conglomerates. Similarly, a firm with foreign investment

Table 13.1   Characteristics of sample firms related to their age

	Date of establishment			(No. of firms) Total
	Up to 1970	1971–80	After 1980	
Total no. of firms	11	8	5	24
1.1 Type of firm (our guess)				
Personal firms	5	5	4	14
Affiliates	3	2	1	6
Subsidiaries	2			2
Small public enterprises	1	1		2
1.2 Legal form				
Private limited companies	3	7	5	15
Wholly Indian	2	4	3	9
With foreign investment[a]	1	3	2	6
Public limited companies	7			7
Wholly Indian	5			5
With foreign investment[a]	2			2
Government firms				
Owned by Centre	1			1
Owned by a state		1		1
1.3 Employment				
Up to 50 workers	2	2	3	7
51–200		4	1	5
201–800	3	2	1	6
Over 800	6			6
1.4 Annual average growth rate of sales, last 5 years				
0 or less	1	1	1	3
1–10	3	4	3	10
Over 10	3	1	1	5
Not known	4	2		6
1.5 Suppliers' market structure				
Concentrated	3	4	3	9
Competitive	8	4	2	15
1.6 Buyers' market structure				
Concentrated	2	2	3	7
Competitive	9	6	2	17
1.7 Market shares – principal product				
Up to 25 per cent	3	2	2	7
26–50 per cent	2	3	1	6
51–99 per cent	4	1		5

continued on p. 382

Table 13.1   continued

	Date of establishment			(No. of firms) Total
	Up to 1970	1971–80	After 1980	
100 per cent		2	2	4
Not known	2			2
Total number of firms	11	8	5	24

	1.8 Market shares – all products			
Up to 25 per cent	10	6	2	18
26–50 per cent	2	5	2	9
51–99 per cent	5	2		7
100 per cent	2	3	2	7
Total	23	17	6	46

	1.9 Reasons for importing technology			
Strengthening competitive position	5	2		7
Process improvement	1			1
Reaction to new entry		1		1
Import substitution	1	1	2	4
Diversification	4	3	3	10
Reaction to customer requirements		1		1

	1.10 Introduction of new product			
New product introduced	3	3	4	10
Product already in the market	8	6		14

Note:
^a Not necessarily from the current technology supplier.

may be a subsidiary, a personal firm, or an affiliate. So in Table 13.1 we give our guesses about the character of firms, together with a more unequivocal, legal classification of the firms, and divide them into groups based on the age of the firm which imported technology (and not the age of its parent firm, or of the leading firm in the conglomerate to which it belongs). The results are very clear: affiliates and subsidiaries are relatively older, whilst personal firms are relatively newer (1.1). The legal classification is equally explicit: public limited companies, such as affiliates and subsidiaries tend to be, are relatively older, whilst private limited companies, which is the form personal firms which import technology tend to take are relatively newer (1.2). The largest firms are all old, and the newer firms are relatively small (1.3). This is consistent with the hypothesis that small firms gained at the expenses of large firms, but could also be due to the fact that the older firms had more time to grow.

The firms' view of their markets is rather more ambiguous. If our view of small and new firms winning in competition against old and large firms is correct, then the older firms should feel the pinch of competition. So apparently they do; eight of the 11 firms founded before 1970 said they faced a competitive market structure; the proportion is distinctly lower for newer firms (1.5). But market-structure distributions do not show them to be less concentrated for older than for newer firms.

The defensive posture of old firms in competition is more evident in the reasons they gave for importing technology. Five of the 11 firms founded before 1970 imported technology to improve their competitive position, and one for process improvement. Two out of the nine firms founded in 1971–80 gave these reasons, and none of the newest firms (1.9). Also, eight of the 11 oldest firms imported technology in respect of a product that was already being produced in India; whereas all of the newest firms introduced new products (1.10).

13.4 SOURCES OF INITIAL TECHNOLOGY

All industrial firms need technology to start with. The technology may be very simple: for instance, a cold storage for potatoes may be capable of operation by an illiterate worker. But the side-ranging shift from large to small firms such as we have described in section 13.3 must involve the application of a larger number of packages of initial technology. Where did these packages come from?

Our recent survey of small and medium enterprises enquired into the sources of technology (Desai and Taneja, 1989). 80 per cent of the firms were engineering and which were hence in a technology-intensive industry; but a formal transfer of technology was exceptional. A majority of the owners said that they had either 'invented' the technology or imitated it; in other words, technology had simply diffused through trained or educated people. The next most important answer was that they had got it from large firms. Even there the purchase of technology was quite uncommon; generally, the large firms gave technical assistance to their suppliers and subcontractors. A small number of respondents said they got the technology from equipment suppliers. Only 5 per cent had imported technology.

Thus the stock of technology earlier imported by large firms was the pool from which the technology required for the emergence of small firms was drawn. Almost all the technology was acquired without payment. Professional employees of large firms ('technological entrepreneurs') started their own firms and took with them the technology they had learned in the large firms. (But it was unusual for such professionals to take employment in small firms.) Large firms passed on to small ones the technology required to produce the components they bought. They also gave technology with the equipment they sold to small firms.

The new mechanisms of free transfer of technology within the country reduced the demand for technology imports and the date when this reduction took place can be tentatively, fixed at 1967 thanks to Cooper (1988). He ran regressions of the number of technology import agreements between India and the Benelux on the Indian index of industrial production, and found that the slope (which measures the technology import-intensity of increases in industrial production) fell from 0.92 in 1953–66 to 0.29 in 1967–80. Although he has not published his results of similar regressions for total technology imports, they confirm the Benelux results.

Cooper explained the fall in terms of the import restrictions on technology introduced in 1965–8. They were:

(a) Royalty ceilings were prescribed for various industries
(b) The standard permitted duration of agreements was reduced from 10 to 5 years; renewals were not allowed unless they involved more advanced or different technology
(c) Export restrictions were allowed only to countries where the technology supplier had subsidiaries, affiliates or licencees
(d) The use of the technology supplier's trade mark in India was not allowed (patent protection was significantly weakened by the Patent Act of 1971)
(e) No restrictions were allowed on the technology importer's right to sell or sublicense the technology (National Council of Applied Economic research, 1971).

I attributed the fall in the demand for imported technology to a fall in the demand price of technology (Desai, 1988). The reasoning was that as the number of firms in an industry increased, profits would be divided up amongst a larger number of firms. As long as technology imports had some overhead costs, the number of firms that could afford to import technology would fall. I also argued that as competition in Indian industry intensified, the income from royalties on technology sold to a single firm had become less certain, foreign firms were inclined to take a larger proportion of the price of technology in the form of fixed payments, and thus to increase the overhead costs of imported technology.

This explanation is still broadly correct, but the underlying assumption that the emergence of small firms left total industry profits unchanged was wrong. The small firms came up because of lower wages and higher profits, so we cannot assume that the profits per firm would be lower, leading to lower demand for technology. The fall in technology imports was more certainly due to the rise in the supply of costless domestic technology, and less to the new firms' lower capacity to pay.

Did the tightening of the technology import policies in the late 1960s have no effect on technology imports? It probably did, but more by increasing transaction costs, delays, and uncertainty than by directly cutting down the costs. It was shown in Desai (1988) that royalties approved on imported technologies did not go down at all between 1951–67 and 1977–80, whilst lump-sum payments went up enormously. The Government did not manage to reduce the cost of technology, so the fall in technology imports cannot be attributed to lower supply at the lower price. But after 1967, the responses of the Government to technology import applications were more varied, and (in the eyes of the prospective technology suppliers and buyers) more arbitrary. In response to an application, the Government may ask the Indian firm to start doing R&D, shift from a lump-sum payment to a royalty, reject an export restriction, accept an export obligation, or accept a combination of such conditions. An applicant never knew what the reaction of the Government would be, and why it reacted in a particular fashion; and often it could get the Government to change its mind by reapplying. Thunman's description of the Swedchem case is typical of the hassles generally faced by technology importers (Thunman, 1988, pp. 87–107). That is how India came to acquire a reputation for having an impossible bureaucracy, which according to the Indo – EC survey of technology imports was the biggest barrier in the eyes of technology suppliers (Hoffman *et al.*, 1985). It is a reputation the government still has to live down despite the liberalisation after 1984.

13.5   THE BLESSINGS OF OLD AGE

For a foreign firm the Indian bureaucracy was an impossible one; but for an Indian firm it had to be lived with. If the Government said a technology importer must do R&D, the Indian firm would set up a show-piece R&D unit. If the Government said only new technology could be imported, the firm dressed up the application to show that the technology related to 'new' products. And – exceptionally and with great delays – the firms brought political pressure to bear on particularly obstructive policies and emasculated them – for instance, the Government's attempt to force firms to buy technology from its laboratories was given up in 1975, whilst in the early 1980s it relaxed its definition of 'new' technology to permit modernisation.

In exerting political pressure as well as in learning to get around policy obstacles, the older and larger firms had more experience and expertise, so many small firms that managed to import technology were their affiliates. Policy made import of technology generally difficult, but most so for the independent small firm.

The older and larger firms also had a better choice of technology suppliers. With a longer history and an established position in India's protected market, they were better known abroad (or more information could be obtained about them). They also often had imported technology before, and therefore had a record of payments and business dealings which could be checked. Our survey, which covers only accomplished technology imports (except for one, where the Indian firm backed out because it would have had to buy the intermediate product from a monopoly Government firm), can throw little light on the vicissitudes of firms trying to import technology. But it furnished some evidence on the supply of technology to older and newer firms (Table 13.2).

Thus, there were six cases in which the Indian firm had a prior relationship with the technology supplier (2.1). In three cases of prior acquaintance, the Indian firm was founded before 1970. One was the renewal in the 1970s of an agreement which dated earlier. The fifth was a company dating back to the 1950s which had set up a subsidiary in the 1970s to produce equipment in collaboration with its erstwhile supplier. The sixth was a company set up in the 1980s by an import agent of long standing. Thus all the prior relationships that led to the import of technology were of long duration, and they were available only to the older firms.

Apart from the three cases of import agency, six of the older firms had chosen the technology supplier for its prestige (2.2). Two of the

Table 13.2   Technology buyer's information about technology supplier

	Date of establishment			No. of firms Total
	Up to 1970	1971–80	After 1980	
Total no. of firms	11	8	5	24
2.1 Prior relationship				
Personal acquaintance	3		1	4
Technology supplier recommended by customer		3		3
Renewal of agreement	1	1		2
Technology buyer used equipment made by supplier			1	1
None	7	4	3	14
2.2 Choice of technology supplier				
Agency relationship	2		1	3
Prestige of technology supplier	6	2		8
Technology supplier an exporter to India	2	2	1	5
Technology supplier offered a better deal	1	2	1	4
Grounds not known		2	2	4
2.3 Country of technology supplier				
United Kingdom	8	3	1	12
Canada	1	2	3	6
United States		2	1	3
West Germany	1	1		2
France	1			1
2.4 Sales of technology supplier				
Up to $30 million	1	6	3	10
Over $30 million	5	1		6
Not known to Indian firm	5	1	2	8
2.5 Employment of technology supplier				
Up to 200 workers	1	2	2	5
201–400 workers	4	2	1	7
Over 400 workers	3	2	1	6
Not known to Indian firm	3	2	1	6
2.6 Employment of technology supplier – actual figures				
Up to 200 workers	5	2	3	10
201–400 workers	2	2	1	5
Over 400 workers	4	3	1	8

continued on p. 386

Table 13.2   continued

	Date of establishment			No. of firms Total
	Up to 1970	1971–80	After 1980	
Total no. of firms	11	8	5	24
2.7 Domestic market share of technology supplier				
1–40 per cent	2	3	4	9
Over 40 per cent	3	1		4
Not known to Indian firm	6	4	1	11
2.8 Technology supplier's position in his domestic market				
Leader	8	6	2	16
Non-leader	3	2	2	7
Not known to Indian firm			1	1
2.9 International investment and technology transfer				
Negligible	1	3	1	5
Some	4	3	2	9
Much	3	1	1	5
Not known to Indian firm	3	1	1	5
2.10 Ratio of technology supplier's to technology buyer's sales				
3 or less	2	2		4
4–10	5	2	3	10
Over 10	1	4	2	7
Not known to Indian firm	3			3
2.11 Relative diversification				
Technology supplier more diversified	3	3	1	7
Buyer more diversified	6	4	1	11
Both about the same		1	2	3
Not known to Indian firm	2		1	3

eight 'middle-aged' firms founded in 1971–80 had chosen on the basis
of prestige, and none of the newest firms. Since every technology importer
would like to have a 'prestigious' technology supplier, this distribution
is based, not on the Indian firms' preferences, but on the technology
suppliers'; prestigious technology suppliers preferred the older and more
established firms. Also, two of the middle-aged firms and one of the
newer firms said that the technology supplier offered them a better
deal. In other words, they had obtained a number of offers and hence
made a search, which only one of the older firms claimed they had.

This goes back to an earlier difference of interpretation. The NCAER – ICRIER survey showed that 70 per cent of Indian firms that imported technology had approached more than one potential supplier, and that 36 per cent had approached more than three (Alam 1988, p. 138). Scott-Kemmis and Bell (1988, p. 41) were inclined to think on the basis of such evidence that Indian firms had considerable experience in negotiation and bargaining over technology. My view was that the large number of unsuccessful initiatives by Indian firms was the result of a large number of small firms looking for and not finding cheap technology abroad (Desai, 1988, p. 19). Clearly, there are large and old Indian firms which not only have experience in negotiating technology imports but have more technology on offer to them than they can use; at the other end there are unknown small firms which have to scrounge around for technology.

There are other indications of older Indian firms getting better or bigger technology suppliers. The older firms had more technology suppliers with sales over $30 million; the newer firms had smaller technology suppliers (2.4). This point is reinforced by employment figures (2.5). The older firms had more technology suppliers with a domestic market share over 40 per cent (2.7), more with a leading position in their domestic markets (2.8), and more with experience of foreign investment and technology transfer (2.9). Their sales of products under collaboration were larger relatively to those of the technology supplier – though still considerably smaller than the supplier's in general (2.10). However, some caution is warranted about this set of conclusions, because the Indian firms' knowledge about their technology suppliers is modest and often inaccurate. For comparison, we have given the technology suppliers' employment figures as given by themselves (2.5). They certainly weaken the impression, arising from the figures given by the Indian firms, that the older Indian firms collaborated with the larger technology suppliers. The difference between 2.5 and 2.6 could be due to ignorance by the Indian firms about their technology suppliers; or it could be due to the fact that in large firms, the person we interviewed was not always the one who dealt with and knew about the particular technology imports; or, finally, it could be due to confusion between the firm that was the immediate supplier of technology and its parent firm that might have dealt with the Indian firm. We have not been able to sort out which of these is the most important reason.

13.6   TECHNOLOGY ACQUISITION AND ABSORPTION

We now come to more difficult questions: those relating to technology absorption and dynamism. They are important to policy, which has tried actively and unsuccessfully to impart technological dynamism to Indian industry. At the same time, the use and production of technology are hidden inside firms, and we know little about them.

The most important contribution on this subject is that of Scott-Kemmis and Bell (1988). They attribute the low achievement of Indian industry to the modest level of technological ambition of Indian entrepreneurs and managers. This is the kind of social/psychological argument that leaves economists unsatisfied – as it does the authors themselves. They point to the need for further enquiry into the impact of technology import policy on the one hand, and into the structure of Indian industry on the other.

We have described the changes in the industrial structure in this chapter, and we think that they have an important bearing on technology generation and absorption. Technology absorption and innovation are closely allied activities, and both require that a corps of professionals – professionals in technology as well as management – work together for years on the problems of a single firm. The personal firm does not provide the right milieu for such sustained cooperative activity. The personal firm, which is subject to the arbitrariness of the owner and the instability arising from his life cycle, provides a poor home for the professional: whilst many professionals start personal firms of their own, they do not prefer to be employed there. Those of them who can manage it find employment in large private firms, which are less subject to the whims of owners (though not entirely free of them) than personal firms and where there are some rules to control arbitrariness; the rest of the professionals congregate in the Government and public enterprises, which have absorbed about three-quarters of them (Desai and Desai, 1988). The public sector provides a poor milieu for technological activity for another reason, namely that professionals have little freedom; centralised controls and bureaucratic rules together make public enterprises too slow to react to external circumstances. Thus in our view, the Indian industrial structure has evolved in the last four decades so as to reduce technological dynamism.

If this hypothesis is correct, we should find differences in the efficiency of technological absorption between affiliates and subsidiaries on the one hand and personal firms on the one hand. Unfortunately, our survey generated little useful information about technology ab-

Table 13.3   Ownership type and technological distance

	Affiliates and subsidiaries	Personal firms Technological jump		Total
		Short	Long	
Total no. of firms	8	10	6	24
3.1 Year of origin[a]				
Before 1960	5	3	2	10
1961–70	3	4	2	9
After 1970		3	2	5
3.2 Employment				
Under 200	3	7	2	12
201–800	2	2	2	6
Over 800	3	1	2	6
3.3 Structure of market supply				
Concentrated	4	5	2	11
Competitive	4	5	4	13
3.4 Market share (principal product)				
25 per cent or less	1	2	4	7
26–50 per cent	3	3		6
51–99 per cent	4	2		6
100 per cent		3	2	5
3.5 Reasons for importing technology				
Strengthening competitive position	3	3		6
Diversification	3	2	5	10
Import substitution	2	1	1	4
3.6 Basis for the choice of the technology supplier				
Prestige	2	5	1	8
Exporter to India	3	2		5
Import agency	1	2	2	5
3.7 Time it took to negotiate an agreement				
6 months or less	4	5	1	10
7–12 months	4	4	3	11
Over 12 months		1	2	3
3.8 Royalty rate				
None	5	6	1	12
1–3	1	3	1	5
4–5	2	1	4	7

continued on p. 392

Table 13.3   continued

	Affiliates and subsidiaries	Personal firms Technological jump		Total
		Short	Long	
3.9 Period of agreement				
None	1	3		4
1–5 years	2	4	5	11
More than 5 years	3	3		6
Total no. of firms	8	10	6	24
3.10 Technicians sent abroad for training				
None	2			2
1–4 weeks	4	3	2	9
Over 4 weeks	2	7	4	13
3.11 Foreign technicians brought in				
None	3	4	5	12
Some	3	6	1	10
3.12 Content of imported technology				
Inputs imported	3	3	5	11
Product modified	5	3		8
Equipment imported				
61–100 per cent	2	2		4
21–60 per cent	2	3	2	7
1–20 per cent	2	1	3	6
None	2	4	1	7
Equipment imported from third countries				
61–100 per cent	2			2
21–60 per cent	2	1	1	4
1–20 per cent	2	3	2	7
None	2	6	3	11

Note:
[a] Of the conglomerate where relevant; of the firm elsewhere.

sorption. A large number of questions was asked on the subject, but what we got in return was the views of the respondents, which were uniformly self-congratulatory. Nevertheless we got a few relevant results; they are presented in Table 13.3.

At this point we shall abandon the age-based classification we adopted in the earlier section. A track record is useful for a technology importer in finding technology suppliers and persuading them to sell technology, but it has only a limited bearing on technological dynamism. An older firm will have some technological resources in the form of professionals and equipment, but their quantity and quality would depend to a great extent on how the firm was managed and how successful it was in attracting and retaining trained manpower. So we now make a distinction between affiliates and subsidiaries on the one hand, the personal firms and Government firms on the other.

Apart from this distinction which we hoped would reflect technological resources, we needed to have some indicator of the magnitude of the technological task. The resources would be more useful if the imported technology was closely related to the technology being used by the firm, and pretty useless if the technologies were utterly different. (This idea of technological distance came from an interview done by Scott-Kemmis with a large Indian firm, where he was told that if the collaboration being negotiated was for an unfamiliar technology, the negotiators 'felt naked'.)

We distinguished between those cases where the product or process for which technology was imported was closely related to the firm's (or the conglomerate's) existing line of production, and the cases where it was not. We discovered that none of the affiliates or subsidiaries had gone into an unrelated line. So we ended up with three classes: cases where the technology importer was an affiliate or a subsidiary, cases where it was a personal firm and the technological jump was narrow, and cases where it was a personal firm or a government firm and the technological jump was broad. Where the firm was entirely new and inexperienced, the technological distance was naturally assumed to be large. For brevity, the three types of firms will be called A, B and C respectively.

Let us begin with age distributions since we classified the firms by age earlier. Here, however, we have classified the firms by the age of the conglomerate if any, and not the firm importing or founded through the import of technology, since the technological resources that the firm can draw on are those of the entire conglomerate. A-firms are older, but there is no difference in the age distributions of B- and C-firms; of the newer firms, some took a short technological jump, others a long one (3.1). C-firms were larger than B-firms, and no smaller than A-firms despite the difference in age (3.2). We have shown in section 13.4 how Indian firms tend to be more diversified at a smaller size than their technology suppliers. In section 13.8 we attribute this tendency to Indian trade policies. Here, in C-firms, we have firms that have grown through diversification and are in the process of continuing to do so.

Most of the A-firms had substantial shares in their principal markets; more of the B- and the C-firms had either small shares or a monopoly. In other words, most A-firms were successful competitors, and fewer monopolist.

Market performance is related to the reasons for importing technologies. Some of the A- and B-firms which had built up substantial market shares imported technology to buttress their competitive position (3.5). None of the C-firms did; almost all of them imported technology to diversify into areas remote from their current markets. If we recall that four of the six C-firms had achieved poor market penetration, it would appear that for one reason or another they had not done too well in their current markets and were cutting their losses and going into new areas instead of building on their existing technological resources.

Since A- and B-firms were building on their technological achievements, they were more attractive to technology suppliers; this shows up in their choice of technology suppliers. Only one of the 6 C-firms chose its technology supplier for its prestige (3.6). We argued earlier that a prestigious technology supplier chooses the firm to sell technology to; and if chose more often to sell it to a firm with a good track record in its current market and which wanted to build on its specialisation. Still more interesting is the record of import substitution. All three types of firms produced goods being imported earlier. But whilst C-firms took the technology from firms for which they had earlier acted as import agents, A- and B-firms also attracted erstwhile exporters who were earlier unrelated to them. The greater difficulty of the C-firms in attracting technology is also reflected in the longer time it took them to negotiate the agreement (3.7).

It was noted in the 1970s that new and inexperienced technology importers not only needed more comprehensive know-how, but also an assurance, in terms of a term agreement and preferably equity investment, that the technology would work (National Council of Applied Economic Research, 1971). The same factors are still at work: C-firms made more term agreements, and paid higher royalties (3.8). But it was the more experienced A- and B-firms which persuaded their technology suppliers to make longer agreements at lower royalty rates or for a lump-sum payment (3.9). A-firms tended less to send technicians for training abroad. They tended to send technicians for shorter periods (3.10), or to bring in technicians from abroad (3.11). B-firms brought in more technicians from abroad, C-firms hardly any. There are also differences in what technology the firms imported, and what they made up for themselves (3.12). A-firms tended to import more equipment and thus process technology; but they imported less inputs and modified the products more often, thus generating product technology on their own. C-firms bought more of their equipment at home, but more often imported inputs, and never modified the product. More revealing is the fact that A-firms more often imported equipment from third countries, and imported more of it. In other words, when they imported technology they exercised judgement (no doubt in consultation with their technology suppliers) on where best to get equipment from. C-firms tended more often to be pure licensees: they took a licence on a product. They bought much of the equipment within the country because their scales were much smaller and their processes of production had to be less automatic; and in this indigenization of plant they were undoubtedly encouraged by the Directorate General of Technical Development (which prevents competitive imports of equipment) and helped by local equipment producers. But they could not – and did not – put in broader technological judgement or inputs; nor did they seek them from their technology suppliers. A- and B-firms did.

These comparisons do not throw up pronounced differences between affiliates and subsidiaries on the one hand and personal firms and Government enterprises on the other in the choice of technology suppliers, in negotiating technology imports or in using imported technology; our hypothesis that the difficulty of attracting professionals would adversely affects the performance of B- and C-firms is not supported. But it may instead affect their growth, for B-firms are distinctly smaller than C-firms (3.2). It is also possible that our classification is faulty, and that some B-firms in fact have ties with more experienced firms.

The results throw up unmistakeable differences between the firms that import technology in their own specialisation, and the firms which go well outside it. The latter firms import technology as an escape route from the difficulties they are facing in their current markets – difficulties that arise more often than not from their own technological incapacity. They find it difficult to attract good technology suppliers, they tend to imitate the technology very closely, they probably experiment less, depend more on their technology suppliers, and learn less. The firms which import technology within their specialisation, on the other hand, use it to build up their technological capacity.

The modification of or experimentation with imported technology was stressed by Ito (1986) as a key element in Japanese technological learning, and the lack of it in India. Clearly, a firm that regards technology as a black box to be obtained ready-made from the technology supplier will learn little from it. At the same time, innovation is a modification of the technological base, which may either be built up within the firm or with imported or otherwise acquired technology. The essential difference is not between own and acquired technology; the conflict between the two assumed by nationalist economists is an illusory one. The important distinction is between a tendency constantly to modify – to improve and to adapt – a firm's technology, and a tendency to leave it alone. Our survey suggests that the former tendency is not entirely absent in India, and that it is more present in firms that specialise.

13.7   THE SME FACTOR

Does the fact of the technology supplier being an SME make a difference to technology transfer? We tried to get a handle on this question in two ways. The firms were asked whether the fact of the technology supplier being an SME had a positive effect, a negative effect, or neither, and their answers were correlated with other variables. Since 10 of the firms had said that it made no difference or that they did not know, they were lumped together with the three firms which thought it had a negative effect, and the 13 firms were compared with 11 firms which thought it had a positive effect.

This comparison revealed no strong differences that could not be attributed to other factors. In most important respects the two samples were very similar. The only variable that showed a considerable difference was the search factor – whether the Indian firm had made a search before choosing the technology supplier, or whether it made no search, generally because it knew the technology supplier beforehand. None of the 11 firms which thought the SME factor was positive had made a search, whereas eight of the 13 firms which thought the SME factor was neutral or negative had made one. What this showed was that technology transfer was likely to be much smoother if the technology supplier had earlier relations with the buyer of technology – as supplier and buyer, or principal and agent, or in some other way; conversely, a 'cold start' was less likely to work. This factor is obviously unrelated to the SME factor. There is no reason why an SME is more likely to have prior relations with Indian firms than a large firms: if anything, the reverse is the case. And if the Indian firms' reply to the

Table 13.4   Characteristics related to size of technology supplier

	Technology suppliers employing			Total
	100 or less	*101–400*	*Over 400*	
Total no. of firms	9	7	8	24
4.1 Type of Indian firm and technological distance				
A-firms	2	4	2	8
B-firms	4	2	4	10
C-firms	3	1	2	6
4.2 Employment in the Indian firm				
50 workers or less	5	2	0	7
51–200 workers	0	1	3	4
201–800 workers	3	2	2	7
Over 800 workers	1	2	3	6
4.3 Choice of technology supplier				
Earlier exporter to India	1	1	3	5
Prestige	2	1	5	8
Agency	0	3	0	3
4.4 Relative diversification				
Supplier more diversified	4	1	2	7
Buyer more diversified	2	5	4	11
Both about the same	1	1	1	3
4.5 Ratio of technology supplier's output to buyer's				
3 or less	1	2	1	4
4–10	4	4	3	11
More than 10	2	1	4	7
4.6 R&D in Indian firms				
Indian firms doing R&D	5	5	8	18
4.7 Time taken by negotiations				
1–6 months	5	4	1	10
7–12 months	3	2	6	11
Longer than a year	1	1	1	3
4.8 Period of agreement				
None	2	4	2	8
5 years	5	2	4	11
Longer than 5 years	2	1	2	5

continued on p. 398

Table 13.4   continued

	Technology suppliers employing			Total
	100 or less	101–400	Over 400	
4.9 Royalty				
No royalty	4	4	4	12
1–3 per cent	2	1	2	5
4–5 per cent	3	2	2	7
Total no. of firms	9	7	8	24
4.10 Lump-sum payment				
Positive lump-sum payment	4	4	7	15
4.11 Content of technology				
Product	7	7	7	21
Process	5	2	7	14
Other	3	1	5	9
4.12 Proportion of imported equipment				
None	5	1	1	7
1–20 per cent	3	2	1	6
21–60 per cent	2	2	3	7
61–100 per cent	0	1	3	4
4.13 Technicians sent abroad or brought in				
Technicians brought in	3	4	3	10
Technicians sent for training	9	6	7	22
– 4 weeks or less	5	3	2	10
– more than 4 weeks	4	3	5	12

question of the SME effect was conditioned by unrelated factors, further analysis of their reply could only mislead. Hence we dropped this line of exploration.

Next we divided the technology suppliers into three classes of firms employing fewer than 100 workers, 101–400 workers and over 400 workers – respectively termed small, medium and large firms. This is where some patterns began to emerge (Table 13.4).

The size of the technology supplier showed no relationship with our classification of firms according to type and technological distance (4.1). On the other hand, there is a relationship between the size of the technology supplier and that of the buyer. In our analysis of earlier evidence we had argued that technology suppliers preferred larger technology buyers who would command larger markets, but that technology buyers had no size preference in reference to technology suppliers; and from this we had inferred that larger technology suppliers, who had greater choice of buyers, would collaborate with larger buyers, but that larger buyers would collaborate with both large and small technology suppliers (Desai, 1988c). The present data are consistent with this hypothesis (4.2).

Larger technology suppliers were more often chosen for their prestige or because they exported to India – evidently because larger firms were more likely to be exporting or to have an international reputation. Technology suppliers which collaborated with their erstwhile agents were, on the other hand, medium-sized (4.3).

In section 13.4 we observed the tendency of Indian firms to be more diversified even when they were much smaller than their technology suppliers. This tendency stands out more clearly in the present context. By and large, the larger the technology supplier, the greater was the ratio of its output (of the product under collaboration) to that of the technology buyer likely to be, and the more diversified the Indian firm was likely to be than its technology supplier (4.4 and 4.5). Clearly, the tendency to diversify as they grew was much stronger amongst Indian firms than their partners abroad.

Negotiations with large technology suppliers tended to take longer (4.7). This may have been due to their greater bargaining power. Being larger, they presumably had fewer competitors who might pre-empt the market by selling technology in India before them. They more often had an international reputation, based on international sales, and the Indian market was not so important to them. But we suspect they also had technology which was more proprietorial, more valuable and less imitable. It may be noted that a larger proportion of the Indian firms to which they sold technology had R&D establishments, and were therefore presumably capable of some imitation or adaptation (4.6). Thus larger firms had technology that could be less easily or cheaply imitated – technology for which it was worth while paying a higher price.

There is some evidence, though weak, that a higher price was paid. The period of agreement tended to be no longer for larger technology suppliers than for others (4.8); nor did they receive higher royalties (4.9). But a larger proportion of them received lump-sum payments (4.10). As we have shown elsewhere (Desai, 1988c), lump-sum payments were the commonest form of evasion of official controls on royalties: between the 1960s and 1970s, the proportion of agreements with lump-sum payments greatly increased, and the size of the payments also grew considerably.

Admittedly, the evidence that larger technology suppliers received a higher price is thin. However, the evidence that they sold better, or more, or deeper technology is somewhat stronger. Whilst almost all technology imports covered product technology, the proportion of agreements that covered process and other technology was considerably higher for larger technology suppliers. Smaller firms were more likely to license out their product, with little accompanying production technology; larger firms were more likely to sell a comprehensive package containing both (4.11). They also more often suggested, insisted on, or led to the use of more imported equipment – another indicator that a more advanced process technology was being transferred (4.12). And they were likely to train Indian technoicians for a longer period (4.13).

If, therefore, our interpretation is correct, small and large technology suppliers supply different technologies, and it would be a mistake to assume that they are in the same technology market. One reason for the increased interest in SMEs in recent years is that they are regarded as better or more desirable technology suppliers than larger firms – more specifically, than TNCs. The difference is attributed to their lower ability or desire to control LDC markets and set up monopolies, as well as to invest in subsidiaries and compete with indigenous firms.

This debate centres on two questions: are the objectives or behaviour patterns of SMEs different from those of TNCs? And do they compete with one another in the technology market? The present survey, which covers only Indian firms that imported technology from SMEs, can throw no light on the first question. But it does give some grounds for doubt whether SMEs and TNCs can be treated as alternatives or competitors in the technology market. In particular, differences in firm size are associated with differences in process technology, and LDC firms which need to improve their processes may well have to go to progressively larger technology suppliers.

13.8 THE COST OF SELF-RELIANCE

We showed in section 13.6 that there is a subset of firms amongst personal firms and government enterprises which is weak in its internal technological resources, and which seeks unsuccessfully to compensate for this weakness by importing technology. However, this set of firms cannot explain the lack of technological dynamism in Indian industry as a whole. We may begin to work towards an explanation by going to another result: namely, that the Indian firms are generally at least as diversified as their technology suppliers whose output (of the products under collaboration) is several times greater (2.11). There is no difference in this respect between old firms and new, between *A*-firms, *B*-firms and *C*-firms: all tend to be considerably more diversified at their level of output than firms elsewhere. This fact was noted by Edquist and Jacobsson (1988, pp. 191–2) in respect of machine tools and hydraulic excavators, who attributed to it the high costs and low technological dynamism of Indian firms:

> A strategy of diversification in the local market can have a number of effects. Firstly, economies of scale may be difficult to reap for individual products . . . This further increases the difficulties in going for exports. Secondly, the low output per basic design would tend to make it unattractive to spend resources, as well as take risks, to develop own designs . . . A reliance on a strategy of diversification on the local market would therefore tend to require a very heavy reliance on licences from abroad for the technological input . . . basic design development is 'squeezed out' by the adaptive design work involved in buying a lot of technology.

Why then do Indian firms diversify? Edquist and Jacobsson related it to India's trade and industrial policy. Across-the-board import substitution with Quantitative Restrictions (QRs) and high tariffs raised production costs and confined the industry to the domestic market, and as one market after another was saturated, the firms diversified into new markets. The same tendency was encouraged by industrial licensing: firms which were bumping against the ceiling of their licensed capacity sought new products to make.

There are other ways in which an inward-oriented trade policy encourages diversification. Competition between small and large firms based on wage differences is not peculiar to India. It is to be found in other countries also, was particularly prevalent in Japan in earlier phases of industrialisation. The way in which large firms elsewhere defend themselves against the encroachment of small firms is by mechanising. Differences in techniques are to be found in India as well, but mechanisation is greatly slowed down by the trade restrictions on the import of equipment. Their effect was deadly as long as the rule of domestic availability was followed: any local producer could get the imports of some equipment banned by saying that he was producing a substitute. The rule has been somewhat relaxed in the last 10 years. But the tariffs on equipment imports are so high that mechanisation based on imported equipment is unprofitable unless it relates to a new product for which a high price can be charged in India. Prevented by import restrictions from mechanising, large firms looked instead for new products to produce; product proliferation was favoured at the cost of process innovation.

In doing so, they are helped in two ways by trade policy. If they spot a new product to produce, they can, by moving to produce it, get its imports restricted. Second, they are given a Phased Manufacturing Programme (PMP) as a part of their industrial licence, which requires them to reduce the import content of the product according to the programme laid down. But the PMP also implies that they are allowed to import components and inputs in the initial years of production. Later entrants would find the market pre-empted by the early entrants, and would get less generous PMPs than the first producers. And if, by chance, later entrants get equally favourable terms from the Government and manage to compete effectively, the first entrants abandon the product and move on to new import substitutes. Indian firms are well aware of the importance of being first, and try to jump into every new market as early as possible. The need to get into production ahead of others militates against R&D, which requires time, and favours technology imports. As a number of early entrants try to pre-empt the market, production gets fragmented and diseconomies result from small scale. The government latterly recognised this and tried to counter it by laying down minimum scales of production for a few industries, but it has not recognised the root cause of fragmentation, which lies in an inward-looking trade policy.

This policy has led over the years to a trade ratio for India that is the lower amongst industrial as well as comparable developing countries (with the exception of Japan). And the low volume of trade also restricts the volume of technology that becomes available through trade. For just as small firms obtain technology from larger firms to which they sell, exporters also learn from their buyers abroad. And imports constitute a stream of new goods in which new technology is embodied. A great deal of technological change arises from the embodiment of improved components or ingredients – new metals, chemicals, designs – into existing products; premature import substitution in materials and components blocks off this source of new technology. Local people get technology by repairing, servicing and imitating new imports. The restriction of imports to permitted importers and to established inputs especially discriminates against such new products.

With a low volume of free, informal technology transfer through trade, demand for formal technology imports is increased. At the same time, the small domestic markets and their fragmentation limit the price that individual technology importers can pay for technology, and make them unattractive to potential technology suppliers. So the government has to force them to sell technology by closing the market as soon as import substitutes begin to be produced. This is how trade restrictions have created low-volume equilibria in the markets for imported technology as well as domestically produced goods.

It should perhaps be added that the other explanations of India's lack of technological dynamism emanating from the Lund School are not convincing – in particular, those based on lack of competition and on culture. Edquist and Jacobsson (1988) as well as Matthews (1986) refer to lack of competition in India. The evidence for this is the dominance of the Hindustan Machine Tools (HMT). But the impression of HMT's market dominance rests on official production figures, which ignore the considerable production of simple machine tools by backyard manufacturers, especially in Punjab. And there are many markets which are not so concentrated as the machine-tool market. Once the rise of small firms in India is taken cognisance of, the belief that Indian markets are not competitive is unsustainable. But it is all competition between firms with low technological capacity; technological improvement based on technology imports plays a small part in it, and so does local innovation.

And the cultural arguments, to which Swedish students pay obeisance in the wake of Myrdal's (1968) work, are either tautological or ignore inconvenient evidence. For one thing, to attribute performance characteristics (such as technological dynamism or lack of it) to countries may be convenient terminological shorthand; but to treat countries as monolithic, rational (or irrational) decision-makers or culturally homogeneous collectives is hazardous. The governments of countries do have policies, even policy documents. But policies do not cover all economic life; and the economic thinking of most governments is so primitive that policies often have quite different effects from those intended. Take, for instance, Matthews' critique (1986, pp. 184–5):

> India's development has been characterised by the way in which it has been 'genetically strait-jacketed' to the established direction of trade with Britain and other already industrialised countries. In addition, technological progress was fostered through the promotion of foreign collaboration, not only because 'West means best' but also because by following a Western model of machine-tool manufacture

innovation became the *modus operandi*, and India was totally reliant on its collaborators for the supply of new designs. Even today, India continues to offer significant concessions to transnational companies prepared to establish manufacturing facilities in the country, especially those geared to export markets. The ill-planned use of foreign collaboration in the machine-tool industry has resulted in the present situation in which the machine-tool sector lacks the capability to innovate because it has never had to try.

Far from any strait-jacketing, genetic or otherwise, the Government of India tried hard in the 1950s and 1960s to foster closer trade and technological ties with the Soviet bloc; the indifferent success of its efforts was not for lack of trying, but because of the limits to what Eastern Europe had to offer. Maybe the people responsible for industrial decisions (more those outside the Government than inside) believed then that West meant best; but then, who did not? Even the Japanese assiduously emulated and learnt from the West till the 1960s. Now that Japanese firms have better technology to offer, Indian firms readily turn to them. The Indian Government has severe restrictions on foreign companies producing in India, which are relaxed if they (not just transnational companies) restrict themselves to exporting. Judging from the paltry foreign investment attracted into the 100 per cent export units, the transnationals hardly regard the concessions as significant. And to argue that 'India' relied too much on foreign collaborations and, by implication, too little on local innovation requires the neglect of the entire experiment in technological self-reliance which spanned the 1970s – the restrictions on technology imports, the insistence on technology importers doing R&D, the efforts to promote national laboratories as sources of technology. It would be possible to dismiss all these efforts as 'ill-planned'; but a more reasonable explanation is that the Government understands little about what technological dynamism means and requires. After all, it cannot be expected to know more than economists, who do not know much about it either. These remarks are not directed particularly at Matthews; it just happens that his passage encapsulates with admirable brevity what is wrong with the Myrdal-inspired 'Swedish approach'.

13.9 CONCLUSIONS

We have tried in this chapter to establish a relationship between two sources of profits which are the driving force of industrial growth in India: the substitution of cheap for expensive labour, and the induction of foreign technology. Domestic wage competition leads to the emergence of new firms and generates demand for new technology. Much of this demand is met by technology diffusion within the economy; but it also spills over into technology imports by firms which find their domestic market shares threatened, as well as by firms which have done poorly in their existing markets and are looking for diversification. The explanation of why the demand for new technology is met more through technology imports and less by technology generation at home is best sought in trade policy, which places a premium on market pre-emption and limits the informal inflow of costless technology that can accompany international trade. We also found traces of product differentiation in the technology market: of evidence that large and small technology suppliers have different technologies to sell, and are therefore not competitors in the technology market.

14 The Case of Korea

Won-Young Lee

14.1 INTRODUCTION

The purpose of this chapter is to summarise the experience of technology transfer by small and medium-sized enterprises (SMEs) of advanced countries in the Republic of Korea. Interviews at 13 technology recipient firms were carried out, the results of which comprise the major part of this chapter.

In section 14.2, the general features of technology transfer in the Republic of Korea are introduced. Section 14.3 explains how the SMEs were selected and their general characteristics. Section 14.4 describes the motivations and means of technological transfer and pattern of adaptive efforts and section 14.5 deals with the issue of the impact of the subsidiaries of SMEs on the Korean economy. Section 14.6 concludes with some policy recommendations for host and source countries.

14.2 GENERAL PATTERN OF FOREIGN DIRECT INVESTMENT AND TECHNOLOGICAL LICENSING

Overview

Tables 14.1 and 14.2 show the annual flow of Technological Licensing (TL) and Foreign Direct Investment (FDI) from 1962 to 1986. On an approval basis, the inflow of FDI increased very rapidly until 1973. The trend, however, was halted in 1973 and the amount of FDI stagnated until the early 1980s, picking up more recently. The annual flow of TL shows a similar pattern. There is, however, a slight difference in the pattern of FDI and that of TL flows, in that TL increased continuously during the 1973–8 period when the inflow of FDI was stagnating.

The flow of TL and FDI is affected by various factors, such as the business cycles of the Korean economy, stages of economic development, political environment, and Government policy. Of these factors, the influence of the business cycles of the host countries and Government

406

Table 14.1   Trends in technology licensing, 1962–86

	Technological licensing (no. of cases)	Royalty payments (million US dollars)
1962–6	33	0.78
1962–72	338	26.52
1973	67	11.49
1974	88	17.49
1975	99	26.54
1976	127	30.42
1977	168	58.06
1978	297	85.07
1979	271	93.93
1980	222	107.25
1981	247	107.10
1982	308	115.69
1983	262	149.50
1984	437	213.23
1985	454	295.50
1986	517	411.00

Source: Ministry of Finance.

policies are most apparent. The stagnation of FDI and TL during 1979–81 seems to be correlated with the lower growth rate of the Korean economy for that period. Caused by the second world oil crisis and domestic political unstability, the Korean economy experienced negative growth in 1979 for the first time since major developmental efforts began in the early 1960s. The annual growth rates were 7.0 per cent, -4.8 per cent, 6.6 per cent in 1979, 1980 and 1981 respectively, which were far below the average growth rate of 10 per cent during the period from 1968 to 1978.

The influence of Government policies on the inflow of FDI and TL is also evident from the annual pattern. In 1973 the first significant measures to regulate the quality of FDI were introduced. These measures, which lasted until 1982, undoubtedly depressed the inflow of FDI during a period when the Korean economy was growing very rapidly. The outstanding balance of FDI in 1978 was US $ 1.1 billion, while in 1982 it was US $ 1.5 billion. On the other hand, foreign loans during the period grew very rapidly. The total outstanding foreign debt in 1970 was US $ 20.3 billion while that in 1982 was US $ 37.1 billion. The restriction on the entry of FDI was lowered in 1983, and the number and amount of FDI has been increasing very rapidly since then.

Table 14.2   Korea: trends in FDI 1962–86 (unit: million of U.S. dollar)

	Approved FDI (A)		Reinvestment (B)	Disinvestment (C)	Withdrawn (D)		Remaining (E) $E=(A)+(B)-(C)-(D)$		Arrived FDI (F)
	No. of firms	Amount of investment			No. of firms	Amount of investment	No. of firms	Amount of investment	
1962–6	39	47.4	2.4	2.3	0	0	39	47.6	24.3
1967–71	349	218.6	3.4	15.6	22	27.8	366	226.1	117.2
1972–6	851	878.5	69.9	61.0	368	219.8	849	893.7	535.8
1977	54	83.6	6.2	7.4	53	31.5	850	944.7	142.9
1978	51	149.4	33.2	4.4	56	32.1	845	1090.9	181.0
1979	55	191.3	19.5	11.3	60	88.5	840	1201.9	195.3
1980	40	143.1	83.2	6.2	62	126.0	818	1296.1	130.9
1981	44	153.2	51.3	4.5	83	41.0	779	1455.0	150.2
1982	56	189.0	66.3	19.7	34	83.0	801	1507.6	128.6
1983	75	69.4	19.3	4.5	29	9.6	847	1752.2	122.5
1984	104	422.3	17.2	5.5	18	25.3	933	2160.9	193.3
1985	127	532.0	14.7	4.8	92	45.6	968	2657.1	235.8
1986	203	353.7	19.3	26.0	30	138.7	1141	2685.4	477.4

Source: The data here are based on a new series released by the Ministry of Finance in 1987. Theres is a significant difference between the old and new series, primarily because the latter includes the purchase of existing companies. In addition, mistakes in the compilation of the raw data are corrected in the new series.

Table 14.3   Ownership structure of FDI (unit: no. of cases), %, 1962–86

	Minority-owned		Co-owned		Majority-owned		Wholly-owned		Total	
1962–6	14	35.9	8	20.5	11	28.2	6	15.4	39	100.0
1967–71	149	42.7	83	23.8	59	16.9	58	16.6	349	100.0
1972–6	383	45.0	255	30.0	87	10.2	126	14.8	851	100.0
1977	34	63.0	12	22.2	6	11.1	2	3.7	54	100.0
1978	32	62.8	13	25.5	4	7.8	2	3.9	51	100.0
1979	34	61.8	14	25.5	3	5.5	4	7.3	55	100.0
1980	24	60.0	11	27.5	1	2.5	4	10.0	40	100.0
1981	18	40.9	16	36.4	9	20.5	1	2.3	44	100.0
1982	17	30.4	21	37.5	13	23.2	5	8.9	56	100.0
1983	30	40.0	30	40.0	11	14.7	4	5.3	75	100.0
1984	52	50.0	26	25.0	15	14.4	11	10.6	104	100.0
1985	63	49.6	27	21.3	18	14.2	19	15.0	127	100.0
1986	100	54.2	33	16.3	26	12.8	34	16.8	203	100.0
Total	960	46.9	549	26.8	263	12.8	276	13.5	2048	100.0

Source: Ministry of Finance.

The influence of Government policies on the flow of TL is also obvious. The number of TL contracts in 1978 increased to 297, from the previous year's 168. Further relaxation of restrictions in 1983 also had an immediate and positive impact on the number of licensing contracts in 1984. The number increased to 437 from 262 in the year before.

The composition of equity versus non-equity forms of technology transfer has been also affected by Government policies. Between 1978 and 1982, the ratio of the cases of TL to the cases of FDI was 5.47 while during 1983–6 it was 3.28. The period from 1978 to 1982 was an era in which the Government had applied more lenient criteria for licensing contracts compared to the restrictions imposed on FDI.

The ownership pattern of FDI has also been influenced by Government policies. As can be seen from Table 14.3, the official relaxation of ownership restrictions in the early 1980s resulted in an increase the proportions of majority-and wholly-owned subsidiaries during 1982–6 compared to those during 1979–81.

Distribution by Source Country and Industry

Japan and the United States account for an increasing proportion of the transfer of technology. Japan and the United States together have a 78 per cent share of the technological licensing in Korea, while their

Table 14.4   Country distribution of technology licensing and FDI (unit: no. of cases), 1962–86

	Japan		United States		West Germany		France		Others		Total	
	TL	FDI	TL	FDI	TL	FDI	TL	FDI	TL	FDI	TL	FDI
1962–76	164	187	494	985	23	20	7	5	64	68	752	1265
1977	45	16	82	27	16	0	3	2	22	12	68	57
1978	67	11	158	31	12	3	9	0	51	7	297	52
1979	61	13	159	32	17	3	8	2	45	8	291	58
1980	54	15	124	19	10	3	9	0	25	3	222	40
1981	75	12	108	23	15	1	11	0	38	8	247	44
1982	68	20	164	20	14	1	16	0	46	18	308	59
1983	77	19	201	37	20	2	10	1	54	17	362	76
1984	99	37	217	52	36	3	23	3	62	13	437	108
1985	114	43	228	58	29	8	14	1	69	21	454	131
1986	157	49	264	109	23	7	19	1	54	39	517	205
Total	981	422	2199	1393	215	51	128	15	532	214	4055	2095

Source: Ministry of Finance.

share in FDI is 87 per cent (Table 14.4). If we look at the trend of FDI in Table 14.4, that from Japan and the United States show different patterns. The level of Japanese investment and licensing increased to double that of United States in the late 1970s. This trend was reversed in the early 1980s, when licensing and FDI from the United States increased very rapidly.

There are, in addition, significant qualitative differences between direct investments from these two countries. A recent study found that Japanese investment tends to be concentrated mostly in the low-technology industries, while its American counterpart is equally divided between the low-and high-technological industries; see Chung Hoon Lee, 1984. It was also found that the technologies associated with US investment were comparatively more capital-intensive and sophisticated.

The transfer of technology from West Germany and France shows little difference to that from the United States and Japan. There is a strong inclination for licensing as a mode of technology transfer, rather than FDI. The ratio of the cases of licensing to FDI are 4.2 and 8.5 for West Germany and France. The relative preference for licensing as a mode of entry seems to be related to geographical and cultural backgrounds. It can be argued that European firms are less informed about the production and marketing environment in Korea. Thus, they tend to prefer an arm's-length transfer of technology while avoiding deeper

Table 14.5 Industrial distribution of technology licensing and FDI inflows, (unit: no. of cases), 1962–86

	1962–71		1972–6		1977–81		1982–6		Total	
	TL	FDI	TL	FDI	TL	FDI	TL	FDI	TL	FDI
Agriculture, dairy and fishing	6	18	0	65	5	14	15	16	26	113
Manufacturing	285	336	391	734	1095	191	1878	450	3649	1711
Food Processing	8	13	7	24	30	13	101	45	146	95
Pulp and Paper	4	7	3	17	7	6	3	5	17	35
Textile and Apparel	14	50	24	100	41	10	127	19	206	179
Chemical and Petroleum	64	43	85	79	194	22	317	64	660	208
Ceramics, Cement and Fertiliser	12	18	9	28	34	7	50	9	105	62
Drugs	19	10	8	9	31	9	55	35	113	63
Metals	29	20	45	66	105	21	112	24	291	131
Machinery	65	45	126	119	448	58	640	105	1279	327
Electric and Electronics	70	64	84	189	205	31	473	99	832	383
Other Manufacturing	21	66	32	103	63	14	122	45	238	228
Electricity	2	0	7	0	37	0	24	0	70	0
Construction	4	3	4	0	25	1	39	4	72	8
Hotel	–	5	–	29	–	11	–	16	–	61
Financing	–	2	–	5	–	7	–	8	–	22
Others	–	24	–	18	–	20	–	71	–	133
Total	318	388	434	851	1225	244	2078	565	4055	2088

Source: Ministry of Finance.

involvement in the local production or financial arrangements that may arise in FDI.

The manufacturing sector received the major portion of FDI and licensing. Among the manufacturing subsectors, chemicals, machinery, and the electric and electronics sectors have absorbed the largest proportion of technology transfer. In these industries, the licensing contract has increased very rapidly. The ratio of the total number of licensing contracts to that of FDI is the highest in the machinery industry, amounting to 3.9, followed by the chemical and electric and electronic industries. These industries usually require a high level of sophistication, which necessitates a greater reliance on foreign technology.

In the agricultural and service sectors, FDI is the predominant form of foreign firms' involvement, with the exception of the electricity industry where FDI is not possible due to the Government monopoly. In the services sector, capital transfer, as well as the transfer of technology, is an important aspect. The amount of investment in the service industries on average is much larger than that in manufacturing industries (see Table 14.5).

14.3   CASE STUDY OF THE ROLE OF SMEs IN KOREA: DESCRIPTION OF THE SAMPLE

The survey on the affiliates of SMEs in Korea was carried out in coordination with other researchers in technology-supplying countries who were also members of the transfer of Technology by Small and Medium Enterprises Project organised by CEDREI. In an effort to interview the firms directly involved in technological licensing, the following steps were taken: first, a list of foreign firms in Korea was sent to the researchers in the advanced countries. In the cases of FDI, the entire list of foreign firms as of 1985 was submitted. In the case of TL, those approved between 1981 and 1985 were covered. The list thus contained approximately 1500 cases of TL and 1000 cases of FDI. The researchers in the advanced countries then identified the size of the source firm, and the list was provided to the author. (In some countries, the willingness to participate in the survey was also considered.)

In total, 39 cases were provided from various countries: 14 from the United States, three from Japan, 12 from the United Kingdom, six from Germany, and one each from Canada, Italy, and France. On this list, there were only two cases of FDI and 37 cases of TL. I conducted a preliminary survey, there companies as to their willingness to participate and managed to get interviews for 17 cases, all of which turned out to be TL. Among these, two were sales agents and two were solely intended for import of capital goods involving no technology transfer. 13 cases were thus left for analysis.

Industry and Country Distribution

Table 14.6 shows the industrial distribution of the 13 sample firms. Of the 13, five belong to machinery, excluding the electrical industry, four are associated with fabricated metal products, and the rest are distributed in electric and electronic equipment, transportation equipment, chemicals and allied product industries. The country distribution of the technology-supplying firms is shown in Table 14.7. The US-based firms were the largest in number, followed by Japan, United Kingdom, and W. Germany.

The size of the recipient firms varied widely (Table 14.8). Of the 13 firms reviewed, seven recipients were SMEs employing less than 500. The remaining six recipients were large firms employing more than 5000.

Concerning the production modes of the recipients, nine firms produced to order, while four firms produced to meet an expected demand

Table 14.6 List of products manufactured by technology-receiving firms

SIC code	Industry Description	Products manufactured by technology-receiving firms
283	Drugs	Biological products
341	Metal Cans and Shipping Containers	Aluminium containers for liquefied gas
343	Plumping and Heating, except Electric	Oil burners
344	Fabricated Structural Metal Products	Boilers
344	Fabricated Structural Metal Products	Heat exchanging equipment
354	Metalworking Machinery	Coating machinery for automobile
354	Metalworking Machinery	Vertical machining centres
354	Metalworking Machinery	Automatic positioning equipment
356	General Industry Machinery	Transmission equipment
362	Electrical Industrial Apparatus	Jumper-coupler
367	Electronic Components and Accessories	64K DRAM
371	Motor Vehicle and Equipment	(a) Brake pad and lining (b) Auto-carburettor

Table 14.7 Country distribution of the sample

SIC Code	United States	Japan	United Kingdom	West Germany	France	Canada
28	1					
34	2		1			1
35	1	1	1	1	1	
36	1	1				
37				1		
Total	5	2	2	2	1	1

(Table 14.9). If we classify production mode by the size of the recipients, six out of seven in the case of small and medium-sized recipients and three out of six in the case of large recipients, produced on an order basis.

Features of Technology Contracts

We will now describe the characteristics of technology contracts: types of transferred technology, forms of payment, length of agreement and

Table 14.8   Size distribution of the recipient firms

SIC Code	10–99	100–299	300–499	500–4999	over 5000
28					1
34	2				2
35	1	1	1		2
36	1				1
37	1				
Total	5	1	1	0	6

Table 14.9   Mode of production by industries

SIC	Custom-order	Production for expected demand
28		1
34	4	
35	4	1
36	1	1
37		1
Total	9	4

contractual conditions, such as export restraints. In addition, a comparison of the results with another survey is provided. The survey used for the comparison in *A Survey of Technology Transfer by Foreign Firms* (1986), which was conducted by the Korea Industrial Research Institute (KIRI). The survey covers 328 cases of TL, regardless of the size of the supplier during the 1980–4 period.[1]

Types of Transferred Technology

Types of technology include know-how, patents or trademarks. Table 14.10 shows the distribution of the types of transferred technology. Not much difference in the composition of the types of technology transfer seems to exist between the recipients of SME and recipients in the KIRI survey. About 50 per cent of the sample firms intended to get patents and trademarks in addition to technical know-how.

Forms of Payment

There are three kinds of royalty payments: lump-sum payment, running royalty, and a combination of the two. Table 14.11 shows the

Table 14.10   Types of transferred technology

| | SME | | | KIRI |
	Small recipients	Large recipients	Total (%)	survey (%)
Only know-how	4	3	7 (54)	201 (47)
Know-how and patent	1	2	3 (23)	138 (32)
Know-how and trademark	1		1 (9)	44 (10)
Know-how, patent and trademark	1	1	2 (15)	49 (11)
Total	7	6	13 (100)	432 (100)

Table 14.11   Forms of payment

	SMEs (%)	KIRI survey (%)
Lump-sum payment	1 (8)	160 (37)
Running royalty	9 (69)	110 (26)
Running royalty and initial payment	3 (23)	162 (38)
Total	13 (100)	432 (100)

distribution of firms by the forms of payment. It seems that the recipients of SMEs were more likely to prefer running royalty schedules as opposed to a fixed-payment schedules. The rates of the running royalty varied from 1 per cent to 5 per cent of the sales. In eight out of 12 cases, the running royalty fell between 3 and 4 per cent, suggesting that this range is the most common in technological licensing.

Length of Agreement

The distribution of the length of agreements is shown in Table 14.12. There is a significant difference between the recipients of SMEs and recipients in the KIRI survey. The length of agreement in the case of SMEs is longer than that in the KIRI survey, but it seems to be the result of the difference in the forms of royalty payments. In other words, the life of the agreement is not much different between the two samples if we exclude the licensing arrangements with only fixed initial payment, which amount to only 8 per cent of the total in the recipients of SME survey, but as much as 37 per cent of the total in the KIRI survey.

Table 14.12   Length of agreement

	Small SME and medium recipients	Large recipients	Total (%)	KIRI survey (%)
1–4 yr	0	1	1 (8)	175 (41)
5–9 yr	4	3	7 (43)	212 (49)
More than 10 yr	3	2	5 (39)	45 (10)
Total	7	6	13 (100)	432 (100)

Table 14.13   Nature of export restraints

	SMEs (%)	KIRI survey (%)
No restrictions	8 (62)	20 (10)
Export restricted to all countries	3 (23)	92 (46)
Export restricted to some regions	1 (8)	77 (38)
Amount of export restricted	1 (8)	13 (6)
Total	13 (100)	202 (100)

Export Restraints

Among the various contractual conditions, export restraints are used the most often. Table 14.13 shows the nature of export restraints in the sample. Contracts made by SMEs, it seems, contain less restrictions on exports as compared to those in the KIRI survey.

14.4   THE TRANSFER PROCESS

This section describes the mechanism of technology transfer. We will, first, examine the motivations for technology contracts. Second, we will describe the selection process of the partners. Third, we will then characterize what measures and steps are taken in the actual phases of technological transfer. Fourth, adaptive efforts by the recipients are summarised.

Motivation

We can think of two different reasons why recipient firms import foreign technology. First, technology licensing (TL) results in an opportunity to produce goods that are not produced domestically. It is well known that TL and FDI in many instances are used as substitutes for the import of goods. For example, by establishing production facilities locally, the source firm can save international transportation costs and other transaction costs.

Secondly, TL provides a chance to improve the efficacy of the production of goods that are already manufactured by the recipient. The need for the improvements may come from many sources. Firms may have to react to the entry in the local market of a competitor. Major customers may demand that the present level of technology be upgraded. A weakening competitive position requires upgrading of present technology by means of TL.

The response by the sample firms shows that the production of a new product is the main motive in all but one case considered. For large recipients, TL contributed to diversifying the present line of production. The product manufactured by TL was in most cases related to the products that had been produced before the TL. In three out of six cases, technology licensing made it possible to substitute for imported parts (see Company *A* in the Appendix). In the other three cases, products produced by TL were complementary to previously produced goods (see Companies *B* and *F* in the Appendix). For example, they were the ones that could be sold by existing marketing channels. For small recipients, six out of seven cases represented new business that had become possible by licensing. In other words, firms were established mainly to manufacture the product whose technology was licensed. In four out of six cases, importing agencies had become the recipient. In two cases, the recipients were spin-offs from established companies which had experienced initial contact with the technology supplier. The established companies did not want a licensing contract directly because this might create legal and financial difficulties; for example, the calculation of the sales-based royalty payment can be very complicated if a firm produces many products.

It is surprising to find that only one firm in the sample licensed technology to improve the quality of products already being manufactured. This firm had produced goods on an order basis and had difficulty in meeting the demand of a certain segment of the market due to a lack of technology (see Company *C* in the Appendix).

In conclusion, TL is in most cases intended to produce goods that are not manufactured domestically. Among 12 such cases, one produced a good, the import of which was prohibited by the trade law. For the remaining 11 cases, the products were not subject to import

Table 14.14   Share of export in total sales

Share of export (%)	Large recipient	Small recipient
0	2	3
1–30	1	3
30–70	2	0
70–100	1	1
Total	6	7

licensing. In most cases, however, tariff rates were higher than 20 per cent. In addition, the major markets of these firms were domestic. Table 14.14 shows the distribution of sales between domestic sales and exports.

In five cases, the firms produced solely to supply the domestic market. One firm had a condition in the contract that explicitly prohibited exports. Thus, it can be concluded that the most important motivation for TL was to serve the domestic market. To put it differently, TL is an instrument to substitute for imports.

Selection of Partners

In this section, we discuss issues related to the selection of partners. First, the means of contact are discussed. Second, the answer to the question 'who is the initiator?' is provided.

The survey shows that four recipients as importers of parts or final products, had commercial contact with the supplier before TL. In the remaining nine cases, there was no previous contact. In those cases, the initial contact was made through various means. In four cases, exchange of letters was the means; three cases, personal contact; one case, product exhibition; one case, intermediation by a government organisation (the Small and Medium Industry Promotion Organisation in Korea facilitated an initial contact between the license and the licensor).

As for the question 'who initiated the TL?', six replied that the recipients were the initiators while four replied that the suppliers were the initiators. For the remaining three cases, two firms responded that both the recipients and suppliers had played equal roles.

In the six cases in which the recipients were the initiators, the reasons for the choice of the supplier were asked. The responses were: supplier's reputation (two cases), suggestion by a related firm (three cases), and good contractual conditions (one case).

In the four cases where the suppliers were the initiators, the reasons for the choice of the recipient were asked. The responses were: recipient's reputation (three cases) and to get access to the market (one case).

Negotiations on average took about one year.

Means of Technology Transfer

We can divide industrial technology into product technology and process technology, both of which are transferred through TL. The survey shows that combination of product and process technologies were transferred in 12 cases while process technology was transferred in only one. The result is not surprising considering that the major motivation for TL was to produce goods that had not been produced domestically.

Different mechanisms were relied upon for the transfer of technology: blueprints, designs, drawings, special equipment, export of critical parts or components, and technical assistance. The response shows that blueprints, designs, drawings happened in 11 cases; export of critical parts in four cases; and special equipment in three cases. Blueprints, designs, drawings were thus the most important means of technology transfer.

Personal contact also is an essential part of technology transfer. In nine cases, the training of local technicians was included in the contract. 12 firms, however, sent local technicians to the supplier. The length of the stay usually lasted about a month or two although there were a few cases in which the length was longer than 6 months. Technicians of SMEs were also sent to the recipient in nine cases. Their length of stay varied from 1 week to 3 months.

Adaptation

Imported technology may not suit the economic environment of the recipient country. The relative prices of the factors of production may be different. Technology imported from advanced countries may be too capital-intensive for the recipient country. The difference in the market size may also require changes in the scale of production. It is also conceivable that part suppliers and subcontractors lack of technological capacity to adjust to imported technology. This also requires adaptation of imported technology.

The survey reveals some characteristics of the adaptive efforts by the technology supplier and recipient. First, the recipients were asked whether the products had been changed in the home country. Three out of 13 firms indicated that the design had been changed, while others

Table 14.15   Relative size of the recipient compared to the supplier

Supplier size/Recipient size	Large	Small
About the same	2	
About 50%		2
About 25%		1
Less than 10%		3
Total	2	6

answered that it had not been changed. The reason for the change in all three cases stemmed from the fact that demand patterns were different. In addition, the availability of inputs or components were the factors that forced the change in two cases. More specifically, parts available in the domestic market did not meet the specification of the licensed technology.

Secondly, a comparison of the output size was made between the suppliers and recipients. In two cases, the suppliers was not producing the product: thus direct comparison was not possible. In three cases the recipients did not know the size of the supplier. Of the eight firms that provided a comparison, two cases were similar in size while in six cases the recipients were smaller less than 50 per cent. The smallest was 2 per cent of the size of the supplier. It seems that the larger the size of the recipient, the more likely is the similarity in size with the supplier (see Table 14.15).

Third, the difference in the degree of product diversification was asked. Of 13 firms, seven firms responded that the supplier had a more diversified line of production while the other six firms replied that the degree of diversification was about the same. It also turned out that the smaller the recipient, the more likely was the supplier to be more diversified than the recipient.

Fourth, the differences in the equipment for the production were asked. Of the nine firms that responded of this question, two firms indicated that their equipment was different from the technology supplier's while the rest replied that there were no significant differences. The main reason for the difference turned out to be the difference in the scale of the output. In other words, the market for the recipient was smaller than that the supplier, so the scale of production was smaller, resulting in the difference in equipment.

In sum, the extent of the adaptation of transferred technology was not as significant as we had expected. The majority of the recipients did not change the design and used similar equipment. The degree of local subcontracting was similar to that of the suppliers. Only a small proportion changed imported technology. Some changed the design to adjust to the difference in the demand pattern; some used different equipment to adjust to local market conditions. It can thus be concluded that adaptation or modification of imported technology was carried out to adjust to the difference in demand. It is surprising that the technology was not modified to adjust for local supply conditions. Not a single firm mentioned that the consideration of labour cost, for example, was a factor that forced the modification of imported technology.

14.5   THE ECONOMIC IMPORT

The most obvious economic benefit for the host country is in getting foreign advanced technology. It is well known that FDI and TL have been the major sources of much-needed technology in the economic development of Korea. The benefit of technology transfer, however, has to be weighed against the costs involved in order to determine welfare implications. The royalties paid to the technology-supplying firms are the most obvious cost. For those countries with a chronic balance-of-payments problem, the compensation paid to foreign firms implies a significant cost. Second, the appropriateness of the transferred technology needs to be examined. There is a possibility that foreign technology suitable for the source country with higher *per capita* income, and with different factor endowments, may cause an undesirable pattern of consumption or production in the recipient country.

The survey sheds some light on the economic costs and benefits mentioned above. First, we will discuss the issues related to the appropriateness of the technology transferred. Secondly, we will examine the linkages between recipient firms and the local industries. The relevant questions here are: Has TL increased or decreased the competition in the domestic market? Has TL contributed to export earning? What are the patterns of purchase by the recipient firms? Thirdly, the composition of the royalty payment is examined; more specifically, the size of monopolistic rents in the royalty payment are reported.

Appropriateness of Technology Transferred

It is often argued that TL (or FDI) is carried out as a means to exploit market opportunities created by trade barriers. Korea has adopted an import-licensing scheme in which imports in various commodities may be restricted. During the early 1980s, prohibited and restricted items (by trade programmes and other special laws) amounted to almost 3000 out of 7500 items in the trade classification. In addition, the average tariff rate was kept high at 22 per cent. In this respect, the extent of the trade barriers on the products manufactured under licensing is of interest.

The survey results reveal that only one case is associated with products that were restricted by the trade law. Products associated with the remaining cases did not belong to items restricted or prohibited by the trade law. The average tariff rates for those 12 cases, however, were about 20 per cent, implying the existence of some trade barriers.

If we consider that the major motivation for TL by the sample firms is to serve the domestic market, then trade barriers encourage TL. The welfare implications of this inducement effect is not clear, however. If the recipients master the technology and become cost-effective in the long run, trade barriers in effect have provided an opportunity to obtain appropriate foreign technology. In other words, trade barriers function as a means to protect infant industries. On the other hand, if recipients cannot compete effectively without trade barriers, both in the short and long run, one can argue that inappropriate technology may have been transferred. In other words, TL simply to exploit market opportunities created by trade barriers may distort the pattern of comparative advantage.

An evidence of the long-run appropriateness of technology transferred may be inferred by observing the types of technology. Licensing intended to acquire foreign trademarks is more likely to result in the transfer of inappropriate technology. On the other hand, licensing intended to get patents is unlikely to waste royalty payments just to bypass trade barriers.[2] The survey results show that three out of 13 samples were intended for the acquisition of trademarks. If we compare that proportion with that of licensing in general, the proportions are about the same.[3] For patents, five firms licensed technology for that purpose. If we compare with the KIRI survey, the proportions are about the same.

In sum, the survey results show that there is some evidence that licensing may be intended to bypass host-country trade barriers. On average, however, licensing is more likely to get technology that is beneficial for the economy.

Table 14.16   Share of imports in the total inputs

	Recipients	
	Large	*Small*
0–5%	4	4
5–20%	2	1
20–50%	0	2
Total	6	7

Industrial Linkages

The industrial linkages of the recipients with the domestic economy can be evaluated on many dimensions. First, the backward and forward linkages of the recipient firms are important. With respect to backward linkages, the survey shows that the majority of the recipients used domestically produced inputs (Table 14.16). Furthermore, the proportion of imported inputs was low, amounting to less than 50 per cent. As for the direct linkage between the technology suppliers and recipients, the survey shows that in two cases the supplier of technology also supplied parts and raw material. These two firms had an explicit contract that specified royalties as a percentage of sales minus the amount of imports from the technology supplier.

The share of exports in the total sales has already been summarised in Table 14.14. It is obvious that the majority of the sample firms were more inclined to sell domestically than to export. The pattern seems consistent with the motivations for technology contracts. In other words, the most important motive for TL is to serve the domestic market. Only one firm sold products to the technology supplier on a regular basis, but the sales arrangement was not specified in the initial contract. A similar result was found in the KIRI survey, in that the recipients were asked about the target markets. Out of 454 firms that replied to the question, 9 per cent replied that the foreign market was the target; 50 per cent said the domestic market was the main target; and the remaining firms stated that both markets were targets.

Secondly, the survey also allows us to infer the licensee's impact on the competitiveness of the relevant markets. In response to the question about are the economic and commercial effects of the transfer, all the firms replied that TL allowed them to secure a leading position in the local market. This is also supported by Table 14.17, which shows the distribution of the number of domestic competitors.

Table 14.17   Number of domestic competitors

Competitors	Recipients	
	Large	Small
1–2	2	1
3–5	4	3
6–9	0	1
Total	6	7

The result is consistent with the observation on the motivations for TL. As we have already mentioned in section 14.4, TL in most cases is associated with production technology. Domestic markets are thus likely to be monopolised by the licensed firms.

The results, however, do not lead to the conclusion that TL contributed to the increase of market concentration in Korea. If we take foreign suppliers into account, the presence of the licensed firms implies increased competition from the perspective of users of the product. There was no non-tradable sector and foreign import was allowed in all but one case.

In conclusion, TL in general enhanced the competitiveness of domestic industries. No case existed in which TL led to more concentration of the domestic markets.

Determination of the Royalty Payment

In evaluating the welfare implications of technological transfer, it is important to understand how the compensation for technology is determined. Compensations to technology suppliers need to include not only the direct costs of transferring technology, but also the opportunity costs and monopolistic rents. More specifically, direct costs include: salary of despatched technicians, lawyers' fee, travelling expenses, the cost of making blueprints, etc. Opportunity cost can be defined as the profit opportunity foregone to technology suppliers by licensing, as opposed to commodity sales or FDI. Monopolistic rent is the contribution margin to technology suppliers due to a monopolistic market situation. It could also be regarded as compensation for R&D expenses incurred by a technology supplier.

If direct costs are the major portion of the compensation, TL is not much different from trade in services. On the other hand, if opportunity costs or monopolistic rents are the major portion of the compensation,

Table 14.18   Estimates of technology suppliers' costs

% of direct cost	No. of cases	% of indirect cost	No. of cases
0–5	5	None	3
6–10	3	1–10	6
11–20	3	11–20	1
30 or more	1	40 or more	1
Cannot tell	1	Cannot tell	2
Total	13	Total	13

the welfare implications of the governmental policy measures on TL are different from that of trade in services. For example, tax on the royalty payment is mostly borne by the technology supplier in the latter case, while the major portion of the tax is borne by the recipient in the former case.[4]

The response of sample firms as to the composition of direct and opportunity costs is shown in Table 14.18.

The results can be compared to a survey by Lee and Kim (1987) in which 114 recipients were asked the same questions. In Lee and Kim's survey the size of the suppliers were not taken into account; their survey thus represents licensing in general. The comparison shows that there is not much difference in the distributions. In both Lee and Kim's and the present survey, the most frequent range of direct costs is between 0 and 5 per cent and the median falls between 6 and 10 per cent.

As for the distribution of opportunity cost, 85 per cent of the response belongs to the range below 10 per cent in Lee and Kim's survey, while 82 per cent (nine out of 11) of the response belongs to the same range in the present survey.

In conclusion, direct and indirect costs are only a small fraction of the total compensation to the technology supplier. The median of direct cost falls between 6 and 10 per cent while that of indirect costs is between 1 and 10 per cent. The comparison of this result to that of Lee and Kim shows that the cost structures of both surveys are very similar.

14.6   SUMMARY AND CONCLUSIONS

This survey on technology transfer by SMEs of advanced countries to Korea produces many interesting findings. First, SMEs are an important source of foreign technology. In a wide range of industries, transfer of technology by SMEs has allowed Korean firms to produce goods that would not been produced domestically. SMEs have also contributed to the transfer of process technology.

Secondly, SMEs rely more on TL as a channel of technology transfer rather than FDI.[5] This, in part, is caused by the governmental policy of unpackaging. In other words, the Korean government had been relatively restrictive on FDI, while encouraging TL. In addition, this tendency may also be partly explained by the intrinsic characteristics of SMEs. By undertaking arms-length contracts, SMEs do not have to bear the risks involved in capital transfers. In addition, the remuneration from the technology is more stable if arm's-length contracts are used.

Thirdly, transfer of technology is a very complex process and much different from trade in goods and services. The market for the technology is very imperfect, and it takes considerable time to find the partners and to transfer technology. Personal interaction, such as training and technical consultancy, is an essential element in the successful transfer of technology.

Fourthly, adaptation of imported technology is usually carried out to meet differences in demand. The modification of technology to local production conditions, such as the relative prices of factors, does not seem to be part of the adaptation, however.

Fifthly, recipient firms are not isolated from domestic industries. They have very strong forward and backward linkages with domestic industries. They have also contributed to strengthening the competitiveness of the domestic economy.

Efforts have been made to judge the comparative performance of SMEs and large multinationals by utilising previous surveys on TL. The evidence, however, is not conclusive in most cases, due to the lack of a study on multinationals and licensing in general. Further research is necessary to for a more concrete comparison.

It is very difficult, moreover to test the hypothesis that SMEs can be as efficient as multinationals in the transfer of technology. On the other hand, SMEs are more likely to transfer technology to SMEs in the host country and are less likely to increase the concentration of the domestic markets. There are thus good reasons for the host

Government to prefer SMEs as a source of technology.

The main obstacle to SMEs going abroad lies in the high transaction costs associated with this process. Markets for technology are inefficient, thus it is costly for SMEs to collect or analyse information. Equity participation or contractual arrangements take time and are usually costly. It therefore seems desirable from the recipient country's point of view, for the Government to reduce these transaction costs for SMEs and their local partners.

Appendix: Case Studies

COMPANY A: FROM IMPORTS TO LICENSING

Company A was formed in 1980 by the merger of two smaller firms. Its employment level is about 70, and it produces jumper couplers for electric locomotives.

In producing jumper couplers, Company A receives orders from the Office of Korean National Railroads. The major production process involves the assembly of imported parts according to the drawings provided by the office. Company A is the largest in size out of 3–4 domestic competitors.

Company A was advised by the Office of Railroads to start producing locally the previously imported parts for making jumper couplers. Lacking the technological capability to produce those parts, the company contacted a Japanese firm which was one of the suppliers of the parts. The Japanese company, employing around 400 people, is a leading firm in the production of jumper couplers. It was willing to offer the technology for making the parts because the operation is no longer profitable in Japan.

The contract specified the royalty at 3 per cent of sales for a 5-year period. Through technology licensing (TL), Company A was able to lower the price of jumper couplers and to improve the quality significantly. Furthermore, Company A could export the parts. Presently, about half of the exports are shipped to the licensor. In other words, the licensor and the licensee have formed an international production division. Both Company A and the Japanese firm are satisfied with the outcome of TL.

COMPANY B: LICENSING WITH A FOREIGN ENGINEERING COMPANY

Company B is a producer of steel pipes; it was established in 1960 and at present employs more than 1000.

Expecting high demand from automotive manufacturing firms, Company B planned to produce machinery used for the coating of automobiles. TL was initiated by the company division in charge of the production of industrial machines. The division originally produced machines used by other branch of the firm.

The company actively sought a foreign source of technology and chose a French engineering firm from among several alternatives. The negotiation process took about a year. The royalty was set at 3 per cent of sales. In addition, fees for drawings, supervision, and training are paid separately.

Technology transfer occurs mainly through the despatching of engineers from the licensor. When the licensee receives an order for a machine which it has no experience in producing, it invites engineers from the licensor to supervise the production. In most cases, the mastery of technology is possible after the production of similar products twice. When the despatched engineers' supervision is not sufficient for mastery, the licensee sends its engineers to the licensor for training.

The division has now separated from Company *B* and formed a new company. The new company presently has a 5 per cent share of the domestic market.

COMPANY *C*: RESPONDING TO IMPORT COMPETITION

Company *C*, employing 20 people, specialises in industrial burners. Burners are very much differentiated by their purpose and the fuels used. Thus, each firm in Korea specialises in some segment of the market. In addition, the share of imports is high, approaching 70 per cent of total sales.

Imports flourish because domestic producers are inefficient. They lack technological capability. In addition, the domestic market is too small to achieve economics of scale. In other words, domestic manufactures produce on an order basis, while foreign manufactures produce according to the batch mode.

Company *C* accumulated technology by imitating foreign products; however, its level of expertise was not high enough to compete with imports and it lost market share, especially in high-pressure injection oil-burners. Foreign technology was sought to strengthen the firm's competitive position. Contact was made with an American company which is a major producer in the US burners industry and has concluded hundreds of technology licences with firms all over the world.

The American company also wanted to have a Korean partner to compete with a Japanese firm which had previously been a licensee of the firm. By having TL arrangements in some product lines, the licensor can also utilise the licencee as a sales agents for its many other products. Because the main motive of the licensor is to strengthen marketing channels in Korea, the royalty for the technology was minimal, at 1.7 per cent of sales, without any other payment. However, exports were prohibited for 3 years following the contract. The licensor does not wish to repeat the same experience that it had with Japanese firms.

The technology transfer involved mainly sending drawings and written technical information. Company *C* had the capability to comprehend and modify the drawings. For example, a change in the fuel tank capacity was made by the licencee without the help of the licensor. Company *C* was also able to apply the licensed technology to other products, and it acts as a domestic sales agents for the licensor.

COMPANY *D*: GETTING HIGH-TECH THROUGH LICENSING

Company *D* was established in 1947 and is a leading firm in the chemical industry. It employs over 8000 people and belongs to one of the largest conglomerates in Korea.

The company wanted to produce bio-engineered products to diversify its product lines and therefore sought a foreign technology supplier. With the help of a Korean–American professor, the company was able to contact US laboratory. The laboratory specialises in research and development in bio-engineering without actually being involved in production.

Through a TL contract, Company *D* was able to get the technology to make interferon and test drugs for hepatitis type B. The royalty was set at US$ 2.2 million as up-front payment and 12 per cent of sales as a running royalty. Company *D* also got assistance in choosing machinery and marketing information.

In addition to the licensing arrangement, Company *D* set up a subsidiary in the US to carry out joint research with the licensor. The company sent 10 researchers to the US. After 2 years of joint research, Company *D* has accumulated a considerable amount of technical know-how. At present, the company is ready for large-scale production of interferon and to test drugs for hepatitis B type. The subsidiary of Company *D* is still actively engaged in R&D in bio-engineering and is able to get technical assistance from the licensor, although the period of the contract is over.

COMPANY *E*: DIVERSIFYING PRODUCT LINES

Company *E* produces steel-made structures for ships. Since the early 1980s, the shipbuilding industry has experienced trouble due to a decline in world-wide demand and in consequence the company has also experienced a drastic decrease in its sales of steel-made structures. To compensate for the loss of sales, Company *E* sought new business.

A trading company suggested that Company *E* produce welding equipment to substitute for import and promised to help find a technology supplier. In addition, the trader agreed to assist in marketing the output if Company *E* commenced production.

With the help of the trading company, Company *E* found an American firm willing to provide technical know-how for the production of welding equipment and a contract was concluded a year later. The royalty is set at 8 per cent of the sales and the duration of the contract is 10 years.

The technology transfer consisted mainly of the provision of drawings and blueprints for basic system mechanisms. The absorption of the technology, however, took a very long time for many reasons. First, Company *E* had never produced welding machines before, and so their learning capacity was low. Secondly, the technology supplier was not very cooperative. It had management problems and was reluctant to offer services beyond those specified in the contract. Thirdly, differences in the specifications of parts between the US and South Korea made direct adoption of drawings from the supplier difficult.

After a long struggle, Company *E* was able to produce welding machines. However, they admit that their products are low in quality and that they will not be able to compete with imported products from Japan and the US in the near future.

Notes

1. The KIRI survey was conducted by mail and it is not a comprehensive as the survey by the author. But it contains much relevant information that allows an opportunity to compare characteristics of recipient of SMEs to technology recipients in general.
2. This conjecture is based on the fact that many licensing arrangements are intended to acquire brand names without actually transferring any technology. If there is no trade barriers, the conjecture may be wrong because increased efficiency may be gained by changing production sites.
3. In 1986, there were 108 cases of licensing with trademarks out of 517.
4. In the extreme case in which monopolistic rents consist of 100 per cent of the total royalty payment, taxation on the royalty payment will only reduce the supplier's share, without imposing any extra burden on the recipient.
5. This argument is based on the finding in the sample selection which is described above. Among the 39 cases out of 1500 of TL and 1000 of FDI (chosen as the candidates for the case studies) by the researchers in the advanced countries, 37 cases turned out to be licensing while two cases are associated with FDI.

15 The Case of Mexico

Miguel H. Márquez

15.1 REGULATIONS RELATED TO TECHNOLOGY TRANSFER, FOREIGN INVESTMENTS AND SMEs

In 1981, the Government decided to revise the law on the Register of Technology Transfer and the Use of Patents and Brand Names (RNTT) in effect since December 1972. The main reason underlying this revision was to adopt new mechanisms that would lay the groundwork for an effective transfer of technology.

The new law adopted in 1982 maintained payment control and the elimination of certain limiting factors as in the previous regulations, but also made the process of technology transfer more selective.

The following parameters were adopted, *inter alia*, as evaluation criteria:

- The share of foreign direct investment (FDI) in the recipient enterprise
- The degree or level of technology to be transferred
- The recipients' technological and industrial experience
- The size of the recipient's enterprise, and
- The industrial sector the recipient belongs to.

The National Development Plan adopted at the beginning of 1982 also included a series of policies and instruments which give special attention to FDI and the role of small and medium-sized enterprises (SMEs). In 1985 a series of Regulations were designed with the primary goal of facilitating the flow of FDI to Mexico.

With respect to SMEs, there have been even more important changes in the regulations. In effect, General Resolution No. 15 was adopted after accepting that SMEs, both on a national and an international scale, have been the main agents in Mexico's industrial development, as well as the promotors of technological innovation that have contributed to the process of industrial conversion. This Resolution is aimed at encouraging the flow of capital from these enterprises and their technology contribution to Mexico in the only way possible under a regulatory regime, by making an exception to the application of this regime.

432

Table 15.1   Firm size criteria

	Large	Medium-sized	Small	Total
Official*a*	7	6	4	17
GR No. 15*b*	2	7	8	17

Notes:
a In accordance with the criteria adopted by the Federal Ministries and in general, official institutions and agencies (Diario Oficial, 30 December 1986). These criteria are:

Industry	Employees	Sales (million pesos, 1986)
Micro	1–15	–80
Small	16–100	80–1000
Medium-sized	101–250	1100–2000
Large	251–	2100–

b In accordance with the criteria adopted by the National Commission for Foreign Investment in General Resolution No. 15 related to Small and Medium-sized Enterprises. These criteria are:

Industry	Employees	Sales ($ million)
Small	–249	–3.9
Medium-sized	250–500	4–8
Large	501–	8.1–

The criteria adopted to define what are considered to be SMEs were the following:

- Total amount of annual sales (8 million dollars)
- Number of employees (500).

In addition to these criteria there were four conditioning factors: the destination (by sector); employment and annual maximum volume of sales; minimum amount for export purposes; geographical location.

Table 15.2 Size of recipient enterprises, by no. of employees and type of recipient enterprise, no. of cases

No. of employees	Type of enterprise	Total	Subsidiary	Joint venture[a]	National
−25	Small	1	1	–	–
26–50		3	–	1	1
51–100		5	2	2	2
101–250		4	1	1	2
251–500	Medium-sized	3	2[b]	–	1
500–600	Large	–	–	–	–
601–700		1	–	–	1
Total		17	6	4	7

Notes:
[a] With the SME supplier of technology and whose share is less than 50 per cent of the capital assets.
[b] This includes a subsidiary that has only one technology contract with a SME.

15.2 DESCRIPTION OF THE MEXICAN SAMPLE

The number of local enterprises surveyed for this study included 17 companies. According to *official* criteria (Table 15.1), the sample included: seven large enterprises, six medium-sized and four small ones; however, the classification varies if we take into account the criteria adopted by the National Commission for Foreign Investment. According to Table 15.1 (GR No. 15), which is similar to the classification criteria used in Table 15.2, which was finally adopted for this study, the samply includes: one large enterprise, three medium-sized and 12 small. None of the enterprises surveyed has more than 700 employees.

The 17 enterprises interviewed belong to the manufacturing industry, 11 manufacture metallic products, machinery and equipment, and six produce chemicals.

A more specific breakdown by branches and types of industrial activities (Table 15.3) shows that five enterprises are in the field of chemicals (351 according to CIIU). Of those enterprises that belong to the metalworking sector, five manufactured metallic products (3819), two machinery and non-electrical appliances (3824), two machinery and

Table 15.3   Distribution by sector for technology transfer in the sample, no. of cases

Branch	CIIU	Total (no. of cases)
Paper		
Manufacture of paper-based articles	3419	1
Chemicals (351)		
Manufacture of fertilisers and pesticides	3512	1
Manufacture of resins, plastics		
Manufacture of synthetic or artificial fibres	3513	1
Manufacture of medicine	3522	1
Manufacture of perfume and cosmetics	3523	1
Manufacture and regulation of lubricants and additives	3540	1
Metallic products (3819)		
Manufacture and repair of metallic structures	3819	1
Manufacture of wires, metallic sheeting and other wire products	3819	1
Work involving thermal treatment, galvanoplasty and metal work in general	3819	2
Manufacture of other processed metallic products	3819	1
Machinery and non-electric Equipment (3824)		
Manufacture of machinery for assembly purposes and industrial equipment in general	3824	2
Machinery and electrical equipment (3831)		
Manufacture and assembly of machinery and equipment to generate and transform electricity	3831	2
Plastic articles (3560)		
Sheeting, profiles, fittings and others	3560	2
Total		17

electrical appliances (3831), two plastic articles (3560), and one is in the paper industry (3419).

With regard to the supplier firms, most of them (15) are medium-sized. Only two could be classified as small enterprises (Table 15.4). It is worth mentioning that two of those classified as 'medium-sized' enterprises sell over $100 million a year, but in spite of this, one does not surpass 400 employees, and its share of the home market is less than 30 per cent; the other has less than 600 employees.

11 of the companies are of US origin, three are French, two are German, and one Canadian (Table 15.4).

Regarding the forms of transfer adopted (Table 15.5), in 15 out of 17 cases there is a technology transfer agreement. Of these, for a majority

Table 15.4　Size of supplier by country of origin, by no. of employees, no. of cases

Country of origin	No. of employees				
	100	*101–250*	*250–500*	*500–750*	*Total*
United States	1		7	3	11
France			1	2	3
Federal Republic of Germany			1	1	2
Canada	1				1
Total	2		9	6	17

Table 15.5　Forms of technology transfer, no. of cases

SMEs share in the capital assets of the recipient (%)	Contract	No contract	Total
100	3	2	5
+ 50	–	–	–
– 50	3	–	3
0	9	–	9
Total	15	2	17

(nine cases), the SMEs have no share in the recipients' ownership. In three cases there was a contract, and the SMEs had a share under 50 per cent, and for the other three, in spite of being subsidiaries, a contract was signed. In only two cases surveyed (both subsidiaries) was there no contract signed for the transfer of technology.

According to data on the total number of technology transfer contracts in the Mexican manufacturing sector, the share in the overall number of contract of chemicals and metallic products, machinery and equipment, is important.

In effect, in both 1984 and 1987 almost 50 per cent of the overall number of contracts for technology in the manufacturing sector can be attributed to the chemical sector and to metallic products, machinery and equipment (Table 15.6).

The representativeness of our sample is corroborated also by the data included in Table 15.7.

In effect, of a total of 767 contracts for technology transfer registered

Table 15.6   No. of contracts registered in manufacturing, chemical and metallic products sectors, 1984 and 1987

	1984	(%)	1987	(%)
Chemicals	157	22.9	191	22
Metallic products	185	27.0	230	26
Other branches of the manufacturing sector	344	50.1	452	52
Total manufacturing sector	686	100	873	100
Total all sectors	969		1 810	

Source: General Direction of Technology Transfer, SECOFI.

Table 15.7   Main foreign suppliers of technology to the manufacturing sector and chemical, metallic products, machinery and equipment branches, 1986–7

Country	Contracts, manufacturing sector, no.	Chemicals, no.	Metallic products, mach. and equipment, no.	Others
United States	508	94	176	–
France	23	16	2	–
Federal Republic of Germany	35	10	16	–
Canada	10	1	6	–
Other countries	191	47	57	87
Total	767[a](100)	168[a]	257[a]	342

Note:
[a] There is a discrepancy between the overall figure for Table 15.6 and Table 15.7 because the figures do not take Mexico into account as a supplier of technology.

during 1986/87, 508 came from the United States, 35 from the Federal Republic of Germany, 23 from France, and 10 from Canada. 74 per cent of the total number of contracts for the transfer of technology registered in 1986–7 originated in these four countries. Technology contracts that involve enterprises from these four countries in the chemical area surpass 72 per cent of the overall number, and in the areas of metallic products, machinery and equipment, they account for 77 per cent of the total.

15.3   INTERSECTORAL ANALYSIS OF THE SAMPLE

Most of the recipient enterprises (15) began to operate in 1950; six during the 1950s; seven during the 1970s; two between 1981 and 1982; one in 1984; and only one initiated operations before the 1950s. Some of the companies established before 1970 were family-owned enterprises that turned into corporations as they developed and grew; 11 of the companies surveyed began to operate or to develop under the incentives derived from the import-substitution policy, and at least four were established during the high growth period of the Mexican economy in the mid-1970s (including the oil boom). These four companies directly or indirectly produce inputs for the energy sector.

In accordance with the previously adopted classification system (Table 15.2), 13 of the recipient enterprises are considered to be small; three medium-sized, and only one a large enterprise. The great majority operate in competitive global markets (eight) or in intermediate markets (five). For a few SMEs (four) competitors are three or less. The situation becomes even more complex if we try to evaluate the degree of competitiveness in specific markets, according to the enterprises' three most important products. In the majority of cases these are the same three products involved in the technology transfers. In spite of this, we can state that only in 2 per cent of the cases surveyed did the recipient enterprises control 100 per cent of the market for one or two products. In only four cases did one of the products represent more than 60 per cent of the market; in three cases it was between 40 and 50 per cent; and in just one case did it go beyond 30 per cent; in the seven remaining cases the enterprise controlled less than 25 per cent of the market.

In addition and due to the fact that in general we are dealing with relatively high customs duties in these industries (Table 15.8), competitive imports are not relevant. In effect, in seven of the cases studied

Table 15.8   Levels of customs duties for import of products similar to those manufactured by the recipient enterprises

Intervals	No. of cases
–	5
1 – 10	7
10 – 15	2
15 – 20	1
25 – 30	2

there were import duties of up to 100 per cent; in two cases between 10 and 15 per cent; in one case between 15 and 20 per cent; and in two cases between 25 and 30 per cent. Even for the cases surveyed who declared that there were no customs duties for those products similar to the ones they produced (a result of Mexico's entry into GATT), competition was still almost negligible.

According to the interviews, in 12 cases price appears as the most frequently-mentioned factor in terms of market competition. In second place we find quality (10), after-sales service (five), brandname (three), and only in one case was customer relations mentioned.

With respect to demand, a large number of cases interviewed (12) pointed out that the degree of concentration was low and that the number of users or buyers was broad. In a limited number of cases (four) they mentioned that the degree of concentration was high. Of these cases, one of them was limited to the demand exercised by the SME abroad, which absorbed almost 100 per cent of production; in two of them the customers were Government-owned (Pemex and the Federal Light and Power Commission), and finally, in only one case was the degree of concentration average, that is, limited to four large clients.

With respect to the modes of production (Table 15.9), we see that for the case of the subsidiaries a larger number (four) base their production on expected demand, and only two on orders. The two enterprises whose SMEs share in the recipient enterprise's capital assets is less than 50 per cent base their production on orders, and one of them combines both modes of production. Local enterprises include four which manufacture according to order and other four which combine both modes of production.

Finally, most of the recipient enterprises carry out some R&D activities (Table 15.10). Nine are domestic enterprises, of which six have a department devoted exclusively to these activities, with more than five but less than nine professionals or technicians. In only one of these cases are there eight full-time professionals and eight part-time employees.

Table 15.9 Mode of production and ownership of recipient enterprise, no. of cases

	Subsidiary	Joint venture	Domestic
Production based on orders	2	3	8
Production based on expected demand	4	1	1

Table 15.10　R&D activities and enterprise ownership, no. of cases

	Yes	No	Total
Subsidiary (or equity-controlled joint venture	2	4	6
Contracts (or minority joint venture)	9	2	11
	11	6	17

Of the remaining six enterprises that do not carry out research and development activities, four are subsidiaries and the other two deal with enterprises where the SMEs have a minority share in the capital of the recipient enterprise.

15.4　BACKGROUND INFORMATION REGARDING TECHNOLOGY TRANSFER

Among the six subsidiaries surveyed, in four cases the SME had no contact with the recipient company, and in only two cases did the SME export to the subsidiary (Table 15.11A). In four of these cases the initiative to make the investment in Mexico was taken by the SME. In all, the decision was based on good perspectives for economic growth in Mexico, and in three on lower export production costs. In one case, the initiative was taken by the local firm. In another case, the interests of the SME and the local enterprise were similar since the local company, which faced economic difficulties, wanted to sell the enterprise, and the SME wanted to buy a local enterprise given that the outlook for domestic market growth was favourable (and also to establish a 'beachhead' in Latin America).

In most cases (five) (Table 15.11B) no local partners were taken in and in only one did this take place, for legal reasons. In four of the cases the SME did not carry out market or feasibility studies, and for the one case where these were carried out, they were not useful.

The resources contributed by SMEs were frequently in the form of foreign currency, and to a lesser degree in capital goods and technology. Practically no enterprise had a problem in getting authorisation for its investment, and for the one case that did have a problem, it was because the legislation in effect did not allow for 100 per cent

Table 15.11   Background information: 1

A   Transfer of technology to subsidiaries (six cases)

Previous links	SME	none	4
		exported	5
Initiative taken by:		SME	5
		local enterprise	2
Resources contributed		foreign currency	4
		capital goods	3
		technology	2

B   Transfer of technology to subsidiaries (six cases)

	Yes	*No*	*Does not know*
Includes local members	1	5	–
Previous marketing studies	1	4	1
Problems in obtaining approval for the investment	1	5	–

subsidiaries in that field. In spite of this, an arrangement that was hard for the SMEs to implement in terms of subcontracting, exporting, rendering of accounts, etc. was made.

With respect to domestic enterprises (11 cases), the reason most frequently mentioned to justify the introduction of technology imported from SMEs was the need to modify the productive process(es) and, to a lesser degree, the need to diversify the lines of production, as well as to reinforce the enterprise's competitive edge. Only in one case was technology introduced to initiate activities, (Table 15.12A).

Of the 11 cases covered (Table 15.12B), seven had not made previous search efforts (three minority joint ventures and four 100 per cent local); however, where search efforts were made, in seven cases the recipient enterprises pointed out that there were other potential suppliers (six of them were domestic enterprises). In four cases the technology transferred was not available through other potential suppliers (two domestic and two minority ventures).

Most of the domestic enterprises surveyed (Table 15.12A) had some type of relationship previous to the contract with the SME. Frequently this contract involved trade or representation agreements and to a lesser degree, the import of parts and/or components from the SME. In only three cases was there no link whatsoever, and contact came about after

Table 15.12 Background information: 2

A   Transfer of technology through contracts or minority joint ventures

		Domestic (8)	Minority joint ventures (3)
	Initiate activities or product	1	2
Reasons	Diversification	3	1
for	Modification product processing	4	–
import-	Reaction to competition	1	–
ing	Reinforce due to competition	2	1
technology	SME image	1	–
	None	3	1
Previous	Marketed products	4	–
relations	Other contracts	1	–
with the	Imported parts	1	1
SME	Personal links	–	2

B   Transfer of technology through contracts or minority joint ventures

	Domestic (8)		Minority joint ventures (3)		
	Yes	No	Yes	No	Total
Previous search efforts	4	4	–	3	11
Transferred technology and other potential suppliers	6	2	1	2	11

the personal visit of a local partner from the recipient enterprise, or through a trade-exhibit organised by the SMEs embassy.

Among SMEs with minority joint ventures, in one case there was no previous contact, and in another they exported parts, and there was personal contact; in a third case it was only due to personal contacts that already existed.

15.5   CONTENT OF TECHNOLOGY TRANSFERRED

In all cases surveyed, the production know-how transferred was quite broad in scope, except technology for plant design. In effect, in the six subsidiaries, the know-how included processes and products; only for two cases was plant design technology included.

Know-hows were novel and not available in the local market for five subsidiaries. Only in one case could the know-how transferred be

Table 15.13   Nature of transferred know-how and transfer mechanism, frequency

	Know-how transferred in:			Mechanism of transfer in:			
	Plant	*Design of* Process	Product	Blue-prints	Special equip-ment	Export compo-sition	Techni-cal criteria
Subsidiary (or equity-controlled joint ventures) (6)	4	6	6	3	4	3	6
Contracts (or minority joint ventures) (11)	2	11	11	11	5	7	11

found on the local market. These process and products technologies were considered to be standard.

In nine of all cases that include both domestic and joint ventures with minority shares, the know-how transfer was still not being used in the local market by other enterprises, which in most cases was the reason why these enterprises continued to be competitive in spite of the presence of other competitors. In only two cases was the know-how transferred already in the market. In one of these cases, it was used by competitors.

For the whole sample, a wide array of mechanisms was used for the transfer of know-how.

Technical assistance was included in all cases with no exceptions (Table 15.13). In 14 cases blueprints, diagrams, designs or formulas (enterprises with a contract and three subsidiaries), were used, in 10 cases there were critical components (seven enterprises with contracts and three subsidiaries), and finally in nine cases special equipment was imported (five enterprises with contracts and four subsidiaries).

Most of the subsidiaries sent local technicians to the SME plant for training. Less frequently they accepted specialised personnel from the SME, and to still a lesser degree offered formal training courses, be it in Mexico or in the SME country of origin.

Of the six subsidiaries, four sent local technicians to the SME plant to learn the know-how and three others received technical staff from the SME to introduce the technology.

Table 15.14   Volume of production of local plant v. SMEs

	10 times smaller	Between 5 and 9 times smaller	Between 2 and 4 times smaller	Others
Subsidiaries (6)	4	1	–	Larger locally: 1
Contract (11)	7	1	1	Don't know: 2
Total	11	2	1	3

Among the enterprises with contracts or minority joint ventures, for only five of the 11 did the technology contract included a training programme for the staff. It was more common to send personnel to the SME for training or to a lesser degree to accept specialised staff from the SME.

Finally in the overwhelming majority of cases (11), the role played by local technicians was considered very significant; significant for six others, and of little significance in only one case.

15.6   ADAPTABILITY/ADAPTATION OF TECHNOLOGY TRANSFERRED

In four of the six subsidiaries the original plant design was changed locally. In the other two cases the plant design was imported from the SMEs country of origin. This effort had to be carried out, in one case, due to the size of the local market, or to the characteristics of local raw materials, or local labour. In the other case, the design of the original plant had to be modified due to limitations imposed by the local industrial park.

11 of the recipient plants operate with plants 10 times smaller than their respective SMEs. Two produced a volume two–four times smaller. Another two did not know much about the SMEs production. In only one case was the volume of production of the local plant greater than the SMEs (Table 15.14). In spite of this difference in volume, the technology used was the same for an overwhelming majority (14 cases). In the other three cases, technology had to be modified.

In spite of the fact that there is a great deal of heterogeneity regarding the origin of the equipment, most of the local plants (15) used equipment similar to the SME's. It should be pointed out that in two of these cases minor changes had been made to obtain products similar to those manufactured by the SME.

Only in two cases was the equipment used local different from that used by the SME. This can be explained in one of the cases by the fact that the products sold in the domestic market were less sophisticated than those sold by SME in their markets, and in the other case, because the equipment offered by the SME guaranteed the local enterprise more versatility than did equipment from other sources.

Undoubtedly the fact that most of the local enterprises used equipment similar to their respective SMEs influenced a large number of local enterprises in the design of the products similar to those manufactured by the SMEs.

In 13 cases the products manufactured locally were similar to those manufactured by the SMEs, and only in four cases – all of them enterprises with a technology contract – were the product(s) different. The factors behind those differences had mainly to do with the availability of inputs or components and the nature of local demand, factors outside the enterprise and, to a lesser extent, with the degree of vertical integration or the nature of the manufactured parts or components.

With regard to diversification, 12 cases confirmed that the SME's degree of diversification was greater than the local enterprise's. It was only in three cases that it was more diverse in the local plant, and in two cases they were not familiar with the SME's degree of specialisation. Perhaps the common elements in those cases for which the degree of diversification in the SME was higher than in the local enterprise resides in factors outside the companies themselves, in other words, the characteristics of the markets they are active in, their size, and especially the nature of the demand.

Regarding the degree of vertical integration, it was greater for the SME in two of the six subsidiaries; similar in another three and only in one case was there more vertical integration in the local enterprise.

Local subcontracting (Table 15.15), was utilised by five subsidiaries. In two cases this represented less than 5 per cent of the enterprise's overall production; in one case the percentage was between 5 and 10 per cent, and for two cases it went beyond 50 per cent. In one of these last two cases, the high percentage was due to conditions imposed by official agencies, since these were subsidiaries that operated in an industrial branch that the SMEs could not legally invest in.

In only two cases was the SMEs subcontracting much lower than the subsidiaries, and in four cases the percentage that the purchases

Table 15.15   Sub-contracting

	Does not exist	5	5–10	10–20%	20–30%	50%	Total
Subsidiaries	1	2	1	–	–	2	6
Contracts	2	2	1	3	1	2	11
Total	3	4	2	3	1	4	17

from regular subcontractors represented in the SMEs' overall production was not available.

Among the 11 domestic enterprises, two had no regular domestic subcontractors. In three of the 11 cases the purchase of inputs parts or components represented between 10 and 20 per cent; in two cases less than 5 per cent, and for another two it was equal to or above 50 per cent. In another case it was between 5 and 10 per cent, and finally for one last case between 20 and 30 per cent.

15.7   TECHNOLOGY CONTRACTS

As can be gleaned from Table 15.16, and given the special situation of the subsidiaries, negotiations are restricted to domestic enterprises and to those SMEs that have less than a 50 per cent share in the capital assets. Normally negotiations are shorter for domestic enterprises, generally less than a year. The longest time for negotiation (4 years) was for an enterprise with a supplier with less than 50 per cent ownership.

The most common problems that arise during negotiations are related to the royalties, the characteristics and types of technical assistance, and the use of brandnames. Official authorisation is more expedient in the case of subsidiaries and presents more stumbling blocks for the domestic enterprises (only two out of eight domestic cases did not have unusual delays), and for those enterprises with less than a 50 per cent share in the capital assets. The most frequent factor in the delay of official authorisation has to do with the percentage of royalties. For three out of eight cases involving domestic enterprises a programme of technological assimilation was required.

With respect to subsidiaries, the technology contract (present in four out of six companies in the sample) was adopted for various reasons, including the possible use of brandnames and patents, as well as their suitability as a way of taking money out of the country, covering legal

Table 15.16 Negotiation and official authorisation

Negotiation and authorisation		Total	Type of enterprise		
			Minority joint ventures (3)	National (8)	Subsidiaries (6)
Negotiation	No	6			
	Yes	11	3	8	
Problems	Royalties	10	3	7	
	Technical assistance	3	3		
	Brandnames	3		3	
	Input import	1		1	
Duration	6 months	4		4	
	1 year	2	1	1	
	2 years	1		1	
	4 years	1			
No problems		7		2	5
Some problems		10	3	6	1
Authorisation	– of royalties	5	1	3	1
	– of technological assimilation programme	3		3	
	– bureaucratic	3			

obligations in force at the time of the contract, etcetera.

Of the 17 cases surveyed, in 15 there was a technology contract. Only two subsidiaries did not use contracts.

According to Table 15.17 (which covers the whole array of contract objectives in the cases surveyed), for all the contracts more than one transfer objective was involved. Know-how was included in all transfers; in all cases it was a transfer of process and product know-how, and there were above know-how transfers for plant design in six cases (for more details see section 15.5).

13 contracts included brandnames. In three of these cases the enterprises surveyed claimed that this was not an important point in the process of technology transfer, but that it had been included in the negotiation 'package' and had to be accepted. In 10 of the cases patents were involved.

In more than half of the enterprises surveyed, the contracts included

Table 15.17   Objectives, duration, renewal and form of payment for contracts[a]

			Type of enterprise		
			Minority joint ventures	Domestic	Subsidiaries
Negotiation and authorisation		Total	(3)	(8)	(6)
	Know-how	17	3	8	6
Contract	Brandnames	13			
	Patents	10	2	5	3
Objectives	Technical service	9	3	6	
	Technical assistance	6			
	Marketing	2	1	1	
	Basic engineering	1		1	
Duration of The Original Contract	10 years	12	3	5	4
	5 years	3		3	
Contract Renewal	No	7	1	2	4
	Yes	8	2	6	
	– by use of permit	5	2	3	
	– by technology updating	5	2	3	
	– % share based on net sales	13	2 (3% and 5%)	7 (0.6% to 5%; most between 3% and 5%)	4
Form of Payment	– % share in the enterprise and input purchase	1	1		
	– % of invoiced sales[b]	1		1	

Notes:

[a] There is no technology contract for two subsidiaries. For the other four the form of the technology transfer is not similar to the other enterprises.

[b] This includes transportation, packaging, credit slips and returned goods.

technical services. According to data obtained, not all the contracts explicitly included this item from the beginning of the technology relation or transfer. It seems that subsequent problems during the productive process and in the design of products made these companies include technical services in the contract.

A smaller number of cases (six) included technical assistance in the technology agreements (help in the selection of materials, assembly operations and training). In only two cases did the technology contract include support and commercial expertise for the products included (not in the case of the subsidiaries), and in one of them it also included representation of the granting enterprise's products. Finally, only one of the cases included the provision of basic engineering.

Regarding the duration of the contracts, we should point out immediately that according to present legislation technology contracts should in principle not exceed 10 years. Changes would be granted only after evaluation of the justification of the request for a longer period and/or renewal of the contracts.

Practically all (12) of the enterprises entered into 10-year contracts. Only three of the contracts were for 5 years. With respect to renewal, eight were renewed, seven were not renewed, and only one was terminated before the period stipulated, at the request of the granting enterprises.

The reasons most frequently cited by the recipient enterprises for contract renewal were: (1) the need to keep abreast of process or product technology advances; (2) the possibility of manufacturing new products; (3) the continuation of a technology assimilation process which was still incomplete.

With regard to payments, nearly all recipient enterprises (13) made their payments based on a percentage of net sales of the products involved in the transfer. In one case the contract stipulated the payment of raw materials whose price had been set by the supplier. In only one case was the contract free of charge, but the recipient had to buy inputs, from the main office. (Most enterprises fell in the 3–5 per cent range and were obliged to stay under 5 per cent to obtain official authorisation.)

With respect to geographical limitations placed on the recipient enterprise (Table 15.18), there were a lot of restrictions in the contracts. In effect, 13 of the contracts had this problem, despite the fact that regulations in force in principle do not allow contracts with these restrictions to be registered. It is even more surprising to note that of the 13 cases mentioned, 11 are recipient enterprises where the SMEs either had no share in the capital assets or their share is less than 50 per cent.

Perhaps this situation is due to the fact that this geographical restriction mostly limited the recipients to the local market and to countries where there are no branch offices or representatives of the supplier.

Table 15.18   Geographical marketing conditions

Geographical aspects	Total	Type of enterprise		
		Minority joint ventures (3)	Domestic (8)	Subsidiaries (6)
No market restriction	4			4
Export restrictions to specific countries	8	2	5	1
Total export restrictions	5	1	3	1

For five cases (only one of the subsidiaries) the supplier limited the recipient to operating exclusively on the local market. A large number of those interviewed, as can be seen in section 15.8, felt that exports were secondary or marginal.

15.8   IMPACT OF TECHNOLOGY TRANSFER

Most of the cases surveyed (13) reported having achieved full assimilation of the transferred technology. In two cases assimilation was still incomplete due to the fact that technological changes implied constant modifications in processes and products. In the two remaining cases the degree of assimilation achieved could be considered very limited. In one case this was due to the scarce resources earmarked for training (added to the excessive turnover of technical staff), and in particular to the lack of time and sufficient experience.

A more detailed analysis of those cases where we could detect assimilation of the technology transfer allows us to see that in 15 cases (the 13 cases previously referred to, plus two cases where assimilation was incomplete), carrying out modifications and minor changes in the technology acquired was possible. The number of enterprises dropped to 12 when this assimilation eventually allowed them to design new products based on the technology acquired. There were even fewer enterprises (eight) that were able to transfer the same technology to other enterprises.

In general terms, the reason why most enterprises claimed to have reached full command of the technology was due to the fact that these companies already had previous experience before signing the contract or before the direct investment was made.

Table 15.19   Export of recipient enterprises

	Exports		
	Regular	*Occasional*	*Does not export*
Subsidiaries (6)	4	1	1
Contracts (or minority joint ventures) (7)	7	–	4
	11	1	5

Not less important in the process of technology assimilation was the role played by the suppliers. This can be grasped not only from the continuity of the technical relation that meant keeping the recipient enterprise up to date on technological innovations, but because most of the recipients incorporated technical training courses into their contracts and into their technological relations with the SME.

More than half of the interprises surveyed (11) exported on a regular basis (Table 15.19).

Of the five subsidiaries that exported, in only two cases did the exports have the SME as a destination. In one case the total amount of exports went to the SME, and in the other about 40 per cent of the total amount.

Among the seven cases of enterprises with a contract or minority joint ventures that exported on a regular basis, in three the total amount of exports had the SME as a destination, while for another three the exports had other destinations. Only in one case were the exports sent to the SME close to 30 per cent of the overall amount exported.

Of these 12 exporting enterprises, seven of them send their exports, or part of them, to Central America; five to the United States; four to South America; two to Europe and Canada; and in only one case are the exports or part of them earmarked for Japan.

With respect to imports, five of the subsidiaries had the SME as a source of supply of raw materials. In one of these cases the SME contributed 80 per cent of the supplies; in three cases it ranged from 20 to 30 per cent, and in one case it was close to 10 per cent.

With regard to enterprises with a contract or minority joint venture, two cases were registered where the imports came from the technology-granting SME. We do not know the impact of these enterprises on the total number of imports made by the recipient enterprises, although in both cases this operation was stipulated in the contract.

Table 15.20 Importance of technology transferred for local sales of recipient enterprises (10 cases) and exports (7 cases)

%	Local sales	Total exports
0	–	–
10–24	2	–
25–49	1	2
50–74	3	–
75–100	4	5
Total	10	11

The importance of technology transfer in terms of the enterprise's local sales can be appreciated by the high percentages that products related to the transfer of technology represent (Table 15.20).

In four of the 10 cases the share of the products related to the process of technology transfer in the total amount of local sales was very high (in two of these cases it was the total amount). In three of the cases this share was high, ranging from 50–74 per cent; in one case it was 40 per cent; and in two cases above 10 per cent but less than 24 per cent.

With regard to the importance of technology transfer in relation to total exports, it can be considered high if these seven cases export. Five of them export 100 per cent of the products manufactured with the technology received. In the two remaining cases, this share is between 25 per cent and 49 per cent.

15.9 RELATIONS WITH SMEs

As we can see in Table 15.21, in seven of the 10 cases of enterprises with a contract or minority joint ventures that considered the technology relation to be ongoing, the SME had sent improvements on more than one occasion, and in all 10 cases they had transmitted expertise in relation to technical problems.

In the case of the five subsidiaries that had defined constant technology relations with the SME, we found that all had received technical assistance in the form of new designs and quality control; in four cases under process engineering; in three cases for product marketing; in two cases for administrative organisation, and in only one case was technical support used for purchases to be made by the branch. Also,

Table 15.21   Technology relations with the SME

	Continuity		Modifications made by the recipients	
	Constant	*Sporadic*	*Yes*	*No*
Subsidiaries	5	1	3	3
Contracts (or minority joint ventures)	10	1	7	4
Total	15	2	10	7

and in keeping with Table 15.21, the 10 recipient enterprises had carried out improvements or modifications in the acquired technology (three subsidiaries and seven with a contract), while seven did not make any changes. For those cases where modifications were made, the SME agreed with nine of them and in the other case provided collaboration.

The nature of the intra-enterprise relations between SMEs and their respective subsidiaries went beyond the mere sphere of technology relations. In none of the six cases surveyed was the subsidiary contributing to the SMEs overheads or general expenses. In the six cases referred to, the General Director was appointed by the SME, but only in one case was the Production Manager appointed. Operation manuals used by the SME were used in four of the cases.

With respect to control mechanisms, all of the subsidiaries needed authorisation by the SMEs for their budgets; in two cases for budgets which would bring possible dividends, and in only one case for a budget or sales accounting. In three of the cases mentioned was there permanent control by the SME to such an extent that both budgets and accounting had to be produced monthly. In only two cases were these accounts made quarterly, and in another case they were made annually.

For the three cases out of the six that make up the group of subsidiaries, the maximum sum that could be spent by the enterprise without consulting the SME was $US10 000; in one case this limit was US$ 200 000; for another there was no limit; and finally for the rest of the subsidiaries there had never been a limit and it depended on how important the investment was. The General Director had to decide whether or not to consult the SME.

The diligence shown by the SME in terms of control through budgets or accounting is also confirmed by the frequent visits of SMEs authorities to the subsidiaries. Thus in four cases these subsidiaries received visits from SME employees at least twice a year for a period of at least 3 days, but not more than a week. In these same four cases the frequency and length of visits by the enterprise's officials to the SMEs were reciprocal or almost reciprocal, although at different times.

In one case the SME representatives visited the enterprises once a year for 5 days and the enterprise's counterparts visited the SME twice a year for 7 days, Lastly, in just one case the SMEs representatives never visited the subsidiary; on the other hand, the enterprise's representatives never visited the SME twice a year for 3 days.

Of the six cases analysed, two of them did not remit in royalty payments or any administrative fees on net sales. The other four paid royalties according to the clauses of the technology contract. Apparently this was the only type of payment made by the subsidiary to the SME.

15.10   EVALUATION

Virtually all of the enterprises under study considered the technology relationship with the SMEs positive and beneficial. only in two cases was it considered not to be valuable because the SME was not interested in the technology transfer, for two related reasons: first, the profits obtained from the contract entered into were not attractive, and secondly, they preferred to produce and sell their own products.

Of the 17 cases surveyed, eight of them considered as a favorable characteristic for the process of technology transfer the fact that the supplier was not a multinational or, in other words, that the enterprise was a SME. According to the persons interviewed, the smaller size made it possible to have permanent and close contact with executives of the SMEs, which in principle facilitated decision-making and eliminated the problems that might arise from the technology relationship.

In five cases the recipient enterprises surveyed stated that size was not a positive factor in the technology relationship, but four of these companies do not have any other previous experience to make a comparison with. The most important feature was the technology offered, and not the size of the enterprise.

Of the 11 enterprises with a contract or minority joint venture, four of them stated that they had no important problems in their relationship with the SMEs. In another four cases the problems that arose were derived from the overall financial or economic context, particularly related to financial costs (high interest rates), inflation, uncertainty, etc. In one case, the problem originated when trying to register the contract with the Mexican authorities, resulting in a loss of time and controversy with the SME. In another case, the biggest problem cropped up because of not having specified in the contract the forms and amounts of the payments for technical consultations, which led to the cumbersome discussions on this matter. It was only in one case that the problem of the non-transfer of know-hows and the termination of ownership of these rights arose and led to the cancellation of the contract.

There were no important problems for five subsidiaries. In another two the most common problems were the excessive delays in payments by Government-owned enterprises. A less frequently mentioned problem was the delay by suppliers and the quality of raw materials. It was only in one case that the biggest problem faced by the recipient enterprise was to win the confidence of the SME and liven up a contract that was until then only on paper.

Most of the subsidiaries agreed that the best point in their favor in the market with respect to their competitors was the quality of their products, especially in properly used technology transfer. Of less importance, one could mention administrative flexibility and freedom when compared to the SMEs and the possibility of resorting to foreign financing, which proved quite advantageous to the subsidiaries.

Three of the five subsidiaries under study surpassed the objective outlined at the beginning; two fulfilled their objectives, and only in one case did the subsidiary not meet the initial targets.

Only six of the 11 cases with contracts or minority joint ventures had subscribed other contracts in addition to those entered into with the SMEs. Of these, five underlined that the SMEs' record for technology training *vis-à-vis* other suppliers was good in terms of flexibility for adaptation to local conditions. The number increases to six if we compare the record of the SMEs with other suppliers in terms of the degree of formalisation of know-how. Responses are even more heterogenous if we evaluate their record in terms of cost of the process of transfer. In effect, in three cases the SMEs record was acceptable; in two cases it was held that the costs involved in the transfer programmes were slightly more expensive than those of other suppliers, and in one case they were considered very expensive.

The outlook of local enterprises is obviously strongly influenced by the critical economical, financial, and social situation of Mexico. The high degree of uncertainty that exists in the Mexican economy, in spite of the achievements attained through the 1970s' economic policies, means that in general enterprises are cautious with respect to increasing operations, and planning expansion.

16 The Case of Singapore

Pang Eng Fong and Annukka Paloheimo

Despite their growing importance in world trade and investment, Small and Medium Sized Enterprises (SMEs) have not received the research attention they deserve. In particular, not much is known about their performance and technology transfer experiences in developing countries. This chapter analyses the technology transfer experiences of a small number of Singapore firms that are subsidiaries or licensees of SMEs from industrial countries.[1] It is based largely on information collected in an interview-based survey carried out in May-June 1988. The survey covers 16 manufacturing firms in key industries, enough to provide a first look at the ways SMEs (defined as parent companies with less than 1000 employees) have transferred technology to Singapore, a newly-industrialising city-economy with a long-standing policy of openly welcoming foreign investment and technology. Foreign investors of many nationalities are represented in the sample. The sample firms account for around 15 per cent of the foreign manufacturing firms in Singapore whose parents fall within the definition used here for a SME.[2] Though small in number, the sample firms reveal an instructive range of experiences on technology transfer. Their experiences have, however, to be placed in a historical and policy context, namely that of a rapidly-industrialising, open city economy that imposes few restrictions on foreign investments.[3]

16.1 SINGAPORE'S DEVELOPMENT AND THE GOVERNMENT'S ROLE

Since independence in 1965, Singapore's economy has expanded very rapidly.[4] Its GDP growth rate averaged 9 per cent a year in the 1960s and 1970s, and 6 per cent a year in the 1980s, despite two world recessions, and a domestic recession in 1985–6.

Rapid growth has led to dramatic changes within the manufacturing sector itself. In the 1960s, most manufacturing firms produced for the domestic and regional markets, and the key industries were petroleum-refining, food and beverages, and printing and publishing. In 1970, the three largest industries were petroleum and petroleum products (with 20 per cent of the manufacturing value added), electrical machinery and electronic products (11 per cent) and transport equipment (mostly shipbuilding and repair, 15 per cent). In the 1970s and 1980s, many industries, including clothes, metal products, chemicals, electrical machinery and electronics products, expanded rapidly, creating a more diversified manufacturing sector. The electronics industry expanded fastest, its growth sustained in the 1980s by the influx of computer and disk-drive manufacturing firms. By 1986, it had become the largest industry, with a 32 per cent share of manufacturing value added, compared with 9 per cent for transport equipment, the second largest industry, and 7 per cent for petroleum and petroleum products. In 1988, the manufacturing sector exported over three-fifths of its output of $S55.4 billion.

Singapore's export growth was led by foreign firms. Wholly-owned foreign firms dominate Singapore's manufacturing sector. In 1986, they employed two-fifths of all manufacturing workers and accounted for two-thirds of Singapore's manufacturing exports. Wholly-owned local firms employed one-third of all manufacturing workers, but their share of manufacturing exports was only 11 per cent.

Though Singapore follows a free-trade policy, it is not a *laissez-faire* economy. The Government plays a highly interventionist role in Singapore's polity and economy (Lim, 1983). The ruling party, in power since self-rule in 1959, wields complete political control through its near-exclusive representation in parliament (it won all but one seat in the 1988 general elections), and its *de facto* control of the Government bureaucracy, the labor movement (through the National Trades Union Congress, whose Secretary-General is also a Deputy Prime Minister), and local community organisations. From the beginning, and especially since 1965, the Government has emphasised the importance of private enterprise and foreign investment to Singapore's industrial development. It affirmed the philosophy of economic freedom established in the colonial period, but added selective and powerful state controls to guide the economy and society. There are today only a few import tariffs, and most of these are aimed at deterring consumption of 'luxury' items such as cigarettes, alcohol, and automobiles. There are few controls on private investment or enterprise, no anti-monopoly laws, no technology transfer controls, or compulsory registration of contracts. Firms do not have to meet minimum local content requirements. Nor are they subject to restrictions on the remittance of profits and the repatriation of capital.

The absence of regulation on the flow of capital and goods does not make Singapore a free-market economy like Hong Kong. The government participates in the economy through its ownership, control or investments in 450 companies (excluding the subsidiaries of statutory boards), of which 65 are in the manufacturing sector. These companies which are run by professional managers are expected to be efficient and to make profits.

State involvement in the economy is not limited to Government-owned enterprises and statutory boards. The state exercises considerable leverage on the rest of the macroeconomy, through its monetary, fiscal, exchange rate, wage and manpower policies, as well as through its extensive and selective interventions in various factor markets. Compared to its interventions in factor markets, Government interventions in product markets are minimal. There are no direct controls on private sector production. Restrictions on investment in the services sector are not to protect local firms, but for social, strategic, and other reasons.

16.2 ROLE OF SMEs IN THE SINGAPORE ECONOMY

SMEs have played an important role in Singapore's economy. They form 90 per cent of all firms, produce 30 per cent of value added, and account for 40 per cent of total employment in Singapore (Lee, 1988). In the manufacturing sector, 86.7 per cent of the establishments in 1985 had between 10 and 99 workers. They employed half the manufacturing workforce but accounted for only a third of the manufacturing value added and capital expenditure.

SMEs in Singapore face a host of problems relating to technology, productivity, human resource development, business development, and finance – problems that affect their ability to innovate, upgrade and grow. These problems are particularly severe for local SMEs because of their low worker productivity. Local SMEs in the manufacturing sector, for example, are 34 per cent less productive than larger, foreign companies.

The Singapore Government is aware of the problems of SMEs. It has set up a SME Committee to coordinate the efforts of various government agencies including the Economic Development Board, the National Computer Board, the National Productivity Board, and Singapore Institute of Standards and Industrial Research. It has helped SMEs of all nationalities by improving the business environment and infrastructure, and by expanding the number of assistance schemes specifically tailored to help SMEs. The Small Industry Technical Assistance Scheme, Product Development Assistance Scheme, and Market Development Assistance Scheme have awarded S$15 million worth of grants to SMEs, while the Small Industry Finance Scheme has provided concessional loans amounting to S$1 billion for 4000 projects. Only a small proportion of SMEs have taken advantage of these schemes, and the government is expanding its efforts to tell SMEs about its programmes which are directed primarily, but not exclusively, at local firms. The government is also encouraging the private sector – banks, Multinational companies (MNCs), consulting firms, trade associations, business groups, and local chambers of commerce – to involve themselves in SME development.

16.3 ROLE OF FOREIGN INVESTMENT IN THE SINGAPORE ECONOMY

Foreign investments have been crucial to Singapore's rapid industrialisation since the late 1960s. In 1981, one-third of all firms were wholly or majority foreign-owned, and foreign funds amounted to two-fifths of all investments (Pang, 1987, pp. 89–92). In manufacturing, foreign direct investment (FDI) commitments formed 83.1 per cent of total net investment commitments in 1987 (Lim and Pang, 1988).

In 1981, the five leading investors were the United Kingdom, the United States, Hong Kong, Malaysia and Japan, which together accounted for 80 per cent of total foreign equity investment in all sectors of the economy. British investments were concentrated in petroleum refining, US investments in manufacturing, mostly oil-refining and electronics, while Japanese investments were mainly in manufacturing, trade and banking (Lim and Pang, 1988).

The most important foreign-dominated industries are petroleum, electronics and machinery. Nearly 60 per cent of the Economic Development Board's (EDB) figure of the cumulative stock of foreign manufacturing investment – S$12.7 billion in 1985 (Lim and Pang, 1988) – was in the first two industries which are characterised by high capital intensity and the use of high technology.

Direct investments accounted for 93.0 per cent of total foreign equity investments in 1981. The bulk of these investments were in wholly-owned subsidiaries, a characteristic that differentiates foreign investment in Singapore from those in neighbouring countries where foreign investment is mostly in joint ventures. Since 1981, with the increasing emphasis Singapore given to industrial restructuring and the attraction of high-tech firms for whom ownership is critical to control, the share of wholly-owned subsidiaries in the manufacturing sector has risen further (Lim and Pang, 1988).

16.4 KEY CHARACTERISTICS OF SAMPLE FIRMS

All but two of the 16 firms in our sample are wholly-owned subsidiaries of SMEs (Table 16.1), a distribution that is similar to that of foreign-owned firms in Singapore's manufacturing sector. The two exceptions are a joint venture with a European partner and a licensee. The joint venture came about because the European investor, even though it was allowed to set up a wholly-owned subsidiary, wanted to limit its equity involvement. The licencee case is unusual – the manager of the Singapore licencee met the technology seller, a chemist with long years of experience in developing specialty sealants, at a trade exhibition in North America. He bought from the seller for a one-off price and a small royalty special formulas for preparing industrial sealants. As the seller had neither the capital nor the experience to invest in other countries, he was eager to sell his formulas.

The large proportion of wholly-owned firms in the sample is the consequence of Singapore's open-door policy on foreign investment. The Singapore government imposes no restrictions on foreign ownership and allows foreign investors into most sectors of the economy. It does not restrict capital and profit repatriation. Nor does it require foreign investors to meet local content and other performance requirements. Also, as Singapore does not have a large domestic market, most firms investing in Singapore are export-oriented. Foreign firms therefore need not team up with a local partner for market access and regulatory reasons – the two main reasons for joint ventures in many developing countries. Technology level and international experience, two determinants found in previous studies (Davidson and McFetridge, 1985; Contractor, 1985) to explain the choice of a wholly-owned subsidiary over licensing and other forms of foreign involvement, are perhaps less important in the case of Singapore.

11 of the 16 sample firms employ fewer than 100 workers. Japanese and North American firms are on the average larger than European firms; one of them has a workforce of over 400 people. Most investments by SMEs from industrial countries are small, reflecting their

Table 16.1 Selected characteristics of sample firms, by country/region of origin

	Country/region of origin				
	Japan	US	UK	Europe[a]	Total
Ownership structure					
Wholly-owned subsidiary	7	2	3	2	14
Joint venture	–	–	–	1	1
Licencee	–	1	–	–	1
No. of workers					
Less than 50	2	1	2	2	7
50–99	2	1	1	–	4
100 and above	3	1	–	1	5
Size of foreign investment[b]					
Less than $US250,000	–	–	1	–	1
$US250,000–750,000	1	1	1	2	5
$US750,000–1 million	1	–	1	–	2
$US1 million–4.9 million	4	1	–	–	5
$US5 million and above	1	–	–	1	2
Investment sector					
Chemical/Plastics	1	–	2	–	3
Electronics	1	1	–	2	4
Machinery[c]	3	–	1	–	5
Other manufacturing[d]	2	2	–	1	5
Year of establishment					
1970–5	2	–	2	–	4
1976–9	4	–	–	1	5
1980 and after	1	3	1	2	7
Total	7	3	3	3	16

Notes:
[a] Excluding the United Kingdom.
[b] Excludes one firm which is a licencee.
[c] Includes industrial machinery and oil rigs and electrical machinery, apparatus and appliances.
[d] Includes fabricated metal products and precision equipment.

weaker financial capacity compared with large multinationals. Among sample firms, only two have invested more than US$5 million in Singapore. European and British SMEs invest largely in chemicals and electronics, two high value added and knowledge-intensive sectors. Japanese SMEs, in contrast, are represented in a wider range of industries.

Nine of the 16 sample firms were in Singapore before 1980. In com-

Table 16.2 Market structure of sample firms, by industry sector

	Industry sector				
	Chemicals/ Plastics	Electronics	Machinery[a]	Other Mfg[b]	Total
Product market structure					
Competitive	2	3	3	3	11
Concentrated	1	1	1	2	5
Industry structure					
Competitive	3	3	4	3	13
Concentrated	–	1	–	2	3
Local competition					
Yes	2	4	2	3	11
No	1	–	2	2	5
Import competition					
Yes	3	3	4	3	13
No	–	1	–	2	3
Total	3	4	4	5	16

Notes:
[a] Includes industrial machinery and oil rigs and electrical machinery, apparatus and appliances.
[b] Include fabricated metal products and precision equipment.

parison with Japanese SMEs, European SMEs are latecomers to Singapore. In part, this reflects their unfamiliarity with the Asian region compared with Japanese SMEs.

Most sample firms operate in competitive industries and sell in competitive markets (Table 16.2). Five firms – one each in chemicals/plastics, electronics and machinery, and two in other manufacturing – are in concentrated product markets. Three companies say they are in concentrated industries where a few sellers account for a large share of the world output.

Most of the firms, especially those in electronics, face competition in the local market from other suppliers. Only five firms do not have local competitors; four of them are in high value added industries including industrial chemicals, pharmaceuticals, non-electrical machinery, electrical and electronics products, and instrumentation equipment. All but three of the firms face stiff import competition, a direct result of Singapore's free-trade policy which allows firms to import duty-free supplies from anywhere in the world.

16.5 INVESTMENT MOTIVES AND STAGES OF INVOLVEMENT

Reasons for Investing Singapore

Foreign firms established themselves in Singapore for a variety of reasons. For sample firms, the single most important factor for choosing Singapore as a production location is growth prospects in the region. For Japanese SMEs, cost reduction is also a powerful motivation factor. Only one firm said Government incentives and the presence of other firms of the same national origin were important factors in their decision to move to Singapore. This finding that outward investments by SMEs are demand- and not supply-driven confirms that of Cheng (1986). It is also consistent with studies by Berger and Uhlman (1984) and Onida *et al.* (1985). Ozawa's study (1985) suggests that the development of new markets is the main factor motivating Japanese SMEs to internationalise. Our survey supports this conclusion only partially – many Japanese SMEs said cost considerations were just as important as market prospects.

Table 16.3 suggests that sample firms which are in high-tech, that is, high value added industries are more growth- and cost-oriented than those in low-tech, that is low value added and mature industries. This finding is consistent with Vernon's product life cycle theory (1974), which suggests that once a product enters a mature phase in its growth cycle and requires more unskilled labour in its manufacturing process, its production will shift from industrial countries where labor costs are high to developing countries where labor costs are low.

Government Incentives and Investment Decision of SMEs

Since 1960, the Singapore government has offered a growing number of tax and other incentives to promote foreign investments that meet its development priorities. The basic incentive remains 'pioneer status', which provides for exemption from the 33 per cent company tax for a period of 5 or more years, depending on such factors as the size of the investment, the number of skilled jobs created, R&D spending, etc. A second incentive encourages exports by taxing approved export profits at only 4 per cent. The normal incentive period is 5 years, but it can be as long as 15 years for unusually capital-intensive projects. The Government administers its incentive schemes flexibly and has been known to offer highly-desired companies specially-tailored incentives.

Table 16.3 Investment motives of sample firms by country/region of origin and technology level

	Investment motive				
	Growth	*Cost*	*Growth and cost*	*Growth, cost and Govt incentives*	*Total*
Country/region of origin					
Japan	3	–	3	1	7
United States	2	–	–	–	2
United Kingdom	3	–	–	–	3
Europe (excluding United Kingdom)	2	1	–	–	3
Technology level					
High[a]	7	–	2	1	10
Low[b]	3	1	1	–	5
Total	10	13	1	1	15[c]

Notes:
[a] High-technology firms are in the following industries: industrial chemicals/gases (industry code 351); chemical products (industry code 352); industrial machinery and oil rigs (industrial code 382); electronic products and components (industry code 384) and precision equipment (industry code 386).
[b] Low-technology firms are in the following industries: plastic products (industry code 357); fabricated metal products (industry code 381) and electrical machinery, apparatus and appliances.
[c] Excludes one firm which is a licencee.

Over the years, the government has also developed many schemes to help SMEs, especially the local ones. But is does not have incentives that are especially intended to promote investments by foreign SMEs. In recent years, the Government's investment promotion agency, the Economic Development Board, has expanded efforts to identify and persuade high value added foreign SMEs to set up operations in Singapore. These efforts reflect the government's recognition that high-tech foreign SMEs are needed to broaden and deepen Singapore's industrial sector.

Only seven out of the 16 SMEs applied for pioneer status at the time of entry. Most of the rest did not apply. For them, tax breaks were not the most important consideration. Their reason for investing in Singapore had more to do with the island's excellent infrastructure and institutional efficiency.

Table 16.4 Exports of sample firms by country/region of origin and technology level

	Exports as % of total output			
	Less than 25%	25–49%	50% & more	Total
Country/region of origin				
Japan	1	–	6	7
United States	1	–	1	2
United Kingdom	–	–	3	3
Europe (excluding United Kingdom)	–	1	3	4
Technology level[a]				
High	1	–	9	10
Low	1	1	4	6
Total	2	1	13	16

Note:
[a] See notes in Table 16.3 for classification of high- and low-technology firms.

Export-orientation, Firm-specific Skills and Market Position

Most sample firms are highly export-oriented. 13 out of 16 sample firms export more than half of their Singapore output, a proportion not much different from that of the manufacturing sector as a whole (Table 16.4). This finding does not bear out the hypothesis of White and Campos (1986, p. 23) that SMEs are more export-oriented than large MNCs in export-oriented countries. In Singapore, most foreign firms, regardless of their age and nationality, must export because Singapore's domestic market is too small to absorb most of their output. Only two firms, both of them very small and producing low value added goods, export less than a quarter of their output.

Dunning's eclectic theory of international production (1988) postulates that the possession of firm-specific skills partly explains why a firm can successfully enter foreign markets. The survey provides some evidence in support of the theory – most responding firms say they possess some firm-specific technological advantages which give them an edge over local firms. The experience of the sample firms is also consistent with a study by Borner *et al.* (1985) which attributes the international success of Swiss SMEs to their firm-specific skills and technology.

Table 16.5 Market position and prior experience of sample firms by country/region of origin

| | Country/region of origin | | | | |
	Japan	US	UK	Europe[a]	Total
Parent company market share					
Less than 25%	2	1	1	1	5
25–49%	1	–	–	–	1
50% and more	4	1	2	3	10
Position in industry					
Leader	5	1	2	2	10
Follower	2	1	1	2	26
Prior experience					
Exports	2	–	3	–	5
Local agent/sales subsidiary	–	–	–	2	2
Business/personal contacts	2	–	–	1	3
Exports and local agent	2	2	–	–	4
Local agent and business contacts	1	–	–	–	1
No contacts	–	–	–	1	1
Total	7	2	3	4	16

Note:
[a] Excluding the United Kingdom.

A large number of the SMEs are market leaders in their home country (Table 16.5). About half of them report market shares of over 50 per cent in their home market, a clear indication that they possess a competitive technological edge over their rivals within and outside their home country. Japanese and US firms are more likely than European firms to characterise themselves as leaders rather than followers. The survey suggested that 'leader' firms follow a more aggressive policy of developing new markets while 'follower' firms tend to adopt strategies to defend their market shares against competitors by moving some production to lower-cost locations.

Stages of Involvement in Singapore

The survey reveals that sample firms took the initiative when they decided to invest in Singapore. None came to Singapore as a result of overtures made by Singapore companies or the Economic Development

Board (EDB), the Government's investment promotion agency. There is no common pattern of entry stages among sample firms, but entry via exports by itself or with the help of a local agent was the most common mode (Table 16.5).

Japanese SMEs reveal a variety of experiences with Singapore prior to setting up manufacturing facilities in Singapore.

Technology influences the mode of entry into new markets. As hypothesised by Teece (1981), and empirically tested by Paloheimo (1986), Anderson and Coughlan (1987), and Davidson and McFetridge (1985), high-technology firms are more likely to use internal or high-control entry modes, i.e. modes which allow them to retain control over their proprietory technology in entering new markets. Such modes include exporting, setting up their own sales subsidiary in the importing country, and direct investment. Evidence from the survey lends some support to this hypothesis. Eight out of the 12 SMEs which exported directly and/or through their own subsidiary prior to investing in Singapore are high-tech firms.

Most SMEs had already established one or more foreign subsidiaries in other countries before they invested in Singapore. In most cases, the first subsidiary was in a developed country. This finding supports White and Campos (1986, p.20) who suggest that firms from developed countries are more likely to invest first in other developed countries, before committing resources to developing countries, and also Davidson (1980) who suggests that a firm's first international investments are likely to be in culturally and physically close countries. Internationalisation is greatest among European SMEs. Japanese SMEs fall into two polar groups: they either have no other overseas plants or they have more than one.

16.6 TECHNOLOGY TRANSFER AND TRAINING

Half the sample firms received technology from their parent in a package (Table 16.6). Japanese SMEs were more likely than firms of other nationality to transfer plant design, process and product technology in a single package. This finding is similar to that of Cheng (1986). Seven firms said their technology was unique and not used by their competitors in Singapore. Japanese SMEs were more likely than European SMEs to bring in unique technology.

10 of the 16 firms reported that local technicians played a significant or very significant role in the technology transfer process (Table 16.7).

Table 16.6   Technology level and transfer of sample firms, by country/region of origin

		Country/region of origin			
	Japan	*US*	*UK*	*Europe*[a]	*Total*
Technology transferred					
Plant design and process technology	–	1	–	1	2
Process and product technology	1	–	3	1	5
Product technology only	–	1	–	–	1
Plant, process and product technology	6	–	–	2	8
Technology of SME					
Unique compared to local competitors	5	–	–	2	7
Not unique	2	2	3	2	9
Total	7	2	3	4	16

Note:
[a] Excluding the United Kingdom.

Five of the seven firms that rated the role of local technicians to be highly significant were European (including British) firms. Only one Japanese SME suggested that local technicians played an unimportant role in transferring technology. This finding differs from that of Cheng (1986), who found that most Japanese SMEs relied primarily on Japanese engineers and technicians to transfer technology to Singapore, with local technicians playing a small supporting role. One possible reason for the conflicting result between this study and that of Cheng is that the mix of firms in the two surveys is different. Another is that the question may not have been interpreted in the same way by responding firms in the two studies.

The role of local expertise is significant regardless of the technology level of the firm – both high- and low-technology firms depend heavily on local technicians for the successful transfer of technology. This finding suggests that local technological capability is sufficiently well-developed to absorb new foreign technologies, whatever their level.

Most sample firms train their technical personnel in Singapore and the home country. All Japanese firms sent local technicians to Japan for training. They do so not only to transfer technical skills but also to familiarise local technicians and engineers with the corporate culture

Table 16.7 Training in sample firms, by country/region of origin

	Country/region of origin				
	Japan	*US*	*UK*	*Europe[a]*	*Total*
Role of local technicians in technology transfer					
Very significant	1	1	2	3	7
Significant	3	–	–	–	3
Fairly significant	2	1	–	–	3
Not significant	1	–	1	1	3
In-house training conducted by home SME					
Yes	6	2	2	2	12
No	1	–	1	2	4
Local technicians sent to home SME					
Yes	5	2	1	2	10
No	2	–	2	2	6
On-the-job training only					
Yes	1	1	1	2	5
No	6	1	2	2	11
Local technicians sent to home SME					
Yes	7	2	2	2	13
No	–	–	1	2	3
Total	7	2	3	4	16

Note:
[a] Excluding the United Kingdom.

of the parent company. They believe head office training will help local technicians and engineers to work better with the head office.

Japanese SMEs also send their engineers and technicians to their Singapore plants, in most cases for periods of up to 3 months. Compared to SMEs from other industrial countries, Japanese SMEs are more likely to encourage a two-way flow of personnel between the head office and its subsidiaries, a practice that improves cooperation and understanding between the head office and the Singapore subsidiary. European firms, on the other hand, depend more on local on-the-job training, especially when introducing low-tech products. Two reasons explain the lower reliance on home-country training among European firms. First, home-country training if it involves many persons is more costly for them than sending their technicians to Singapore. Secondly, European SMEs view home-country training mainly in technical terms and do not see it as an important element in fostering company spirit and cooperation between themselves and their Singapore plant.

The technology level of the subsidiary also strongly influences whether home-country training takes place. An SME is more likely to provide home-country training for local technicians if it is introducing new or high-techlines in its Singapore subsidiary. Technology transfer involves the transfer of both engineering and technical know-how as well as non-technical know-how such as management organisation, marketing techniques, personnel relations, etc. Less than half of the SMEs provide both engineering and non-engineering assistance to their Singapore plants. In keeping with their close relationship with and control over their Singapore plants, Japanese SMEs are much more likely than SMEs from other industrial countries to ensure that both types of technology transfer occur.

Except for the licencee firm, no other firm in the sample has a formal agreement with its technology supplier. For all but one firm in the sample, technology transfer occurs as part of the process of setting up and managing a new enterprise. It involves the transfer of both propriety and non-propriety knowledge, technical as well as management know-how. It is consequently a complex, on-going process that requires close interaction between the technology supplier and the local firm (Teece, 1981). Manuals are not enough, and formal agreements unnecessary, especially since most sample firms are wholly-owned subsidiaries rather than licensees.

16.7   TECHNOLOGY ADAPTATION

Sample firms make a narrower range of products than their parent companies, a finding consistent with a study of Swiss SMEs (Borner *et al.*, 1985) which finds that, among successful companies, internalisation and internationalisation are limited to the central core functions and products (Table 16.8). They also operate plants that are much smaller than their parent. Six of the 16 sample firms are less than one-tenth the size of their parent company. Only in two cases is the Singapore plant of the same size as the parent company. Japanese subsidiaries are more likely than American and European ones to be closer in size to their parent companies.

Most firms said they manufactured products similar to those made by their parent company. They also used equipment similar to that

Table 16.8 Product development, product design, plant size and equipment of sample firms, by country/region of origin

	Country/region of origin				
	Japan	*US*	*UK*	*Europe*[a]	*Total*
Product diversification					
SME products more diversified	5	1	3	2	11
Same	2	–	–	2	4
Not applicable	–	1	–	–	1
Plant size					
Same size as SME	1	1	–	1	3
2–4 times smaller	2	–	–	–	2
5–9 times smaller	1	–	2	–	3
More than 10 times smaller	3	1	–	2	6
Not applicable	–	–	1	1	2
Product design					
Different from SME	1	1	3	1	6
Same	6	1	–	2	9
Not applicable	–	–	–	1	1
Equipment used					
Same as SME	6	2	1	4	13
Different from SME	1	–	2	–	3
Total	7	2	3	4	16

Note:
[a] Excluding the United Kingdom.

used by their parent company. Six firms said that their product design was different from that of their parent. In most of them, however, the difference was small, involving minor modifications to equipment and machinery to suit the smaller scale of production in Singapore. One British SME, for example, modified its process technology to accommodate the smaller output of its Singapore plant. It substituted more labor-intensive methods for the more machine-intensive methods used by the parent company. None of the firms that had to make design changes report any difficulty in making the changes.

There is no evidence to suggest that product adaptation is related to technology level. Both high- and low-tech firms make product design changes to reduce production costs rather than meet the needs of the domestic market.

Table 16.9 Vertical integration and domestic subcontracting in sample firms, by country/region of origin

	Japan	US	UK	Europe [a]	Total
			Country/region of origin		
Vertical integration					
SME more integrated	6	1	2	2	11
Same level of integration	1	1	1	1	4
Not applicable	–	–	–	1	1
Domestic subcontracting					
Yes	7	1	–	2	10
No	–	1	3	2	6
Total	7	2	3	4	16

Note:
[a] Excluding the United Kingdom.

Only three firms used equipment that was different from that of their parent. This was because their product mix was different from that of the parent. Most of the equipment of sample firms were bought from or purchased through the parent. Local firms supplied only about 20 per cent of the equipment bought by sample firms.

16.8 VERTICAL INTEGRATION AND SUBCONTRACTING

Most sample firms are much less vertically integrated than their parent companies (Table 16.9). This difference arises largely because of their smaller plant size and narrower product range. Their high export-orientation reduces the scope for forward linkages, while Singapore's poor natural resource base limits opportunities for backward linkages.

10 of the 16 firms buy some of their inputs from local suppliers, even though Singapore imposes no local content rules. Compared to firms of other nationalities, Japanese firms buy more of their inputs locally, though not necessarily from locally-owned firms. In fact, a sizeable proportion of their inputs are purchased from Japanese suppliers operating in Singapore. Only two firms buy local inputs that exceed 50 per cent of their output value. 10 firms said local suppliers provided only a small proportion of their inputs; six of them were in high-tech industries which had difficulties finding local suppliers which could make the parts and components they needed. The survey suggested

that linkages developed more strongly among low-tech firms than among high-tech firms, a result similar to that of Lall (1980), who found that low-technology firms, partly because they are older, have better-established relations with many suppliers who have the capacity to make the inputs they need.

Local purchases of sample firms have increased absolutely but not relatively. Sample firms still depend highly on imported inputs. This finding is not surprising as firms are free to buy inputs from anywhere in the world. For almost half the sample firms, relative dependence on local inputs has fallen. This decline reflects a number of separate factors, including the unavailability of local supplies, particularly for high-tech firms, cheaper imports (because of the strong Singapore dollar) and stronger ties with home-country suppliers.

Low forward and backward linkages are to be expected, given Singapore's small, open, resource-poor economy. The lack of a well-developed indigenous parts industry also adds to the weakness of backward linkages (Lim *et al.* 1988, p. 266). The high export-orientation of sample firms accounts for the lack of forward linkages, though still weak, linkages are growing with the broadening of Singapore's industrial sector. High local linkages, it is important to remember, are not an end in themselves. They are important only if they strengthen technological capability and quicken industrial growth. Policies that compel firms to forge local linkages may harm productive efficiency.

16.9 TECHNOLOGY ASSIMILATION

The success of technology transfer can be assessed in several ways. These include the degree of technology assimilation by the local subsidiary, the extent of local R&D activity, the success of the subsidiary in achieving various output, sales and other objectives, and so on.

All 16 firms in the sample said they had assimilated the new technology provided by their parent company. All but two claimed to have mastered the technology transferred by their parent company (Table 16.10). Several said they had also developed a capability to modify technologies provided by their parent company. One reason why Singapore firms can assimilate technology quickly is the absence of language barriers and the high education level of Singapore's technically-qualified workforce. Almost all engineers and technicians are competent in English, the language of government, commerce and industry in Singapore. This competence facilitates learning from foreign instructors as well as from

Table 16.10　Technology assimilation and performance of sample firms, by country/region of origin

	Country/region of origin				
	Japan	US	UK	Europe[a]	Total
Assimilation of transferred technology					
Yes	5	2	3	4	14
No	2	–	–	–	2
Performance					
Better than expected	5	1	3	1	10
As expected	–	1	–	–	1
Did not meet expectations	2	–	–	2	4
Not applicable	–	–	–	1	1
Output exported to parent company					
Yes	3	–	–	1	4
No	4	2	3	3	12
Annual sales growth, past 5 years					
Less than 10%	1	–	–	1	2
10–20%	6	2	2	2	12
More than 20%	–	–	1	1	2
Total	7	2	3	4	16

Note:
[a] Excluding the United Kingdom.

training manuals, video programs, etc. A second factor quickening technology assimilation is the high motivation of Singapore's workers who share a success and work ethic uncommon among developing countries.

Sample firms carry out little R&D work in Singapore. Only one high-tech German firm making multi-layered printed circuit boards has a formal R&D unit staffed by three engineers. The main reason for the low level of R&D work in Singapore is that most firms manufacture products similar to those of their parent company which carries out the R&D. There is no need for subsidiary firms to adapt their products to local conditions, a requirement that encourages R&D. Also, most SMEs are too small to support cost-effective, decentralised, applied R&D work in their subsidiaries (Mansfield, Teece and Romeo, 1979).

10 firms had more than met the objectives set by their parent company (Table 16.10). Four firms did not achieve their targets, not because

they had had problems assimilating the technology provided by their parent, but because of other factors including unexpected shifts in demand, labour shortages, and high operating costs in Singapore.

Most firms reported significant improvements in worker productivity and plant efficiency. Many firms said the gap in worker productivity between the Singapore plant and the home-country plant was narrowing. Even so, according to Japanese and German firms, workers in Singapore still have a long way to go before they match their counterparts in Japan and Germany in productivity and experience.

Despite their rapid expansion, sample firms are still small compared to their parent company. Most expect to continue to grow rapidly in the future, but with little expansion in employment. Most firms have problems hiring workers, particularly production workers and experienced engineers, because of the widespread shortage of labour in Singapore. All of them are expanding their training and automation programmes to reduce their labour requirements. Several are planning to relocate some of their more labour-intensive products to lower-cost, more labour-abundant locations in the Southeast Asian region.

16.10 LINKS WITH TECHNOLOGY SUPPLIERS

Only four firms send their output back to their parent company. Japanese firms are more likely to have intra-firm trade with their parent companies than American and European firms. They also rely more on their parent company for exporting marketing, unlike European subsidiaries, most of whom handle their own marketing. This difference reflects the greater control Japanese SMEs exercise over their subsidiaries in Singapore compared with American or European SMEs.

Only six firms pay royalties based on sales to their parent company. Royalty payments, however, do not appear to be related to the nationality of the SME or its technology level.

10 SMEs set the prices for inputs they provide to their Singapore subsidiaries. Japanese SMEs are more likely than American and European SMEs to determine the prices of inputs purchased by their subsidiaries. All but one Japanese SME said they fixed the prices of inputs exported to Singapore subsidiaries. In imports from their parent company, as in other areas, Japanese subsidiaries have less autonomy than their American and European counterparts.

All but two Singapore subsidiaries submit monthly reports to their parent company. One German firm said it did not have to submit monthly reports, while another, a British firm, said it had to submit weekly reports. Compared to SMEs of other nationality, Japanese SMEs impose much stricter reporting requirements on their Singapore plants.

16.11 CONCLUSIONS

Three conclusions can be drawn from the experiences of the 16 sample firms. First, there is a large difference between the behaviour of Japanese SMEs and SMEs from other industrial countries. Japanese SMEs exercise greater control in many areas (e.g. training, reporting requirements, technology decisions, equipment purchase, etc.) over their Singapore subsidiaries than American and European SMEs. Nationality is an important variable in determining parent – subsidiary relations, but it is not a crucial determinant of effective technology transfer. Most firms in the sample have successfully assimilated the technology transferred by their parent company. This finding leads to the second conclusion of the study, which is that effective and speedy technology transfer requires an economically liberal and politically stable environment in which firms can freely pursue their profit goals. Through its various policies which expand economic opportunities for firms, Singapore has created such an environment.

Finally, the experiences of the sample firms suggest that the best way to speed up technology transfer is not to hurry it up with local content and other performance requirements. SMEs will transfer technology to their subsidiaries or partners at a speed that reflects local capabilities. If local conditions are not suitable, firms will be slow or reluctant to transfer technology. The proper role of the Government should be to ensure that there is an adequate supply of motivated and educated workers who can be trained quickly and retrained to learn new skills that new technologies demand. Judging from the positive experiences of most sample firms in this study, it is a role that the Singapore government has played with some success.

Notes

1. The study was carried out as part of an international collaborative programme on SMEs coordinated by the Centre for the Study of Development and International Economic Relations (CEDREI) in Buenos Aires. Financial support for the study was provided through CEDREI by the

Canadian International Development Research Corporation. Originally as part of the study, 30 firms with SME involvement were to be interviewed, but some could not be traced and a few were discovered to be involved only in trading activities.

2. In 1986, out of 3449 manufacturing firms in Singapore, 701 or more than one-fifth were wholly or more than half-owned by foreigners. They accounted for 55 per cent of the manufacturing workforce of 246 682. Most of them are subsidiaries of large multinationals. Probably no more than 100 of them have parent companies which employ less than 1000 workers.

3. Trade is very important to Singapore's economy. In 1969, the ratio of total trade to GDP was 2.1. In the 1970s, trade expanded faster than GDP, with the result that by 1980, the ratio stood at 3.8, one of the highest in the world. In the period, 1969–88, total trade multiplied more than 16 times. Imports exceed exports, giving Singapore a merchandise trade deficit which was more than offset by the inflow of long-term capital and the exports of services.

4. For a further discussion see Pang (1989).

Select Bibliography

Acs, Z.J. and D.B. Audretsch (1988) 'Innovation in Large and Small Firms: An Empirical Analysis', *American Economic Review*, 78(4).

Aharoni, Y. (1966) *The Foreign Investment Decision Process*, Graduate School of Business Administration, Boston: Harvard University.

Alam, G. (1988) 'India's Technology Policy: Its Influence On Technology Imports and Technology Development', in Desai (1988a).

American Business Conference (1987) *Winning in the World Market*, Washington: McKinsey & Co., Inc.

Anderson, E. and A.T. Coughlan (1987) 'International Market Entry and Expansion via Independent or Integrated Channels of Distribution', *Journal of Marketing*, 51.

Andrews, K.R. (1971) *The Concept of Corporate Strategy*, New York: Dow Jones-Irwin.

Aoki, M. (1984) 'Innovative Adaptation Through the Quasi-Tree Structure: An Emerging Aspect of Japanese Entrepreneurship', *Zeitschrift für Nationalökonomie*, 4.

Balanco Anual, (1988) Gazeta Mercantil, São Paulo.

Barca, F. (1988) 'La Dicotomia dell'industria Italiana: le Strategie delle Piccole e delle Grandi Imprese in un Guindicennio di Sviluppo Economico', paper presented at Bank of Italy seminar *'Ristrutturazione economico-finanziaria delle imprese'*, Rome (27–28 June).

Becattini, G. (ed) (1987) *Mercato e Forze Locali: il Distretto Industriale*, Bologna: Il Mulino.

Berger, M. and L. Uhlman (1984) 'Auslandsinvestionen Kleiner und Mittlerer Unternehmen', *IFO Schnelldienst*, 30/84.

Bertin, G.Y. (1986) *Transfer of Technology to Developing Countries by France's Small and Medium-sized Enterprises*, UNCTAD/TT/84, Geneva: UNCTAD.

Bertin, G.Y. and S. Wyatt (1988) *Multinationals and Industrial Property*, Atlantic Highlands, NJ: Humanities Press.

Bertsch, R., (1964) *Die industrielle Familienunternehmung*, Winterthur: Schseurberg.

Birley, S. (1982) 'Corporate Strategy and the Small Firm', *Journal of General Management*, Winter.

BMZ (1982) *Deutsche Unternehmen und Entwicklungslander*, 2nd edn, Bonn.

Borner, S.B., *et al.* (1985) 'Global Structural Change and International Competition Among Industrial Firms: The Case of Switzerland', *Kyklos*, 38.

Braun, H.G. (1983) 'Strukurelle Probleme Mittelstandischer Unternehmen bei Direktinvestitionen in Entwicklungslandern', in *Direktinvestitionene in Entwicklungslandern, Info-Studien zur Entwicklungsforschung*, 11.

Buckley, P.J. (1979) 'Foreign Investment Success for Smaller Firms', *Multinational Business*, 3.

Buckley, P. J. (1981) 'The Optimal Timing of a Foreign Direct Investment', *Economic Journal*, 91.

Buckley, P.J. (1983) 'A Critical View of Theories of the Multinational Enterprise', *Ausenwirtschaft*, 36.

Buckley, P.J. (1989) 'Foreign Direct Investment by Small and Medium Sized Enterprises: The Theoretical Background', *Small Business Economics*, 1.

Buckley, P.J. and M. Casson (1976) *The Future of the Multinational Enterprise*, London: Macmillan.

Buckley, P. and M. Casson (1985) *The Economic Theory of the Multinational Enterprise*, London: Macmillan.

Buckley, P.J. and M. Casson (1987) 'A Theory of Co-operation in International Business', University of Reading, *Discussion Papers in International Investment and Business Studies*, 102, January.

Buckley, P.J., Z. Berkova and G.D. Newbould (1983) *Direct Investment in the United Kingdom by Smaller European Firms*, London: Macmillan and New York: Holmes Meier.

Buckley, P.J., G.D. Newbould and J. Thurwell (1978) 'Going International – the foreign direct investment behaviour of smaller United Kingdom firms', University of Reading, *Discussion Papers in International Investment and Business Studies*, 41.

Buckley, P.J., Newbould, G.D. and Thurwell, J. (1988) *Foreign Direct Investment by Smaller United Kingdom Firms* London: Macmillan, Republication of 1978 book.

Campos, J., J. Cardozo, A. Herrera, E. White and M. Sierra (1993) *Technology Transfer to Developing Countries* by *Small and Medium-Sized Enterprises*, Ottowa: DRC.

Campos, J., S. Feldman and E. White (1985) *Implications of the Transfer of Technology by Small and Medium-sized Enterprises for the Economic and Technological Development of Developing Countries: A Case Study of the Metal Working Industry in Argentina and Brazil*, New York: UNCTAD.

Carstairs, R.T. and L. S. Welch (1981) *A Study of Outward Foreign Licensing of Technology by Australian Companies*, Licensing Executives Society of Australia.

Casson, M. (1979) *Alternatives to the Multinational Enterprise*, London: Macmillan.

Casson, M. (1982) *The Entrepreneur: An Economic Theory*, Oxford: Martin Robertson.

Caves, R.E. (1971), 'International Corporations: The Industrial Economics of Foreign Investment', *Economica*, 38.

Caves, R.E. (1982) *Multinational Enterprise and Economic Analysis*, Cambridge: Cambridge University Press.

CESPRI–CESAG (1988) *International Agreements of Italian Firms: An Analysis With Specific Reference to the Role of Intra-EEC Cooperation*, Milan: CESPRI–CESAG.

Chandler, A.D., Jr (1900a) *Scale and Scope: The Dynamics of Industrial Capitalism*, Cambridge: Harvard University Press.

Chandler, Alfred D., Jr. (1990b) 'The Enduring Logic of Industrial Success', *Harvard Business Review*, vol. 90, no. 2, March/April, pp. 130–40.

Chee, Y.H. and W.Y. Lee (1986) 'Characteristics of Technology Transfer Agreements and Policy Implications', *Korea Development Review* 8 (1) (in Korean).

Cheng, A.N.M. (1986) 'Technology Transfer and Economic Development: The Role of Small and Medium Enterprise in Singapore', unpublished MBA project dissertation, Strathclyde Business School.

CNR (1988) *Relazione Generale Sullo Stato Della Ricerca Scientifica e Technologica in Italia Per L'anno 1988*, Rome: Consiglio Nazionale della Ricerche, .

Contractor, F.J. (1980) 'The Composition of Licensing Fees and Arrangements as a Function of Economic Development of Technology Recipient Nations', *Journal of International Business Studies*, vol. xi, no. 3, pp. 47–62.

Contractor, F.J. (1985), *Licensing in International Strategy*, Westpoint: Quorum Books.

Cooper, C. (1988) 'Supply and Demand Factors in Indian Technology Imports: a Case Study', in Desai (1988a).

Crossick, S. (1988) 'Comparative Assessment of the Impact of 1992 on SMEs and MNCs', *European Affairs*, 3.

Cruz, H.N. (1985) 'Mudança Technológica No Setor Metal-Mecanico do Brasil', São Paulo: IPE/USP.

Daniels, J.D. and L.H. Radenbaugh (1988) *International Business: Enviroments and Operations*, Reading, Ma. Addison-Wesley.

Davidson, W.H. (1980) 'The Location of Foreign Investment Activity', *Journal of International Business Studies*, vol. xi, no. 2, pp. 9–22.

Davidson, W.H. and D.G. McFetridge (1985) 'Key Characteristics in the Choice of International Technology Transfer Mode', *Journal of International Business Studies*, 16(2).

Desai, A.V. (1985a) 'Market Structure and Technology: Their Interdependence in Indian Industry', *Research Policy*, 9.

Desai, A.V. (1985b) *Technology Imports and Indian Industrialization*, Indian Council for Research on International Economic Relations.

Desai, A.V. (1988a) *Technology Absorption in Indian Industry*, Delhi: Wiley Eastern.

Desai, A.V. (1988b) 'Technological Performance in Indian Industry: The Influence of Market Structures and Policies', in Desai (1988a).

Desai, A.V. (1988c) 'Technology Acquisition and Application: Interpretations of the Indian Experience; in R.E.B. Lucas and G.F. Papanek (eds), *The Indian Economy: Recent Development and Future Prospects*, Boulder and London Westview Press.

Desai, A. and E. Desai (1988) 'Public Sector Employment in India', in G. Edgren (ed.), *The Growing Sector*, Delhi: ILOARTEP.

Desai, A. and N. Taneja (1989) *Small and Medium-Scale Enterprises in India's Industrialisation*, Delhi: Indian Council for Research on International Economic Relations.

Doz, Y., G. G. Hamel and C.K. Prahalad (1986) 'Strategic Partnerships: Success or Surrender? The Challenge of Competitive Collaboration', paper presented at AIB EIBA Joint annual meeting, London, (20–23 November).

Dunning, J.H. (1979) 'Explaining Changing Patterns of International Production: In Defence of the Eclectic Theory', *Oxford Bulletin of Economics and Statistics*, 41.

Dunning, J.H. (1981) *International Production and the Multinational Enterprise*, London: George Allen & Unwin.

Dunning, J.H. (1988) *Explaining International Production*, London: Unwin Hyman.

Edquist, C. and S. Jacobsson (1988), 'State Policies, Firm Strategies and Firm Performance: Production of Hydraulic Excavators and Machining Centres in India and Republic of Korea', in Desai (1988a).

Emmanuel, A. (1981) *Technologie Appropriée ou Technologie sous-developée?*, Paris: PUF.

Fayerweather, J. (1978) *International Business Strategy and Administration*, Cambridge: Cambridge University Press.

Fayerweather, J. (1981) 'A Conceptual Framework for the Multinational Corporation', in W. Wacker, H. Haussman, B. Kumar, (ed.), *Internationale Unternehmensfuhrung*, Berlin: Erich Schmidt.

Gantzel, K., (1962) *Wesen und Begriff der Mittelstandischen Unternehmung*, Koln: Wesrdeutscher Verlag.

Ghoshal, S. and Bartlett, C.A. (1988) 'Innovation Processes in Multinational Corporations', in M.L. Tushman and W.L. Moore (eds), *Readings in the Management of Innovation*, Cambridge, MA: Ballinger.

Hackett, D.W. (1977) 'Penetrating International Markets: Key Considerations for Smaller Firms', *Journal of Small Business Management*, vol. 17, no 1.

Hall, G.R. and R.E. Johnson (1970) 'Transfers of United States Aerospace Technology to Japan', in R. Vernon (ed.), *The Technology Factor in International Trade*, New York: Columbia University Press for the National Bureau of Economic Research.

Hamel, G. and C.K. Prahalad (1985) 'Do You Really Have a Global Strategy?', *Harvard Business Review*, vol. 85, no. 4, July/August, pp. 139–48.

Hennart, J.F. (1982) *A Theory of Multinational Enterprise*, Ann Arbor: University of Michigan Press.

Hirschman, A. (1959) *The Strategy of Economic Development*, New Haven: Yale University Press.

Hoffman A., L.H. Reile and F. Vardag (1985) 'Technology Transfer to India: the Interaction of Company Behaviour and Government Policy', in W.M. Callewaert and R. Kumar (eds.), *EEC India: Towards a Common Perspective*, Leuven: Inforient.

Hoorn, Th.P. van (1955) 'Strategic Planning in Small and Medium-Sized Companies', *Long Range Planning*, 12.

Horst, T. (1972) 'Firm and Industry Determinants of the Decision to Invest Abroad: An Empirical Study', *Review of Economics and Statistics*, vol. 54, pp. 258–66.

Hörnell, E. and J.E. Vahlne (1986) *Multinationals: The Swedish Case*, New York: St Martin's Press.

Hymer, S. (1976) *The International Operations of National Firms*, Cambridge, MA: MIT Press.

Inter-American Development Bank (1988) '*Economic and Social Progress in Latin America*', Washington, ADB.

ISTAT (1986) *Indagine Sulla Diffusione dell'innovazione Tecnologica Nell'industria Manifatturiera Italiana*, Rome: ISTAT.

Instituto Nazionale per il Commercio Estero (ICE) (1988) *La struttura delle esportazioni italiane: un'analisi per impresse*, Rome: ICE.

Ito, S. (1986) 'Modifying Imported Technology by Local Engineers: Hypotheses and Case Study of India', *The Developing Economies*, 24(4).

Jansson, H. (1982) 'Interfirm Linkages in a Developing Economy: the Case of Swedish Firms in India', Acta Universitatis Upsaliensis, Studia Oeconomiae Negotiorum, 14, Uppsala: Uppsala University.

Japan Overseas Development Corporation (1984) *Chushokigyo Kaigai Toshi Kyoryoku Shikin Yushi Jigyo Jireishu* (Case Studies on Small and Medium Firms' Overseas Investment and Loans from the Cooperation Funds), Tokyo.

Jéquier, N. and Blanc, G. (1983) *La Technologie Appropriée dans le Monde*, Paris: OECD.

Johanson, I. and I. Vahlne (1977) 'The Internationalisation Process of the Firm – A Model of Knowledge Development and Increasing Foreign Market Commitment', *Journal of International Business Studies*, vol. 8, pp. 23–32.

Johnson, H.G. (1970) 'The Efficiency and Welfare Implications of the International Corporation', in C.P. Kindleberger (ed.), *The International Corporation*, Cambridge, MA: MIT Press.

Kayser, G. and Schwarting, U. (1981) 'Foreign Investments as a Form of Enterprise Strategy: On the Results of a Survey', *Intereconomics*.

Kayser, G. *et al.* (1981) Munich: *Deutsche Auslandsinvestitionen in Entwicklungslandern*, Munich: Weltforum Verlag.

Kent, C.A., D.L. Sexton and K.H. Vesper (eds) (1982) *Encyclopedia of Entrepreneurship*, Englewood Cliffs, NJ: Prentice-Hall.

Khan, S.M. (1978) *A Study of Success and Failure in Exporting*, Stockholm: Akademilitteratur.

Kim, I.H., 'Small and Medium Enterprises in Korea', *Korea Exchange Bank, Monthly Review*, 22(7).

Kindleberger, C.P. (1970) (ed.) *The International Corporation: A Symposium*, Cambridge, MA: MIT Press.

Kitterer, B., W. Hebing, B. Kumar, H. Steinmann, A. Wasner, and H. Wilkens (1983) *Privatwirtschaftliche Kooperation mit Entwicklungslandern*, Munich: Weltforum Verlag.

Knickerbocker, F. (1973) *Oligopolistic Reaction and Multinational Enterprise*, Boston: Harvard University.

Kogut, B. (1983) 'FDI as a Sequential Process', in C.P. Kindleberger and D. Audretsch (eds), *Multinational Corporations in the 1980s*, Cambridge: MA: MIT Press.

Kohn, T.O. (1988) 'International Entrepreneurship: Foreign Direct Investment by Small US-Based Manufacturing Firms', DBA Dissertation, Harvard University.

Koike, K. (1987) 'Human Resource Development and Labour-Management Relations', in K. Yamamura and Y. Yasuba, *The Political Economy of Japan, Vol. 1: The Domestic Transformation*, Stanford: Stanford University Press.

Kojima, K. (1978) *Direct Foreign Investment: A Japanese Model of Multinational Business Operations*, New York: Praeger.

Korea Industrial Research Institute (1986) *A Survey on the Status of Technology Transfer by Foreign Firms*, Seoul.

Kumar, B. (1975) *Fuhrungsprobleme Internationaler Gemeinschaftsunternehmen in den Entwicklungslandern*, Meisenheim.

Kumar, B. (1982) 'Die Multinationale Unternehmung und das Grundbedurf-niskonzept', in E. Pausenberger (ed.), *Entwicklungslander als Haundlungs-felder Internationaler Unternehmungen*, Stuttgart: Poesche.

Kumar, B. (1987) *Duetsche Unternehmen in den United States. Das Management in den Amerikanischen Niederlassungen Deutscher Mittelbetriebe*, Wiesbaden. Gebler.

Kumar, B. (1988) 'Investment Strategy of German Small and Medium-Sized Firms in the United States and the Theory of Direct Investment', in F. Khosrow. (ed.), *International Trade and Finance. A North American Perspective*, New York: Praeger.

Kumar, B. and H. Steinmann (1978) 'Future and Emergence of German Multinationals', in M. Skully (ed.), *A Multinational Look at the Transnational Corporation*, New York: 16.

Kumar, B. and Steinmann, H. (1985) 'Internationalisierung von Mittelbetrieben – Managementprobleme und Forderungsmöglichkeiten', *Betriebswirtschaftliche Forschung und Praxis*, 6.

Lachner, J. and W. Meyerhofer (1985) *Stellung und Entwicklung der Kleinen und Mittleren Unternehmen in Bayern*, Munich: Ifo-Institut.

Lall, S. (1980) 'Vertical Inter-firm Linkages in LDCs: An Empirical Study', *Oxford Bulletin of Economics and Statistics*, vol. 42, pp. 203–6.

Lall, S. (1987) *Learning to Industrialize: the Acquisition of Technological Capability by India*, London: Macmillan.

Lee, C.H. (1984) 'Transfer of Technology from Japan and the United States to Korean Manufacturing Industries: A Comprehensive Study', *Proceedings of International Convention of Korean Economists* (August).

Lee, H.L. (1988) 'The Importance of Small and Medium Enterprises', speech given at World Trade Center Auditorium, Singapore (4 May); reprinted in Ministry of Communications and Information, Singapore, *Speeches*: bimonthly selection of ministerial speeches (May–June 1988).

Lee, T.Y. (1987) 'The Government in the Labour Market,' in L.B. Krause, A.T. Koh and T.Y. Lee (1987) *The Singapore Economy Reconsidered*, Singapore: Institute of Southeast Asian Studies.

Lee, W.Y. (1987) *Direct Foreign Investment in Korea: Pattern, Impacts and Government Policy, Working Paper*, 8706, Seoul: Korea Development Institute.

Lee, W.Y. and J. H. Kim (1987) 'Determinants of the Royalty Payment in Technology Licensing', *Korea Development Review*, 9 (1).

Levin, R.C. *et al.* (1984) 'Survey on R&D Appropriability and Technological Opportunity, Part I: Appropriability', mimeo.

Lim, L.Y.C. (1983) 'Singapore Success: The Myth of the Free Market Economy', *Asian Survey*, 23(6).

Lim, L.Y.C., *et al.* (1988) *Policy Options for the Singapore Economy*, Singapore: McGraw-Hill.

Lim, L.Y.C. and E.F. Pang (1988) *Foreign Investment, Industrial Restructuring and Changing Comparative Advantage: The Experience of Malaysia, Thailand, Singapore and Taiwan*, Paris: OECD Development Centre.

Little, I., D. Majumdar and J.M. Page (1987) *Small Manufacturing Enterprises: a Comparative Study of India and Other Economies*, Oxford: Oxford University Press.

Litvak, I. and C. Maule (1978) 'Canadian Small Business and Investment in the US – Corporate Forms and Characteristics', *Business Quarterly*, 43 (4).

Lupo, L.A., A. Gilbert and M. Liliestedt (1978) 'The Relationship between Age and Rate of Return of Foreign Manufacturing Affiliates of US Manufacturing Parent Companies', *Survey of Current Business*, 58.

Malerba, F. (1988), 'Apprendimento, Innovazionie e Capacita; Technologiche: Verso una Nuova Concettualizzazione Dell'impresa', *Economia e politica industriale*, 58.

Mansfield, E., A. Romeo and S. Wagner, 'Foreign Trade and US Research and Development, *Review of Economics and Statistics*, 61, 49–57.

Mansfield, E., D.J. Teece and A. Romeo (1979) 'Overseas Research and Development by US-based Firms', *Economica*, 46.

Mariotti, S (1989a) 'Gli investmenti Industriali Italiani All'estero ed Esteri in Italia: un Quadro Aggiornato a fine 1987', in III Rapporto CESPRI-Bocconi per la Camera di Comercio di Milano, *Processi di mondializzazione e transformzioni strutturali dell'industria nel nascente Mercato Unico Europeo*, Milan.

Mariotti, S. (1989b) 'Italian Inward and Outward Direct Investments: A New Pattern of Internalisation', *Rapporto Interno* 89-014, Dipartimento di Elettronica-Politecnico di Milano (January 1989), Table 4.

Markensten, K.L. (1972) *Foreign Investment and Development: Swedish Companies in India*, Stockholm: Scandinavian Institute of Asian Studies, *Monograph Series*, 8.

Marshall, H., F. Southward and K.W. Taylor (1936) *Canadian–American Industry*, New York: Carnegie Endowment; reprinted, Toronto (1976).

Mascarenhas, B. (1986) 'International Strategies of Non-Dominant Firms', *Journal of International Business Studies* (Spring).

Matthews, R. (1986) 'Technological Dynamism in India and Japan: The Case of Machine-Tool Manufacture', in E. Baark and A. Jamieson (eds), *Technological Development in China, India and Japan: Cross-Cultural Perspectives*, London: Macmillan.

Ministero dell'Industria, del Commercio e dell'Artigiananto (1988), *Rapporto Della Commissione Per lo Studio Delle Problematiche Delle Piccole e Medie Imprese*, Rome.

Ministry of International Trade and Industry (various issues) *Wagakuni Kigyo no Kaigai Jigyo Katsudo (Japanese Firms' Overseas Business Activities)* Tokyo.

Ministry of International Trade and Industry (1986) *Wagakuni Kigyo no Kaigai Jigyo Katsudo (Japanese Firms' Overseas Business Activities) The 5th Survey*, Tokyo: Okura-sho Insatsu-kyoku.

Ministry of International Trade and Industry (1983) *Dai Iikai Kaigai Jigyo Katsudo Kihon Chosa: Kaigai Toshi Tokei Soran (The 1st Basic Survey on Overseas Business Activities: Statistical Compilation of Overseas Investment)* Tokyo: Toyo Hoki Shuppan.

Ministry of International Trade and Industry (1986) *Dai Ni-kai Kaigai Jigyo Katsudo Kihon Chosa: Kaigai Toshi Tokei Soran (The 2nd Basic Survey on Overseas Business Activities: Statistical Compilation of Overseas Investment)* Tokyo: Keibun.

Ministry of International Trade and Industry (1989) *Dai San-kai kaigai Jigyo*

Katsudo Kihon Chosa: Kaigai Toshi Tokei Soran (The 3rd Basic Survey on Overseas Business Activities: Statistical Compilation of Overseas Investment), Tokyo: Keibun Shuppan.

Monteverde, K. and D.J. Teece (1982) 'Supplier Switching Costs and Vertical Integration in the Automobile Industry', *Bell Journal of Economics*, 13.

Myrdal, Gunnar (1968) *The Asian Drama*, London: Penguin.

Namiki, N. (1988) 'Export Strategy for Small Business', *Journal of Small Business Management*, vol. 26, no. 2.

National Council of Applied Economic Research (1971) *Foreign Technology and Investment: Their Role in India's Industrialisation*, Delhi.

Nelson, R. and S. Winter (1982) *An Evolutionary Theory of Economic Change*, Cambridge: Harvard University Press.

Newbould, G.D. *et al.* (1978) *Going International: The Experience of Smaller Companies Overseas*, New York: John Wiley.

Niosi, J. (1982) *Les Multinationales Canadiennes*, Montreal: Boreal (English translation, Toronto, 1985).

Niosi, J. and J. Rivand (1990) 'Canadian Technology Transfer to Developing Countries by Small and Medium Enterprises', *World Development*, 18 (11), 1529–42.

OECD (1987) *International Investment and Multinational Enterprises. Recent Trends In International Direct Investment*, Paris: OECD.

Oman, C. (1984) *New Forms of International Investment in Developing Countries*, Paris: OECD Development Centre.

Onida, F. (1988) 'Patterns of International Specialisation and Technological Competitiveness in Italian Manufacturing Industry', in F. Onida and G. Viesti (eds) *The Italian Multinationals*, London: Croom Helm.

Onida, F. *et al.* (1985) *Technological Transfer to Developing Countries by Italian Small and Medium-Size Enterprises*, Geneva: UNCTAD/TT/81.

Onida, F. and G. Viesti (eds) (1988) *The Italian Multinationals*, London: Croom Helm.

Oppenländer, H.H., (1985) 'Auslandsinvestitionen und Aussenwirtschaftlicher Technologietransfer: Ubersicht über Uraschen und Ausmass, in *Zielsetzung Partnerschaft*, Edition Drager-Stiftung, Band 9, Stuttgart: Bonn Akhiel.

Ozawa, T. (1979) *Multinationalism, Japanese Style*, Princeton: Princeton University Press.

Ozawa, T. (1985) *International Transfer of Technology by Japan Small and Medium Enterprises in Development Countries*, Geneva: UNCTAD/TT/68.

Ozawa, T. (1988) 'Technology Transfers by Japan's Small and Medium Enterprises', mimeo.

Paloheimo, A. (1986) 'Foreign Market Entry Forms: An Information-Transactions Cost Approach', unpublished doctoral dissertation, New York University.

Pang, E.F. (1987) 'Foreign Investment and the State in Singapore, in V. Cable and B. Persaud (eds), *Development with Foreign Investment*, London: Croom Helm.

Pang, E.F. (1988) 'Developing Strategies and Labour Market Changes in Singapore', in E.F. Pang (ed.), *Labour Market Developments and Structural Change: The Experience of ASEAN and Australia*, Singapore: Singapore University Press.

Pang, E.F. (1989) 'Structural Adjustment in Three Manufacturing Industries in Singapore', in H. Patrick (ed.), *Structural Adjustment, Trade and Declining Industries in the Asia-Pacific Region*, New York: Columbia University Press.

Penrose, Edith T. (1959, 1980) *The Theory of the Growth of the Firm*, White Plains: M.E. Sharpe originally published by Basil Blackwell (1959).

Pfohl, H.-Chr. and P. Kellerwessel (1982) 'Abgrenzung der Klein und Mittelbetriebe von Grossbetrieben', in H.-Chr. Pfohl (ed.), *Betriebswirtschaftslehre der Mittel und Kleinbetriebe*, Berlin: de Gruytes.

Porter, M.E. (1980) *Competitive Strategy*, New York: The Free Press.

Porter, M.E. (1985) *Competitive Advantage*, New York: Free Press.

R&P-Ricerche e Progetti and OSPRI-Bocconi (1986) *L'Italia Multinazionale. L'internazionalizzazione Dell'industria Italiana*, Edizioni del Sole 24 Ore, Milan.

Rattner, H.N. (1985) 'Pequena e Media Empresa no Brasil', São Paulo: Ed. Brasiliense.

Rothwell, R. (1989) 'Small Firms, Innovation and Industrial Change', *Small Business Economics*, 1 (1).

Sabel, C.F. and M.J. Piore (1984) *The Second Industrial Divide*, New York: Basic Books.

Savary, J. (1981) *Les Multinationales Françaises*, Paris: IRM.

Scarda, A.M. and G. Sirilli (1982) *Technology Transfer and Technological Balance of Payments*, Quaderni ISRDS, National Research Council (CNR), 10.

Schreyogg, G. (1984) *Gundlagen der Unternehmensstrategien*, Berlin: de Gruyter.

Schumacher, E.F. (1973) *Small is Beautiful*, London: Blond & Briggs.

Schumpeter, J.A. (1949) *The Theory of Economic Development*, Cambridge, MA: Harvard University Press.

Scott-Kemmis, D. and M. Bell (1988) 'Technological Dynamism and Technological Content of Collaboration: are Indian Firms Missing Opportunities?', in Desai (1988a).

Sen, A. (1962) *Choice of Techniques*, Oxford: Basil Blackwell.

Sharkey, T.W., S. Lim and K.I. Kim (1989) 'Export Development and Perceived Export Barriers: An Empirical Analysis of Small Firms', *Management International Review*, 29 (2).

Shoko-Sogo Kenkyusho (1988) *Chushokigyo Shinjidai* (A New Era for Small and Medium Firms), Tokyo: Nikkan Kogyo Press.

Sirilli, G. (1986) 'Indicators for the Measurement of Technology Transfer', in Seminar on the importance of technology transfer in ECE Member countries, Warsaw (20–24 October).

Sirilli, G. (1987) 'International Technology Transfer by Italian Firms. Aspects, Problems and Perspectives', International Conference on the History of the Enterprise, Technology and Enterprise in a Historical Perspective, Terni (1–4 October).

Small Business Corporation (1986) *Chushokigyo Kaigai Shinshutsu Jireishu* (Case Studies of Small and Medium Firms' Overseas Operations), Tokyo: SBC.

Small and Medium Enterprise Agency (various issues) *Chusho Kigyo Hakusho*

(White Paper on Small and Medium Enterprises) Tokyo: Government Printing Office.

Smith, J.G. and V. Fleck (1987) 'Business Strategies in Small High-Technology Companies', *Long Range Planning*, 20 (2).

Statistics Bureau, Management and Co-ordination Agency (various issues) *Report on the Survey of Research and Development*, Tokyo.

Statistics Canada (annual) *Canada's International Investment Position*, Ottawa, Cat. 61–202.

Steinmann, H. and B. Kumar (1984) 'Personalpolitische Aspekte von im Ausland Tatigen Unternehmen', in E. Dichtl and O. Issing, (eds), *Exporte als Herausförderung für die deutsche Wirtschaft*, Koln: Deutsch Institut Verlag.

Steinmann, H., B. Kumar and A. Wasner (1977) *Internationalisierung von Mittelbetrieben. Eine Empirische Untersuchung in Mittelfranken*, Wiesbaden: Gabler.

Steinmann, H., B. Kumar and A. Wasner (1981) 'Entwicklungspolitische Aspekte der Direktinvestitionen deutscher Mittelbetriebe in Brasilien', in W. Wacker, H. Haussman and B. Kumar (eds.), *Internationale Unternehmensführung*, Berlin: Erich Schmidt.

Stevenson, H.H., M.J. Roberts and H.I. Grousbeck (1985) *New Business Ventures and the Entrepreneur*, Homewood, Il.-Irwin.

Stewart, C. and Y. Nihei (1987) *Technology Transfer and Human Factors*, Lexington, MA: D C Heath.

Stopford, I. and L. Wells, (1972) *Managing the Multinational Enterprise*, New York: Basic Books.

Sweeney, J.K. (1970) 'A Small Company Enters the European Market', *Harvard Business Review*, Volume 48, Sept/Oct., pp. 126–32.

Teece, D.J. (1977) 'Technology Transfer by Multinational Firms: The Resource Cost of Transfering Technology Know-How', *Economic Journal*, 87.

Teece, D.J. (1981a) 'The Multinational Enterprise: Market Failure and Market Power Considerations', *Sloan Management Review*, 22, 3, pp. 7–10.

Teece, D.J. (1981b) 'The Market for Know How and the Efficient International Transfer of Technology', *Annals*, 458.

Teece, D.J. (1986), Innovazione Technologica e Successo Imprenditoriale, *L'Industria*, 3.

Thunman, C.G. (1988) *Technology Licensing to Distant Markets: Interaction Between Swedish and Indian Firms*, Acta Universitatis Upsaliensis, Studia Oeconomiae Negotiorum, 28, Uppsala: Uppsala University.

Toyo Keizai Shimposha (1988) *Gyoshu-betsu Kaigai Shinshutsu Kigyo Soran (Japanese Multinationals Facts and Figures, Sectoral Edition)*, Tokyo: Toyo Keiza, Shinposa.

United Nations Centre on Transnational Corporations (UNCTC) (1978) *Transnational Corporations in World Development: A Re-examination*, New York: United Nations Publications.

UNCTAD (1987) *Impact of Technology Transfer by Foreign Small and Medium-sized Enterprises on Technological Development in Kenya*, Geneva: UNCTAD.

United Nations Centre on Transnational Corporations (UNCTC) (1987) *Transnational Corporations and Technology Transfer: Effects and Policy Issues*, New York: United Nations Publications.

United Nations Centre on Transnational Corporations (UNCTC) (1988)

Transnational Corporations in World Development, Trends and Prospects, New York: United Nations Publications.

US Department of Commerce (1985) *US Direct Investment Abroad: 1982 Benchmark Survey Data*, Washington, DC: Government Printing Office.

US Small Business Administration (1982) *The State of Small Business: A Report of the President, 1982*, Washington, DC: US Government Printing Office.

US Small Business Administration (1984) *The State of Small Business: A Report to the President 1984*, Washington DC: US Government Printing Office.

US Small Business Administration (1985) *The State of Small Business: A Report to the President 1985*, Washington DC: US Government Printing Office.

US Small Business Administration (1988) *The State of Small Business: A Report to the President 1988*, Washington DC: US Government Printing Office.

Vernon, R. (1966) 'International Investment and International Trade in the Product Cycle', *Quarterly Journal of Economics*, vol. 80, pp. 190–207.

Vernon, R. (1970a) 'Organisation as a Scale Factor in the Growth of Firms', in J.W. Markham and G.F. Papanek, *Industrial Organization and Economic Development*, Boston: Houghton Mifflin.

Vernon, R. (1971) *Sovereignty at Bay*, New York: Basic Books.

Vernon, R. (1974) 'The Location of Industry', in H.J. Dunning (ed.), *Economic Analysis and the Multinational Enterprise*, London: George Allen and Unwin.

Vernon, R. (1977) *Storm Over the Multinationals, The Real Issues*, Cambridge, MA: Harvard University Press.

Vernon, R. (1979), 'The Product Cycle Hypothesis in a New International Environment', *Oxford Bulletin of Economics and Statistics*, 41, 255–67.

Viesti, G. (1988) *Gli Accordi fra Impresse: Nuove Strategie per la Crescita Internazionale e L'apprendimento Tecnologico?*, Working Paper, CESPRI, 11, Milan.

Vlachoutsikos, C. (1989) 'How Small-to-Mid-Sized US Firms Can Profit from Perestroika', *California Management Review*, vol. 31, no. 3, Spring pp. 91–112.

Wasner, A. (1985) *Internationalsierung von Deutschen Mittelbetrieben in Brasilien*, Göttingen: Göttingen Verlag.

Watanabe, S. (1983) 'Inter-Sectoral Linkages in Japanese Industries: A Historical Perspective', in S. Watanabe (ed.), *Technology, Marketing and Industrialisation*, Delhi: Macmillan.

Welch, L.S. (1985) 'The International Marketing of Technology: an Interaction Perspective', *International Marketing Review*, vol. 2, no. 2.

Wells, L.T., Jr (1972) *The Product Life Cycle and International Trade*, Cambridge, MA: Harvard University Press.

Wells, L.T., Jr (1983) *Third World Multinationals: The Rise of Foreign Investments From Developing Countries*, Cambridge, MA: MIT Press.

White, E. and J. Campos (1986) *Alternative Technology Sources for Developing Countries: The Role of Small and Medium-Sized Enterprises from Industrialised Countries*, Buenos Aires: CEDREI.

White, E. and S. Feldman (1982) *Organizational Forms of Transfer of Technology to Developing Countries by Small and Medium Enterprises: a Case Study of Equity Joint Ventures and Technology Agreements in Latin America*, Geneva: UNCTAD.

Williamson, O.G. (1975) *Markets and Hierarchies: Analysis and Anti-Trust Implications*, New York: Free Press.

Wolf, C. and S. Sufrin (1965) 'Technological Change and Technological Alternatives', in C. Wolf and S. Sufrin, *Capital Formation and Foreign Investment in Underdeveloped Areas*, Syracuse: Syracuse University Press.

Index

The editors

Peter J. Buckley is Professor of International Business and Director of the Centre of International Business, University of Leeds, and Visiting Professor at the Universities of Reading and Paris I: Panthéon, Sorbonne. He has published and edited numerous books and articles on international business. He is a former Vice-President of the Academy of International Business and former Chair of its UK region. In 1985 he was elected a Fellow of the Academy for 'outstanding achievements' in that field, and in 1995 elected a Fellow of the British Academy of Management.

Jaime Campos is a consultant to various international organisations and Director of CEDREI (Centre of Studies on Development and International Economic Relations). He is currently Executive Director of Argentina's Investment Foundation. He is the co-author of *Technology Transfer to Developing Countries by Small and Medium-Sized Enterprises*.

Hafiz Mirza is Professor of International Business at the University of Bradford Management Centre. He has published widely, including many articles in *The Journal of International Business Studies, Management International Review* and *International Business Review*. He is currently involved in a number of projects, with UNCTAD, the UN Economic Commission for Africa and ASEAN, on foreign direct investment and the international transfer of technology and business culture.

Eduardo White was a consultant to various international organisations and adviser for the Centre on Transnational Corporations of the United Nations. He was Director of CEDREI and is the author of *Las Empresas Multinacionales Latinoamericanas*.

INTERNATIONAL TECHNOLOGY TRANSFER BY
SMALL AND MEDIUM-SIZED ENTERPRISES

International Technology Transfer by Small and Medium-Sized Enterprises

Country Studies

Edited by

Peter J. Buckley
Professor of International Business
University of Leeds

Jaime Campos
Director
CEDREI

Hafiz Mirza
Professor of International Business
University of Bradford Management Centre

and

Eduardo White
sometime Director, CEDREI

First published in Great Britain 1997 by
MACMILLAN PRESS LTD
Houndmills, Basingstoke, Hampshire RG21 6XS
and London
Companies and representatives
throughout the world

A catalogue record for this book is available
from the British Library.

ISBN 0–333–56487–1

First published in the United States of America 1997 by
ST. MARTIN'S PRESS, INC.,
Scholarly and Reference Division,
175 Fifth Avenue,
New York, N.Y. 10010

ISBN 0–312–12883–5

Library of Congress Cataloging-in-Publication Data
International technology transfer by small and medium-sized
enterprises : country studies / edited by Peter J. Buckley ... [et
al.].
p. cm.
Includes bibliographical references and index.
ISBN 0–312–12883–5 (cloth)
1. Technology transfer—Economic aspects—Developing countries.
2. Small business—Developing countries. I. Buckley, Peter J.,
1949– .
HC59.72.T4157 1996
338.9'26'091724—dc20   95–34282
                                                        CIP

This book is printed on paper suitable for recycling and made from fully managed and
sustained forest sources.

10   9   8   7   6   5   4   3   2   1
06   05   04   03   02   01   00   99   98   97

Printed in Great Britain by
The Ipswich Book Company Ltd
Ipswich, Suffolk